Cellular Phones, Public Fears, and a Culture of Precaution

This book is the first account of the health panic surrounding cellular phones and their supporting network of transmitting towers that developed in the mid-1990s. Treating the issue as more "social construction" than evident scientific problem, it tells the story of how this originally American anxiety diffused internationally, having an even bigger impact in countries such as Italy. Burgess highlights the contrasting reactions to the issue ranging from positive indifference in Finland to those such as in the United Kingdom, where precautionary measures were taken. These differences are located within a culture driven by institutional insecurity with regard to alleged health risks that first appeared in the United States and is now most evident in Europe. Anxieties about cell phone radio waves are also related historically to reactions to technologies such as x-rays and "microwave suspicions" about television. In addition, Burgess outlines a history and sociology of what is, despite media-driven fear, a spectacularly successful device.

Adam Burgess received his undergraduate degree from the University of London and his Ph.D. from the University of Kent. He is the author of one previous book and numerous journal articles and book chapters. Burgess has been a lecturer at the University of Reading and is now a lecturer in sociology at the University of Bath.

D0050461

For my two boys, Carl and Alec

Cellular Phones, Public Fears, and a Culture of Precaution

ADAM BURGESS

University of Bath

PUBLISHED BY THE PRESS SYNDICATE OF THE UNIVERSITY OF CAMBRIDGE
The Pitt Building, Trumpington Street, Cambridge, United Kingdom

CAMBRIDGE UNIVERSITY PRESS
The Edinburgh Building, Cambridge CB2 2RU, UK
40 West 20th Street, New York, NY 10011-4211, USA
477 Williamstown Road, Port Melbourne, VIC 3207, Australia
Ruiz de Alarcón 13, 28014 Madrid, Spain
Dock House, The Waterfront, Cape Town 8001, South Africa

http://www.cambridge.org

First published 2004

Printed in the United States of America

Typeface   Sabon 10/13 pt.   *System* LATEX 2$_\varepsilon$ [TB]

A catalog record for this book is available from the British Library.

Library of Congress Cataloging in Publication Data

Burgess, Adam.
Cellular phones, public fears, and a culture of precaution / Adam Burgess.
    p.   cm.
Includes bibliographical references and index.
ISBN 0-521-81759-5 – ISBN 0-521-52082-7 (pb.)
1. Cellular telephones – Health aspects.   2. Low-level radiation – Health aspects.   I. Title.
RA569.3.B87   2004
363.18'9–dc21   2003043591

ISBN 0 521 81759 5 hardback
ISBN 0 521 52082 7 paperback

Contents

Acknowledgments

It is simply not possible to thank all of the hundreds of people who have helped with this project, in the main by providing and confirming information. I can only single out some of the individuals who "went beyond the call of duty" and those who helped me as a friend and colleague. On the activist side I thank Sue Ferguson, Libby Kelly, and Kathy Moran. On the industry side I'm grateful to Marianne Olson at Ericsson, who was the only person from a cell phone manufacturer or operator who proved helpful in providing illustrations and permission to use them. Mike Dolan from the United Kingdom's Federation of Electronic Industries was also very supportive, as well as providing useful information on Australian developments. Professors John Adams, Joel Best, and Frank Füredi all encouraged the project along, and the energy and high standards of Professor Roberto Franzosi were particularly valuable in the early stages. My father, Mike, and Martina Cortesi, Brendan Craigie, Koen Delbeke, Keyhan Delibas, John Gillott, Susannah Quinn, and Dominic Standish all provided useful information and comment. Particular thanks go to the Italian scientist Paolo Vecchia, who allowed me to draw on his valuable insights. Far and above all, thanks go to Tracey Brown – my inspiration, discipline, and editor. Without her this book would never even have gotten off the ground, let alone been completed.

List of Abbreviations

BSE	Bovine spongiform encephalopathy
CPRE	Council for the Protection of Rural England
CTIA	Cellular Telecommunications Industry Association
CWA	Communications Workers of America
CWTI	Council on Wireless Technology Industries
ELF	Extremely low frequency
EPA	Environmental Protection Agency
EPL	Environmental Protection Law
ERMAC	Electromagnetic Radiation Management Advisory Council
FACA	Federal Advisory Committee Act
FCC	Federal Communications Commission
GPRS	General Packet Radio Service
GSM	Global System for Mobile Communications
IARC	International Agency for Research on Cancer
IEGMP	Independent Expert Group on Mobile Phones
ICNIRP	International Committee on Non-Ionizing Radiation Protection
ISPESL	National Institute for Prevention and Safety at Work (Italy)
KCC	Kent County Council
LGA	Local Government Association
MAUK	Mast Action U.K.
MCF	Mobile Carriers Forum
NCI	National Cancer Institute
NIFATT	Northern Ireland Families Against Transmission Towers
NRPB	National Radiological Protection Board (U.K.)
SAR	Specific absorption rate

SIM   Subscriber Information Module
SMS   Short Message Service
3G   Third Generation
VDT   Video display terminal
WAP   Wireless Application Protocol
WHO   World Health Organization

Themes and Influences; Phones and Risk

Discovering the Issue

This book examines the origins and development of health concerns associated with cellular phones, focusing principally on Western Europe, North America, and Australasia. Like so many other intellectual projects, this one began more by accident than design. Telephones of whatever sort do not hold any special fascination for the author. What sparked my initial curiosity was the succession of sometimes bizarre newspaper stories that began to appear in the United Kingdom following the infamous headline that cell phones might "fry" the brain (*Sunday Times*, 4 April 1996). Even past their 1997–9 peak, and four years after the "frying brain" story, the British media's fascination with cell phones and health has not entirely abated. On 17 October 2000, for example, London's newspaper, the *Evening Standard*, carried two whole pages on the subject. The first was concerned with the risk of (associated) violence: "Suburban crime surge is blamed on mobile phone thefts," ran the report, describing the trend for young people to be robbed of their cell phones on the streets. Further on, the more conventionally defined health problems were raised in a story announcing: "Sickly pupils 'recover' after leaving cell phone mast school." The article repeated the claim of longtime anti–cell phone tower campaigner Debbie Collins that removing her daughter from a school sited close to a tower had led to dramatic improvements in the girl's health. Discounting the skepticism of "the experts," Debbie claimed: "She's a different child now – it's all the proof I need to convince me there is a link between those wretched masts and the health of children." Another mother similarly dismissed the word of the unspecified "experts," declaring: "I needed no more proof than that. This term he started at a new school and I can already see the change in him. His memory has improved and his headaches have gone." Such anxieties are not restricted to parents or the vulnerable. The manager of London's top soccer team, Arsenal, insisted at the end of 2001 that his players fit a crystal device called the "PhoneShield" to their cell phones on the basis that radiation might somehow sap their strength.

Stories about health risks from radio-frequency radiation from cell phones and their communication towers have become common in the British media in the last five years. It is important to emphasize that these stories cannot be dismissed as of the *National Enquirer*, "aliens abducted my mother" variety. This remains a seriously regarded issue, and it was the United Kingdom's most influential "quality" weekend newspaper, the *Sunday Times*, that began the whole episode, and its sister daily, *The Times*, that reinvigorated the issue toward the end of 2000. Alongside the *Sunday Times* story, reports featured by the BBC television shows *Health Watchdog* and *Panorama* were the other influential moments in the evolution of cell phone health risk's public profile. In both their more populist and "up-market" formats, the stories about health risks follow a standard pattern of "revealing," "disturbing" new research about the link between cell phones and health. A week after the *Evening Standard* stories, for example, the leading middle market newspaper, the *Daily Mail*, announced: "Warning over mobile link to nerve damage" (24 October 2000). One of the two new studies in the report claimed that "excessive use" of the mobile phone could damage nerves around the ears, while the other described a "significant increase in skin temperature" with "unknown long-term health consequences."

None of the studies made public so far has offered verifiable evidence of negative health effects from cell phone emissions. It is *potential* rather than *actual* harm that has prompted concern. Unsurprisingly, perhaps, it is in relation to children that special measures on the basis of potential harm are most widely endorsed. Following research at the University of Utah suggesting that *if* mobile radiation were harmful, then children would be especially vulnerable, for example, an article in the left-liberal daily, the *Guardian*, advised that minors should take precautionary steps such as holding the phone at a distance while dialing and sending text messages (*Guardian*, 20 November 2001). By contrast, not a single British media source reported on an official report for the Dutch government that firmly concluded that there was no evidence of a health hazard from cell phones, and therefore no need for the precautionary limiting of children's usage

(Health Council of the Netherlands 2002). Good news appears to be no news for a media apparently fascinated only with the possibility of harm.

Claims of harm from cell phones seemed less than compelling to the author, given their largely hypothetical basis. Imperfect a guide as it is, experience also contradicted these news stories; many people I knew had been using these devices since their introduction in the mid-1980s, without ever reporting any ill effects. Even in retrospect it is clear that there was something quite unique about the treatment of the issue in the British media. More distinctively still, British newspapers developed public warning campaigns about potential dangers as an explicit campaigning focus. Stories were typically created out of obscure, single studies from which the possibility of more generalized human harm was illegitimately extrapolated or inferred. Ominous implications are suggested by the "significant increase in skin temperature" and "unknown long-term health consequences" described above, for example. The far greater increase in skin temperature from getting into a hot bath or sitting in the sun might also be described as having "unknown consequences" (including cancer in the latter case), but we can recognize in these instances that portentous language means little. Similarly, the suspicions of a parent who consciously rejects any expertise in considering whether his or her child's health is related to cell phone towers is only "news" insofar as the media have chosen to make it so. The uncritical way in which the British media announced unreviewed research on the effects of microwave radiation and encouraged readers to draw unwarranted conclusions suggested that many journalists, editors, and producers made an early decision that the possibility of harm being proved at a later stage was worth gambling on. On the assumption that cell phones might turn out to be the "new tobacco," even barely credible fragments presented themselves to the British media as potentially part of a bigger picture. An interview with the journalist who most determinedly sought to promote the issue, becoming a fulcrum for organized campaign activities in the process, confirmed this impression.[1]

The U.K. media's determination to alert audiences to potential dangers from cell phones was relatively unsurprising given their and indeed the American media's similar obsession with health scares. A diet of worries about food products is served on an almost daily basis on both sides of the Atlantic. But an important dimension that marked out this from many other media alarms was that the British authorities commissioned a comprehensive survey by a group of experts into possible health effects,

[1] Interview with Cathy Moran of the *Express* newspaper, 23 August 2000.

apparently in response to the media's campaigning. In March 1999, Minister for Public Health Tessa Jowell initiated an Independent Expert Group on Mobile Phones (IEGMP) to assess the current state of research on possible health risks. The inquiry was an explicit response to "public perceptions and concerns," as the opening section of the final report was entitled.

The IEGMP was unusual in many ways, not least the fact that the official radiation regulator, the National Radiological Protection Board (NRPB), was deliberately marginalized from the inquiry, and that several of the scientific experts were consciously drawn from those without specific expertise in the field of possible effects from weak electromagnetic fields. Personnel for the inquiry were selected in order to limit the possibility of a simple reaffirmation of accepted scientific orthodoxy that only direct heating effects from radiation can be considered, and that these are simply too weak to cause human harm. The IEGMP, or simply the Stewart Inquiry (after its chair, former Chief Medical Officer Sir William Stewart), went on to heavily criticize the NRPB for not being sufficiently proactive in raising radiation concerns, and demanded that their safety standards be rejected and the threshold for exposure to low-level radiation be raised by several times. Overall, the enquiry concluded, in May 1999, that "the balance of evidence does not suggest that mobile phone technologies put the health of the general population... at risk" (IEGMP 2000: iii). Nonetheless, the expert group recommended, among many other proposals, a "precautionary" approach, particularly with regard to children's usage, which it suggested should be "limited." What appears a somewhat contradictory endorsement of unsubstantiated worries was made even more curious by the fact that it could hardly be suggested to be a straightforward response to wider "public concern."

Rightly or wrongly, the British population had evidently proven by their actions that using cell phones was a potential risk they were prepared to accept. In the face of the media campaign of stories linking cell phones to ill health, Britons continued to use cell phones in greater numbers. Some 42 million (out of a population of around 58 million) Britons owned one in late 2001, an exponential increase that has come about precisely during the post-1996 period when the public profile of the cell phone was principally in relation to health risks. The British government, meanwhile, was devoting well-publicized efforts to investigating an issue that appeared principally driven by media concern, in spite of public acceptance. Special leaflets on mobile phones and health are distributed through sales outlets that summarize the precautionary warnings of the Stewart Report. They warn, for example, of children's special vulnerability *if there were* a danger and recommend that under-sixteens use them only for "essential purposes" and for short periods (Department of Health 2000). The recommendation flew in the face of the almost entirely recreational cell phone usage of British teenagers to the extent that it is unclear what the advice could mean, let alone how it might be implemented. Was the precautionary approach embodied in the Stewart Inquiry a case where public authorities decided for, rather than in any meaningful sense, on behalf of the population that they really should be more careful about their choices, despite the fact that cell phones were not "putting the health of the general population at risk"?

Digging deeper, other aspects of cell phone health concerns were intriguing; an obvious question being, Was it actually true that radiofrequency radiation could cause harm? Yet it was quickly apparent that what appeared to be the key issue was only a beginning rather than an end. Specific allegations of actual harm from cell phones had indeed begun the whole episode, following a famous lawsuit in the United States. Similar attempts have been made subsequently to prove a connection between cell phones and cancer. A class-action suit for "biological injury" is still being vigorously pursued in the American courts at the time of writing in August 2001. As has already been suggested, however, the case for cell phone risk is not based on clear evidence of specific harm. The heart of the cell phone matter, like so many other contemporary risk issues, is that we, and the manufacturers, *cannot rule out the possibility* of future harm. A further layer of complication is added by the argument that this is a possible risk that might affect only a minority of especially sensitive individuals, in which case it is difficult to see how it could ever be either proven or disproven. In any event, whatever may be proven, cell phone risk remains an idea rather than a demonstrable reality, and how we view it depends on the inclination of our beliefs and suspicions, rather than knowledge. In this respect the more compelling question for me became, Where had this idea come from and how had it spread?

It also became necessary to explain the very different reactions and responses to these issues in different countries. Health fears about cell phones and base stations are by no means confined to the United Kingdom. Although the media profile and governmental response have been more concerted in the United Kingdom than in any other country, cell phone health concerns have already been consolidated in Australia, several European societies, and a growing number of others, as mobile telecommunications spread internationally. In December 1998, for example, a businessman sued mobile operators in South Africa alleging that his brain cancer had been caused by the electromagnetic fields from his cell phone. Reporting on the incident, the pre-eminent monitor of such "microwave news" noted that South Africa could now "be added to the list of countries" to which mobile EMF suspicions had diffused (*Microwave News*, January/February 1999).

However, the pattern of an increasing number of countries sharing cell phone health concerns is uneven. Some societies appeared almost actively disinterested in even considering the possibility of harm from these devices, and, at the other end of the spectrum, there were those societies that appeared to be reacting in an even more anxious way than in Britain. But these patterns bore little relationship to the actual number of cell phone users. Finland, for example, the country with the highest percentage of cell phone users in the world, is largely immune to the issue of cell phones and health. In Italy, on the other hand, where there are also very high levels of usage, it is quite a different story. Italians visibly love their mobile devices; a modern young Italian appears to feel hardly dressed if not walking down the road animatedly speaking into his or her cell phone. Yet alarm about the radiation "electrosmog" they produce is a common subject of discussion; hence the entry of this highly distinctive and loaded expression into their vernacular. Such is the Italian authorities' concern about radio-frequency emissions from these and other sources that they have passed the most stringent laws in the world limiting their radio-frequency fields. This has had some dramatic consequences. Diplomatic war broke out with the Vatican in early 2001 over allegations that the Papal radio station's emissions were causing cancer among local villagers. While a frosty compromise was eventually reached, this was not before the Italian authorities threatened to cut off the station's electricity supply. In other countries, such as Turkey, disputes over transmitters have led to them being destroyed, and even to the murder of neighbors, as well as the more typical stories of parents blaming towers for a wide variety of minor health complaints.[2]

---

[2] A retired night guard, in Kucukcekmece, a sub-district of Istanbul, killed two and injured three from the family of his neighbor after they allowed the installation of a tower on top of their apartment block, leaving a mast opposite his home (*Hurriyet Istanbul*, 6 December 2000). More generally, mobile phone masts (*baz itasyonlari*) were referred to 135 times between 1997 and 2000 in *Hurriyet Istanbul*, one of the biggest daily Turkish newspapers. Most of these were in 2000, when towers became more prolific. A typical story is "Furious parents" (13 December 2000), where parents of children at an Istanbul school blamed

One thing was certainly apparent; anxieties about ultra-high-frequency radio waves (or microwaves) not only had appeared in an increasing number of societies, but there was a discernible sequence to their development. As with so many other contemporary ideas and sensibilities, the issue first appeared in the United States, in this case at the beginning of the 1990s. While its profile waned in America, public reaction emerged in Australia and several European countries. It was as if health fears about radio-frequency radiation had run their course in America, only to somehow reappear in other continents. What's more, in the process their focus and character had changed. Beginning life as a lawsuit focused on an alleged cancer connection to cell phone handsets in the United States, when similar "microwave fears" then exploded in Australia a few years later, it was cell phone towers that were the objects of concern. Rather than pursuing legal action, Australians staged community direct action with parents chaining themselves to the fences of the offending tower. Elsewhere, concerns were very clearly absorbed into distinctive national preoccupations and organizations. In Northern Ireland, for example, anti–cell tower feelings revived and refocused existing suspicions of military facilities among residents.

I set about the task of answering these questions with an open mind, and endeavored to gather as much information and speak with as many people connected to the evolution of the issue as possible, given the inevitable constraints of time and resources. In so doing, I sought some distance from established sensibilities of social science. It is almost an axiom of environmental sociology, for example, that the author should proceed from sympathy with the "community" against the corporation or state. Arguably, such an approach effectively limits the scope to investigate beyond superficial appearances; to see whether battle lines are really so clear-cut, and that "right" necessarily lies with an innocent "people." It is difficult to imagine a more value-laden approach than that betrayed by the title, *No Safe Place: Toxic Waste, Leukemia and Community Action* (Brown and Mikkelsen 1990), for example, an influential book on the growth of community protest against waste dumps in the United States. Before a line of the book is even read, a connection between toxic waste and leukemia is asserted in the title, as if self-evident fact. So pervasive (and thereby, presumably powerful) is its human impact that there is "no safe place" of shelter. The notion that any response emerged through

headaches, stomach aches, and coughs on a newly installed tower following the suggestion of a doctor that the illness of a teacher might be due to the structure.

media intervention and other influences is also effectively discounted by the title of the book, as reaction is endowed with the legitimacy and authority of "community action." Brown and Mikkelsen's title, and assumptions, are by no means exceptional in the literature of "environmental justice."[3] So many interesting questions are simply not investigated because the values that inform contemporary research are accepted: we might ask how a word such as "toxic" has become so powerfully evocative, for example, and how neutral terms such as "pesticide" or "chemicals" have become synonymous with the dreaded "toxic."[4] These were the sorts of questions that animated this inquiry into cell phones and health fears.

Attitudes toward Cell Phones

The author has no particular agenda with regard to the cell phone's fortunes, its good or bad public image. I am not driven by any impulse to promote the virtues of cell phones and the part they might play in a more communicative society, for example; as if this were an exciting vision only held back by "irrational" concerns about health and safety. Certainly, the cell phone is not so personally indispensable that I would be inclined through experience to set about its defense. Were I a traveling salesman, no doubt I would be a more enthusiastic proponent of the "mobile revolution." For some people, the cell phone has greatly enhanced and even, on occasion, saved their lives.[5] It is certainly clear that the cell phone is central to the lives of the younger generation, in particular.

Members of the author's own generation (born in the early 1960s) are perhaps the last to have a more or less functional attitude toward communication, with a rather more limited appreciation of the value of phones, whether mobile or fixed-line, for "idle chat" or entertainment.

---

[3] For example, Vyner, *Invisible Trauma: The Psychosocial Effects of Invisible Environmental Contaminants* (1987); more recently, *Roberts and Toffolon-Weiss, Chronicles from the Environmental Justice Frontline* (2001).

[4] See Slovic et al. (1997) for an interesting account of how "chemicals" have become coterminous with "toxic" and "hazardous."

[5] Mobile industry representatives and commentators – to some extent quite justifiably – often highlight instances where cell phones have saved lives in a counter to the presentation of mobiles as increasing health risks. On 9 April 2001, for example, thirty ferry passengers were rescued from a reef in Fiji after one of the passengers used his mobile to summon help. A survey of 720 users by Chapman and Schofield (1998) found that one in eight users have reported a traffic accident; one in four a dangerous situation; one in 16 a nonroad medical emergency; one in 20 a crime; and one in 45 being lost or having difficulty at sea.

Cell phone usage among the under-thirties in Europe, by contrast, is extraordinarily extensive. Having not considered it significant enough to warrant investigation in 1997, the authoritative Eurobarometer monitor found in 2001 that some 80 percent of Europeans aged between fifteen and twenty-four used cell phones at least once a week.[6] A survey for a U.K. cell phone retailer found that on average British students spent more on their mobile phones than on food! (*Mobilex Environment Monthly*, October 2001). Quite grand claims are being made for this greater volume of conversation. Recent research argues that the constant "gossip" characteristic of cell phone use is the human equivalent of social grooming among apes, and essential to our social, psychological and physical well-being (Fox et al. 2001).[7] This researcher argues that such interaction improves teenagers' social skills. In an age where the specter of teenagers "communicating" principally with video games looms large, the impulse to elevate basic conversation with peers is perhaps understandable. The actual evidence for improved social skills among British teenagers since the arrival of the cell phone is more questionable, however.

Whatever one's opinion about the centrality of the cell phone to contemporary interaction, it is clearly changing the nature of communication. Communication and entertainment are becoming difficult to distinguish, for example. This is borne out by the rise of short message service (SMS) or, more simply, "text messaging," in the late 1990s. In April 1999 alone, users in Europe sent more than one billion text messages, and some operators were reporting 800 percent increases in the number of messages over the previous year (OECD 2000: 66). "Texting" has become routine for those in their teens and twenties, in particular, for everything from arranging blind dates and receiving football scores to interacting with television game shows. It was not lost on British politicians that, in July 2001, over 15 million electronic "votes" were cast by viewers of the elimination show *Big Brother*, many via SMS, three months after a general election that had seen the lowest voter turnout of modern times. Somewhat desperately, the British government is looking at ways in which it can utilize the ease and popularity of cell phones to address the problem of democratic participation. The British Electoral Commission announced in October 2001 their

---

[6] Eurobarometer Survey: European Communities, Young Europeans in 2001. Brussels: Eurobarometer. Available at www.http://europa.eu.int/comm/dg10/epo/eb/eb55/young_summary_en.pdf.

[7] The research was carried out for the BT Cellnet operator in the United Kingdom and was based on a survey of 1,000 mobile users and focus group discussions.

plans to look at voting by mobile phone as a means of improving voting figures (*The Times*, 6 October 2001).

Texting has become an interesting sociological phenomenon. At the end of 2001, British Telecom introduced a home phone (the Diverse 4010) that can send text messages, a development suggesting that texting has grown into a medium of its own beyond the particularities of communicating on the move. While there are signs in 2001 of texting becoming more common among other generations, it remains a distinctive youth activity in Europe. In a survey of 1,000 British eleven- to fifteen-year-olds in 2001, the vast majority sent between one and six messages per day; 15 percent sent more than ten per day.[8] Young people appear transfixed by the features and appearance of mobiles, reflecting the way in which they have become a fixture of identity and status. Evidently, the cell phone is a cherished personal object in itself, illustrated most extravagantly by the Motorola Bezel mobile, studded with diamonds and available for around £2,300!

The inescapable use of cell phones in public places, most notoriously on trains, has become a source of vexation for those, often middle-aged, less enamoured with their ubiquity. "Hell is other people talking web-speak on mobile phones," as British journalist John Humphrys entitled a newspaper opinion piece (*Sunday Times*, 27 August 2000). Australia and Japan already allow jamming of cell phones in public places such as theaters, with others set to follow. A theme explored more fully in the next chapter is the way the cell phone intrudes on what was once a relatively clear division between our public and private worlds. Such a distinction appears to have less meaning for younger generations. Having said this, certainly in Europe, cell phones have so rapidly become a part of everyday life that they often now go virtually unnoticed. Cell phone public "intrusion" appears to have become culturally absorbed much like the initially irritating experience of "mobile music" from the Sony Walkman.

Beyond simple generational differences and particular professional needs there is a more serious reason for qualified enthusiasm about claims for a mobile and wider information technology "revolution." The implication is clearly that technological innovation, in itself, can have a transformative impact on social life. Such claims can be interesting, as in the work of "futurologist" Alvin Toffler, but are more often simply rather banal, and basically untrue (Toffler 1981). During a recent U.K. television

---

[8] The survey was carried out by the Pupil Researcher Initiative managed by a team at the Centre for Science Education, Sheffield Hallam University. The project site can be visited at www.shu.ac.uk/pri.

program documenting the rise of the mobile, for example, a cellular company representative spoke of what he regarded as a startling utopia where one's whole life could be organized by an advanced "third generation" (3G) cell phone.[9] Such a "vision" is not only personally unappealing, but it comes at a time when informed opinion recognizes that the "mobile revolution" has badly stalled.

Transformative claims for information technology seem especially hollow at a time when any sense of more real, social transformation – even the idea of social change – has been virtually extinguished. As an insightful American book recently explained, we live in an age of "the end of utopia" (Jacoby 1999). Without any serious intellectual contestation or even discussion of larger ideas, the idea of real democratic debate, let alone more compelling visions of the future, has diminished. There is instead, "the end of politics," as a more recent volume from a similar perspective suggested (Boggs 2000). Puttnam (2000) impressively documents the associated processes of how American society has been distinctively and destructively individualized. Although there is some dispute over whether similar trends are apparent in the United Kingdom, particularly following the election of 2001, informed observers rightly recognize a similar decline in the stock of "social capital."[10] A greater volume of electronic communication can be regarded as a poor and depressing alternative to effecting real social improvement, even simply reviving a climate of greater intellectual contestation and debate.

Approaching the Issue: "Social Construction"

The approach taken by this book can be broadly described as "social constructionist"; that is to say, it proceeds from the assumption that the particular focus of concern has been actively, if not necessarily consciously created through the interaction of different actors and institutions. This perspective demands that we interrogate even the most apparently self-evident of social reactions, such as the contemporary abhorrence of child abuse or the fear of dying. The starting point of social constructionism usefully establishes some detachment and (potentially) greater objectivity

---

[9] *The Mobile*, by Philip Loft and Stephen Pidgeon, broadcast on Channel 5 on 28 May 2001.

[10] The argument that the United Kingdom is not experiencing similar individualizing trends to America is put forward by Hall (1999). The review of Puttnam (2000) in the *Times Higher Education Supplement* (10 August 2001) suggests an opposite conclusion.

from what are often very contemporary issues and therefore subject matters in which researchers might find themselves emotionally involved. Such
dangers can be lessened, so that powerful contemporary preoccupations
such as with pedophiles and child abuse can be treated as demanding explanation with the same level of detachment as earlier obsessions such as
with witches.

The process of social construction is one of originally marginal concerns becoming institutionalized. The first step in this process is when a
concern is taken seriously by authoritative individuals and institutions. It
is one thing, for example, if "ordinary" individuals choose to believe in
flying saucers, angels, or horoscopes. It is evidently a different matter if
respected and higher profile figures begin to also take such beliefs seriously, and thereby endow them with a legitimacy that makes it far more
difficult for them to be dismissed. Contesting what he calls "voodoo science," for example, the physicist Robert Park points to how the bizarre,
if relatively widespread belief in alien abduction has been patronized by
respected American academics (Park 2000: 174–5). Any kind of attention
from larger authorities helps to construct an issue as legitimate, often irrespective of whether it affirms or denies the claims. Horoscopes have
had some endorsement in Europe comparable to that of alien abduction
in the United States, through being made the subject of academic inquiry.
Drawing the attention of only one disconcerted journalist, the University
of Southampton in the United Kingdom established a research group for
the study of astrology.[11] Funded by an astrology-promoting body, one of
its projects is setting out to examine the "apparent relationship" between
the position of Jupiter at the time of birth and subsequent alcoholism
and drug dependency. Meanwhile in France, former adviser to President
Mitterand, Elisabeth Teissier, has been granted a doctorate on the subject
by the country's most prestigious university, the Sorbonne.[12]

Where traditional assumptions are concerned, the ground has been
cleared for a social constructionist approach by a universal undermining
of previously unquestioned beliefs about family, state, and nation. We are
more amenable to the idea that these institutions are not self-evident and
everything must have been somehow socially created. Interesting academic work that demonstrates how even cherished national traditions
and customs were all relatively recently "invented" has found its time
(Hobsbawm and Ranger 1992). A social constructionist approach is more

[11] See Catherine Bennett, the *Guardian*, 22 March 2001.
[12] See Magnus Linklater, *The Times*, 16 August 2001.

contentious, however, on issues that have not been widely challenged and that appeal to contemporary sensitivities, and this might include an environmental health issue such as low-level radiation. Yet the very fact of dramatically contrasting national reactions to the issue itself suggests a very active and differential process of social construction.

A social constructionist approach has become influential in numerous fields of social science and history. In the United States, the "construction of social problems" approach was pioneered by Blumer (1971), and Spector and Kitsuse (1987), and is now exemplified by the work of Best (1995, 2001b). The aim is to "shift the focus of analysis from the causes of objective social conditions to the processes by which members of a society define those conditions as problems" (Spector and Kitsuse 1987: 59). Central to the constructionist perspective is a radical challenge to the conventional understanding of the way problems are created. Problems do not simply accumulate to the point that they demand recognition. The rise of concern about environmental pollution examined in one study, for example, could not simply have been a response to a decline in the quality of air and water, for there was no such deterioration (ibid.: 128).

The general pattern of human problem creation and resolution indicates that a problem becomes defined as such only when the possibility of a solution becomes real. Otherwise, conditions are absorbed in a fatalistic fashion, simply "routinely accommodated" (ibid.: 84). An important consequence of approaching social processes in this way is that the "common sense" view of political and institutional "responses" being driven "from below" by public concerns is effectively challenged. The author has suggested elsewhere, for example, that the unprecedented prominence of "the consumer" and consumer affairs in Europe not only has been driven "from below" by greater public spending power and consumer choice. It has been decisively fueled "from above" by the encouragement of consumer safety concerns by a European political class seeking an effective and engaging identity – in this case as health guardians of the European population (Burgess 2001).

Social constructionism is sensitive not only to the constructed character of original claims but to the transformations undergone in the process of a "pre-problem" becoming recognized as of wider concern. Using the example of neighborhood complaint about unpleasant smells, Spector and Kitsuse note how in the process of finding a responsive agency the grievance would be transformed in accordance with the remit of the particular agency that pursues the problem. The creation of mental health provision within the community might mean that a complaint that previously would have been directed towards the police is, instead, laid at the door of health professionals. In the process, a problem of "order" becomes one of "health." This process is comparable to the way in which esthetic, economic, and consultation concerns about cell phone towers were transformed into issues of health in some countries such as Britain. In Spector and Kitsuse's example the issue became one of health not simply because mental health professionals shaped it in the process of response. Prior to this it is likely that locals will have, consciously or otherwise, interpreted the issue to themselves in terms they imagined would gain a sympathetic ear, thereby already beginning the process of constructing the new health problem (Spector and Kitsuse 1987: 84). Similarly, in the case of cell towers, campaigners began to consider and present their objections through the prism of health in response to the agenda promoted by the media and government.

Perceptions of whether something is a problem or not also reflect the changing levels of confidence and trust we have in our institutions, and in their ability to resolve those problems. British academic Alan Irwin recalls the story of visiting a factory in England during the 1980s to discuss problems of occupational health with managers and trade union officials. As an environmental sociologist he arrived with a strong sense of the human harm that chemical exposure might cause. Given a hostile reception, he recognized very honestly that whatever the "facts" (of marginal dangers),

my sense of a significant hazard was totally at odds with his sense of security, employment and an exceptionally rigorous set of workplace controls. . . . my assumption of a major health issue was matched by his notion that this was merely the temporary and controllable side-effect of an otherwise successful technology. . . . My (inevitably partial and selective) use of scientific evidence conflicted with his trust in the technical competence of the company's medical staff. (Irwin 2001: x)

What constitutes a problem reflects dominant beliefs and identities. It is also subject to modification, as values and relationships change. It is likely that were Irwin to return to a trade union official today, he would encounter a greater receptivity to the notion of workplace health risks. As the ability and inclination of British trade unions to exercise traditional industrial power has receded, so they have absorbed and extended the "safety first" ethos of contemporary British society. The continued and repeated threats of industrial action on the London Underground train system are now legitimized on the grounds of ensuring customer safety, for example, rather than the need for higher wages.

Social constructionist approaches have become increasingly common. There is some work examining scientific controversies, for example, reflecting debate among philosophers of science about the constructionist method.[13] Research in the constructionist tradition remains unusual with regard to the other key themes of this book, however: risk and the environment. More traditional shibboleths connected to race, family, nation, and faith are subject to often merciless "deconstruction." Yet what might be regarded as their contemporary equivalents, even replacements, have largely escaped attention. While social constructionism is identified as an approach to studies of the environment, there is only one work that can be adequately referenced as an example of this "school."[14] This is a particularly European absence; there are some American texts that have adopted a social constructionist approach to environmental risk (Johnson and Covello 1987; Leviton, Needleman, and Shapiro 1998). Yet what remains a relative lack of critical writing in these areas appears to be because the very act of socially (de)constructing a theme or concern is interpreted as an act of criticism, whatever the intentions of the author. To undertake a social constructionist approach to the environment suggests that the agenda of environmentalism is somehow illegitimate. Even the factual contesting of the environmentalist case appears almost sacrilegious, evidenced by the bemused and hostile reaction in August 2001 to the publication of *The Skeptical Environmentalist* by a former ecologist (Lomborg 2001).[15]

Diffusion and Contamination

This study proceeds from an assumption that cell phone risk not only was socially and politically constructed, but also was informed and shaped by the ways in which it had presented itself elsewhere, in other societies. Internationalized perceptions of cell phone risk here fit into a much wider pattern, with countless examples. To some degree, and in some fashion, it spread from one society to others. A focus on processes of international diffusion established within the study of social movements (McAdam and

---

[13] Englehardt and Caplan (1987) took a constructionist approach to issues such as nuclear energy and workplace safety. MacHamer, Pera, and Baltas (2000) contest what they describe as "extreme" social constructionism.

[14] In the most recent book in the field, Alan Irwin's *Sociology and the Environment* (2001), Hannigan (1995) stands as the only real example of a constructionist approach.

[15] Lomborg's book was the subject of very personalized attacks in many publications; a website was even set up: www.anti-Lomborg.com.

Rucht 1993; Snow and Benford 1999) is beginning to emerge within social constructionism (Best 2001b).

This process of international diffusion of sensitivities and concerns appears increasingly in evidence in relation to a range of ideas and even emotional responses in the modern world, from "road rage" (a term now common to several societies) to an emphasis on the emotional and therapeutic (Nolan 1998). Returning from a conference in Israel in August 2000, for example, the author struck up a conversation with a law teacher from London about the in-flight movie, *Erin Brockovich*, based on the true story of the class-action lawsuit brought against an American chemical company over the chromium penetration of the ground water of a local community. The alleged consequences ranged from cancers and miscarriages to deformed chickens and dead frogs. The law teacher reported that a friend had convinced herself after also seeing the film that her failure to get pregnant (after twelve months) might also be due to "something in the water." Her friend apparently saw enough similarity between her complaints and those afflicting people in the American town of Hinkley to arouse her suspicions about water quality in Redbridge, Essex. The idea that contaminated water might explain difficulties in becoming pregnant was diffused, in this case via popular dramatization.

This study is concerned not only with the process of diffusion in general but with the diffusion of sensibilities suspicious of "modernity" more particularly. An ill-defined, often unuseful term, "modernity" here refers simply to "the modern" and its consequences, as opposed to what is assumed to be more "natural" and traditional. While some of the fruits of modernity, such as cell phones, are embraced, there is now a widespread assumption that there is a longer-term price to pay for the accumulated advance of modernity. A transnational concern with "contamination" from modernity has been spread via the now global environmental agenda. Suggestions of life-threatening conditions from relatively routine aspects of modern life have themselves become routine.

Although little research has been carried out in this area, one innovative study suggests that modernity is indeed "bad for your health," or at least perceived to be. Researchers in New Zealand attempted to investigate more closely what they describe as "a growing public fascination with how features of modern life pose threats to personal health" (Petrie et al. 2001).[16] They found that concerns about modernity affecting health

---

[16] In the first study, 526 university students completed a questionnaire measuring health worries, symptom reports, and health perceptions. A second study utilized an existing

consisted of four principal components: environmental pollution, toxic interventions, tainted food, and radiation. Heightened concerns about possible harm from these sources "were significantly associated with somatic complaints and ratings of the importance of health to the individual." They found additionally that those with higher levels of modern health anxieties had correspondingly higher rates of food intolerance and chronic fatigue syndrome. Heightened and negative fears about selected aspects of modernity, in other words, appear to have some role in undermining people's confidence in their health. In its more extreme forms, such as "magnetic deficiency syndrome," the outlook behind the trend toward "natural" medicine," is the notion that industrialization has left humans "starved of the natural energy that was once supplied by Mother Earth" (Park 2000: 58).

Perhaps the most widespread of contemporary anti-modernity concerns is the extraordinary reaction against even the testing, let alone consumption, of genetically modified food. The concern has not yet been embraced in the United States to the same degree as in Europe, partly because of a more positive popular attitude toward science and more devolved regulatory system. Indeed, the issue has become part of a "global food fight" where a more pro-scientific American stance chastises a backlash created by "scare-mongering" European consumer groups (Paarlberg 2000). Popular European reaction is largely uninformed scientifically and based on the feeling that it is wrong to interfere with nature. It is historically curious to single out this particular instance of human "interference" in the whole history of (man-made) agriculture. The consequences of this "playing God" are likely to be disastrous, according to contemporary sensibilities. This is summed up by the epithet "Frankenfood," a description approved by influential environmentalists (Porritt 2000: 33–6). Despite a more positive attitude toward genetically modified food, comparable anxieties about modern interference in nature appear to be also evident in the United States, but fixed on other issues, most notably stem cell research.

The belief that a "return to nature" offers protection against the risks of modernity is pervasive. In the context of hostility toward genetically modified Frankenfood, organic produce, wrongly perceived to be free of "contamination," has been overwhelmingly embraced. The latest figures show sales rising by 40 percent year by year, making it the fastest growing

national survey database of 7,869 New Zealanders. The survey examined people's concerns of modernity affecting their health in the past twelve months.

retail sector in Europe. The number of organic and in-conversion farms in the European Union is estimated to have exceeded 100,000 in 1998, from only 6,300 in 1985.[17] Sales of organic food in Australia have grown from $100 million in 1995 to more than $250 million, a trend described by one commentator as similar to the safety-driven fashion for hands-free kits for mobile phones.[18] World sales are tipped to reach U.S. $100 trillion by 2006. Somewhat ironically for a type of food bound up with "the local," it has itself become a global industry.

The case of organic food clearly illustrates that concern is not with "contamination" in general, but with only that deemed "unnatural." As in the popular perception of risk more generally, reaction is highly selective and inconsistent (Hammitt 1990). Indeed the exclusive reliance on "natural" animal fertilizers involves dangers of its own. Organic food has not been safety tested to anything like the degree that has its genetically modified equivalent. Fertilized with human and animal sewage, it is seen to carry health risks itself, among other problems. It is not surprising that the embracing of organic food (despite its high price) is beginning to be described in popular commentary as a "new religion, the truths of which are based on mythology and unsupported by any scientific or empirical evidence."[19] The natural or organic represents something of a statement, even a personal opting out, or at least an expression of a desire to do so. The germs of a new secular morality can be discerned, which strives not for purity in the moral sense but for being free of contamination by modernity.

It is interesting to note that perceptions of contamination from modernity are not particular to the classical West. A number of experts suggest that the legacy of the Soviet experience has been one of environmental catastrophe, which has had in its turn a disastrous impact on human health. One focus of perceived Russian "contamination" are the problems of the Altai region of Siberia, where a cluster of health complaints are attributed to the impact of the Soviet – now Russian – space program. Soviet rockets have been launched from the Baikonur Cosmodrome in Kazakhstan for the last three decades, powered by the toxic propellant hepthyl. Debris from these rockets has landed on a nature reserve in the

---

[17] Cited in *Trends* (occasional publication of Canadian High Commission in London), January 2000 edition: 4.
[18] For statistics and comparison, see Rodney Chester, "Healthy Scepticism," *Courier Mail* (Queensland), 7 September 2000.
[19] Robin Young, "All Things Bright and Beautiful?" *The Times*, 7 October 2000.

Altai Republic of Southern Siberia. Some inhabitants of the Altai region believe that health problems with children are somehow attributable to the rockets. Of particular concern is the high incidence of (extremely jaundiced) "yellow babies." These claims have interacted with those of Western environmentalists concerning the "deadly fuel" hepthyl. Alexei Yablokov, President Yeltsin's former scientific adviser, has claimed that 30 million hectares are routinely subjected to rocket fuel pollution.[20] A village head from the affected village of Ploskaya believes that the fuel is contained in everything they eat: "for us there is no escape."[21] Interestingly, the phrase is almost identical to the "No Safe Place" of American "environmental justice."

According to the most extreme environmental discourse, the Altai case is hardly surprising, and fits a general thesis of an environment ruined by the ultimate modernity of Soviet industrialization. Murray Feshbach, a research professor at Georgetown University, has posited a possible "ecocide," as the population is decimated in various ways by the environmental legacy of the Soviet experiment in "ultra modernity" (Feshbach, Friendly, and Brown 1993). He has had some success in diffusing his ideas within Russia. Yet no matter how intuitive it might be to imagine that the impact of Soviet programs was likely to have been destructive, it is by no means self-evidently the case. Fuel experts have pointed out that while the dangers of hepthyl are real, the vast majority of the propellant would evaporate very quickly and be confined to the immediate crash site.[22] Considered academic opinion suggests that ecological factors have not played a determinant role in the post-Soviet health crisis. Indeed, the relationship has been the inverse of that supposed by an ecological interpretation; the general increase in mortality is linked to socioeconomic decline, not increased industrial output (Ellman 1994: 337).

It would appear from emotive interviews with parents of afflicted children in the Altai that a possible connection of their child's ill health to a major Soviet technological program was loaded with meaning, even if proof of any specific connection was lacking. If the argument to indict the environment is only hypothetical, desperate Russian parents of sick children continue to point to a mysterious "contamination," much like the British parents with which this chapter began. "It's all around us – we're

---

[20] Kathy Brewis, "Deadly Harvest," *Sunday Times* magazine, 12 November 2000.
[21] Ibid.
[22] According to Craig Covault, a senior editor with *Aviation Week and Space Technology*, in special international report in the *Washington Times*, 20 December 2000.

being poisoned!" exclaimed one distraught mother of a desperately ill child in a BBC documentary.[23] While sympathetically covering the plight of Russian families, the program itself strongly intimated that pointing to a degraded environment infecting children was driven by the desire to come to terms with misfortune. The parents of afflicted children in the Altai appeared to find some comfort in identifying a cause for their state despite the absence of any evidence. Under circumstances where social institutions were barely functioning and there was no other means of salvation or even recognition of their desperate plight, individual tragedy appears to acquire meaning as a by-product of the ill-fated Soviet experiment with nature. A spontaneous environmentalism thereby plays one of the roles of a secular religion in a society where there is no proper recognition for personal tragedy, or any means of redress.

Claims and Claims Makers

The sharper edge of indicating the intellectual origins and motivation for a study such as this is the powerful contemporary suspicion of hidden agendas, and even more so the hidden sources of research funding. It is this pervasive suspicion that has led, for example, to the creation of a website in the United States that reveals the names of some 1,100 university researchers whose work is claimed to be underwritten by the private sector.[24] Such a concern might be viewed as particularly relevant to a study such as this. The very act of socially "deconstructing" perceptions of mobile phone risk could suggest such a hidden agenda, one that is in league with cell phone companies obviously keen to promote the idea that mobile phones are not harmful to health. Especially in the United States there has been considerable controversy related to the cell phone industry's relationship to scientific research on health effects. Dr. George Carlo, a man once entrusted with overseeing the industry-sponsored research program into possible health effects, subsequently fell out with his former sponsors. He has vigorously pursued the claim that his downfall was precipitated by a desire to cover up disturbing findings (Carlo and Schram 2001). On the wider issue here, and whatever the truth of these specific charges, it should be noted that industries such as mobile telecommunications find themselves in an unresolvable situation. Corporations

---

[23] Documentary in the BBC's *Assignment* series by Julian Pettifer, entitled *The Russian Disease*, broadcast on BBC2 on 21 March 1998.

[24] Center for "Science in the Public Interest" website at www.integrityinscience.org.

are attacked for not providing sufficient funds for effective long-term studies, thereby suggesting lack of concern. At the same time, when they do sponsor studies, they are open to the accusation that they have done so only in order to influence the findings.

The author received no funding from cellular phone companies, either directly or indirectly. Following interviews with anti–cell phone campaigners, I spoke with some representatives of the cell phone industry, mainly individuals from operators and national trade associations whose job it was to coordinate an effective response to public concerns and who had therefore monitored developments closely.

What is intellectually striking about the contemporary suspicion of hidden agendas, corporate funding, and research "cover-ups" is that it is largely absent when evaluating the claims of nongovernmental lobbying organizations, alternative experts, and claims makers. The possibility that such groups and individuals might be working to an agenda, promoting safety products, or simply furthering careers is not widely entertained. Married to this prejudice is the assumption that any party suggesting something to be more dangerous than we supposed is doing a public service and should be taken seriously. Yet, of course, agencies more in accord with contemporary sensibilities are themselves in the business of selling and promotion. At the time of writing, the (U.K.) Soil Association produced a report, based on selective sources, revealing that organic foods are better for you.[25] It is hardly surprising that this, the principle representative of small, "alternative" farmers and other promoters of organic produce, would come to such a conclusion. Sometimes those keen to promote particular dangers may well be selling products such as hands-free mobile phone kits that purport to reduce radiation emissions. The publicizing of fears is often now followed by entrepreneurial "risk products," such as the promotion of special socks and "airogym" cushions for the feet following the panic over deep vein thrombosis on long air journeys in 2000.[26]

---

[25] *Organic Farming, Food Quality and Human Health* was released by the Soil Association on 7 August 2001. In its review of 99 scientific papers, the author, Shane Heaton, rejected 70 of them for alleged defects in study design or, technique or because they were not "fair and accurate" comparisons of organic and nonorganic foods. Unsurprisingly, the methodological defects of Heaton's own work led it to be rejected as unscientific by the British Nutrition Foundation and Food Standards Agency.

[26] Scholl began promoting "flight socks" in 2001, while retired British Airways pilot Paul Richards successfully publicized his invention of an "Airogym" to exercise the feet while flying (see *Daily Mail*, 19 April 2001).

It is commonly assumed that "discovering" new risks is a selfless act. Yet we should be aware of the possibility that any voices of alarm have their own, less transparent agendas. More importantly, the absence of direct commercial motivation does not necessarily denote independence. Simple self-promotion, or the advertising of an agenda bound to the fortunes of a particular lobby group, may inform the publicizing of "independent" advice, and should be treated with as much caution as information tied to more obvious financial gain. This is hardly an insignificant problem where environmental and consumer groups and their agendas are so pervasive.

It goes without saying that media claims about previously unheard – of threats and risks should be considered with caution. As Marcia Angell's excellent dissection of the breast implant controversy in the United States points out, such stories are actively sought and promoted because of the "... fascination with newly discovered, mass health hazards and the penchant to assume a cover-up in any disaster" (Angell 1997: 31). But knowledge of the "risk messenger" is as important as knowledge of the media's risk message itself. It is important to be aware of the possibility that individuals popularizing risks are bound up with particular environmental and consumer agendas or are often promoting their own careers through monopolizing particular risk concerns as their own. Such suspicions are particularly important in the many instances where the scientific authorities in question choose to pursue their suspicions in the public domain, rather than allow their experiments to be repeated and confirmed by their peers.

It has become increasingly common for preliminary risk research in particular to be released to the media in a blaze of publicity. It is stretching credulity to accept that every instance of pursuing such a media attention–grabbing course is because the "whistle-blower" has been backed into a corner by the blindness or corruption of his peers. Park (2000) documents the fascinating case of the much publicized yet now totally discredited discovery of "cold fusion" in 1989, for example. The very fact that the scientists in question were more interested in generating media interest in their discovery than in publishing their results in scientific journals and carefully validating their findings with their peers rightly aroused scientific suspicions. They had (unsurprisingly) not managed to overturn the laws of thermodynamics and generate energy from nothing, thereby enjoying infamy long after their moment of fame.

In the case of a number of defining contemporary health panics in the United Kingdom it is often middle-ranking academics and scientists who have put themselves at the center of public attention with their claims of unrecognized dangers. The continuing alarm over a purported relationship between the measles/mumps/rubella (MMR) vaccine and autism has been generated in the United Kingdom by Dr Andrew Wakefield, formerly a consultant gastroenterologist at the Royal Free Hospital in London where his work was heavily criticized.[27] Another doctor, Peter Mansfield, has subsequently made a name for himself as the only practitioner prepared to administer single, separate jabs in place of the triple vaccine MMR. Similarly, the scientific doubt central to consolidating the reaction against the American multinational corporation Monsanto, and genetically modified food more generally, was provided by Dr. Arpad Puzstai, who revealed subsequently unsubstantiated claims about possible health effects in a sensationalist television documentary.[28] Most of the newspaper stories substantiating British concern about cell phones have included quotes from Dr. Gerard Hyland, a senior lecturer in physics at the University of Warwick. Hyland has become the principal source of scientific doubt for British anti-mobile campaigners.

An obvious question to consider about whistle-blowing scientific claims makers is why their colleagues and peers do not appear to agree with their alarming conclusions. It is implausible to work only on the jaundiced assumption that they are bravely revealing a truth that others are afraid to tell. Certainly, none of the above risks is driven by overwhelming evidence; rather, there is only the possibility of indirect or future harm. It is consequently at least questionable whether the individuals concerned were simply compelled by manifest dangers that only they had been able to identify.

While it is important to encourage an attitude of skepticism toward claims and claims makers, this is not to endorse cynicism. Whatever the merits of their case, claims makers such as Wakefield and Hyland appear genuinely motivated by a desire to do something positive, if not for society at least for some of its apparent victims. Yet it should be recognized that

---

[27] Typical headline: "Parents are being deceived on MMR jab, warns doctor," *Daily Mail*, 22 January 2001.

[28] In ITV channel documentary, *World in Action*, screened on 23 April 1998, one of the scientific researchers, Dr. Arpad Puzstai, gave an unauthorized comment on the preliminary, unpublished results of tests in which modified potato was fed to rats. He suggested that immune system damage was possible. Despite refutations of Dr. Puzstai's claims by senior scientists at the Rowlett Institute laboratory where he worked, fears about the health effects of genetically modified organisms became the front-page story in many national papers.

the starting point for particularly the more organized health risk claims makers is a pre-determined conviction that the environment or the consumer is under threat. There is nothing wrong with this in principle, but it can be argued, at the very least, that it involves a degree of self-deception. It is as if such claims makers imagine themselves to have become "people's champions" only reluctantly, rather than through a semiconscious process of self-promotion. And while we are all engaged to some degree or another in self-promotion, when its consequences fuel public alarm, and even create the possibility of a measles epidemic – as in the case of MMR panic – a considerable degree of caution and responsibility is, or should be involved, on the part of those promoting possible risks.

To conclude these remarks on claims and claims making, it is important to add that the claims makers themselves are ultimately unimportant. There are thousands of potential risk claims to be made, not least because in sufficient quantity, and in the wrong circumstance, almost anything can be said to pose a hypothetical risk. Yet only a few risk claims succeed in making even a momentary public impact. Some strike a chord, resonate with, even capture certain themes and preoccupations that a particular society has or is beginning to establish. Others do not. The merits of the particular claim and the skill with which it is put forward are not decisive. What is more important to understand and question is why particular concerns manage to accord public and institutional anxieties. Such a question is likely to provide insights into the way in which society is heading.

Risk and Risk Taking

Risk concerns over cell phone radiation cannot be seen in isolation. They form part of a wider culture that is highly amenable to claims of possible harm from everyday foods and objects. It is because this particular risk concern is situated within a wider climate of heightened sensitivity to everyday risks that it has struck a chord. "We live in fearful times where the pursuit of personal safety has become a religion, and risks seem to lurk everywhere. The shining symbol of this new era is the mobile phone," suggested an editorial in the influential *New Scientist* magazine (10 April 1999). Had cell phones become popular before the 1960s, it is unlikely that there would have been so much interest in suggestions that they might cause harm, as is illustrated below in the book.

An exaggerated reaction to everyday risk appears to have been routinized and culturally embedded in American society from the late 1960s.

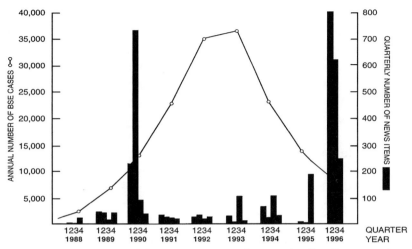

FIGURE 1. Comparison of the press coverage of BSE with officially reported cases. *Source:* House of Lords, Select Committee on Science and Technology.

Health concerns about asbestos, alar on apples, and toxic contamination are some of the defining episodes in the coming of the American "risk society" (Wildavsky 1995; Foster, Bernstein, and Huber 1999). Europe has come more recently to embrace such concerns, as consumer health became politicized in the 1980s and 1990s. In Europe it was the reaction to "mad cow disease" (bovine spongiform encephalitis, BSE) and its human form (variant Creutzfeldt-Jakob disease, vCjD) that consolidated the politicization of risk. As Figure 1 illustrates, the reporting of BSE bore little relation to its actual incidence, instead reflecting the extent to which it became a wider "panic" spread through the media.

The United Kingdom is at the center of the European risk storm. News stories in an unexceptional week between 21 and 28 June in Britain, for example, included a panic over soy sauce links to cancer, a cancer alert in connection with eggs produced near an animal incinerator, chemicals in hair dye also presenting cancer risks, and a purported threat to male fertility from the phthalate group of chemicals. It is only in the United Kingdom, among the countries of the developed world, that the possibility of discontinuing the MMR vaccine has been raised.

Of course, media risk headlines are not necessarily of any social consequence, even if they are read by millions of people in newspaper-loving Britain. It is interesting to consider what the impact of these often momentary and episodic risk concerns actually is. In one sense it can be confidently suggested that there is a law of diminishing returns. At one time, like in the United States, asbestos stood relatively uniquely as the invisible workplace and later more general domestic hazard, and society's anxious energies were singularly focused on its impact. Today, so many and so constantly shifting are moments of risk alarm that they often barely merit a mention beyond the day on which the story appeared. Little further was heard about the media-generated concerns listed above, for example. Indeed, what is so curious about announcements of new risks today is that risk alarms are rarely put forward with any serious conviction, and are quickly forgotten as society moves on to another. Announcing risk concerns has become a sort of habit shorn of any relationship to consequences. At the same time, some of these panics really do affect people's behavior. Thousands of British parents are now actively seeking out ways to receive single vaccines, rather than the triple MMR jab. Even more importantly when the state takes action with bans, license withdrawals, and official inquiries, people's choices are necessarily and involuntarily affected.

The cumulative effect of these and many other examples has been to create something of a culture shift in Anglo-American societies. Sociologists on both sides of the Atlantic have written identically titled books describing a "culture of fear" (Furedi 1997; Glassner 1999). Whilst usually more intangible than earlier, external fears such as of communism and nuclear annihilation, cultural change in this regard has been dramatic. Angell's description of America may be now true of European societies: "we feel we live in a sea of toxins and dangerous habits" (Angell 1997: 155). Such sensibilities are very much in evidence among some of those drawing attention to possible health risks from cell phones and their towers. British campaigners in particular drew most of their strength from a wider cultural and political climate that insists on precaution, rather than any specific evidence.

This book has not, however, been informed by a cavalier attitude toward risk despite a critical attitude toward the advancing of such claims. Besides a cautious, sometimes quite irrational attitude toward a number of possible hazards, there are some risks associated with cell phones that appear plausible. An increased risk of accidents while driving and using a cell phone is by no means unreal, even if American cell phone industry representatives say there is little evidence to single out mobiles from other distractions. The latest research, by the British Transport Research Laboratory in March 2002, suggests that talking on a cell phone while driving is more dangerous than being drunk. The results demonstrate that drivers' reaction times were, on average, 30 percent slower when talking on a hand-held mobile phone compared with being drunk and nearly 50 percent slower than under normal driving conditions (Direct Line Insurance 2002). It is unsurprising that around thirty-one countries, as well as New York and thirteen other American cities, have banned hand-held cell phone use while driving.

The author would not posit himself as a distinctively rational person, against those "irrationally" campaigning against what are invariably only relatively small risks. Many of those who have contested what are perceived to be "panics" over risk issues do so by challenging the scale of the purported problem, often using statistics to demonstrate how unfounded and remote the probabilities involved really are.[29] Yet while basic facts are important, a focus exclusively on this purely quantitative dimension is very one-sided, as writings on risk perception have long established (Starr 1969; Douglas and Wildavsky 1982; Slovic 1987). It is the character of perceived risks as much as their scale that is at least as important. While everyone knows "flying is the safest form of travel," the fact is that one does not feel in control (unlike car driving – even if it is, of course, actually an illusion as you are subject to the actions of other drivers). That the consequences of anything going wrong when flying suggests fatality rather than only injury further determines greater fear of air travel for some people. Straightforward risk statistics are also often of little use because risks are always balanced against perceived benefits that are notoriously difficult to quantify. How do we measure the lives actually saved in emergencies by cell phones against the potential for harm from their radiation? No matter how strong one's fear of flying, the attractions of far speedier travel are a considerable incentive to overcoming anxiety in even the most nervous traveler.

Having private, irrational fears is not essentially a social problem, if actions and reactions are largely inconsequential. Pragmatism and possible benefits are often the incentive to discard or review irrational concerns. What is so striking about so many risk concerns today, however, is that they do indeed threaten to overshadow people's lives. Besides damaging one's quality of life through increasing anxiety, minor risk concerns can then take on a life of their own. An ironic consequence can be to diminish more important and more real risks that we confront elsewhere. Once the preoccupation with "phantom" risks begins to consume individuals' lives, perspective can be lost to the point where, in effect, a hypothetical

---

[29] The website of the Harvard Risk Analysis Unit, for example, centers on revealing how surprisingly remote many apparently everyday risks really are.

risk is traded for a real one. The speculative link between MMR and autism is leading parents to leave their children unvaccinated, for example. Arguably, the "phantom" connection of autism to the triple jab has been traded for the real risk of measles, a disease that can cause deafness, blindness, brain damage, and even death. In the case of cell phone tower campaigns, some prominent campaigners have involved their own children in campaigning and have even withdrawn them from schools where masts are present. Responding to "phantom" risk here involves accepting possible consequences for the child's education and socialization. Yet acting on remote threats to our children's physical welfare is now often regarded as the "responsible thing to do," forgetting the wider impact of obsessively protecting children from any phenomenon or experience that suggests physical dangers (Furedi 2001).

There is an important distinction between sensitivity to social dangers and contemporary risk aversion. Risk in the sense in which it is understood today is ultimately nonsocial; it is not rooted in our real experiences of society. This is reflected in the most influential European sociological work on risk where we are all, regardless of social position and context, susceptible to risk (Beck 1992). This is risk associated with the environment: all-pervasive, even invisible dangers emanating from humanity's impact on nature. Assumed as an article of faith in European societies, the factual basis for many of these threats is, at the very least, limited (Lomborg 2001). The undoubted quantum leap in the *perception* of everyday risk needs to be understood sociologically, rather than as mechanically determined by objective environmental hazards. In outline, heightened risk perception can usefully be understood as driven by the processes of individualization and of the dissolution of beliefs, social institutions, and practices. It is principally a transformation or, rather, breakdown of traditional patterns of social life that generates a distinctively individuated and fragile conception of existence. Like the proverbial old lady living alone in an inner city apartment scaring herself to death with "real life" crime shows, I detect that our perceptions have become more disconnected from reality in an increasingly lonely society. Where the elderly person develops an exaggerated sense of vulnerability to violent crime, society as a whole appears to now experience everyday relationships and phenomena as harboring potential menace and damage. This is not to suggest that a distinctively atomized conception of the world is the principal driving force behind cell phone fears. It may have created greater receptivity to this and many other everyday risk alarms, but without the institutionalized response to the cell phone and health issue, it is unlikely that it would have been sustained and diffused through so many societies. Overcautious institutions appear to have been more central to the issue's development than local campaigners and fragmented societies. Before the evolution of cell phone fears is outlined, however, it is necessary to consider the scope and impact of the "mobile revolution" witnessed in the last decade.

2

The Mobile "Revolution"

The Global Expansion of the Cell Phone

Cell phones have become a ubiquitous feature of life at the beginning of the twenty-first century. As the deputy editor of the British political weekly, *New Statesman*, put it: "The mobile is the vibrating, ringing or bleeping tool that keeps us connected in a society that is constantly on the go." The heartbreaking final calls from the airliners about to crash into the Twin Towers on September 11, among other things, suggest for her that "Mobile phone calls will provide the soundtrack of our twenty-first century."[1]

Between 1992 and 1997, the number of mobile subscribers grew at a compound annual growth rate of 52 percent in OECD countries (OECD 2000: 7). In June 1999 there were more than 293 million subscribers in the OECD area alone, with Scandinavian countries showing the highest rates of cell phone usage (see Fig. 2). Leading manufacturer Nokia estimates the total global market in 2000 to be about 405 million phones. In several European countries, between a half and two-thirds of the population now own a cell phone. In the United States, meanwhile, only around one in three people were owners in 2000, as the market continued to be held back, relative to Europe, even into 2002 by conflicting technologies and a lack of radio spectrum.

Market penetration in Finland, which has the highest rates of ownership in the world, stands at around 70 percent of the population. It is no longer simply owning a cell phone that counts in this part of the world, but owning a certain model. Distinctively Finnish "mobile etiquette" involves

[1] Cristina Odone, "Our Mobile Homes," the *Observer*, 13 January 2002.

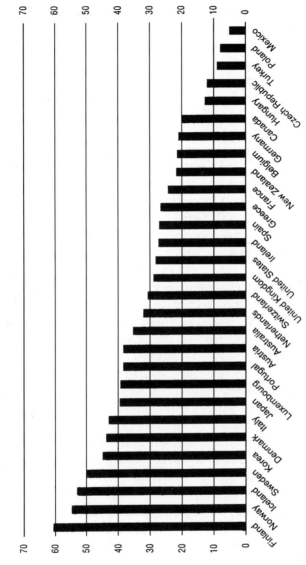

Mobile subscribers per 100 inhabitants, June 1999

Finland
Norway
Iceland
Sweden
Korea
Denmark
Italy
Japan
Luxembourg
Portugal
Austria
Australia
Netherlands
Switzerland
United Kingdom
United States
Ireland
Spain
Greece
France
New Zealand
Belgium
Germany
Canada
Hungary
Czech Republic
Turkey
Poland
Mexico

FIGURE 2. Mobile penetration in the OECD area. *Source:* "Mobile Phones: Pricing Structures and Trends."
© OECD, 2000.

laying one's cell phone on the table when meeting friends, whereupon the person with the most outdated model has to buy the drinks! Such rates of ownership, let alone new cultural patterns around cell phones, vastly exceed academic expectations of the early 1980s that penetration levels might reach 20 percent by the end of the twentieth century (Muller and Toker 1994: 182). Similarly, the consultancy firm McKinsey reportedly estimated in a commission for U.S. telecoms giant AT&T that the total market for cell phones would be around 900,000 by the turn of the century. Basing its prediction on the poor quality of the devices and prohibitive cost of calls, Brown notes how the example illustrates the perils of projecting the present into the future (B. Brown 2002: 1). They have turned out to be "the most successful communication devices of all time," as one account describes (Helyar 2002: 355).

The expansion of cell phone usage continues to be both extremely rapid and global in scope. In September 2000, Vodafone became the first U.K. cellular operator to pass the 10 million subscribers mark. This was just fifteen years and eight months after launching its service. Vodafone is now the world's largest mobile phone operating group, half owning the main U.S. operator, Verizon. There were 43 million subscribers in China at the end of 1999, compared with only 3.6 million in 1995 (WHO 2000). Korea, along with Portugal, was the outstanding performer of 1998 with growth rates of over 100 percent (OECD 2000: 15). Other emerging nations such as South Africa enjoy extensive and highly advanced systems. Authoritative forecasts predict Asia supplanting Europe as the center of cell phone usage (see Fig. 3). This follows the early American lead in 1990 being taken over by Northern Europe, as it became the continent of the cell phone. Southern European countries were typically late starters before catching up in the late 1990s. It is doubtful whether these trends can be taken as any sort of developmental indicator, however, still less a sign of a shifting balance of power. This globalization of usage does suggest, however, that if a health risk were posed, then it would be of global proportions, as suggested by a recent summary of cell phone EMF and health by the head of the World Health Organization (WHO)'s program on EMF (Repacholi 2001).

Rates of usage are a reflection of many factors, principally the comparative cost of fixed-line local call rates, the extent of competition, and the marketing of innovative tariffs, especially the "pay-as-you-go" system that requires no subscription contract (OECD 2000). These have only an indirect relationship to social and economic development. The patterns of cell phone adoption have been internationally varied, to some extent

Regional shares of fixed-telephone lines, worldwide, on 1 January 1990, 2000 and 2010 (forecast)

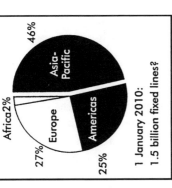

Africa 2%
Asia-Pacific 23%
Europe 40%
Americas 35%

1 January 1990:
490 million fixed lines

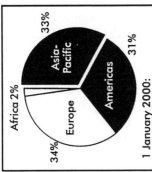

Africa 2%
Asia-Pacific 33%
Europe 34%
Americas 31%

1 January 2000:
905 million fixed lines

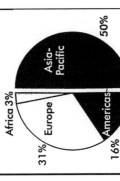

Africa 2%
Asia-Pacific 46%
Europe 27%
Americas 25%

1 January 2010:
1.5 billion fixed lines?

Regional shares of mobile-phone subscribers, worldwide, on 1 January 1990, 2000 and 2010 (forecast)

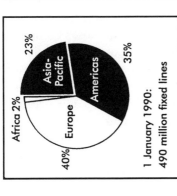

Africa 0%
Asia-Pacific 13%
Europe 34%
Americas 53%

1 January 1990:
7.5 million mobile-phone users

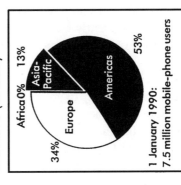

Africa 2%
Asia-Pacific 35%
Europe 36%
Americas 27%

1 January 2000:
490 million mobile-phone users

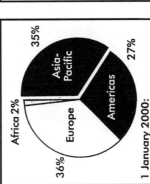

Africa 3%
Asia-Pacific 50%
Europe 31%
Americas 16%

1 January 2010:
2.2 billion mobile-phone subscribers?

FIGURE 3. Regional shares of fixed-telephone lines and mobile-phone subscribers. Courtesy of ITU, "Asia-Pacific Telecommunication Indicators," 2000.

mirroring the initially uneven adoption trends for fixed-line telephones. Telephone usage has reflected different relationships between service providers, particularly the private/state relationship. The Swedish arrangement, for example, where private telephone operating companies competed with a government provider, was unusual. It led to the highest per capita penetration rate for telephones in the world in the early 1990s (Steinfield 1994: 6). The Finnish telecommunications system has long been distinct from other systems. Reacting against Tsarist centralization, the independent Finnish government after the First World War established a public long distance network and a myriad of small local operators (Davies 1994: viii). Overall, the Scandinavian countries already had extremely high densities of conventional telephone usage, and because it is possible to use the same technology in all of the Nordic states, they have been at the forefront of cell phone adoption (Muller and Toker 1994: 191). High levels of demand stimulated competition and a rapid reduction in price.

There is a clear relationship between cost, the way in which people are charged for conventional phone calls, and the extent of cell phone expansion. The OECD notes, "Since 1997, growth of mobile service has been much faster in those markets with measured rather than unmeasured fixed-network local calls" (OECD 2000: 30). In the United States, for example, intense competition with cheap, unmeasured local telephone services has recently led to dramatic reductions in the cost of usage. The expansion of more advanced mobile services, in particular, is related to the cost of connecting to the Internet. An important factor behind the remarkable rise of the "I-mode" mobile Internet service in Japan is that it is the cheapest way to access to online services. This is mainly because of the state of the country's conventional phone system. In other countries, land-line Internet connections are cheaper than mobile Internet connections, but in Japan the land-line system is hampered by government regulation. The lumbering Nippon Telegraph and Telephone (NTT) levies the highest service charges in the world for telephone calls, and has a virtual monopoly on the land-based system. Against this background the deregulated cell phone market flourished in Japan during the late 1990s.

In some instances accelerated expansion of mobile telecommunications suggests an undeveloped telecommunications infrastructure that necessitates a "jump" to the cell phone. Mobile communication potentially allows societies with relatively undeveloped telecommunications systems to bypass the need for fixed telecoms infrastructure. In less developed African countries mobiles allow the wealthy and educated, at least, "to leapfrog entire generations of technological progress."[2] In Eastern Europe, mobile services have been specifically promoted "as a short cut to closing the technology gap that exists in telecommunications" (Muller and Toker 1994: 199). The corollary of this is that in some countries that were extensively "hard-wired" from the beginning there was less of an imperative to innovate in cellular phone technology. Although still high, American rates of penetration remain lower than in many European countries. The relative cheapness of local land-line calls in the United States has been an important factor in slowing market expansion.

Whatever the impulse behind it, cell phone expansion to the less developed world symbolizes a process of modernization. The cell phone is a visible and unambiguous symbol of being "connected" to the twenty-first century. The title of the book *The New Rich in Asia: Mobile Phones, McDonald's and Middle Class Revolution*, an academic account on East Asia, captures the sense in which the cell phone is at the perceptual forefront of technologically driven change (Robison and Goodman 1996). One commentator described surreptitious efforts of Iranian women to establish greater social space where "a headscarf instead of a chador, sunglasses, and the ubiquitous mobile phone, mark the march of progress in Iran."[3] Yet equally as the cell phone is a potent symbol of modernism in the less developed world, patterns of usage clearly reveal the limits of modernizing, rather than globalizing influences.

As in other spheres, Africa is an important exception to the purported worldwide "mobile revolution." Extremely low rates of ownership provide some measure of the developmental gap, and a timely reminder of the limits of "globalization" and the existence of a "digital divide" (see Fig. 3). There is an acknowledged lack of a mobile strategy for Africa in the twenty-first century. Nigeria's cell phone license contest in the summer of 2001 failed to attract the interest of a single European company, even though it is Africa's most populous nation. This was reported to be due to worries over frequent changes of government, and the reputation for widespread corruption (*Mobile Communications* 310, 26 June 2001). Perhaps more important, however, in stark contrast to the aggressive expansion strategy of the 1990s, operators are now narrowing their focus to core business in more developed regions. Growing concerns in 2001 about the economic future of the cell phone industry, indeed the whole information technology sector, have limited its global expansion.

[2] John Simpson, "21st Century Travel," *High Life* (British Airways), September 2000.
[3] Christine Toomey, "Veiled Threats," *Sunday Times* magazine, 1 October, 2000.

The Cell Phone: Past and Present

A cell phone is a type of two-way radio.[4] Barry Brown of Hewlett-Packard research laboratories in the United Kingdom outlines an interesting history of its development, or rather the "history of non-development" of initial possibilities (Brown 2002: 9–13). The first commercial mobile phone systems were operational in the 1940s; it was another thirty years before they became widely available, as other historical outlines concur.[5] In general terms this is explained as an "example of how a technology can be delayed by decisions to favor other technologies." Brown cites artificial intelligence, computer graphics, and nuclear weapons as examples of research areas that were prioritized in the Cold War years, as research into cellular communications languished.

The 1940s predecessor of the modern cell phone was a car-based system. Radios broadcast and received signals from a base station, where the radio channel would be connected to a land phone line. The system required the user to search manually for a free radio frequency, pick up the receiver, and be connected on that channel to an operator at the base station, in the manner of early telephone exchanges. After quoting their subscription number and asking for a particular number, they would be connected by the operator, who connected the land-line phone with the radio channel (ibid.: 9–14). Crude but effective, the system was chronically hampered by the lack of channels available for use. The frequency used by a particular call could not be simultaneously used by another, and radio transmissions travel a considerable distance, thereby barring other users far and wide. The system could not cope with demand. As late as 1976 there half as many people again on five- to ten-year waiting lists as the 44,000 Americans lucky enough to own a car phone (ibid.: 10).

The breakthrough necessary to resove the lack of available frequency was made in the late 1940s. AT&T's Bell Laboratories' innovation was to split geographical coverage into individual "cells." Transmissions were broadcast within each "cell" at a power insufficient to interfere with others, allowing frequencies for calls to be duplicated between cells. Even greater capacity could be created by lowering power and dividing cells into four smaller units. At least in theory, the "cell" phone was born. There remained significant problems: the phone needed to be able to maintain a call as it passed from one cell to another, had to be small, and had to

---

[4] On its workings, see Webb (1998) and Stetz (1999).
[5] See Smyth (2000) and also the useful website on the cell phone's history at http://inventors.about.com/library/weekly/aao70899.htm.

transmit on a narrow frequency band. These problems were overcome by the time of the first nonexperimental cellular call in 1969, made from a service running on Metroliner trains from New York to Washington, D.C., according to Brown (ibid.). Passengers now could "conveniently make telephone calls while racing along at better than 100 miles an hour" (ibid.: 11). Only four years later, the technology was shrunk to hand-held size. Dr. Martin Cooper, a project manager at Motorola, called his rival at Bell Laboratories from a New York street in 1973 (Farley 2000). An experimental Motorola cellular phone system, designed to employ both portable and vehicular phones, was created in the neighboring cities of Washington, D.C., and Baltimore, Maryland. According to another authoritative account, by 1977, AT&T and Bell Laboratories had constructed a prototype cellular system.[6] A year later, public trials of the new system were started in Chicago, with over 2000 trial customers. By 1982, the slow-moving Federal Communications Commission (FCC) finally authorized commercial cellular service for the United States. A year later, the first American commercial analog cellular service, or AMPS (Advanced Mobile Phone Service) was made available in Chicago by Ameritech. Consumer demand quickly outstripped the 1982 system standards.

The introduction of a widely available American system was delayed throughout the 1970s, held back mainly by the reluctance of regulators to allocate spectrum for an unproven technology in favor of new television channels. The FCC had decided to limit the number of frequencies available in 1947, making only twenty-three phone conversations possible simultaneously in the same service area. This was hardly a serious incentive for research. In a classic "chicken and egg" dilemma, the FCC stated in 1968 that it would be prepared to increase the number of frequencies if a better service were established.[7] Yet of course, the introduction of service improvements and the research that would make this possible was in its turn held back by uncertainty over whether cellular would be allowed to expand.

Despite the early American lead in cellular research, other countries managed to operationalize a working system slightly earlier. In 1979 a commercial cellular telephone system began operation in Tokyo. The Scandinavians established a mass-market cellular system in 1981. Comparable dilemmas continue to hamper cellular development to this day. One way in which the long-awaited introduction of "third generation"

[6] http://inventors.about.com/library/weekly/aa070899.htm.
[7] Ibid.

mobile Internet services is being held back is through handset manufacturers, operators, and service providers each awaiting developments in the other spheres before they fully commit research resources. Suitable services await suitable handsets, and vice versa. A factor in the Japanese success with the DoCoMo system is that service operators dictate more directly to handset manufacturers the exact specifications they require and when they must be ready.

Brown identifies the lack of basic research into cellular technology as the principal reason for the thirty-seven years it took for the first car-phone service to be translated into an operational system. Despite the massive resources at the disposal of Bell Laboratories, there were few scientists and engineers assigned to cellular research. The area was described as "grubby" by one researcher, and compared to being "lost in the desert" by another (cited in Brown 2002: 12). The cell phone is a classic case of the mismatch between the availability of technologies and the foresight to appreciate their social potential. Brown also suggests this is a case where researchers were distracted by other technologies that seemed more appealing. He contrasts the lack of resources devoted to cellular with the considerable funds put into videophone systems (over $500 million was spent by AT&T developing and marketing it in the 1970s); an innovation that, as we now know, failed spectacularly. Technological developments, or lack of them, often appear odd with the benefit of hindsight. In retrospect it is difficult to understand why it was ever imagined that anyone would have wanted to be watched while speaking on a telephone, just as it is difficult now to imagine why the potential of mobile communications was not anticipated. Yet these examples are hardly unique. The recent explosion of text messaging was completely unanticipated. Indeed, it came about in an accidental fashion. According to a now often repeated anecdote, the capacity to transmit short messages was allegedly added to the cell phone only as a result of the need to fill some spare capacity on the chip! It is partly because of this experience that cell phone operators such as Vodafone are now putting more resources into social research. There is particular concern to ensure that the technologies being developed for third-generaiotn (3G) Internet-connected cell phones are not inappropriate to people's expectations, needs, and priorities.

Despite the problems with development, by 1987 there were more than one million cellular telephone subscribers in the United States, and the airways were crowded. Increasing numbers of operators were granted licenses following the introduction of the first commercial systems in the early 1980s, and the system rapidly spread from its American and Scandinavian roots. It was introduced into the United Kingdom in 1985. The subsequent technological history is essentially the quest for ever smaller, therefore more portable handsets (see Figs. 4 and 5). Scandinavian, and, to a lesser extent, American and Japanese models dominated the shrinking cell phones. This history is well illustrated by the British case, where a large and discerning market for cell phones developed particularly quickly, as science correspondent Geraint Smith has detailed.[8] When cell phones were first launched, the widely acknowledged "phone of the year" was presented as being all about mobility; hence it was advertised by racing driver Nigel Mansell. The phone in question, the Nokia Mobira Talkman, weighed 4.8 kg (about 10 lb, 9 oz), cost £3,000, had a battery life of less than a day between charges, and gave only one hour of talk time! Progress was relatively swift, however, as the British case again illustrates. The "yuppie boom" was well under way by 1987, and demand for more, lighter cell phones was considerable. The popular handsets of the year were the 700-gram Ericsson Hotline and the 800-gram Mobira Cityman. The network was reported to be having difficulty coping with demand. New frequencies allowed by the government led to new handsets; typical among these was the stereotypical construction workers' phone, the Motorola 8800 and the 800-gram NEC 9A. The cell phone had broken from its exclusive identification with the "yuppie" into the new social territory of the builder and traveling salesman. The mobility of the cell phone was also beginning to break its restriction to automobiles. One now has to be reminded that the majority of cell phones originally worked from automobiles; Europe's biggest retailer of handsets retains its original name, the Carphone Warehouse.

By 1991 the first acknowledged attempt to standardize the system came with the Global System for Mobile Communications (GSM), which was accepted in the United States in 1995. New consumer tariffs in 1992 marked the end of the exclusive yuppie toy. The same year saw the launch of the NEC P4, the first that you could "forget was in your pocket," as it measured 56 by 153 millimeters, was slim at 21 millimeters, and extremely light at only 225 grams. It also had a talk time of sixty minutes, and a standby time of a full day. Usage remained expensive (£1,000 for what would cost £300 by 2001), but a mass market was targeted with consciously attractive handsets. The Sony "Mars Bar" was much sought after, despite its expensive £299 price tag. Competition really took off

[8] Geraint Smith. See "From the Brick to Pay-as-You-Go," *Evening Standard*, 7 February 2001.

FIGURE 4. Early "portable" cell phone, the Ericsson Hotline 900 Combi. Courtesy of Ericsson Mobile Communications AB.

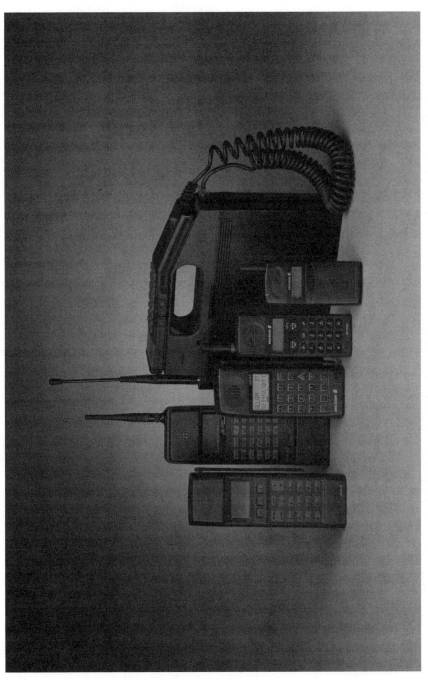

FIGURE 5. The shrinking of the cell phone: Ericsson handsets 1992–1998. Courtesy of Ericsson Mobile Communications AB.

when two new operators, One2One and UK Mercury, were allowed licenses in 1993. Tariffs rapidly fell. Nokia made arguably the biggest impact ever with a cell phone, the Nokia 2110. It weighed 237 grams, had a big screen that showed signal strength and battery life, and a memory that could store a hundred names and numbers. In 1994, "the smallest ever phone, they won't get any smaller than this," was launched. The Sony CMR-111 weighed 185 grams and was so small that a flip-down boom was needed so that the microphone would reach the mouth. The Motorola StarTac followed in 1996; it also flipped open, but this time the screen was inside and it weighed only 91 grams. Although costing £995, it changed hands on the black market for over £1,400. Today there are numerous "lightest" cell phones, such as the Trium Cosmo (69 grams), Sensei sptd88 ((69 grams), and Sendo D800 (68 grams). More significant than their weight, is their price. They typically cost around £100 with a contract. As Smith summarizes his account: "Looking back, the first mobiles weighed 70 times as much and cost 30 times as much."

In the summer of 2001, phone weight still remained something of a sign of cell phone progress, as Nokia's model 8210 was advertised as the smallest ever "pay-as-you-go" cell phone. Previously the popular prepay tariff arrangement meant having to use a bulkier and less stylish phone. Newer cell phones are already becoming heavier, however, as they incorporate other functions such as e-mail and web browsing. More than just a cell phone, the bulky Nokia "Communicator," complete with mini keyboard, is the shape of things to come, according to some analysts. It is anticipated that the 3G cell phones "proper" will be bigger and heavier again. And in October 2001 the first 3G handset was introduced in Japan by NTT DoCoMo, after months of delays and technical glitches. The awkwardly named Foma (Freedom of Mobile Multimedia Access) offers a connection speed that is forty times faster than existing mobile phones, allowing the user to surf the Internet and engage in videoconferences. Prices range from around £375 to £540, with a £57 monthly subscription fee. The first handset weighs 150 grams, and measures 104 millimeters by 56 millimeters by 35 millimeters. Interestingly, press reports described the video capabilities of the handset as of most consumer interest, as a way for parents to be able to monitor their children at a closed circuit TV–equipped nursery, for example (*Guardian*, 2 October 2001).

There is more than just a technological history here; rather, improving technology made possible and interacted with social patterns and changes. The cell phone modified its social identifications and uses, changes that also drove the technological quest for ever lighter phones. The cell phone was, of course, a potent symbol of the "yuppie" 1980s on both sides of the Atlantic, captured by the Gordon Gecko character in the movie *Wall Street*, barking commands and prices into his cell phone. At this time, they remained expensive, mainly automobile-bound, and still inefficient as they used an analogue rather than digital system (see below). They remained the preserve of business users, a distinctively unpopular section of society at this time. A measure of the popular perception of, and hostility toward the "yuppie bear" (as it is known in Sweden) is that in 1990 unpopular U.K. Chancellor of the Exchequer (finance minister) Norman Lamont received the biggest cheer of his political career in Parliament when he announced a tax on business usage of cell phones. A blow against cell phones and their users was at this time perceived as a blow "for the people." It would be only another decade before they became used by the public at large. The decreasing cost of cell phones and usage was obviously central to their popularization. Operators subsidized handset sales in an effort to maintain their position in increasingly competitive markets. A bewildering range of tariff arrangements (which bore little relationship to real costs) targeted ever wider sections of society.

Perhaps the most important innovation that consolidated the universalization of cell phones in Europe and beyond was the introduction of "pay-as-you-go" systems: "The impact of pre-paid pricing cannot be stressed enough in considering changes to the market for mobile communications" (OECD 2000: 11). This is the system whereby users buy pre-paid cards rather than through a subscription commitment. In some Southern European countries operators have more than 80 percent of their subscribers on pre-paid tariff plans. This arrangement is proving crucial in Africa, where there was also 80 percent pre-paid usage at the end of 2001, a level twice the global average (*Mobilex Environment Monthly*, November 2001). A majority of U.K. users are connected through this arrangement. It is a particularly important aspect in driving children's usage, as it was obviously difficult for teenagers to take out a formal subscription agreement. Much of the recent European boom in cell phone sales was driven by sales to teenagers and children, although this remains a more contentious issue in the United States. Recent research in the United Kingdom indicates that 74 percent of older teenagers now own a mobile phone, compared with just over 50 percent of adults.[9] In a further fortuitous development, teenagers then discovered to their delight that it was even cheaper and

---

[9] Survey of over 2,000 people nationwide conducted by Mintel reported in Sean Poulter, "Mobile Generation," *Daily Mail*, 26 October 2000.

more fun to communicate with the text messaging service that became available at the end of the 1990s. The biggest selling book of Christmas 2000 in the United Kingdom was a book on the language of texting, rather than the usual fare of recipe books and autobiographies. Text messaging has now not only established itself as an adult activity but become a serious source of revenue. A watershed in mobile media was reached in the United Kingdom with the June 2002 soccer World Cup. On the day of England's defeat by Brazil a record 60 million text messages were sent, many of them from services sending instant scoreline updates to paying customers.

At the same time, it should be remembered that there is a certain law of diminishing returns with the expansion of mobile services, particularly with regard to "pre-pay" customers. Orange, a leading European operator, announced in 9 April 2002 that 750,000 of its prepaying customers had neither received nor made a call in the last three months. This followed a similar calculation of inactive customers from Vodafone. Clearly, there was some statistically engineered hype to earlier calculations; a lack of acknowledgment that for many cell phone "users" they serve principally as an emergency communication backup, and that old cell phones replaced by new, often company-supplied devices still figure in statistics.

The mobile telecommunications industry anticipates that 3G technology heralds the dawn of a new era where mobile data and multimedia will eclipse speech-only services. The new "mobile Internet" era will also involve an even stronger, more interactive "relationship" with the cell phone. The cell phone is already a distinctive communications device in its very personal character fixed to the individual rather than a place. This trend looks set to increase as 3G opens up the possibility of the cell phone becoming even more intimately enmeshed in contemporary life.

The less advanced forerunners of 3G, wireless application protocol (WAP) and the General Packet Radio Service (GPRS), have already been introduced. On this basis, industry predictions are that there will be one trillion subscribers globally by 2003, and 1.6 trillion by 2005. The Japanese I-mode system, the country's answer to WAP phones, has been a major success. It was launched in February 1999, and by August of 2000 it had signed up 10 million people. Operator DoCoMo is still signing on people at a rate of a million a month in 2001. I-mode is easy and cheap to use, largely because it is a "packet-switched" system (similar to text messaging) that allows many conversations to be carried on a single channel. E-mail is the most popular function of the system, but there are also some 20,000 specially converted websites to visit. The success of the system also reflects the cultural particularities of Japan, where, unlike in the United States, so many people find themselves stuck on public transport systems with time on their hands and no car to steer.

The idea behind 3G is to go a step further than I-mode, and make available services currently possible only on desktop computers, as one account explained (*New Scientist*, 21 October 2000). As well as send e-mail, it will be possible to download music, watch color videos, and buy plane tickets, for example. A 3G mobile will be like an "always on" Internet connection, permanently ready to use. The 3G network will send signals from many mobiles over a single channel, moving voice, text, video, and audio using a packet switching, similar to the way data is sent around the Internet. Packet switching slices up information into packets of data that are sent as separate chunks to their destination. Every packet is treated like a parcel going through the postal system: it is routed through the network according to the address written on its front. Because of this, researchers suggest we will have Internet-style addresses rather than phone numbers. Your phone will be like an e-mail box or a website, with its own unique address. Several technological hurdles are yet to be fully overcome, however, such as maintaining the "always on" connection between base stations.

There are already some services available in 2001 that allow a glimpse of a possible 3G future. A crude data-based service was introduced in the United Kingdom at the end of 2001 that simply builds on text messaging. The "Mobile Channel" offers users a reduction in their phone bills in exchange for signing up for text messages from targeted advertisers. Less openly discussed is the fact that pornography is likely to play a major part in driving mobile communications, much as it was an important driver in the popularization and technological innovation of the Internet.

Some of the wider implications of the shift to interactive, data-based services can be gauged from experiments in "location-based services" already possible using intermediate technologies such as GPRS and SMS. The European cell phone industry is hoping that the improved services available through such interim technologies will both keep users happy in lieu of the arrival of 3G and begin to familiarize them with some of its features. One example of location-based services is that restaurants and shops can call passers-by with advertisements and special offers. Possibilities are not confined to new forms of advertising. The VOXNAV experiment in GPRS-based navigation services is used by haulage firms to interactively deal with breakdowns, allowing continuous instructions to be provided. Of course, many questions are posed even by this relatively limited development towards a 3G cellular system. How many messages will people be prepared to accept, for example? There is an interesting trend toward establishing the cell phone as a "general purpose device." The thinking behind this initiative is that the already indispensable cell phone can further extend its usage, enabling us to dispense with everything else we have to carry around, notably credit cards and money. Vending machines that can be operated with "e-wallet" cell phones are already being tested. British operators are in discussions with the general provider of ATMs to establish a system of cash machines that work with cell phones, allowing functions such as collecting movie tickets. In the British city of Hull during the summer of 2002, drivers are paying for parking using their cell phones in an experiment in "m-payment."

There are plans to make the cell phone an even more indispensable personal item, with moves for it to replace credit cards and even passports. The SIM (subscriber information module) card inside every phone currently holds only details such as your favorite phone numbers. In the future it could identify you to everyone. To pay for a meal, for example, the phone could be used to transfer (the promise of) money through the phone network to a restaurant's computer. Similarly, on boarding a plane there could be no need to wait in line for a boarding pass and seat number. In 2002, the Finnish telecoms company Sonera plans to set up a WAP site that will let travelers do both before they even reach the airport. Unless they have luggage, there'll be no more queuing at check-ins. Also in Finland, the government is looking at using SIMs in place of a national identity card, and eventually a passport. Under this plan, the SIM will become a person's legal proof of identity.

In an even more intimate sense, research points toward making the cell phone an indispensable part of the self. Researchers at Bell Laboratories in New Jersey are looking into ways in which the cell phone will be able to monitor health, following the discovery that it is possible to reveal the pulse and breathing rate from a cell phone signal. British researchers at Loughborough University led by Professor Bryan Woodward are similarly developing "telemedicine." They unveiled a new mobile handset in October 2001 that can monitor the vital signs of housebound patients. During the same month, Korean manufacturer Samsung released its A400 cell phone for women, which among many other "feminine" features can calculate ovulation dates, fertility, and even has a "fatness" calculator! There are now suggestions that the mobile might be able to change rather than only monitor our biology. An extensive Motorola-funded investigation into global "mobile behavior" suggested, among other things, that because of the impact of mobile texting and computer games the thumbs of young adults have overtaken their fingers as the hand's most muscled and dexterous digit (Plant 2002).

Overall the cell phone appears to have become so much a part of modern living that, other than in occasional comic television sketches and newspaper cartoons, its extraordinary expansion seems scarcely to attract attention or discussion. While a few newspaper articles regret the popularity of the mobile, it is invariably in a self-consciously nostalgic and resigned tone. [10] This is not to say they are held in high regard, particularly by the older generation. A letter to *The Times* (13 October 2001) remarked snidely, "The second law of Mobile Phone Etiquette appears to be that the length of the call is in inverse proportion to the meaningful content." Yet the expansion has challenged long-held cultural assumptions. Reflecting on the announcement that more than half of Britons now own a mobile phone, one journalist asked, "What has happened to this nation of technophobes?" referring to renowned British skepticism about new technology (*The Times*, 5 July 2000).

Mobiles have redefined and "particularized" the standard telephone, which is now commonly referred to as a "land line," in much the same way that the consolidation of satellite television led to the description of what was once merely "television," as "terrestrial." Already some 6 percent of Britons have chosen to entirely abandon their "land lines" in favor of exclusive reliance on mobile communications as of 2001. Such a reordering of everyday language and behavior is a powerful measure of the importance of the cell phone to twenty-first-century life.

The Digital Age and Its Limits

Central to the transformation of the cell phone from executive toy to universal communicator is the shift from an analogue to digital system, a development mirrored in other technological areas such as television and fixed-line phone systems. This transition is important to the story of risk perceptions, even though ostensibly only a technical innovation. Technology is itself socially shaped in often crucial ways (MacKenzie and Wacjman 1999), as with the shrinking of handsets and the demand for text messaging.

---

[10] See, e.g., James Bartholomew, "Why I Detest Mobile Phones," *Daily Mail*, 5 July, 2000, and Quentin Letts, "Glad to Be a Luddite," *The Times*, 5 July 2000.

But technology also can have its own social impact, or least provide the basis for one. The move from analog to digital not only made cell phones a more universal and visible part of everyday life but played some role in the popularization of health fears related to their usage. The coming of digital necessitated a massive expansion in both the number and visibility of their supporting network of base stations. Anti–cell phone campaigners describe how there was no widely perceived health problem connected to mobile telephony before the introduction of the digital system. It is unlikely that it is only the number and visibility of towers that explains the extent of the reaction against cell towers, but it is useful to understand something of the difference between the systems in situating health concerns. The character of the digital signal is also important, as some base their argument that there is a significant health risk on the distinctive "pulsed" pattern of digital emissions (Hyland 1999a–c).

The analog system is a means of modulating radio signals so that they can carry information. With the receiver and transmitter tuned to the same frequency, the voice transmitted is varied within a small band to create a pattern that the receiver reconstructs, amplifies, and sends to a speaker. Analog cell phones work much like FM radio. In digital systems, by contrast, the analog voice signal is converted into binary code and transmitted as a series of on and off transmissions.[11]

Early cell phones used an analog system. Most cell phones in the early 1980s were operated from automobiles and powered by the battery. With the analog system, they could operate at greater distances from the base station, and fewer towers were necessary. These could usually be located on high ground away from population centers. Digital arrived in the United Kingdom and Europe with the introduction of the new operating standard GSM in 1991. In Europe at least, this overcame the confusion of different noncompatible standards and frequencies, some of which caused interference between systems. GSM has made operations totally seamless across Europe and is now used in more than twenty countries.

For the user, there are several advantages to digital. There is greater call clarity and a more reliable service as many more calls can be handled by the system. Users can also "roam" between different countries. Phones can be smaller, not least because digital requires smaller battery packs that operate at lower power levels than analog. There is a price to pay for these

---

[11] http://inventors.about.com/library/weekly/aa070899.htm.

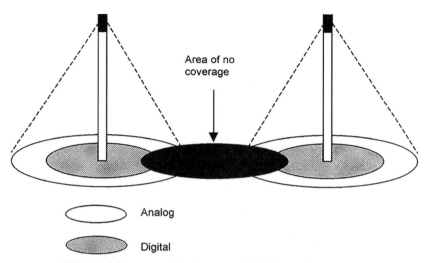

FIGURE 6. The need for more digital towers: digital gaps in coverage.

advantages, however. The lower power levels limits their transmitting power to shorter distances, which in turn means that base stations need to be located much closer to the user. What's more, the digital radio signal itself cannot travel as far. The consequence is that far more towers are required with the digital system, and they have to be located near to where users make their calls (see Fig. 6). There were some 20,000 cell sites in the United Kingdom by the beginning of 2000, and around 82,000 in the United States, with each cell holding one or more base stations (WHO 2000).

There are then basic technological reasons for the controversial siting of towers on or near schools, for example. It is not necessarily the case, as many parents campaigning against towers near their children's schools believe, that these sitings are due to operators taking advantage of easily available sites or are simply unnecessary. Particularly as children are such heavy users of the digital system, there is an inevitability to towers being sited near to them. More widely, there is clearly some relationship between the sheer number and location of towers and the widespread reaction they have provoked. Answering their own question about why there has been so much public concern about cell phone towers compared with far larger structures such as TV and radio broadcasting towers, publicity from the world's largest operator suggests that it is "probably that radio base stations are more numerous...and much more likely to be found nearby to where people live and work" (Vodafone 1999).

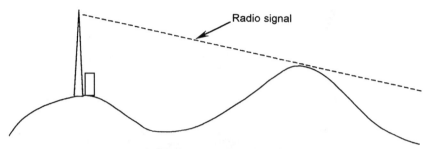

FIGURE 7. The shadowing effect from terrain creates a need for more towers.

It should be added that the siting of cell towers is also influenced by the character, not just the power, of radio signals. The signals are like light. As with a lighthouse, the higher the structure, the greater the distance from which the light can be seen. The higher and more prominent the tower, the further the signal can travel. While radio signals can penetrate certain materials such as brick and stone, an important limitation is that, like light, they travel in straight lines and are affected by obstructions that create "shadowing" (see Fig. 7). The consequence for mountainous regions such as in Italy or Scotland is that more, very visible towers will be needed to provide coverage to the areas left in these shadows. There is some relationship between the relatively intense levels of reaction against towers in both these countries and the number and visibility of towers required to service these regions. By contrast, it is not entirely coincidental that there has been very little public reaction in a largely flat country such as the Netherlands. The Dutch can be provided with a digital cell phone service with fewer base stations.

In response to concerns about these structures, operators have attempted to improve the design of towers. As the handset has become smaller and more discrete, so operators have introduced lightweight, slimmer "lattice" towers in place of the characteristically ugly early structures (see Figs. 8–11). The success of such efforts is dependent on general location, however. Urban transmitters present less of a problem, as they can be more easily blended in to the environment. Small street-level "microcells" that supplement coverage in city centers can now be disguised as street signs. Other technical attempts to limit the number and visibility of towers include the sharing of masts between different operators, although these can be self-defeating as they may involve a considerable increase in the height of the tower.

FIGURE 8 and 9. *Above*: Early British cell tower from mid-1980s, still in use. *Right*: Close-up.

FIGURE 10. Rooftop antennae.

FIGURE 11. Sleeker, late 1990s British tower.

But there is a bigger problem looming. The pending introduction of 3 G cell phones requires a far more extensive network of towers to service this technological leap forward. The 3 G system uses higher frequencies than GSM, which do not travel so well, so it will need three times as many antennas in urban areas, and twice as many in rural locations. Telecoms analyst Ovum calculates that in Britain, for example, 3 G operators will need at least 100,000 new antenna masts to match GSM coverage, a number that dwarfs the 40,000 used for today's GSM network. "Finding sites is becoming very difficult," according to Ovum, because "[p]eople are increasingly worried about health issues."[12] In countries such the United Kingdom, operators are very seriously concerned about whether it will actually be possible to erect the thousands more towers necessary to make 3 G a reality. There are reports of near panic about how the infrastructure will be erected, particularly among operators who are new to the market. These problems are presenting themselves at a time when many analysts are already expressing doubt about the whole future of the mobile Internet.

Many operators agreed to very high license fees; an astonishing £80 billion was paid for licenses to operate the 3 G system across Europe, suggesting prohibitive costs being passed on to the consumer. This is in the context of fears about a worldwide recession that appears to be hitting telecommunications particularly hard in 2001–2. Other, intermediate technologies such as I-mode suggest that a fully fledged mobile Internet service is unnecessary. However, some experts point out that the 3 G system is not simply an optional extra allowing interesting but unnecessary services. 3 G cellular is necessary for expansion in the context of saturated network (McGrath 2001).

The technology on which the cell phone industry's future is staked has very quickly come to be seen in a more sober light. The direct forerunner of the 3 G system, WAP, became widely available in the United Kingdom at the beginning of 2000. It has proven a disappointment in Europe, indeed, the "biggest disappointment to hit the mobile phone world," according to newspaper commentators (Helyar 2002: 367). Particularly with users expecting what was hyped as the "mobile Internet," it became clear that it is not easy to transfer web content designed for the home computer to a portable device. It is also held back by the limits of the existing GSM system where users are charged for airtime rather than how much content is (very slowly) downloaded. This suggests that a switch to packet

[12] "Not in My Backyard," *New Scientist*, 10 February 2001.

systems such as GPRS, already used with the I-mode system, may be better. GPRS is an intermediate technology (sometimes known as 2.5G), and some estimates suggest that 80 percent of 3G applications could be carried out perfectly well on a (lighter) GPRS phone. Other systems also threaten to make 3G redundant before it has even started, such as a cheap in-car digital radio receiver system developed by the U.S. firm Command Audio that will deliver news, traffic, weather, sports, and stock price information in a compressed audio format. An in-car receiver stores the last eight hours of information, which can then be played back whenever is desired. In late 2001, young British entrepreneurs have stepped into the opportunity provided by the slow introduction of 3G internationally with a system that speeds up GSM signals by compressing them, and providing the Internet in full-color, personal computer–like form.[13] It is the success of the Japanese I-mode system that has attracted most attention, however. Perhaps the clearest lesson drawn is one of not exaggerating claims for what technologies are and can achieve. I-mode was presented to the Japanese public as simply a cell phone with added features, rather than a mobile Internet. Overall the idea that the other devices will simply disappear into the mobile, leaving it as the single device of choice appears overstated (B. Brown 2002: 6). Nevertheless, problems need to be kept in perspective; there were still some 8 million WAP users worldwide in 2000.

There are signs that the purported mobile revolution is badly stalling. Nokia, the world's largest mobile phone manufacturer, alarmed the equity markets in January 2001 with a signal that global demand for handsets could be reaching its limits. They reported selling 128 million mobile phones in 2000, well below the 135 million units estimated by many analysts. There are fears that, with key Western European countries having penetration rates of between 50 and 70 percent, the market is reaching saturation point, and replacement sales are more likely to be sensitive to weakening economies. Handset manufacturers have been very directly hit already. By April 2001, it was calculated that 35,000 jobs were lost in the industry worldwide following Ericsson's announcement of 12,000 job losses in April 2001. Motorola also shed 22,000 jobs in 2001. Overall, as a *Financial Times* editorial commented (30 August 2001): "Positive news is scarce in the mobile phone industry."

In 2002, the world's largest mobile operator, Vodafone, revealed the biggest loss in U.K. corporate history. Even the industry's one truly

---

[13] The "Pogo" system was founded by three independent London-based designers, due to be launched in the United Kingdom, in January 2002.

successful nonvoice product, text messaging, is now acknowledged to have reached its limits as it is realised there are only so many such messages people can send and receive in a day. The introduction of services to "mail" photographs rather than only text in mid-2002 (in Europe) has even more obvious limitations in demand. By the summer of 2002 the European industry's hopes were now staked on the success of newly introduced "smartphones" such as the Nokia 7650, all-around entertainment and information devices that combine the functions of a PDA (personal digital assistant), including calendar and e-mail, with a digital camera and even an MP3 player. Significantly, the development and presentation of these devices as "smartphones" represents something of a shift towards more clearly adapting to consumer needs and desires rather than simply what appears to be technologically possible. Instead of being hyped as the "mobile Internet," the new generation of cell phones suggests they are "smart" enough to adapt to the consumers' needs instead of only reflecting the technological brilliance of their manufacturers.

The Impact of Telecommunications

The character of the digital "mobile revolution" is of some importance in contextualizing the reaction against cell phone EMF. It has necessitated the erection of a prominent network of towers that have made an imposing impression on contemporary life. It is also worth giving wider consideration to the speed with which this change has come about in beginning to locate discontents with the "mobile revolution." As with discontents against the process of globalization more generally, it could be understood that the pace of change has increased to a point where it feels out of human control. Unable to cope, individuals and communities can only react defensively by trying to limit the impact of change on their locality, according to this sociological perspective (Giddens 1990, 1991; Beck 1992, 1995). Thus it is perhaps inevitable that the expansion of mobile communications will stimulate reaction. Whether it is meaningful to speak of the pace of contemporary change as qualitatively faster than in the past remains open to debate, however. In other ways the character of the mobile "revolution" might help explain widespread reaction against the infrastructure of cellular communications and the resonance for health fears more widely.

The introduction of the mobile phone is characterized in academic thought as the latest telecommunications revolution. The first was begun with the introduction of the telegraph in the 1830s, the second with the telephone from the 1870s. The national telegraph, telephone, and postal systems, which facilitated the expansion of mass production, were in place by the 1920s. The digital revolution was begun in the 1940s with the emergence of electronic data processing and control technologies (Davies 1994: 3). By the 1970s, corporate demands for a revolution in telecommunications stimulated the consolidation of the digital revolution.

Considerable claims have been made for the impact of this latest, digital, telecoms "revolution." Former U.S. president Bill Clinton said that contemporary communications "could do for the productivity of individuals at their places of work and learning what the interstate highway of the 1950s did for the productivity of the nation's travel and distribution system" (Davies 1994: 1). At the level of perception, at least, the meaning and impact of the cell phone is quite considerable. It is seen as part of the "revolution" of the so-called information society (Sapolsky et al. 1996). New information technologies in this discussion are said to have a transformative impact on society (Toffler 1981). The mobile revolution is part of the coming of the "network society" in the information age (Castells 2000). The cell phone is at the center of this transformation, particularly with the advent of Internet mobiles. Text messaging, e-mail, voice mail, and Internet access give mobile communication a different character, beyond making the traditional telephone more convenient and portable. As it becomes more embedded in our lives, the cell phone appears to symbolize aspects of contemporary society in a way that the original fixed-line telephone did not.

The revolution in communications has not simply quickened communications but changed their very character, as the languages and worlds of e-mail and text messaging illustrate. The implications of being able to contact individuals at any time, in almost any place, are considerable. It suggests a transformation of time and space, or what Marx called "the annihilation of space by time" (cited in Davies 1994: 91). Time becomes less differentiated, as we can converse before we even arrive, and continually rearrange the point of arrival. More generally, the process of globalization is regarded as suggesting far more than greater and quicker "connectedness."

The other side of the process of globalization also needs consideration, and is particularly important in understanding protest against mobile towers in local communities. In sociological terms, such a reaction suggests a palpable feeling of the loss of control in a "runaway world" shaped by the remote decisions of corporate "expert systems" (Giddens

1992). The local here appears as a point of reaction against the sense of being overwhelmed by global forces. In a sense the cell phone example appears a classic case of such a pattern, aggravated by the way in which expansion was carried out. There were some instances where operators erected masts and extended coverage with determination and perceived indifference to complaints from individuals and local residents. Residents were confronted with the end result of this particular aspect of globalization: structures appearing suddenly and unannounced on land around their homes. In the absence of explanation and consultation, such an approach by the cellular phone operators is perceived as an attitude of arrogance and lack of regard. The experience appears as a contemporary tale of all-powerful global corporations riding roughshod over powerless individuals and communities.

While there is some truth to this picture, it is not the case that reactions such as contemporary local campaigning against cell towers are confined to our contemporary period of allegedly unique globalization. In the late 1920s, there was public opposition to the expansion of the National Grid of electricity infrastructure in the United Kingdom, for example. "Triumphalists" who confidently anticipated a boost to employment prospects and economic fortune argued against the anti-pylon movement, which contested the effect on the natural beauty of the English landscape: "the pylon as a symbol of the loss of old England became a powerful mobilizing force" (Macnaghten and Urry 1998: 37). Opposition groups were set up, supported by prominent intellectuals such as Rudyard Kipling and John Maynard Keynes, and *The Times* took on the kind of campaigning role that is today characteristic of newspapers involved in the anti–cell tower campaigns. The parallels between the reaction to the national grid expansion and the anti-mast campaigns are limited, however. Such was the consensus around the necessity and inevitability of infrastructural progress in the 1920s that even apparently implacable opposition was quite transient and uncertain. A leading opponent of pylons could only plead defensively that ". . . we think that this is the type of progress we could do without" (cited in ibid.: 37). In this case there was little suggestion that such progress might be bad for our health. Only in today's climate where individuals appear to feel that scientific and technological development is quite separate from them, even working against them, has the idea that such structures may be destructive of health, rather than just the landscape, become more widely consolidated. A focus merely on an acceleration in the pace of change in this respect thus misses more interesting changes in society's assumptions and preoccupations.

An obvious starting point in historically locating the social impact of cellular technology is to make a comparison with the traditional, fixed-line telephone. A number of studies have elaborated a sociology of the standard telephone, most notably Fischer's impressive social history of its prewar consolidation in the United States (Fischer 1992).[14] However, as Fischer himself notes, studies of the telephone are themselves unusual, relative to other innovations, because its symbolic power and meaning to individuals and society was limited. There was only a partial sense of the telephone "being modern" historically: "the connection between the telephone and modernity probably remained, subtly and below people's consciousness..." (ibid.: 243). Unlike the television or automobile, the telephone provoked little broader social reflection, intellectual or otherwise. It was relatively quickly integrated into everyday routines, principally as a means of enhanced sociability. Fischer notes that "few Americans found the telephone dramatic beyond about 1910." Its very practical function in the vast expanses of America, in particular, ensured a pragmatic absorption of the phone into everyday life.

Perhaps a better historical analogy is between digital telecommunications and the telegraph. There are many parallels between claims made today for a mobile phone and communications revolution, and those made in the mid-nineteenth century about the telegraph. It has become routine to assume that the current transformation of communications technology is unprecedented in scope, yet consider the following description:

a new communications technology was developed that allowed people to communicate almost instantly across great distances, in effect shrinking the world faster and further than ever before. A worldwide communications network whose cables spanned continents and oceans, it revolutionized business practice, gave rise to new forms of crime, and inundated its users with a deluge of information. Romances blossomed over the wires....The benefits of the network were relentlessly hyped by its advocates, and dismissed by the skeptics....(Standage 1998: 1)

Standage is describing the impact of the telegraph, what he dubs "the Victorian Internet." Expansion of the telegraph was most rapid in the Unitted States. At its beginning in 1846, Samuel Morse's experimental

---

[14] Besides Fischer's volume, the most important social study of the telephone remains Ithiel de Sola Pool's edited volume (1977). For an exhaustive survey of other sources, see Fischer's bibliographic essay (Fischer 1992: 273–6).

line spanned the forty miles between Baltimore and Washington, but only two years later there were around 2,000 miles of wire. By 1850 there were more than 12,000 miles, controlled by some twenty companies. The British newspaper *The Daily Telegraph* suggested that "time itself is tele-graphed out of existence" (ibid.: 97). The newspaper's name itself was a testament to the way in which the telegraph transformed information gathering and dissemination. The media was transformed through the ability to report news in a more immediate way.

At least for its proponents, the impact of the telegraph was depicted in the most dramatic terms. The laying of the first (failed) telegraph cable across the Atlantic was described as a momentous occasion. An early American "story of the telegraph" described how it

is regarded, and most justly, as the greatest event in the present century; now the great work is complete, the whole earth will be belted with electric current, palpi-tating with human thoughts and emotions. . . . It shows that nothing is impossible to man. (cited in ibid.: 80)

The author's conclusion could hardly have been more optimistic. In the United Kingdom, *The Times* compared the laying of the transatlantic ca-ble to the discovery of the New World. The accredited inventor, Samuel Morse, was honored by heads of state throughout Europe. He was hailed as "the Columbus of our time" at a dinner in his honor (ibid.: 86). In a way that now seems hopelessly naive, the international communication made possible by the telegraph led to references on both sides of the Atlantic to its peace-making potential.

The pace of the telegraph's introduction was very slow by the standards of subsequent breakthroughs. Puttnam calculates that it took sixty-seven years for the telephone to reach 75 percent of the U.S. population from 1890, whereas the television took only seven years from 1948 to reach a similar level of penetration. Fischer's comparative table, on the other hand, compares the introduction of the telephone and the car with radio, television, and electric light between 1900 and 1980 (Fischer 1992: 22). He finds that the latter three electronic devices diffused more rapidly than either the car or the telephone. Such a comparison poses interesting questions with regard to the mobile phone, itself an electronic device that has apparently followed a pattern of rapid diffusion distinct from the more pedestrian pace of the ordinary telephone.

Yet the example of the telephone illustrates an important point about the pattern of technological diffusion. The number of buyers does not measure abstract enthusiasm for a particular technology, but rather measures demand in relation to the terms of acquisition, particularly the cost of supply. Throughout the history of telecommunications, diffusion has closely mirrored affordable availability. In the United States, the diffusion of the telephone was very rapid following the opening up of competition in 1893; it then slowed when AT&T reconsolidated its control after 1907. Overall, "the correlation of expansion with vigorous competition and price-cutting is plain" (ibid.: 49).

Comparisons between the expansions of different communication systems are confusing, the only relatively clear relationship being a comparative one between different nations based on wealth. The more rapid diffusion of the telephone in the United States compared with Europe was in this sense simply a reflection of its greater resources (ibid.: 55). Despite the many problems confronting early telephone expansion, the pace of developments was not qualitatively distinct from the later "mobile revolution." The establishment of the early telephone system was not simply a process of slow evolution: it had an overnight impact despite the odd route that the cash-poor Bell Corporation established (Davies 1994: 34–6).

Beyond levels of usage, the impact on social consciousness and everyday life of different technological innovations is, by contrast, impossible to measure. How are we to compare the impact of the introduction of electricity with the impact of the Internet, or the telegraph with the cellular phone? What can be suggested is that the particular claims for a contemporary communications "revolution" are difficult to sustain. On the basis of his research into the impact of the telegraph, Standage argues that

> ...the electric telegraph was, in many ways, far more disconcerting for the inhabitants of the time than today's advances are for us. If any generation has the right to claim that it bore the full bewildering, world shrinking brunt of such a revolution, it is not us – it is our nineteenth century forebears. (Standage 1998: 200)

A plausible argument can be made that successive technologies have a declining impact on consciousness, as familiarity breeds, if not contempt, a lack of wonder and interest. Such a change even appears discernible in comparing the excitement that greeted the newfound possibility of telegraphic "talking over the wires" with the more practical and direct means of doing so that arrived with the telephone. At the same time, the telegraph was not able to touch everyday life in quite so intimate a fashion as its technological successor.

Comparisons between the social impact of different technologies might be interesting, but cannot be resolved. In this sense talk of a distinctive mobile revolution is inappropriate as it distinguishes a qualitative distinction from what might also be regarded as the "revolutions" of the telegraph and telephone. Winston's (1998) overview of the interaction between media technologies and society usefully shifts the terms of discussion from difficult comparisons between each new impact to a general pattern of technology's accommodation to social trends. Technologies are subject to the balance of forces encouraging and inhibiting their dissemination, rather than able to initiate significant social changes of their own accord:

> ...there is nothing in the histories of electrical and electronic communication systems to indicate that significant major changes have not been accommodated by pre-existing social formations. The term "revolution" is therefore quite the wrong word to apply to the current situation. Indeed it is possible to see in the historical record not just a slower pace of change than is usually suggested but also such regularities in the pattern of innovation and diffusion as to suggest a model for all such changes. (Winston 1998: 2)

In this respect, the mobile phone as a rapidly adopted new technology cannot account for the reactions that have accompanied it. The speed with which the mobile phone has been adopted does play some role in creating reaction, through the consequent competition to erect masts to improve reception coverage, for example. But the pace of change is perhaps not as important as the context in which these changes have taken place. The cell phone has become intimately bound up with negative social trends in an era that appears more fascinated with the potential negative side effects of innovation than with its possibilities.

Sociological Reflections of the Cell Phone: Promoting Individualization or Encouraging Sociability?

The changes brought about by the communications revolution have placed mobile phones at the center of our lives, but the impact has not been entirely welcomed. Technology in general now brings with it its own fears. According to Edward Tenner's widely cited thesis, an "unintended consequence" of our increasing dependence on technology is increased "revenge effects" as progress creates ever-greater problems in its wake (Tenner 1996).

More direct issues are raised by the increasing sophistication of mobile systems quite apart from the problems with the introduction of 3G mobiles already mentioned. The issue of privacy is posed by the development of location-based services. A European Commission directive already states that positional data on individuals can be processed only if anonymous or with consent. The wider issue of trust is also raised by plans to develop the cell phone as an all-purpose device that even verifies identity. Some analysts believe that people will never find it acceptable to have all their personal information stored in their cell phones. The currently favored solution is to store precious information on secure servers accessible via a WAP connection or the World Wide Web. However, there are grounds for suspecting that in an age where people already effectively limit their privacy in order to gain access to a website, people are prepared to compromise their privacy for a specific return. People don't necessarily value their personal information in itself, but are concerned about its control, particularly when it comes to potential fraud.

There are other ways in which the cell phone is less than enthusiastically embraced. As it is ubiquitous, and so intimately bound up with our lives, it is also implicated in negatively perceived social developments. The cell phone's most potent association at the beginning of the twenty-first century in Europe is with crime. Mobiles are very directly associated with crime, particularly with regard to children. Recorded crime in the United Kingdom is falling in every area other than cell phone robberies. The 2000 annual British Crime Survey, regarded as the definitive picture of crime in England and Wales, showed a decline in overall crime but a 14 percent increase in robberies. Government researchers found the overwhelming majority of the increase was accounted for by attacks on school pupils for cell phones. These conclusions were confirmed by a Home Office report in January 2001, adding that cell phone theft was also a racial issue. *Mobile Phone Thefts* (Home Office 2002) estimated that 710,000 were stolen in the previous year, the most common pattern being gangs of nonwhite youngsters preying on their male peers. It is in such contexts that press coverage of the cell phone dramatically highlighted the "playground plague" (*Daily Mail*, 17 October 2000), the "mobile menace" (*Evening Standard*, 10 July 2000), and the "mobile disaster" (*The Times*, 9 January 2001). Cell phone crime has since become a major target of

U.K. government policy, and manufacturers are being held responsible for not designing them in a way that limits their attractiveness to thieves. In February 2002, Britain's chief justice, Lord Woolf, demanded automatic custodial sentences for cell phone thefts, to the surprise of even government officials.

Popular commentary is replete with references to worrying trends associated with the cell phone; even academic studies are often publicised in the European media if they highlight apparently worrying trends associated with cell phones. British police have warned that a recent case where an estranged wife was sent a stream of threatening messages by her husband highlights the newly emerging problem of "textual (as opposed to sexual) harassment" (*Daily Mail*, 11 January 2001). These references reflect the dominant anxieties of our age, the fate of our children being perhaps foremost in the imagination. Besides the association with teenage crime, the cell phone is blamed for the apparently worrying state of the younger generation. In the summer of 2001, child sociologist Hisao Ishii warned that the addiction of children to their mobile phones could threaten the fabric of society (*Daily Mail*, 29 June). He said that young people would soon be incapable of forming and maintaining relationships without the help of a cell phone. Other sociologists were reported to be warning that the popularity of mobile games and text messaging is affecting other important recreational activities, such as reading. In another clear comparison to the allegedly pernicious influence of television, the cell phone has even been blamed for increasing childhood sloth and obesity. A study by Leeds Metropolitan University announced: "Mobile phone children are the fattest generation" (*The Times*, 4 May 2001). Based on a review of 694 children, the authors argued that cell phones, especially texting, were helping to make the current generation of seven- to eleven-year-olds the fattest ever.

Besides occasional stories of emergency rescues, the cell phone is very rarely associated with good news. Unlike so many other stories from the *British Medical Journal*, a report entitled, "The Public Health Benefits of Mobile Phones" did not make the newspaper headlines.[15] An exception to this was an announcement that cell phone use had led to a decline in youth smoking. Statistics indicating the coincidence of a fall in teenage smoking and increase in their cell phone use at the end of 2000 led researchers to argue that it "satisfies the same needs as cigarettes," offering

---

[15] Debbie Lawlor, "The Public Health Benefits of Mobile Phones," *British Medical Journal* 323 (25 August): 447.

"adult style and aspiration, individuality, sociability, rebellion and peer group bonding."[16] Such observations raise wider sociological issues about the cell phone's place in contemporary life. The first issue to consider is whether, like other technologies such as the television, the cell phone can be implicated in a process of destructive individualization or is actually a tool for greater socialization. A second pertinent issue is the very distinctive qualities of the cell phone, most notably how it erodes the boundaries between our public and private worlds.

Burkart notes that the cell phone combines three of modernity's basic elements: communication, mobility, and individuality (Burkart 2000). An important driver behind the expansion of the mobile phone is the individuation of households:

The greater value of individualized telephone numbers and services is that now only a minority of households conform to the nuclear family model. The world has become a place in which the unit of one – each individual – has greater currency. . . . (Future Foundation 1999: 22)

According to this perspective, the cell phone is simply the logical means of communication for a more individualized world in the positive sense of increased freedom of choice and contact. It is argued that the mobile phone helps to maintain existing ties and relations, particularly within the family, in circumstances where we can no longer geographically, or even temporally, share the same space. The widespread use of mobile phones in East Asian societies, such as Hong Kong and Singapore, is viewed by many as making it possible to retain family contact under the more demanding circumstances of increased mobility and work hours. Italy's main statistical institute recently reported that 70 percent of the population not living at home phone their mothers every day, often on cell phones (*The Economist*, 1 April 2000). The most optimistic analyses even consider the cell phone to help limit the most extreme and anti-social aspects of our more individuated culture. The trend toward living alone alarms many observers, suggesting an almost pathologically atomized society. Those more favorably disposed toward contemporary culture, on the other hand, suggest that such an arrangement need no longer be of significance, as ". . . it is now feasible for an individual to live alone whilst maintaining a healthy network of social contacts . . ." (Future Foundation 1999: 22).

---

[16] Anne Charlton and Clive Bates, "Decline in Teenage Smoking with Rise in Mobile Phone Ownership: Hypothesis," *British Medical Journal* 321 (4 November 2000): 1155.

Other U.K. research argues from its findings that, in an increasingly fragmented and isolating world, mobile phones let us communicate as if we lived in small, close-knit communities. Cell phone gossiping encourages us to develop relationships, learn social skills, resolve conflicts, and make friends; it is an "antidote to alienation" (Fox et al. 2001). Such claims appear one-sided, however, as there is often a less positive consequence to more privatised mobile contact. The Finnish Nufix research project observed, for example, that while the cell phone increased parents' control of their childrens' whereabouts, it also meant that they were increasingly out of touch with their childrens' circle of friends (Kopomaa 2002). More generally, Kopomaa entitles his snapshot of research on that most mobile of societies as one where "Finns keep friends at arm's length."

A similar, more prominent discussion about whether communications technologies signify a more isolated or connected society surrounds the possibilities of the Internet. A common stereotype of the "surfer" is of a loner who retreats from the demands and complexities of real social interaction. On the other hand, Puttnam asks whether small groups organized through the net can go "against the tide" of declining "social capital" in the United States. The web's technical qualities of easy access, high speed, and low cost certainly facilitate organization, "especially for widely scattered like minded groups of citizens." Puttnam uses the example of a Nobel Prize–winning campaign against land mines that was organized principally over the Internet from an individual's home (Puttnam 2000: 173). The campaign around cell phone EMF is another example. Without e-mail and the Internet it is doubtful whether there ever would have been a campaign, certainly not one that existed on an international level. On the other hand, even in these terms Puttnam highlights what he dramatically labels, "cyberbalkanization...the confining of our communication to people who precisely share our interests" (Puttnam 2000: 177). Groups become increasingly particular and specialized, much as the proliferation of niche magazines has led us from what already appear as narrow interests into even more obscure territories.

Some evidence suggests that new forms of communication compliment, rather than substitute for, face-to-face contact. Studies have shown that academics in regular face-to-face contact also engage in more electronic exchange (Puttnam 2000: 179). Puttnam identifies telecommunications as the most important of three countertrends toward *greater* social connectedness. Highlighting the exponential growth in telephone usage throughout the century, he notes that an important component of this has been social calls: by 1982 almost half of all American adults spoke on the phone each day (Puttnam 2000: 166). But "more" is not necessarily "better," of course. There is a significant distinction to be made between quantity and quality, as much is simply "din." Such a sensibility was evident in interviews with some anti–cell tower activists who saw the cell phone as a largely superfluous innovation, useful only in emergencies. By contrast, through their own campaigning, they had established friendships and links to the local community far more worthwhile than anything technology could offer or facilitate.

The cell phone may be about communication, but only in the most banal or unnecessarily businesslike of fashions, in some estimations. As a business accessory, the mobile suggests that the individual and the business itself are somewhat out of control; people are not able to wait until arrival at the office but instead conduct business in public. Meaningful conversation would perhaps not be through any medium at all, but reserved for direct contact. Burkart (2000) suggests that the cell phone may even create problems with face-to-face communication in public space. In July 2002, the Liverpool City Council forbade its 19,500 employees from sending internal e-mails on Wednesdays, in a move designed to help employees realize the extent to which electronic communication might be worsening more interactive, direct contact and the shifting of responsibility for problem solving. Sensitivity to a feeling of loss of community through communications technology is recognized by the cell phone industry itself, illustrated by the award-winning television and cinema advertising campaign by the Orange operating company in 1997. Presenting a future where real contact with other people was rendered superfluous by technology, the dismissed such a vision as distinctly dystopian. It presented an "Orange" future where "real" contact remains as important as ever, assuring us that change would be restricted to communicating faster and more efficiently.

What the Future Foundation describes as an enhancement of choice can also be described as a process of less positive individuation. Puttnam identifies a secular trend toward the decline of wider community, association, and participation in American life. The family household tends toward fewer shared activities. For example, where television once indicated a common, even universal experience, it now reflects a more atomized world, with different family members watching their own sets. American research into television watching indicates that, by the end of the 1990s, over 75 percent of American homes owned two or more sets, "allowing ever more private viewing" (Puttnam 2000: 223). In terms of telephone communication, the fracturing process is reflected in the U.K.

launch of a "call sign" service by British Telecom, whereby the different members of the family have their own designated ring. The cell phone takes this process of personal exclusivity a stage further.

The debate about whether innovations in the technology of communication enhance sociability or promote individuation is not new. Describing the advocates of sociability through telecommunications, Puttnam notes that enthusiasts of a "virtual community" are "very much like nineteenth century futurists contemplating the vistas opened up by the telephone..." (ibid.: 171). Complaints about the telephone included the claim that it "weakened character, made people lazy, broke up home life, and reduced visiting among friends" (Fischer 1992: 261). On the other hand, Fischer reminds us that "socializing" claims for new communications technologies have a long history: "the telegraph, as well as the telephone, was supposed to make 'one neighborhood' of the whole country" (ibid.: 260). Two decades ago, the renowned American futurologist Alvin Toffler dismissed the idea that telecommunications "will deprive us of face-to-face contact and make human relations more vicarious" as naive and simplistic. He argued that innovations can create a new "telecommunity" where telecommunications' shrinking of time and space allows us to devote more energy to chosen relations, rather than wasting our time commuting to the workplace, for example (Toffler 1981: 382).

There are few signs of a newly energized social and civic life in the decades following Toffler's prognosis, however, suggesting there is certainly no clear relationship between the (potential) freeing up of time by improved communications and its redeployment to more sociable ends. A high level of voluntary work is the main trend that suggests a still high level of "social capital" in the United Kingdom as opposed to the United States (Hall 1999) and has, in its own way, been made possible by telecommunications. Yet it is as likely that such activities represent a highly individualized opting out of social commitments as a deepening of social ties and responsibilities. In February 2000 the U.K.'s Voluntary Service Overseas (VSO) reported a 61 percent increase, as 50,000 Britons volunteered themselves to the less developed world. Even the VSO identified "consumer blues" rather than altruism as the reason for greater interest in participation, however. The trend was described as one where "more and more recipients of city bonuses, instead of buying a second home... want to spend their money on feeling like better people. Sorry, on helping others" (*The Times*, 1 March 2000). A former volunteer added: "It's just as much about adventure and exoticism as it is about wanting to help others."

The current discussion about the relationship of media and technology to "social capital" is probably more intense and sustained because of broader anxieties about sociability. The Future Foundation identifies three "revolutions" that are driving the emerging network society: technological, social, and political-economic. It identifies a change in social relations and practices toward a "networked family" that is "more flexible, individualized and democratic ... families, despite some geographic dispersal are continuing to keep in touch" (Future Foundation 1999: 6). Their account asserts the continuing importance of social networks that counter increasing individualization and highlight the transformation, rather than elimination, of interaction: "more complex forms of interaction have emerged to fill their place, creating a new balance between family and informal 'friendship' contacts in peoples lives" (ibid.: 34). These developments are explicitly situated within the framework of a more democratic, individuated family, which concurs with the analysis of Giddens (1991). According to the British Social Attitudes Survey, in the mid-1990s Britons were interacting with a smaller network of people than a decade previously, but meeting with them more often (Jowell et al. 1996). Classic sociological texts have pointed to the way that social networks have adapted over time to change (Wilmott and Young 1960). Smaller but better is the suggestion here with regard to concerns about shrinking circles of social interaction.

Metcalfe's law, which suggests that the more points of contact there are, the more communication will take place, is confirmed by data from the Future Foundation study, which indicates that nearly a fifth of all telephone calls are now made between mobiles. A third of people with *mobiles* would rather keep their cell phones than their normal fixed line when offered the choice, indicating their indispensability. Even people who claim that their mobile phone is principally for work use find that they make more social calls than others who work but don't have access to a mobile (Future Foundation 1999: 43). However, the maintenance of contact does not necessarily compensate for a decline in informal sociability. Studies of American phone usage clearly demonstrate that the majority of calls are to a handful of local numbers (Puttnam 2000: 168). Such developments "hardly outweigh the many other ways in which most Americans are less connected to our communities than we were three or four decades ago" (ibid.: 180). In this sense reassurance that trends such as the dramatic increase in those choosing to live alone and the decline of civic contact are nothing to worry about seem complacent. The concentration of telephone usage suggests a constant, even diminishing pattern of interaction.

Reminding us of an obvious but important point, Puttnam says that "one does not meet new friends on the telephone," although the growth of often sexual "chat lines" on both sides of the Atlantic partially contradicts this notion (ibid.: 168).

Both sides of the debate appear to speak to different aspects of actual experience; mobile communication seems to be double edged as it "appears to both reduce loneliness and face-to-face socializing" (ibid.: 168). But whichever way we look at it, the more important point is that "social patterns are not easily altered by new technologies." Fischer contends that "Americans apparently used home telephones to widen and deepen existing social patterns rather than to alter them" (Fischer 1992: 260–2). Deliberately understating any claims for the transformative impact of the telephone on American life, the historian Daniel Boorstin describes it as "only a convenience, permitting Americans to do more casually and with less effort what they had already been doing before" (cited in Puttnam 2000: 169). This leads Puttnam to conclude that "the telephone has had the effect of reinforcing, not transforming or replacing, existing personal networks" (ibid.: 168). It can be suggested that the same is true of the cell phone. There is a secular trend toward increased individualization, and in this context the phone has played a modest part in cementing a more individualized social psychology. Fischer concludes that the telephone did indeed intensify "privatism," something he defines as the "participation and valuation of private social worlds as opposed to the larger, public community." As suburbanization and the automobile played their roles in this process, so too did telephones, as "they allowed subscribers to conduct from the privacy of their homes some otherwise public activities." Telephone conversations can be understood to privatize contact, in the sense that an individual can conduct social interaction from a private space in a way that avoids the public exposure of face-to-face meetings. It could be argued that e-mail and text messaging take us even further down this route. In this sense, "telephone use may have contributed to a more compartmentalized society during the first half of the twentieth century" (Fischer 1992: 265–6).

The increased use of mobile phones appears to be intimately bound up with wider social trends, particularly those affecting "Anglo-American" culture, toward greater individuation and strategies to compensate for the shrinking of many people's social world. Individual attempts to overcome isolation are manifested in the intensive use of mobile phones to stay in touch at all times, to the point where public space is used for private interaction. Broader social strategies to overcome individuation are symbolized by the opening up of private space and time, typified by the cell phone connection to an employer and the possibility of locating a person at any point in the day. Arguably, while the impact of the mobile on sociability and individualization is limited and not dissimilar to the traditional telephone, it plays a more distinctive role in blurring the boundaries between the public and private in contemporary life. Again, its role may not be decisive, but the mobility of the cell phone does have implications for how contemporary life is ordered.

Eroding Public and Private Boundaries

Too much can be made of technology's impact on society and our lives. The discussion of Internet "cyber-culture," for example, appears overblown and tiresome. Although there is as yet relatively little written about the impact of the cell phone, there is already a tendency toward pretentious and overstated assessment, as with the recent *Heidegger, Habermas and the Mobile Phone* (Myerson 2001). The author suggests a "postmodern encounter" that changes the whole nature of communication. At the same time, a technology so intimately bound up with social life is likely to provide a useful prism through which to gain insights into the changing nature of social interaction. These changes may not be monumental, and may not have actually been brought about by the technology itself, but the cell phone does have specific qualities and meanings; it is "more than just talk on the move" (Leung and Wei 2000). As a renowned sociologist contends: "these devices have something wider to say about society, and even changes in society itself. Perhaps by dismissing the mobile phone we are dismissing the very stuff of society" (Latour cited in Brown 2002: 3).

The cell phone is a personal object in a way that the ordinary telephone and indeed most other technologies are not. The caller to a cell, rather than standard telephone, is virtually guaranteed as to who will answer. Many people "never leave home without it," making it more akin to house keys, wallet, and address book than a telephone. It has acquired distinctive associations given its own history, most notably with the 1980s "yuppie." Some argue it remains a characteristically male item. A recent study suggests that the cell phone is a "lekking device" used by men to advertise their worth, status, and desirability, like peacocks use their tail feathers and Romans embroidered their clothes (Dunbar and Lycett 2000). Whatever the truth of such claims, the fact that the cell phone is principally used in public has consequences for the way in which it is viewed, and has an impact on those using them. It modifies our public encounters, determining a new set of rules of interaction on trains, for example (Murtagh 2002). Private communication is temporarily sacrificed in public for the well-being of the group. The cell phone sets the individual and his or her world apart from his or her surroundings and encounters. The ringing of a cell phone during a concert or academic lecture is more than a simple distraction. A call during class signals personal distance from public commitment; his or her personal world and priorities are evidently at least as important as the classroom. Even if the call is not taken, it is a disruptive invasion of an environment that has temporarily suspended other realities.

An obvious impact of the cell phone is its effect on privacy. The private cell phone identifies us to the state. Like the ubiquitous closed circuit televisions (CCTVs) on street corners in the United Kingdom, the cell phone puts our whereabouts and business at the disposal of authority. If we are all now "connected," we are also thereby part of a "surveillance society." But whereas the ostensibly sinister implications of CCTV are recognized and largely accepted, most people are unaware that a digital cell phone can pinpoint the precise whereabouts of an individual, regardless even of whether it is being used to make calls. This is because the phone transmits a "recognition call," a facility now used in criminal investigation. Following the notorious killing of three drug dealers in the Essex region of the United Kingdom in December 1995, a successful prosecution was based on the ability to trace their movements on the night of the murders. In October 2000, the BBC current affairs program *Panorama* named suspects of the Omagh bombing in Northern Ireland, again identified through their mobile phones. While the cell phone stands at the center of a (mobile) modernity, it is evidently a modernity with a qualified attitude toward the very autonomy that cell phones suggest.

The development of location-based services extends this intrusion, allowing precise whereabouts to be known at any time, and not only by state authority. The impulse behind this move is far from sinister in itself, as is the use of recognition calls in crime prevention. The drive to improve location fixing was initiated in the United States by the Federal Communications Commission (FCC) in a move to ensure that emergency services can pinpoint people who call from mobiles but don't know where they are. The FCC ordained that by the end of 2002 all operators of cellular networks must have decided how they intend to locate cell phones, and a similar initiative has been pushed by the European Commission. Nevertheless, there is obviously another side to this development. Do we all consent to being locatable by the state, and what about for more

commercial purposes? "This technology is rushing ahead without any regard to privacy issues and questions of what the legal standards should
be," says David Sobel of the Electronic Privacy Information Center in
Washington, D.C. (*New Scientist*, 21 October 2000). Unsolicited promo-
tional text messaging has begun a wave of complaints to the U.K. regulator, the Independent Committee for the Supervision of Standards of
Telephone Information Services (ICSTIS) in 2002.

Others highlight the more positive aspects of permanent awareness of location. Sociological contributions suggest that the everyday
"surveillance" capacity of the cell phone (such as the ubiquitous com-
muter call of: "I'm on the train; home in twenty minutes") allows mutual
accountability, the cementing of relationships, and trust (Green 2002).
But this depends of course on the quality of that intimacy. "If the mobile
phones are not increasing the risk of brain cancer they may pose another danger – to the health of a couple's marriage," declared *The Times*
(6 September 2001). Undeleted text messages from alleged lovers have
become the latest weapon in the divorce courts to prove infidelity! On
the other hand, an important counterexample is the greater privacy afforded young people by the cell phone, which allows a precious degree of
independence and space away from the adult gaze (Green 2002). Texting,
as has already been mentioned, emerged principally as a private teenage
world.

The cell phone changes the meaning of personal time, as everyone can
be constantly interrupted and rescheduled; we are "always on" to each
other, something that has changed the whole pace and character of urban
life (Townsend 2002). The individual is now, for better or worse, permanently available. Unfettered access brings its own problems. People may
now be able to maintain constant contact with their loved ones, but there
is the considerable complication of managing more unwanted access. We
may be more "free" of general time and space constraints, but cell phone
conact is obviously also disruptive of present time and space. It has led to
a greater intrusion of work into private life. In the case of mobile workers
constantly on the move and on call, work has extended worryingly into
private, home life, as one study found (Laurier 2002). We have already
become accustomed to the way in which mobile communications have
had an impact on our lives. Back in 1993 one study looked at how a
group of workers' lives were changed through access to "one person, one
number" facilities. It didn't lead to work and private life being directly
merged, as in people making far more calls from work, for example. But
it did lead to more calls and a further erosion of work norms "in settings

where the norms of communication were already weak." One perceptive contribution noted the wider historical curiosity and significance of the cell phone's relationship to work and home. "There is a "paradox," they suggest; "in the previous era, increased mobility led to an increasing separation of work and personal place and life. Wireless technology may be changing this equation and make it difficult to draw a distinction between work and social life" (Gant and Kiesler 2002: 239–44).

There is now no clear division between the "home" phone and the mobile. This means that any advantages in ease of communication are balanced out for many employees by the realization that employers can contact them at any time, any place. To deny this possibility the employee can switch off the phone, but this is itself a self-conscious statement about their availability to the employer. Some recent anthropological research suggests that for those at the cutting edge of technology, at least, private and public worlds have become indistinguishable. Researchers from San Jose University tracked the lives of fourteen families in Silicon Valley, California (Greenbaum et al. 2000). The researchers found that even families' "private" lives were governed by the language and demands of ubiquitous mobile phones and pagers. While they noted that communications technology allowed family members to stay in touch throughout the day (what they termed "pinging"), this constantly threatened their own more direct interaction. One family attempted to draw a line addressing the blurring of work and home life, and decreed a family rule that e-mailing was banned during meal times. Constant availability has led to the screening of calls, which has become a finely crafted art among office workers (Laurier 2002). Cell phone designers are looking at ways in which the technology can be modified to manage calls more flexibly and thereby "relieve some of the burden of clashing worlds" (Sherry and Salvador 2002: 226).

As one sociologist described, the cell phone is a strikingly indiscrete technology: "This is not primarily because it facilitates forms of social indiscretion ... but rather because it has the capacity to blur distinctions between ostensibly discreet domains and categories" (Cooper 2002: 37). The mobile sits curiously within the established contours of social life. The public and the private are no longer so separate; the mobile provides a direct line from one to the other such that they lose their integrity. It is very unlikely that this elision of public and private space is attributable to the cell phone alone, but it is perhaps its clearest expression.

Burkart notes that the "handy" (as it is known in Germany) shifts the boundaries between the public and private spheres (Burkart 2000). Clear demarcation between these two spheres was central to classical modernity (Weintraub and Kumar 1997). This is more than just an interesting sociological observation. Capitalism was founded on a division between public work and private life. The Western family was possible only because of a public world that could assume many of the duties incumbent on more extended families in Eastern Europe and elsewhere (Burguière et al. 1996: 533). The autonomous individual was created through managing to successfully traverse the two very different worlds, and the whole character of modern society was shaped by this ability. We became self-conscious in a distinctively modern fashion as a result, learning the disciplines demanded by society, on the one hand, and the obligations and affections of home life, on the other. In pre-capitalist and still many less developed societies in the world today, the private and public are not so separate. Indeed, there is no private life as such, as "social" activity is not separate from "home," but is subject to the scrutiny and regulation of all in the community.

Numerous contemporary developments now threaten this long established division. Work is no longer confined to "9 to 5," any more than home is an exclusive domestic refuge from the rigors of the workplace. The personal domain of emotions, health, and relationships is no longer so characterized by intimacy and privacy. We increasingly negotiate these areas in a public way. The state has now colonized many functions that were previously in the domain of the individual and the family (Nolan 1998). While these developments are not attributable to innovations in communication, the mobile symbolizes a blurring of public and private, which is perhaps not altogether welcome. It is in this sense that the very public use of cell phones is instinctively and powerfully reacted against by older generations, in particular. It represents a world where the boundaries on which modern society was founded have been broken down. What we are left with is a seamless world where it is hardly possible to separate the business of society from what remains the preserve of the autonomous, private individual.

Any instinctive discomfort with the way in which the cell phone erodes the boundaries between public and private is rarely consciously expressed, however. It is principally only in a far more direct fashion that a focused reaction against the "mobile revolution" has emerged. The next chapter introduces the very concentrated way in which the issue of health risks associated with mobile telephony has developed in the United Kingdom. The United Kingdom is worthy of singular examination because it is here that the risk campaign has been most intense. As the minutes of a global mobile industry forum for responding to health concerns reported in 1998, the British industry "has been on the front line for a while now" (*Microwave News*, January/February 1999). Following an account of the "front line" of cell phone health concerns, the rest of the chapter takes a step back to provide some comparative historical context to the modern emergence of microwave fears.

3

Mobile Discontents and the Origins of Microwave Fears

The Media Campaign Against Cell Phone Health Risks

The cell phone is regarded as an agent of socialization by some. More commonly and undeniably, it is regarded as a positive, certainly indispensable part of modern living. Yet it also has numerous negative associations, some arising from its distinctive attributes and others simply from how embedded it has become in contemporary social life. The most significant and influential misgivings about the cell phone, however, concern the purported connection between cell phone radiation and negative health effects. These first entered the public domain in the United States, following a lawsuit in the early 1990s that alleged a woman's cancer was the result of prolonged exposure to cell phones. Although the story faded fairly rapidly in the United States, similar allegations became commonplace from the mid-1990s in Australia and Europe.

The international cell phone industry has been concerned about these reactions, sufficiently so that it initiated annual "Is there a health risk?" conferences since the late 1990s to discuss the issues and its responses.[1] Industry's concerns led to the establishment of the Wireless Information Network at a meeting in London in December 1998. This new body included industry representatives from Australia, Austria, Canada, Denmark, France, Germany, Ireland, Italy, New Zealand, Norway, Sweden, the United Kingdom and the United States. Stimulated by "increased attention

---

[1] The two-day conference, "Mobile Phones and Health: An Update on the Latest Research," was held in Gothenberg, Sweden, in September 1999, and several others have followed in London.

to wireless issues by the media," according to a spokesperson, the body aimed to be "a vehicle to exchange information worldwide," so that the industry can "share the techniques they find to be most effective in responding to media inquiries and the public" (*Microwave News*, January/February 1999). At a later London conference, in December 2000, cell phone industry representatives from an unprecedented thirty-eight nations attended. Representatives came from the Republic of Georgia in the former USSR, Egypt, and Venezuela, among others, anxious to learn how best to respond to the concerns they are encountering. This is not to say there is a full appreciation of public health concerns about cell towers within the cell phone industry. One industry consultant claimed nonchalantly: "I expect that it will be forgotten in a couple of years. Health implications get a good airing whenever new technology is introduced," apparently oblivious to the fact that these health fears had already been receiving a "good airing" for almost a decade.[2]

There has been an extraordinary volume of stories about cell phones and health effects in the United Kingdom, in particular. In many respects the stories represent the most important pillar of the issue worldwide, as they were drawn on internationally to substantiate concerns about cell phone radiation in other societies. The Stewart inquiry reviewed 641 cuttings from newspapers published in the United Kingdom between January 1999 and February 2000, and examined the content of seventy-six radio and television programs. Some 79 percent of the media reports alleged that mobile phones and base stations were causing adverse health effects, whereas only 9 percent concluded that there was too little rigorous scientific evidence to arrive at a conclusion or reported no adverse effect (IEGMP 2000). In the early days, stories were typically associated with cell phones themselves, rather than towers.

Health concerns associated with mobile telephony first became public in the United Kingdom following reports about European Commission interest in the subject in 1995; there had been little publicity generated by the earlier lawsuit in the United States. This pattern of diffusing risk concerns being initiated by the European Commission in Brussels continues to this day, as some of the examples in the introductory chapter indicate. The European Commission set up an inquiry in 1995, as one report in a distinguished newspaper described, "after a series of scare stories saying that mobile phones could 'cook' users' brains" (*The Observer*, 1 September

---

[2] Declan Lonergan of the Yankee Group Europe consultancy in London, cited in *Mobile Communications* (306), May 1, 2001.

1996). As with the stories that followed, they were based primarily on a study by scientists at the University of Washington in Seattle, which suggested that the brain cells of rats were damaged by microwaves (Lai and Singh 1996). Certainly, the European Commission was not responding to any public expressions of alarm. The initial inquiry's findings reported that users may be at risk from cancer on the theoretical basis that there was insufficient evidence to rule out links between ill effects and cell phone radiation. At this early stage the European Commission was defensive about its self-appointed role as health guardian. A spokesman explained: "The Commission isn't a Euro-nanny but it is important that one looks at the risks because mobile phones are so important to the way people communicate. We needed to find out if there is some public health risk" (*The Observer*, 1 September 1996). The European Commission decided to fund a £20 million program of research into the potential health risks, nonetheless, and nothing more was heard about the dangers of "nannying" the European public.

These early reports made little public impact and were generally confined to small sections of the broadsheet press. The two key items that propelled cell phone risk into public consciousness were an edition of the BBC television consumer health program *Watchdog Healthcheck* and a report in the *Sunday Times* with the now infamous headline claiming the possibility that "Mobile phones cook your brain" (14 April 1996). The story was by Jonathan Leake, who, over the ensuing five years as the *Sunday Times*'s science editor, continued to draw attention to possible health risks. The principal focus for the original story was advance publicity for the Lai and Singh study above, suggesting that rat's DNA molecules could be split by mobile phone radiation (Lai and Singh 1996). In addition, European Commission announcements that it intended to publish new, "safer" emission guidelines and fund new research into mobile phone EMF also provided momentum for these early stories. Leake followed up his article the following week (*Sunday Times*, 21 April 1996), adding that one of the scientists who conducted the experiment was now recommending the use of vitamins to combat radiation. The new story was also prompted by other inferences of harm, with the launch of the "Microshield" microwave protection device (which generated a number of articles in other newspapers) and news of what was purported to be the first person in the United Kingdom to begin legal action alleging that mobiles had damaged health (about which nothing further was heard). By the end of April 1996, the idea of a mobile phone health "panic" began to be referred to casually in the press (*Daily Telegraph*, 26 April 1996; *Sunday Telegraph*, 2 June 1996).

By July, alarmist headlines about mobile phones "cooking the brain" were picked up beyond British waters, in the *Irish Times* (22 July 1996). The *Sunday Times* headline claim was reproduced and reported as part of a series of "scare" stories that had prompted the European Commission to fund new research (*Observer*, 1 September 1996).

The BBC's *Watchdog Healthcheck* (3 June 1996) was more directly influential in promoting awareness of the issue. The program was trailed and reviewed in most of the broadsheet and specialist press, focusing, like the *Sunday Times*, on the rat DNA molecule experiment (*Independent*, 3 June 1996; *The Times*, 3 June 1996). The program and newspaper reviews pointed out that the scientists reporting ill effects either now limited their mobile phone use or avoided it altogether. Two weeks later, with advance publicity from the *Observer* (16 June 1996), *Watchdog Healthcheck* followed up on its original report. The program also now claimed that individuals planned to pursue legal action, and that two local councils were expressing concern about possible health effects on their employees (17 June 1996). By the end of 1996, the influence of the *Health Watchdog* report within the media continued to be acknowledged, with suggestions that it had led to the commissioning of numerous research programs (*Guardian*, 14 November 1996).

Sustained media promotion of the issue, principally through the newspapers, did not begin in earnest until the autumn of 1997, however. It was at this time that cell phone health stories were taken up by the popular, "tabloid" press and became a regular news feature. This wave of alarmist reports reached its peak in the summer of 1998. Even *Microwave News*, the pre-eminent American monitor of developments in the field and a promoter of concerns about microwave health effects in its own right, described a "bad summer for mobile phones in England. The British press has been blaming them for everything from hypertension to miscarriages..." (*Microwave News*, July/August 1998). The tabloids gave the issue an explicit campaigning focus and vied with each other to present themselves as the champions of public concern about health risks associated with cell phones.

The notorious *Sun* newspaper was the first of the popular press to adopt a campaigning stance, with its "menace of our mobiles" slogan, in the autumn of 1998. But the later boast of the *Sunday Mirror* that it had initially "led the way" with its "mobile phone watch" campaign (11 April 1999) was not inaccurate, as the *Sun* did not sustain its interest. The *Sunday Mirror*'s campaign made a wide range of health claims: that mobile phones simply make you ill (16 May 1999), especially if you wear glasses (30 May 1999); that they can affect your liver and kidneys (11 July 1999); and, more generally, that "a mobile puts years on you" (17 October 1999). Introducing a now common theme of risk stories, derived from the smoking and lung cancer connection, the paper claimed that "experts knew 23 years ago mobiles can kill" (25 July 1999). The campaign did not abate in the following year, when the newspaper suggested that the phones "could make your brakes fail" (9 January 2000); that there may be a "cancer link" (26 March 2000); and (perhaps more worryingly!) that they could "reduce your sex drive" (16 April 2000). However extravagant some of the claims, the *Sunday Mirror*'s campaign was organized around the compelling message that future scientific investigation would reveal the dangers of exposure. In an editorial, the newspaper asked the rhetorical question, "Are mobiles the new tobacco?" (7 March 1999). The most successful paper in Britain in recent years, the *Daily Mail*, also featured the issue prominently, with stories such as "Loss of memory link" (1 March 1999) and "Harm to unborn babies" (24 April 1999). It frequently quoted leading U.K. media pundits on EMF damage, Roger Coghill and Dr. Gerard Hyland.

When campaigning journalist Cathy Moran moved from the *Sunday Mirror* to the *Express*, the latter also adopted a campaigning stance on mobile phone risk. Reflecting its more up-market position, the *Express* was less sensationalist than the *Sunday Mirror*. It innovated new angles beyond the unfocused claims of harm that characterized the early stories. *Microwave News* noted that the articles in the *Express* were the first in the United Kingdom to link mobile phones to the health problems of specific individuals (*Microwave News*, November/December 1997). The *Express* became the most vehement media critic of the mobile phone industry and of government assurances of cell phone safety. Significantly, it increasingly focused on publicizing anti–cell tower campaigns, rather than only on claims about handsets. The *Sunday Mirror* had begun to report on the banning of towers from schools (5 December 1999), but did not systematically develop this aspect. The *Express* went much further on the "environmental" angle, publishing articles about people living near mobile phone towers who had developed cancer. It reported ill effects on school pupils in the city of Sunderland from a mast (2 March 2000), and a ruling in the city of Leeds that a tower had to be removed (8 March 2000), culminating in specific advice on "how to fight [the] mobile threat" (11 March 2000). Alongside such stories, *Express* editorials urged a precautionary approach to base station siting (28 February 2000). The *Express* became the most important conduit for anti-tower campaigning, directing many of its subsequent inquiries to the influential campaigners on a local administrative body, Kent County Council.

Despite some evidently silly stories about cell phones, even the *Sunday Mirror*'s coverage was self-consciously precautionary rather than overtly alarmist. It argued in an editorial: "[we are] not scare-mongering over the health risks and we are not against mobile phones, indeed they have revolutionized our lives for the better" (13 August 2000). It was the suggestion of an effect on children that was particularly prominent. "Sickly pupils 'recover' after leaving cell phone mast school" was a typical headline in *The Express*, as indicated in Chapter 1. Cell towers were blamed for cancerous tumors. Although "[a]t first they were concerned only about its impact on the value of the property," a Leeds woman now linked the mast to her husband's cancer. The logic was, typically, inverted. "Nobody can say it isn't down to the mast," she said (the *Express*, 28 February 2000). More common than the "you can't prove it's not the masts causing harm" claims, it was *possible* harm at the center of attention.

At the personal level, at least, the *Express*'s campaign was driven by a sincere conviction of possible harm from EMF. Its key journalist on the issue, Cathy Moran, came to strongly believe herself that mobiles and masts may be harmful. She dedicated a considerable amount of her own time to the issue and directed hundreds of inquiries on to other sources of support. Moran saw raising public awareness about the possible dangers of mobile phones and masts as her opportunity to do something "more worthwhile" in an age where newspapers were typically dominated only by celebrity-driven trivia.[3]

At a wider level, the particularly prominent role played by the *Express* can be explained by its distinctive circumstances during the late 1990s. Under the editorship of radical feminist Rosie Boycott, the paper self-consciously sought to modernize and distance itself from its highly conventional past. Taken over by Lord Hollick, then adviser to the Labour Party, the paper became known for being more "on message" than any other. As a professor of journalism explained, Boycott sought a "successful new identity . . . ditching the paper's traditional conservatism and trying to catch a wave of Blairite popularity."[4] In particular, the paper appeared to try and relocate itself at the center of the public safety issues that continue to be a dominant theme in "risk aware" contemporary

---

[3] Interview with Cathy Moran, 23 August 2000.
[4] Donald Trelford, "Another Editor Gone and Still No Signs of Life," *Evening Standard*, 25 January 2001.

Britain. In September 2000, for example, it railed against the lack of compensation for victims of human variant vCjD ("mad cow disease").

The tone of reporting in the tabloid newspapers was often not dissimilar to that of more "quality" outlets. The leading roles of the *Sunday Times* and BBC television continued. In a major report at the end of 1998, the *Sunday Times* asked again: "Are we being told the truth about mobile phones?" (*Sunday Times*, 20 December 1998). An edition of the BBC's *Panorama* documentary on 24 May 1999 was as influential in generating concern as *Health Watchdog* had been three years earlier, and became a common media reference point. The program was organized around "worrying new research on mobile phone safety." Referring to the American cell phone industry whistle-blower, George Carlo, the program announced that "one of the industry's own leading experts says the public must be told." Representatives from Nokia, Motorola, and the U.K.'s National Radiological Protection Board (NRPB) were aggressively questioned, and appeared defensive and uncommunicative. By June 1999 the *Panorama* broadcast had helped to raise the media profile of the EMF and health issue to new levels; in the same month Education Minister David Blunkett called for "urgent investigation" of masts on schools.

Anti-tower campaigns became more prominent in the rest of the United Kingdom as base stations began to appear more prominently with the introduction of the digital mobile network. At the beginning of 1999, local protests against masts were becoming relatively common and a staple feature of local and regional newspaper reports. Local newspapers have been an important source of publicity because it is at a very local level that anti-mast campaigns operate. They also tended to be highly sympathetic accounts. "You mast be joking" ran a typical headline in one newspaper about a local residents' blockade of an attempt to erect a tower (*Reading Evening News*, 27 June 2000). The Kent-based *Gravesend Reporter* carried headline stories such as "Mobile Warfare" on 27 July, 10 August, 7 September, and 26 October 2000. The *Gravesend Messenger*, meanwhile, tried to outdo its rival with demands that the local council refuse to allow any further towers to be erected without full planning permission. Local newspapers, usually notoriously reluctant to commit themselves to any type of campaigning activity unless absolutely assured of victory, have publicly identified themselves with the issue. Another, *This Is Buckinghamshire*, has even gone so far as to organize a web-based anti-mast campaign. Besides drawing local attention to individual anti-tower campaigns, this extensive local newspaper coverage has provided considerable moral support for otherwise isolated campaigners.

Campaigners refer to the ease with which they managed to get local papers to cover the issue, and this was evidently instrumental in sustaining enthusiasm.

The national media's problematization of cell phones and the local media's encouragement of campaigns against cell towers combined to give considerable momentum to campaigning on the tower issue, in particular. If the government inquiry under Sir William Stewart was expected to allay in any way media concerns about mobile telephony, it was unsuccessful. Press campaigning and promotion of health concerns did not abate after the release of its report in May 2000, despite the extreme precautionary stance of the IEGMP report. The principal newspapers leading the promotion of concern continued to reveal problems. The *Sunday Mirror* demanded a lowering of emission levels in line with American standards (13 August 2000). The *Express* ran a front page declaring: "kids in mobile phone alert" and that children were facing "growing risk" after Disney dropped plans to market phones in the United States (25 November 2000). The *Daily Mail* discovered possible "nerve damage" (24 October 2000). Cell phone health fears reappeared in the national press at the end of November 2000 following the government announcement that safety measures, which arose directly from the Stewart Inquiry, were soon to be implemented. Safety leaflets about children's usage were now to be distributed at the point of sale of mobile phones.

The number of campaigning newspapers actually grew in the aftermath of the government inquiry. *The Times* began to engage in the promotion of mobile phone health issues at the end of 2000. After publicizing yet another cancer-based American lawsuit against mobile phone companies, it later announced that £5 billion had been wiped off Vodafone shares as a result of its report (*The Times*, 29 December 2000). The newspaper also publicized the new national campaign, Mast Action U.K., on the same day. At the beginning of 2001, "disturbing" studies continued to be revealed (*Daily Mail*, 16 January 2001), as well as reported connections between cell phone EMF and tumors (*The Times*, 1 January 2001) and alleged litigation (*The Times*, 4 January 2001). New American research, which again disproved any connection between mobile usage and brain cancer, was barely reported in the British media (Muscat et al. 2000; Inskip 2001). Overall, the British media has maintained a remarkable fascination with the "phantom risk" of cell phone emissions. A few critical voices, meanwhile, suggested that concerns about mobile safety were the latest in a series of unfounded health scares. Peter Preston, a former editor of the *Guardian*, railed against what he saw as a technophobic culture dominated

by "pseudo scientific panics" and lamented the absence of a more rational approach he saw as still common in the United States (*The Guardian,*
15 May 2000).

The Campaign Against Cell Towers and the Elevation
of Health Concerns

While the media campaign highlighting cell phone risk initially centered
on the handsets, it is the towers that have become increasingly central
to the story of health fears. Partly this is because, from the end of 1998,
an increasing number of local campaigns emerged. Many of these were
eventually to merge into an official national campaign, Mast Action U.K.
(MAUK), launched at the House of Commons at the end of 2000. By
its own estimates, in 2000 there were over 300 active campaigns in the
United Kingdom, and the figure continued to rise. Campaign groups have
organized marches and protests and have dismantled masts. There were
almost 100 incidents of parents requesting that masts be removed from
their childrens' schools between 1998 and 2000, and possibly more that
have passed without media comment.[5] Protests and campaigning against
masts have been more intensive and sustained in the United Kingdom than
elsewhere and have involved a range of people and institutions. Yet the
emergence of these groups cannot be divorced from the wider problematization of mobile telephony that preceded it. Campaigners were influenced
by and interacted with the media's own determined campaigns to highlight
health risks. They were also crucially influenced by the extent of reaction
from institutions and government, which increasingly encouraged their
concerns through recognition and indirect endorsement.

The author's own interviews with campaigners suggest that the media
has played an important role in energizing and generalizing local concerns
about "inappropriately" sited masts. This is not to suggest a crude process
whereby people mechanically reacted to media stories about cell phones
by challenging the construction of cell phone towers. The role of the media
and other external influences has rather been one of shifting the balance of
competing issues confronting people faced with the sudden appearance
of unwelcome and ugly structures in their community. Specifically, the
media has been instrumental in elevating *health* concerns about nearby
masts over and above other, more tangible factors such as local democracy,
property prices, and esthetic considerations. Effective media always have

5 Reuters newspaper archives 1998–2000.

an ability to generalize from specific experiences; in the "risk society" this takes the form of promoting health concerns over more "mundane" local issues. Research on local mobilizations against waste incinerators confirms a similar picture whereby spontaneous, NIMBY ("not in my backyard")-style reactions on the basis of visual amenity and property values acquires a health dimension only at a later stage, often as a result of intervention by environmental groups (Rootes 2001).

In specific health terms, the reaction against cell towers is something of a curiosity, however. The government-commissioned Stewart Report explained that even if the possibility of a health risk associated with mobile EMF were to be accepted, towers pose little potential risk compared with handsets. Indeed, it is argued that if cell tower EMF were a problem, it would actually be better to be sited nearer, rather than far away from, the tower (see Chapter 4). The scientific illogicality of reaction to masts rather than handsets underlines the fact that reaction is driven by social influences rather than scientific knowledge or actual harm.

Invariably, protests began simply as a reaction to the sudden appearance of a cell tower near people's homes or schools. The often unannounced appearance of these structures next to people's property has understandably caused annoyance and anger. Interviews with anti-tower protestors indicate that reaction is dominated by indignation about a lack of consultation. Generally only in relation to towers erected on or near schools were more diffuse, health-based anxieties spontaneously triggered. Even in these cases, however, the suspicion was of something unfamiliar appearing close to their children, and was evidently not informed by specific knowledge about how these structures might be dangerous. The extent to which health anxieties appeared also seemed to depend on how developed the media profile was at the time the tower was erected. For many protestors, it was often only at the subsequent stage of finding out more information and publicizing their plight that the possibility of harmful health effects was introduced and frequently came to override other factors. This is illustrated in interviews with campaigners carried out in the summer of 2000.[6]

The media played an instrumental role in creating campaigning momentum and consolidating the health aspect of reaction to masts. One successful campaign began by going directly to the local papers to publicize

---

[6] Twenty open-ended interviews with campaigners in June-September 2000. These included several of the more prominent campaigners, others suggested by them, and campaigns traced through the Internet. Only first names are used, for relative anonymity.

the way in which the offending mobile operator had put up a mast without consulting residents. Important to the launch of an anti-tower campaign of one resident, was the fact that his neighbor was a regional television news producer, so he had the inspiration and potential access through which he could gain coverage of his grievance. Sometimes it was the media that effectively "made" the story for themselves. Tony and Jo's campaign was, in effect, initiated by the web service BBC Online when it began interviewing parents and the headmistress about plans (at that time unknown to the parents) for a tower on the school. The campaign snowballed after this report ("so these things can harm my child, can they?"), with local television station Anglia News wanting a story, as well as local radio stations and newspapers.

An even more common pattern was of individuals hearing about other complaints through the media. Many of them established contact with one another and began to exchange experiences and information. Sue heard on a radio program that Liverpool Council was ordering an operator to take down a tower. She managed to take her own efforts further after eventually establishing contact with the council. Shortly after the mast went up near Mary's property, she saw an article in the *Express* by Cathy Moran. She called Moran and was then put in contact with others. Similarly, an article in the *Daily Mail* was an important catalyst for Tony and Jo, and led them to the main U.K. scientific voice of health alarm, Dr. Gerard Hyland, an academic at Warwick University.

The media promotion of campaigns enabled individuals to identify one another and create campaign links. Establishing contact with others confronting similar circumstances was central to moving from initial outrage to an organized approach. An organizer from an influential campaign fulcrum, the Liberal Democrats at Kent County Council, explained that "many people telephone thinking, 'I really feel as if I'm the only person fighting....' But they quickly realize that it's not the case when I tell them we've had 250 calls...."[7] Campaign links were established through the television and newspaper media. Following their coverage on BBC Online, Tony and Jo were contacted by another organizer, who in turn put them in contact with others who were also contesting the erection of a mast on a local fire station. Similarly, Jan chanced on a television news report about Clive's campaign. Getting his number via Carlton television, she linked up with him. The media appear to have played the role of campaign organizer or at least facilitator.

---

[7] Interview with Rebecca Casson, 26 September 2000.

The new electronic media were also important in establishing campaign links. One campaigner, perhaps overstating the case, suggested that "this has built up into a movement, which has reached global proportions through the aid of the Internet and email facility." Another, Brian, searched the Internet for similar situations and found out about the various campaigns worldwide. Indeed, what often distinguished those who sustained their involvement was access to a computer. The first U.K. campaign centered upon the web page that Roy set up with the help of his son. Many of the early activists had a presence on the web, and this partially determined the significant role they were to play in the campaigning network. Another campaigner, Peter, believes that a book could be written on the role of the Internet in contemporary campaigning. For Dahleen, "it highlighted just how useful the Internet can be." In both of the two early Scottish cases that led Friends of the Earth (FoE) Scotland to its important involvement, the complainants turned to the web. FoE Scotland itself, once it had decided to lead campaigning, found its information on the web.

The Internet provided access to material on the alleged health effects of electromagnetism. Lead campaigner Margaret Dean's witness statement to the Stewart Committee details her first reaction against the tower: "I subsequently updated our computer system, gained access to the Internet and started my investigations."[8] Among other things she was then able to establish international links with individuals from an American anti-EMF group. Once part of the "loop" of activists, individuals were often mailed the latest research findings found on the Internet by fellow campaigners. Large reports and international correspondence could be exchanged at little cost.

Without the World Wide Web it would have been difficult to make such specialized materials as on potential health effects from radiofrequency radiation accessible to ordinary campaigners. This factor is very important because typically it was only through the experience of finding "alternative" scientific materials on the Internet that health concerns began to acquire a consistent focus. This raises questions about the Internet as a source of information, particularly scientific information. Any member of the public has been able to gain access, through the web, to a range of data, news reports, and opinions that might otherwise be unavailable. But there is no quality control, which is particularly important in scientific matters, as they invariably require considerable interpretive

[8] Margaret Dean's witness statement to the IEGMP.

expertise. Good science is dependent on a rigorous process of peer review; without such a process there is no guarantee that research is valid. But the stringent requirements of peer review are no barrier to posting materials on the Internet. For the campaigners, the implications of this lack of quality control may not be fully recognized. Instead, papers by those without specialist expertise have weight on the Internet equal to the published results of elaborate and painstaking research carried out by teams of internationally esteemed scientists.

Institutional Responses

In response to the wave of press coverage in the United Kingdom in 1997 and 1998, some institutions began to express health concerns themselves and even take specific precautionary measures. In August 1997, the National Union of Teachers consulted the Health and Safety Executive about possible health risks. In November 1998, entrepreneur Richard Branson made his health concerns about mobiles public, recommending the use of safety devices for his employees (*Sunday Times*; *Sunday Business*, 15 November 1998). Mobiles were also banned at London's premier luxury store, Harrods. The owner, Mohammed al Fayed, went on to become crucial to establishing early momentum for the anti–cell tower campaign (see Chapter 5). Specific state institutions also responded to concerns about cell phones. In June 1999, the London Metropolitan police service announced that officers were being told to limit mobile calls as a "purely precautionary measure," for example. Its press release made reference to the *Panorama* program of 24 May.

The response of government and public authorities to campaigns against towers was also significant. At the end of 1998 and the beginning of 1999, local protests against the siting of radio base stations had first emerged in Scotland. Following a report by the environmentalist organization FoE, indicating a more restrictive approach to mast siting by some local councils, other councils followed suit. By the end of March 1999, six Scottish councils had adopted a precautionary policy. The government began to respond, most importantly by setting up the Independent Expert Group on Mobile Phones (IEGMP) inquiry, also in March 1999. The campaign then became more dynamic in the rest of the United Kingdom, given added momentum by the growing concerns about mobile phone handsets.

The issue of health risks from masts sited near or on schools in particular came to national prominence following three separate incidents in June

1999. Several local protest groups held their first meeting at the House of Commons in June 1999. In the same month, Secretary of State for Education David Blunkett called for an "urgent investigation" into masts near schools, and the Glasgow Health Board claimed, referring to the debate about masts on schools, that there was a probable link between mast emissions and leukemia. Parliamentary activity increased significantly in the following months. The House of Commons Science and Technology Committee concluded its investigation of the issue in September 1999 with a call for massively increased research funds and an 80 percent cut in permitted radiation levels from phones, which added to the speculation about health effects. In November 1999, Member of Parliament (MP) Howard Stoate proposed an early day motion in the House of Commons (No. 56), which was signed by 181 MPs, calling for restrictions on tower siting and funding for research into possible health risks.[9] By the end of 1999, local councils across the United Kingdom were experimenting with attempts to impose their own unilateral bans or restrictions on mobile masts, especially those sited near schools.

The *Sunday Mirror* boasted that after eighteen months of campaigning against cell phones, it "had blazed a trail all the way to the heart of government" (13 August 2000). This claim was not without foundation. Announcing the formation of the Stewart Inquiry in 1999, the then Minister for Public Health, Tessa Jowell, stated: "To date there has been no consistent evidence suggesting risk to health but there is continuing public concern about the possibility. It would be wrong to ignore that concern." Specifically, the issue of children was singled out for reasons of "public concern": "In giving special attention to schools, the Expert Group was responding very largely to public concern rather than any proven health hazard" (IEGMP 2000: 1). The continuing increase in cell phone usage described in the previous chapter suggests that public concern was far from overwhelming. The inquiry appears to have been initiated in *anticipation* of such a development, with media coverage interpreted by the government as an early warning of public fears. Explaining her proactive approach before a House of Commons Select Committee, Jowell highlighted the "considerable amount of media interest, media concern about the potential ill effects on health from mobile phones." The inquiry was set up by Jowell, "[b]ecause [she] was keen that [they] respond

---

[9] Early day motions are "calls for legislation"; largely tokenistic registers of an MP's concern to their constituents, the closest comparable measure in the American system is "Concurrent and Simple Resolutions."

to what had been quite a wave of public reporting of studies about the impact of mobile phones." She went on to make clear that in, "an area like this...it is very important that we...work very hard to *keep ahead of public anxiety*" (House of Commons 1999: 1–2; emphasis added).

It is important to add that more traditional democratic pressure undoubtedly also played an important role in driving government to an "anticipatory" response. Insofar as any single issue dominated MPs' mail bags during 1999, it was from constituents complaining about the siting of mobile towers. The Stewart Report detailed the quantity of complaint to politicians and the state: 600 letters to ministers (mainly concerning masts), 85 letters to MPs replied to by Health ministers, 80 letters to the Department of Health, 350 to the Department of Environment, Transport and the Regions on planning and environmental issues, and 157 to the Department for Education and Employment about the location of base stations in or around schools (IEGMP 2000: 2). It went on to note that the tower issue had become the most popular early day motion tabled in Parliament.

Considering the relatively large number of public complaints, the government's action would appear to be a good example of "responsive" and "open" government. However, it should be remembered that the relationship is far from direct between this more conventional public pressure and a major government-sponsored inquiry that embraced the spirit of precaution from the outset. These letters of complaint were principally concerned with issues of planning, location, and environment, not with health concerns about electromagnetism alone. It is only through interaction with the long-running and intensive media health problematization of mobiles that this factor came to prominence. In other words, more apparently conventional democratic public pressure cannot be separated from the highly effective media campaign. In this sense, government reaction was indirectly in response to a media-led agenda, not to abstract public concern.

Although the Stewart Committee found no evidence of adverse health effects from cell phones and masts, its recommendations were precautionary and called for further research. This, in turn, has not alleviated concerns about hidden health risks, and the number of campaigns in the United Kingdom continued to rise. Indeed, with some justification, leading U.K. activist Margaret Dean claimed: "The Stewart enquiry was due to our campaign," explaining: "We worked closely with them...we supplied them with information on an almost daily basis." Among many others, Dean submitted her own witness statement. She declared herself "very pleased with the conclusions."[10] The official national campaign was formed in the winter following the publication of the report's findings in May 2000. Activists also cite the endorsement by the European Union of the precautionary principle as compelling grounds for action; to ignore others' prudence becomes necessarily irresponsible. If precaution exists elsewhere, and has even been politically endorsed continent-wide, it becomes a moral imperative.

Although stating that there was no evidence to suggest possible harm, the Stewart Committee's report counseled caution, particularly in relation to mast siting and children, on the grounds that public fears must be accommodated. Some confusion was created by the report's contradictory signals. Sir William Stewart went on to declare in September 2001 at the annual conference of the British Association for the Advancement of Science that cell phone operators are "irresponsible" in marketing their devices to teenagers. He has subsequently repeated the accusation, and has emphasized that he would not allow his own grandchildren to use cell phones.[11] The issue refuses to go away. In June 2002 planning chiefs from some sixty local councils held a conference in Harrow, London, to form a pressure group to lobby for tougher controls on tower siting. Although precautionary health concerns have been encouraged, it remains difficult to legally oppose towers on health grounds. Local authorities are resentful at having to fulfil statutory obligations to allow expansion of mobile networks, at the same time as having to face down health fears expressed by local groups.

The Dynamic of Precaution and "Public Concerns"

Regardless of the specific content of what the government has said about cell phone risk, it is the very high profile given over to the issue that has itself been instrumental in fueling concern and campaigning activity. Precautionary advice and activity itself can animate risk perceptions. Why is this? Previous case studies on comparable technological risks indicate that official reaction to "phantom risks" heightens anxiety, irrespective of the specific content of the message. American psychometric research on public perception of health risks from power lines suggests that the

---

[10] Interview with Margaret Dean, 23 September 2000.

[11] It should be pointed out that cell phone companies do not advertise their products to children in the United Kingdom. Second, advertising in such a market does not create general demand, only determines which particular brand attains greater market share. The cell phone market is very clearly driven by social demands that have taken the cell phone industry completely by surprise, as in the case of text messaging.

very act of officially addressing such concerns through public information leaflets adds to the perception of hazardous risk (Morgan et al. 1985; MacGregor, Slovic, and Morgan 1994). In a study on individual reactions to brochures presenting a balanced presentation of exposure to power-frequency EMF, it was found that they "significantly increased people's concerns about those risks" (MacGregor et al. 1994: 826). Earlier studies related to perceptions of nuclear power confirm this finding (Flynn 1984) and point to the importance of uncertain and conflicting information in leading people to follow the most cautious advice as the best course of action (Mazur 1989). The pattern of response in the contemporary cell phone EMF "panic" indicates a similar process where public concern is fueled by concerted official responses.

Precautionary responses by the state and regulatory bodies can actually be decisive in activating otherwise potentially inconsequential concerns. Almost by definition, what is a risk issue is itself determined by the extent and character of government reaction. The dynamic is not difficult to grasp; it is the inexorable logic of there being "no smoke without fire." This is shaped by the contemporary suspicion of authority that is peculiar to our age; if the government is taking precautionary action, we might only guess at how serious the problem really is. There is also another more particular sense in which official risk responses potentially animate and cohere otherwise diffuse anxieties. More than ever, potential risk is seen to be pervasive. It is notable that new risks from different food products are regularly identified, for example. Yet it is increasingly difficult to measure or even contextualize these many potential hazards, as few cause demonstrable and widespread human harm. Typically, the alarm is sounded on the basis of a possible (future) threat. In these circumstances, it is precautionary official warnings or measures themselves that can provide confirmation that concern is warranted. According to French thinker François Ewald, if a risk is perceived, then it is real, and therefore even a "phantom risk" can acquire a life of its own, and can apparently justify the original precautionary response:

Risk has an allusive, insidious potential existence.... Assumed to be everywhere, it founds a politics of prevention. The term prevention does not indicate simply a practice based on the maxim that an ounce of prevention is worth a pound of cure, but also the assumption that *if prevention is necessary it is because danger exists.* (Ewald 1993: 221; emphasis added)

Ewald's argument that precaution confirms the "reality" of danger appears pertinent in the British mobile phone case. To consider a simple example, parents in the British city of Nottingham were campaigning for the city council to remove a tower from a school. The school is one of only four in Nottingham that has an active cell phone tower, after the council pledged not to install new towers on schools. Existing towers are being used only until the end of contracts. Unsurprisingly, however, in November 2001 parents demanded that the council remove all the masts, arguing that there must legitimate grounds for concern about safety if the contracts are to be terminated.

Public mistrust of official and corporate reassurance is widely discussed. Recent British research indicates that almost half of those questioned said that they thought the government had something to hide when it offered reassurances about the safety of vaccines, mobile phones, or genetically modified food (Grove-White, Macnaghten, and Wynne 2000).[12] Only 40 percent trusted the information from the mobile phone industry about product safety, and only 36 percent believed what the food industry told them about genetically modified foods. These results were used not only to substantiate public skepticism, but also to suggest that a positive "awareness" informs these reactions. However, there is no evidence to suggest such public attitudes are informed by balanced knowledge of the issues.

Analysis and concern about risk invariably focus on public perceptions, rather than the role of institutional actors. Public "risk communication" is a growing field on both sides of the Atlantic (Leviton et al. 1998; Bennett and Calman 1999). New approaches to science and society question the feasibility, even the desirability, of contesting public fears, suggesting it should be far more of an interactive process. The new thinking is that perhaps authorities were themselves wrong to have imagined that people might be "irrational" and arrogant to think that it was the place of science and authority to assume they knew better. Whatever the merits of this approach, it is striking that contemporary reflections on risk still avoid investigating the dynamics of how risk concerns are established in the first place. We can gauge whether real public health concern existed, or was created, about cell phones only from a few fragments.

There is some evidence of a passive fascination with potential risks from cell phones, much like the wider curiosity with health risks of all kinds. The edition of the BBC documentary program *Panorama* on cell phone fears attracted seven million viewers in 1999, compared with viewing figures as low as three million in early 2001 (*Guardian*, 20 February

---

[12] The research carried out at Lancaster University involved questioning 1,002 people between 2 and 4 March 2001.

2001). Clearly, the subject appeals to a far wider number of people than those who are inclined to take concrete action or register concern in any way. Generalized, if qualified and apparently passing concern is also illustrated by the popularity of hands-free kits, which promise enhanced safety precautions with headsets to keep the phone unit away from the head. Having been something of a fad in the late 1990s, sales have dropped and the sight of people apparently talking into their own shoulders is already now much rarer. We should add that the specific health protection qualities of hands-free kits was also tarnished by a campaign by the Consumers Association, which argued that they were probably more dangerous than "ordinary" cell phone usage. A more active measure of concern is provided by the number of inquiries to the official regulatory body, the NRPB (see Fig. 12). Of course, this striking figure for queries about cell phones and masts is relative to the general lack of interest in other forms of radiation. Indeed, from the perspective of society as a whole, these specific queries and complaints are much like the (very limited number of) complaints received from the "moral minority" over the broadcasting of controversial television programs.

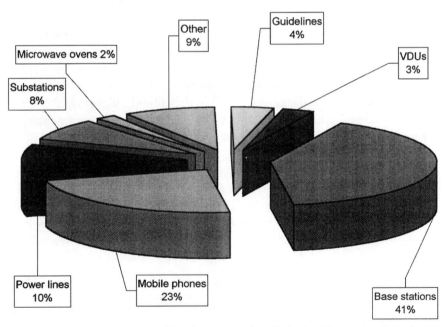

FIGURE 12. Inquiries received by the National Radiological Protection Board on radiological matters by subject area in 1999. Courtesy of the National Radiological Protection Board.

There have been few studies of the extent to which people perceive a danger from cell phone and mast radiation. A 2001 British study of 1000 under-sixteen-year-olds found that while nine out of ten own a mobile, only 11 percent believed they had been affected by radiation from their phones, with the majority highlighting headaches as the main complaint.[13] If passive opinion can be divorced from any apparent consequence, people are evidently prepared to err on the side of caution. According to the Future Foundation's research, some 75 percent of mobile users agreed that government health warnings should appear on handsets (Future Foundation 1999). Despite this approval for warnings, there is no serious demand for the technology to be withdrawn. Indeed, in the contemporary culture of precaution, it is difficult to imagine a polled majority not agreeing to more warnings, inquiries, and research into any such risk, if asked in the abstract. Whether the reply would be the same if the cost of such inquiries was both specified and set against alternative uses, such as treating childhood cancers, is a different matter, however. This is leaving aside whether people would be prepared to limit their own or their children's usage in the name of enhanced safety.

No doubt influenced by the fact of their own decision to use cell phones, even when set against other "worries about modernity," the perception of health risks from cell phones was of least concern, according to one recent study (Petrie et al. 2001). As the graph of their results indicates, cell phones came last out of twenty-five specific modern health worries (see Fig. 13).[14] The results suggested some relationship between heightened perceptions of risks and behavioral changes. Notably, they found a higher rate of food intolerance and greater use of alternative health practitioners among the "worried." There is a striking absence of behavioral changes with regard to cell phone use, however, with the very limited exception of hands-free kits. This illustrates the wider discrepancy between passive engagement with risk and a lack of interest in personal consequences. The absence of active public health concern over cell phones was apparent during the Stewart Inquiry's program of information gathering between September 1999 and March 2000. During that period, the IEGMP held five public

---

[13] Study by the Pupil Research Initiative at the Centre for Science Education at Sheffield Hallam University. Results can be viewed at www.shu.ac.uk/pri.

[14] The study was based on a questionnaire completed by 526 university students, and on a national survey database of 7,869 New Zealanders. A scale was derived from initial surveys that included twenty-five items. Respondents were asked to rate each item on a five-point scale, ranging from "no concern" to "extreme concern." The scale has high levels of internal reliability producing a Cronbach alpha of 0.94 in this sample.

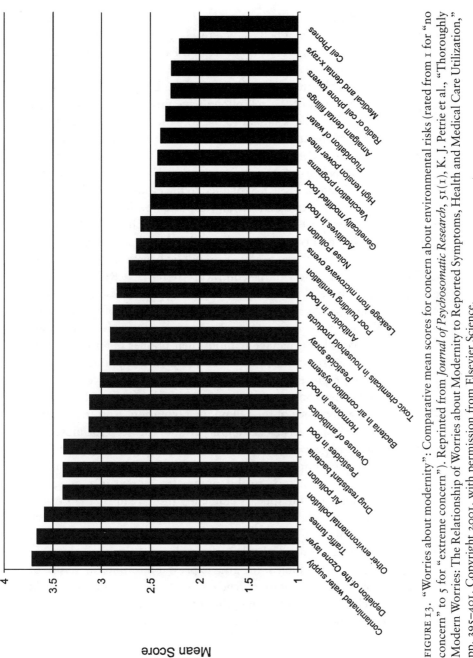

FIGURE 13. "Worries about modernity": Comparative mean scores for concern about environmental risks (rated from 1 for "no concern" to 5 for "extreme concern"). Reprinted from *Journal of Psychosomatic Research*, 51(1), K. J. Petrie et al., "Thoroughly Modern Worries: The Relationship of Worries about Modernity to Reported Symptoms, Health and Medical Care Utilization," pp. 395–401. Copyright 2001, with permission from Elsevier Science.

meetings around the United Kingdom. These attracted only a handful of people with the exception of Belfast, where a larger group had been mobilized by the local campaign, Northern Ireland Families Against Telecommunication Towers (NIFATT).

As suggested in the introductory chapter, the bottom line is that the convenience and utility of the cell phone have more than offset interest in hypothetical risks. This is similar to the way that, in the United States, the convenience of the microwave oven overcame health concerns that initially threatened to destroy the industry. Referring to a representative survey for Motorola in 1998, the chairman of the United Kingdom's leading polling organization, MORI, explained to the House of Lords' Science and Technology Committee that "widely-reported health scares over the use of mobile phones seem to have had no effect in checking the explosion in mobile use and ownership, while other health scares have had a very significant and measurable effects on public behavior (perhaps most notably that over the safety of the contraceptive pill)."[15] Robert Worcester then detailed how almost 90 percent of those interviewed said their phones gave a sense of greater personal safety and peace of mind for the safety of loved ones when away from home. Some 42 percent of mobile users said they could not manage without their phones for personal use; more than half said they couldn't do without their cell phones at work. A similar number reported that it made them more productive.

It is interesting that the anti-tower campaign itself is marked by a somewhat awkward acceptance of the cell phone revolution. Anti-tower campaigners contest their precise location rather than the need for masts per se. Indeed, the emergence of the focus on masts rather than phones, despite the potentially more direct impact of the phone emissions on the body, can itself be understood in this pragmatic context. Campaigning to change a tower location appears eminently more realistic than trying to challenge properly the "mobile revolution." While a handful of very committed campaigners profess complete avoidance of mobile phones (and even domestic cordless phones), the majority appreciate the popularity of mobile communication and express objections in terms of informed choice and consultation. The equivocal nature of even activist rejection of cellular technology underlines the need to establish the origins of concerns about electromagnetism. It is to this subject we now turn,

---

[15] 1998 Motorola Survey by MORI, "The British and Technology." Submission by MORI chairman Robert Worcester to the House of Lords Select Committee on Science and Technology (House of Lords 2000b: 153).

examining also the very different reactions to radiation-based technologies earlier in the century.

Changing Times, Changing Technologies

Radiation fears have spread not only across countries but across technologies and phenomena. They did not originate with recent concern over cell phones. There is a history of comparable fears focusing on different microwave technologies. Steneck's early account (1984) sympathetically outlines the history of concern that microwaves might have a biological effect, even though they are too weak to cause any direct human harm (see Chapter 4).

Anxieties about microwave technologies first made a wider public impact when alleged dangers from color television x-rays were publicized in the 1960s. The concern was short-lived, limited in its impact, and apparently still informed by more traditional hostility to unfamiliar new technology, or "technophobia," rather than more modern health-based sensibilities. The brief alarm and confusion over radiation from televisions is better regarded as an anticipation of the more developed concerns in the following decades. There was a slightly more pronounced reaction to the introduction of microwave ovens in the 1970s, but this alarm was also quickly over and made no enduring impact. The most significant precedent for reactions against cell phone EMF was provided by suspicions about electricity pylons. This was initiated by a controversial and highly influential American study in the 1970s that suggested a link between childhood leukemia and proximity to power lines (Wertheimer and Leeper 1979).

This American study was instrumental in creating microwave concerns in other countries such as Italy. The link between power-line and cell phone EMF alarms was often very direct, despite the different character of the purported dangers. Sometimes the same individuals, such as Louis Slessin, the editor of *Microwave News*, have been involved in raising the possibility of harm from pylons, and then from cell phones. In several countries, campaigning against cell phone towers in the late 1990s became a new focus for groups already contesting the presence of overhead power lines. In the United States, it remains inseparable from a longer established opposition to other forms of microwave facilities and devices. Publicity about microwave effects appears to have registered with the American public more widely, even if it has not generally led to a boycotting of devices with which they are associated. Research by the Edison Electric

Institute suggests that over 50 percent of Americans are aware of research on EMF, with half of these specifically aware of a possible link to cancer. Some 10 percent of the total surveyed felt that the risk was serious or very serious (cited in Sagan 1996: xv).

Video display terminals (VDTs) also became a focus of very modern health anxieties in the 1980s. Around a dozen clusters in various parts of North America from 1980 onward linked VDTs to miscarriages and other problems (Foster 1986, 1999b). Significant also was the more community-based opposition to microwave facilities that developed in the context of Cold War suspicion of technology linked to the military. The cumulative impact of these episodes was the consolidation of the possibility, even the expectation, that radiation from cell phones might be harmful, despite the obvious lack of any demonstrable impact on their millions of users.

In one sense, cell phone health concerns form part of a general twentieth-century fear generated by the technological harnessing of different parts of the electromagnetic spectrum, even simply electricity itself. One useful account of contemporary American science-related controversies describes how "[t]he fear of EMF combines two of man's gut-level emotions: the fear of the invisible and the distrust of new technology" (Fumento 1993: 225). At its earliest and most basic level these suspicions can be dated to the introduction of electric light, as another account illustrates:

"The room is equipped with Edison Electric Light. Do not attempt to light with a match. Simply turn the key on the wall." So ran one of many similar notices that began to appear in hotel bedrooms during the 1880s. But along with the admonition not to try and ignite the light bulb came a further statement to allay fears: "The use of electricity for lighting is in no way harmful to health, nor does it affect the soundness of your sleep." (cited in ibid.: 218)

The reassurances did not convince everyone, as Fumento observes. Even into the 1930s, some of the older generation, at least, remained wary of electricity. The American humorist James Thurber wrote of his grandmother, in a 1933 essay, that she "lived the latter years of her life in the horrible suspicion that electricity was dripping all over the house" (see Fig. 14). She spent her days turning off the wall switches that led to empty sockets, "happy in the satisfaction that she had stopped not only a costly, but a dangerous leakage" (cited in ibid.: 218). Yet overall, electrification was greeted more with wonderment than fear. Concern about harm to health was equal to worries about a possible impact on a restful night's

FIGURE 14. "Electricity was leaking all over the house," cartoon by James Thurber (1933). Courtesy of Barbara Hogenson Agency, Inc.

sleep, suggesting the threat was not imagined to be dramatic. Thurber's grandmother appears more a victim of general ignorance than someone gripped by the possibility of deadly harm. More broadly, it is striking that even innovations such as x-rays that, it transpired, were genuinely dangerous were greeted with such excitement that potential dangers were barely considered or investigated. It is only in the last thirty-five years that the possibility of harm from EMF has been seriously entertained (Sagan 1996: 3).

According to sociological accounts of our contemporary "risk society," the increased receptivity to minor risk is explained by the correspondingly increased pace of change and innovation (Giddens 1990, 1991). We now live in a "runaway world" where we can hardly keep pace with an unsettling process of transformation, according to this account. Yet, as in the case of comparing the impact of the telegraph with contemporary telecommunications highlighted in Chapter 2, such an argument is by no means clear-cut. To an extent, change at the level of technology and everyday life appears more dramatic at the end of the nineteenth and beginning of the twentieth centuries. By way of illustration, one science writer high-lights the new inventions enjoyed by the novelist Henry James over only half a decade. James had electric lighting installed in 1895, rode a bicycle the following year, wrote on a typewriter in 1897, and saw a cinemato-graph in 1898. What were becoming known as "gadgets" were reaching a mass market by the 1890s, and domestic electricity became more widely available to make them work. The difference today is not so much in the extent of change as in the sharply contrasting cultural contexts. These more confident, pre-war decades were far less troubled by any potentially negative consequences of accelerated innovation than the fin-de-siecle pe-riod a century later. During the earlier period science itself was so confi-dent as to declare that all had been discovered, and only mere details remained to be elaborated. The first American Nobel Prize-winner, Albert Michelson, announced in 1902 that "the more important funda-mental laws and facts of physical science have all been discovered and these are now so firmly established that the possibility of their ever be-ing supplanted on consequence of new discoveries is remote" (Appleyard 1992: 115). Michelson was wrong, of course; ironically, it was his own work into the nature of light that led to the questioning of his "firmly established" physics.

To some extent, a pro-science and -technology attitude was distinctively American: "The development and liberal dissemination of technology be-came identified with the history of America itself" (MacLeod 1997: 373). Thomas Jefferson saw the widespread pursuit and application of scientific knowledge as characteristic of a free society. The apparently "value free" nature of scientifically based decision making had strong appeal from the post Civil War years onward. Yet what can be regarded as a more positive or, on the other hand, naive attitude toward technology was not confined to the New World. In Europe, also, enthusiasm for the benefits of benefi-cial technologies overwhelmed latent fears and misunderstandings.

The Magic of X-Rays and Miracle of Radar

An interesting comparison and contrast to contemporary EMF concerns is the social and scientific responses to the harnessing of rays at the danger-ous, ionizing, end of the electromagnetic spectrum. X-rays were discov-ered in 1895 by the German physicist Wilhelm Roentgen (Bleich 1961). Through experimentation with the production of cathode rays, he found that placing a hand or arm between the charged tube and a fluorescent plate or screen rendered the bones clearly visible through the flesh. In a few days he produced a photograph of his wife's hand, with rings and bracelet. By January of the following year he had circulated reports of his discovery of "a new kind of ray" throughout Europe and the United States.

X-rays were an important innovation for the whole future of medicine, science, and society. They were the first "miracle machine" in clinical medicine. As such their discovery heralded a decisive break with the understanding of how medicine was to proceed with combating disease. X-rays shifted the nineteenth-century emphasis on social improvement and hygiene to "the appliance of science."

Initial skepticism about the "new rays" was short-lived. The editors of *Scientific American* described the rapid enthusiasm that spread throughout the world. Notably, they immediately speculated on the even greater possibilities opened up by the invention, in a fashion reminiscent of the terms in which the telegraph was discussed. "It seemed as if the limits of human discovery were being reached," they suggested, "but the wonder of the new photography only emphasizes the possibility of other victories to be won in the world of science." Among the medical and scientific communities, feverish experimentation commenced. Some speculated that they may be able to reveal all of the body's, even the brain's, functions, cure blindness and diseases such as cancer, and provide important clues to longevity. Many of the early experiments betrayed the "extreme hopes for health and longevity that were vested in them" (Knight 1986: 14). They were deployed against the increasing problem of cancer, sometimes "with no apparent rationale other than that the technique was new and untried" (ibid.: 24). This is not to say their reaction was entirely unambiguous. *Scientific American* described a breakthrough so revolutionary that it "almost dangerously increases our power of belief" (cited in ibid.: 13). This Frankensteinian sensibility is far more recognizable to our age, when breakthroughs in biotechnology, in particular, are greeted with as much trepidation as excitement.

Today, it is often single and unverified studies suggesting possible health risks that capture the imagination. Yet at the turn of the century there was "x-ray mania" within society, as the press and the public speculated on the possibilities that might flow from even the most mundane experiment. "Hidden solids revealed," declared the *New York Times*. "Startling results" were declared at Yale where x-rays of uncracked walnuts showed a "splendid view of the kernels" (cited in ibid.: 14). Knight details many other examples of the impact on public consciousness as gauged by x-rays' appearance in popular magazines and cartoons, for example

FIGURE 15. "The March of Science: Interesting result attained, with aid of Röntgen rays, by a first-floor lodger when photographing his sitting-room door." *Source:* Punch, 7 March 1896, p. 117.

(see Fig. 15). Popular enthusiasm was a cause of some bafflement among the intelligentsia, given the typically ungenerous view of "the masses" at the time. One author commented in 1897 that "the unbounded enthusiasm of the unscientific multitude was unlooked for, and [required] special explanation" (cited in ibid.: 26). He suggested that the "multitude" might be captivated by the sensational pictures and flashing lights. Whatever the truth, an undoubted popular fascination with the potential of x-rays endured, as in the science fiction of "ray guns" and "x-ray vision."

An important feature of x-rays was the simplicity of the apparatus. This made it available to the amateur as well as the professional, a fact that added to the sense that "X-rays would be a part of everyday life" (ibid.: 16). All that was required was a power source and an evacuated glass tube with an anode and a cathode. Among the scientifically informed and technically able, "almost everyone wanted to experiment with X-rays" (ibid.: 16). Fabulous claims followed, and not a few entrepreneurial gimmicks such as skeletal portraits and lead underwear for women, advertised to keep out peeping toms! They were also taken up as a more serious educational tool, in initiatives that reflected the reforming priorities of the time. One scheme proposed to combat alcoholism by showing the drunkard a shocking picture of their insides ravaged by the "demon" drink. Popular enthusiasm to an extent reflected a more hopeful sense of the possibilities of science in comparison to today. Yet sentiment also reflected the decidedly nonscientific outlook of the day. There was speculation that x-rays would provide access to thoughts and feelings, coinciding as it did with widespread interest in psychic and supernatural phenomena (ibid.: 18).

Even the most striking quality of x-rays – that in sufficient strength and duration, they destroyed almost everything in their path – was received positively. The fact that exposure caused the hair to fall out was viewed as a potential benefit, as in the cosmetic removal of unwanted hair, for example. But the "new rays" brought with them new dangers: x-rays are very harmful to humans with prolonged exposure. X-rays were initially used to confirm pregnancies until the dangers became established by 1903–4. They caused enormous damage to radiographers before the danger was realized and safety measures introduced. A reaction against all forms of radioactivity followed the discovery of the damage that could be caused; "radioactivity assumed an aura that continues to the present, a confusion of promise and fear" (Cole 1993: 8). These are still rigorously enforced, as in the case of a dentist struck off the practitioners' register in September 2001 in Scotland for unnecessarily carrying out unrecorded x-rays on children. In the light of discovering the extent of harm that could be caused by radiation, it is perhaps hardly surprising that society now appears as sensitive to the smallest doses as it was once oblivious to the largest. It was the experience of nuclear weapons in the 1940s rather than a realization of the impact of x-rays that was far more decisive in stigmatizing a generic danger from radiation, however.

Caufield's "chronicles of the radiation age" explains how the discoveries of radium and then nuclear fission were similarly "greeted with wild enthusiasm." With the discovery that many mineral springs had high concentrations of radium and radon, many attributed supposed curative powers to their newly discovered radioactivity (Caufield 1989: 195). Whilst such claims have been discredited, they are a reminder of important qualities of radiation. Ionizing radiation exists in both natural and unnatural forms; it is all around us. In other words: "In just the time it takes you to read this sentence, several hundred cosmic rays will have shot through your body." Ionizing radiation is also now "the best understood and most tightly controlled toxic substance known to man" (ibid.: 193).

Another interesting and more directly relevant comparison to cell phone EMF is radar. Radar, alongside the electromagnetic energy used in microwave ovens and in telecommunications, is one of the three main everyday uses for the microwave part of the electromagnetic spectrum. An acronym for "radio detection and ranging," radar sends out a beam of microwaves from a rotating aerial. Any objects that cross its path reflect the microwaves back to the aerial, which acts as a receiver. The signals are displayed on a monitor, so the position of the object can be seen. The time taken for the beam to be sent back can be measured, and thus the distance from the transmitter can be found. In this way radar can be used to locate and guide ships and aircraft, among many other uses. The fascinating story of its development at the beginning of the Second World War is not informed by the possibility of negative health impacts, however. There is nothing in its authoritative history, *The Invention That Changed the World* (Buderi 1996), that even broaches the subject of human harm, and there was no widespread social concern about harm from radar (Steneck 1984).

A number of reasons can be suggested for the absence of any comparable reaction to that which developed later around relay towers, power lines, and cell phone towers. First, it was largely only military personnel who came into contact with radar facilities. Among these specialized service personnel there was a degree of consciousness about possible dangers, according to some accounts. Brodeur (1977) suggests that, from the late 1930s, a culture of black humor and apprehension grew up among radio engineers in regular contact with the new technology, and that there were concerns also among sailors who worked with radar. From the beginning of the war, rumors of radar's alleged sterilizing effects spread, and even led to a small-scale navy investigation in 1942 (ibid.: 24). This apparently light-hearted culture of low-level radiation awareness was largely confined to these specialist personnel, however. A second factor in the lack of public response to early microwave technologies was that it was not then common practice to attribute negative health outcomes to exposure from public or military facilities. Social attitudes toward business, government, and technology were much more trusting prior to the late 1960s. Most important, radar was seen as a technology that not only was of general benefit but specifically helped to win the Second World War. In 1943, newspaper articles began to publicize the new microwave technology of radar with headlines such as, "Radar – Our Miracle Ally." Steneck elaborates on the very different perception of microwaves in the 1940s:

When the newly invented ultra-high-frequency radiowaves (later called microwaves) were first brought to the attention of the public in 1942 and 1943 they
could not have been more welcomed. At the time the United States and its allies
were engaged in a bitter war whose outcome seemed heavily dependent on
the abilities of the opposing powers to put science and technology to work.
Inventions that were new, scientific, and technological and that worked were
looked at as the preservers, not the annihilators of peace. (Steneck 1984: 23)

We can speculate that even if allegations had been seriously advanced
about the harm that radar might cause, they would have been overwhelmed by the certainty that it had very directly saved countless Allied
lives, in an unusually clear-cut case of balancing real against unproven
risk.

In the 1950s the positive attitude toward microwaves as military technology also applied to the perception of emerging nonmilitary applications. Microwave technology was seen, long before the arrival of the microwave oven, as potentially allowing us to "perform a multitude of tasks
that will relieve men from drudgery and bring higher standards of living
and culture." This was a time when progress was regarded as "our most
important product," according to a 1950s General Electric advertising
slogan (ibid.: 24).

Any allegations about adverse health effects that were made remained
marginal. A microwave technician with the Sandia Corporation complained of blurred vision in 1951, and his cataracts were attributed to
microwave exposure by at least one medical authority (Brodeur 1977:
26). However, in the immediate post-war years, the cultural climate was
not yet conducive to the generalization of interest in such cases, however;
this required a considerable shift toward more distrustful, even cynical,
sensibilities within society.

This earlier period of optimism appears to have existed until around
the mid-1960s, prior to Vietnam and the Watergate scandal. An important
signal of a changed social and political mood came with the enormous
impact made by Rachel Carson's *Silent Spring* in 1962. This, the seminal
environmental text, began the discussion about negative environmental
impacts, and challenged the notion that low dosages of toxic chemicals
were of little concern. Environmental pollution became increasingly
established as a preoccupation and campaigning target, eventually to
be extended from toxic to invisible electromagnetic "pollution." What
Steneck terms the "public years" of the microwave debate then began in

the late 1960s, as "the federal government extended its environmentalist concerns to the radiation problem" (Steneck 1984: 18).

Paul Brodeur and the Popularization of Microwave Suspicions

"Microwave fears" first systematically developed in the United States from the late 1960s. By the early 1980s Steneck wrote of the United States that "over the past decade nearly every form of RF [radio-frequency] technology has been the target of public concern at one time or another" (ibid.: 15). Radio broadcast towers, microwave relay systems, video display terminals, radar systems, and power lines all became a focus for varying degrees of public concern and the subject of institutional reaction. As with the contemporary case of cell phones, however, few made any lasting impact. Perhaps most prominent among the many reasons is the sheer convenience and utility of devices such as televisions, microwave ovens, computers, and cell phones. It is principally only where the structures associated with them, such as towers, are apparently transportable to someone else's neighborhood that concerns have endured. Unsurprisingly in the age of "not in my backyard," it is unsightly and imposing power lines, radio towers, and now cell phone towers that have generated most focused reaction.

The possibility of more generalized microwave concerns emerged with the appearance of radiation-based technology in society, most notably with the advent of television and microwave ovens. The first time that the potential dangers of "everyday" radiation were brought into the public realm was in May 1967 when General Electric announced that 90,000 of its new color televisions leaked ionizing radiation. The problem was quickly rectified, but not before possible microwave dangers had become public. Steneck notes that "the terms *health hazard* and *peril* became common in all reports" (ibid.: 178). The creator of modern consumer safety politics, Ralph Nader, picked up on the issue. With his extraordinary flair for generating publicity, Nader campaigned for a dose limit from television sets (Caufield 1989: 211). With the input of campaigning consumer safety politics, the accusation became routine that both industry and government had not acted responsibly with regard to public health. This assumption, denoting greater alienation from and suspicion of industry and authority, informed what otherwise appeared to be growing "technophobia" at odds with a society increasingly at ease with technology.

In late 1960s America, the authorities made a concerted attempt to appease this new mood and bridge the growing "confidence gap." Consumer safety became a defining priority of government action. Specifically in relation to radiation, the congressional House Subcommittee on Public Health and Welfare announced inquiries in August 1967 "to provide for the protection of the public health from radiation emissions from electronic products" (cited in Steneck 1984: 122). The Senate followed suit, and the issue then was raised in the annual presidential consumer pledge. President Johnson promised "protection against hazardous radiation from television sets and other electronic equipment" (cited in ibid.: 126). The Radiation Control for Health and Safety Act was passed shortly afterward, in 1968, and $63 million was pledged for research to establish whether microwave radiation posed a health hazard. As in the contemporary cell phone case, the true extent of "public" concern remains uncertain, but the reaction of the state to early microwave scares was not.

While little more was raised about possible dangers from television sets, similar concerns became apparent around microwave ovens, which had been intensively marketed in the 1960s. By the end of the decade, media reports began to emerge about faulty ovens, and microwave oven producers' stocks temporarily plummeted in response to health fears. Most important, the authoritative Consumers Union declared the ovens "not recommended" after its tests in 1973. This was on the precautionary basis that they could not "unequivocally be called safe" (ibid.: 15). They were not approved until 1981, when it was acknowledged that there was minimal risk. In response to the concerns promoted by the Consumers Union, a cautious safety standard was imposed by the federal authorities. The alarm quickly passed, however, as sales of microwaves overtook gas ranges in 1975; in the following year the *New York Times* headlined: "Microwave sales sizzle as the scare fades" (cited in Brodeur 1977: 316). The anxieties promoted around microwave ovens made little lasting impact; they are now no more than a historical artifact subsumed by familiarity and utility.

A more influential and enduring concern has been the purported association between power lines and various health problems, particularly cancer. An early Soviet study in the 1960s suggested some effects among workers at electricity substations, but many subsequent studies failed to confirm these findings and the study's significance is principally retrospective (Sagan 1996: 3). Far more important, and the first study to bring the issue of EMF to widespread public attention, was the childhood cancer study by Wertheimer and Leeper (1979). Although its findings were refuted by many scientific authorities, their suggestion of an association

between illness and the magnetic fields generated by power lines was crucial in creating doubt (Foster 1999a). Three further epidemiological studies also suggested increased risks of cancer among children living near
power lines (Savitz 1988; London et al. 1991; Feychting and Ahlbom
1993). Significantly, these were epidemiological studies, a branch of scientific investigation whose risk findings are so uncertain at statistically
low levels as to cast doubt on the whole enterprise, according to critics
(Dalrymple 1998; Le Fanu 1999; Fitzpatrick 2001). The countless other
studies that failed to confirm any EMF cancer connection were not met
with the same public interest. Instead, some twenty years after they were
first promoted, health concerns about power lines are still periodically
raised. In 2000, for example, one of the British newspapers central to promoting cell phone fears publicized the claims of an academic that those
living near power lines "could be up to three times more at risk from air-
borne cancer-causing pollutants" (*Daily Mail*, 22 September 2000). The
research was set alongside claims by another authority that computer
EMF is also dangerous.

The social and political context within which EMF concerns began to
develop was more important than the evidence of isolated studies, however. Early EMF concerns were shaped by a reaction to Cold War secrecy
and the pervasive suspicion that the technology-based "military industrial
complex" conspired to conceal the long-term dangers of everyday technologies. Some anti–mobile phone campaigners rightly locate the origin
of their "movement" in the development of microwave technology in the
secretive military projects of postwar America. According to (now former)
U.K. campaigner Margaret Dean, "the whole microwave thing began
from American military technology," adding that little of these origins
had been revealed by campaigners for fear of causing too much alarm.[16]
Still today, suspicion of military technology is an influential component
of microwave and other suspicions in Italy, Northern Ireland, and most
recently in Cyprus, where riots broke out in the summer of 2001 against
the erection of British military telecommunications towers.

The influential New Yorker journalist Paul Brodeur, who can be said
to have almost single-handedly given coherence to American microwave
anxieties, ably marshaled radical antagonism toward the Cold War "military industrial complex." All accounts refer to the leading role played by
the work of Brodeur (MacGregor et al. 1994; Sagan 1996; Park 2000). His
articles on microwaves and power lines were later published as books and

---

[16] Interview with Margaret Dean, 23 September 2000.

proved highly influential in engendering widespread concern in American society about electromagnetic and high-power energy (Brodeur 1977, 1989, 1993). Having originated in the United States, these concerns about EMF are now embedded and routinized to a greater extent than in other countries. There is also a clear continuity as well as a striking thematic similarity between the microwave suspicions codified by Brodeur and the contemporary health fears about cell phone EMF.

Paul Brodeur's early articles set about exposing CIA operations. He shifted his attentions to the specific issue of exposure to environmental and occupational hazards in the late 1960s. Brodeur first established a reputation through raising concerns about exposure to asbestos, in many ways the seminal contemporary public health issue of our times. He then became interested in microwaves, not just those emitted from microwave ovens but those used in many other ways, such as in air traffic control. Park describes how, while the issues changed, the sensibilities with which Brodeur approached them did not: "he approached environmental issues with a Cold War mindset," his key question being, "who had something to gain? And what were they covering up?" (Park 2000: 145). Many environmental activists in the United States discovered the microwave issue through Brodeur's *Zapping of America*, which was based on his *New Yorker* articles. Suspicions found apparent confirmation in the fact that the majority of research into the biological effects of microwaves had been carried out with the support of the U.S. Department of Defense. This in itself was presented as evidence of a government attempt to control, even conceal, the issue. According to Park, when industry scientists also reported a lack of evidence of harm, there were claims that the electronics industry must be league with the military (ibid.: 146).

The military emerged as the most important focus for radical health suspicions in the early 1970s. *Washington Post* writer Jack Anderson claimed in 1971 that U.S. spy planes "were so loaded with electronic gear that the microwave radiation may be causing eye damage" (cited in Steneck 1984: 179). He wrote similar articles raising suspicions about military hardware over the following years, eventually spreading the circle of suspicion to the military research community. Anderson also drew attention to the mysterious, "James Bond" world of secret weapons. Most important, he broke the story that the CIA had begun investigating microwave beams directed by the Soviet authorities at the U.S. embassy in Moscow. This later notorious "Moscow signal" episode was important in consolidating the suspicions about microwaves already raised by the television scare and then compounded by the microwave oven alarm.

The American authorities had known and complained about the intensive Soviet electronic surveillance of its Moscow embassy for several years. It had prompted a secret investigation to try and establish what the Soviets were doing, by subjecting monkeys to a simulated "Moscow signal" in "Operation Pandora" in 1965. In the context of Cold War America, electromagnetism was viewed as a more sinister force than the benign power of radar that helped win the war. The very low level of the signal led the scientists involved in the investigation to become suspicious that long-term, indirect effects from radio-frequency radiation were possible and had been discovered by Soviet scientists. It was believed that the beam must be some sort of weapon to control the mind or attack the central nervous system. The American state then took precautionary measures, apparently confirming the possibility of human damage from what had previously been thought to be "harmless" signals. In an "extraordinary step" in February 1976, the U.S. State Department installed aluminum screens in the windows of the Moscow embassy (ibid.: 181).

The State Department's action became public knowledge through the press; in the process an issue of Cold War eavesdropping was transformed into potential public health damage from EMF. Suspicions were further raised by the conspicuous silence of prominent spokesmen. Secretary of State Henry Kissinger stated that it was too sensitive to be dealt with openly in response to the first wave of newspaper articles. Subsequent research studies into effects on embassy personnel then only strengthened suspicions among journalists that something sinister and dangerous was afoot, regardless of the scientific conclusions. The very fact of investigation appeared proof positive in conditions where findings could not be definitive one way or another. Concerns became more focused and humanized following the contraction of leukemia by the American ambassador at the Moscow embassy. Cancer, the most powerful personal fear of our age, became bound up with the discussion of microwaves and their effects.

Paul Brodeur published extensive articles in the *New Yorker* on the Moscow embassy incident, developing the conspiratorial themes first outlined by Jack Anderson. A year later the debate was immortalized with the publication of his provocative book, *The Zapping of America* (1977). With some justification, Brodeur boasted, "A year or so ago one would have had a hard time finding anyone who believed that microwave radiation might turn out to have potent biological effects similar to those associated with x-rays and other ionizing radiation. Today there is considerably more concern..." (Brodeur 1977: 317). The refusal to respond to media concern so characteristic of the Cold War American state meant there was no challenge to Brodeur's account, and the "conspiracy" of silence added further weight to his style of inferential problem creation. Steneck notes that the consequence was that by the time the story reached mainstream America, *Reader's Digest* could blandly state as fact Brodeur's unsubstantiated suggestion that Moscow embassy personnel show a higher than average incidence of cancer (Steneck 1984: 203). It was also Brodeur's *Zapping of America* that was the principally cited influence in Louis Slesin's conversion to the (anti) microwave cause (Slesin 1990; Blumberg 1991). Slesin went on to be the most important source of microwave concerns, including those relating to cell phones.

What is less recognized than the influence of the Cold War climate on early microwave fears is the way in which the state response was also influenced by the newly emerging agenda of environmentalism. Major research programs were initiated both into ionizing and, from the mid-1970s, nonionizing bio-effects. The research agendas appeared to be influenced by the mood of environmental catastrophism prevalent in the United States in the early 1970s. The Electromagnetic Radiation Management Advisory Council (ERMAC), the body charged with coordinating research into radio-frequency bio-effects in 1969, announced the need for more research in dramatic terms:

Unless adequate monitoring and control based on a fundamental understanding of biological effects are instituted in the near future, in the decades ahead, man may enter an era of energy pollution of the environment comparable to the chemical pollution of today. (cited in Steneck 1984: 147)

Their language was quite similar to the alarmist arguments of Paul Brodeur, who claimed that the nation may "one day be faced with a public health disaster of monumental and perhaps irreversible proportions" (Brodeur 1977: 287). The council also appears to have been among the first organizations to officially endorse the expression "electronic smog," later to become "electrosmog," the preferred term of contemporary European anti-radiation activists. In 1971, the ERMAC issued a report entitled, "Program for Control of Electromagnetic Pollution of the Environment." Also in 1971, Anderson used the expression "electronic smog" rather than "pollution" in his articles on the dangers of military gadgetry. Brodeur adopted it later in the 1970s, attributing it to unspecified environmentalists (Brodeur 1977: 13).

Brodeur was also instrumental in publicizing the most direct predecessor of the cell phone controversy: the debate over video display terminals

(VDTs). As Foster (1986) describes, the story began in 1980 when a Canadian newspaper, the *Toronto Globe and Mail*, carried a story on how four employees of the rival *Toronto Star* had given birth to children with birth defects. Perhaps unsurprisingly, as newspaper office workers, all had worked with VDTs during their pregnancies, and this factor was singled out as of significance in the Toronto cluster with which the controversy began. Other newspaper stories followed that effectively began to report their own story with openings such as: "Thousands of Canadians edged away from their television screens this week with a tinge of fear..." (*Toronto Star*, 26 July 1980). More important, unwarranted significance was attributed to the apparent connection between VDTs and birth defects: "Some participants quickly reified the observed connections among the events into 'effects,' a term that embodies the assumptions of causality" (Foster 1986: 164). While the local department of health flatly denied the possibility of harm, other clusters of cases in various workplaces were reported in Canada and the United States.

As in all microwave controversies, the specific social context was important to establishing some dynamic behind the VDT alarm. In this case it was the allegation that conditions of work and even the employer were responsible for individual tragedies. In the scenario reported by Irwin in Chapter 1, employees had felt a common interest in denying the externally imposed prescription of possible harm. What evidently propelled the VDT debate was a very different impulse, as the alleged danger to pregnant staff became a focus for friction between management and employees. Pregnant employees at another Toronto paper boycotted VDTs until their safety was established. Such demands were given support from trade union officials. One hospital union representative asserted: "Enough is enough. We want those VDTs put out of service until they have been completely gone over" (cited in ibid.: 163). In response, the Federal Labor Minister of Canada supported the recommendation of a task force, which had been set up to examine the claims that pregnant workers should have the right to transfer without loss of seniority to jobs not requiring the use of VDTs. Another state body, a public service arbitration board in Ontario, then acknowledged the right of pregnant government employees to refuse VDT-based work because of the belief that it might cause harm. Later, many American states introduced legislation allowing the transfer of pregnant workers and demands for the shielding or monitoring of microwave radiation.

The principal disseminators of microwave anxieties picked up the issue. Louis Slesin was the joint author of a special pamphlet on the topic promoted through *Microwave News* (Slessin and Zybko 1983). Brodeur gave prominence to the issue in his 1989 work, *Currents of Death: Power Lines, Computer Terminals, and the Attempt to Cover Up the Threat to Your Health*. Foster, on the other hand, who explains the lack of any scientific or statistical basis for concern, makes the important point that where many public officials flatly denied the possibility of harm, a better approach would have been to attempt a discussion of the apparent relationships and the issue of causality. As with all such risk issues, it is simply wrong to assert absolute safety and, arguably, also wrong to underestimate the public's capacity to understand factual explanations.

Power Lines and Community Campaigning

Community-based campaigning against microwave installations also began around the same time as the VDT issue. At the beginning of the 1970s the earlier acceptance of radar was called into question, and its safety became a public issue when the U.S. Navy proposed to increase the power levels of its coastal defense units by installing a new system, known as PAVE PAWS. A small campaign group emerged in California, called Citizens Concerned About PAVE PAWS, which brought a National Environmental Policy Act suit to block construction (Steneck 1984: 15). A similar group developed in Cape Cod. Citizens' groups also campaigned vociferously against an attempt by the National Weather Service to install a weather radar system at Brookhaven National Laboratory on Long Island. The radar was canceled after a judge ruled in favor of residents' suspicions about microwaves (Park 2000: 148–9). Concern about the retrospective impact of radar also developed around the case of Joe Towne, a retired air force radar man who had begun to lose his sight.[17] Towne began a campaign, which led to the first meeting of the Radar Victims Network in 1976. The initiative declared its concern not just about radar users but for all those "who have suffered damage to health from their exposure to electromagnetic radiation" (Steneck 1984: 16). The campaign prompted newspaper stories about radar hazards, and this in turn prompted a government investigation.

Attempts to introduce new microwave installations met with growing local community protest in the 1970s. An important example was the

---

[17] Effects on eyesight were the key health issue in the early days of EMF stories. The key early campaigning scientist claiming that EMF could do harm, Milton Zaret, based his claims on their alleged damage to cataracts.

reaction to the attempt by the cable TV network Home Box Office (HBO) to construct an "uplink" facility (a large satellite dish to beam pictures to a space satellite) in Rockaway township, just outside New York. Planned from the mid-1970s, the subject of HBO's meetings with local officials extended beyond simple planning procedures because microwaves were involved and because the proposed site was near a local school. Furthermore, Rockaway residents had been alarmed only a few years previously by a scare about industrial waste and the potential pollution of drinking water. In this context a local campaign was quickly formed in 1983, Concerned Citizens of Rockaway Township, and its pressure led local authorities to require HBO to prove that the facility could not be harmful (ibid.: 4). The Rockaway case anticipates many features of later anti-mast campaigning: local residents' campaigns, the focus on protecting children, and an insistence on the elimination of uncertainty and on corporate guarantees of zero risk. Striking also was the dismissal of scientific findings: "all the evidence doesn't amount to a piddle in the snow," as one campaigner put it (ibid.: 7). The residents' committee voted against the HBO proposal on the basis that evidence about potential harm was inconclusive. In the public hearings expert testimony was treated with suspicion, on the assumption that science was always "for hire." Experts for HBO protested that it was impossible to prove a negative and show that harm was impossible, but eventually gave in to community pressure and withdrew its application (ibid.: 13). The RCA Corporation's attempt to build a microwave facility on Bainbridge Island on the West Coast encountered similar resistance. The County Commissioners in the RCA case eventually agreed with campaigners' objections on health grounds in a ruling in 1982. The commissioners explicitly based their decision on public perception rather than on any proven hazard. The implication was drawn out by Steneck: "public fears themselves could be used to block any building project, regardless of whether the fears are justifiable..." (ibid.: 217). This precautionary approach, regarded as innovative in relation to the Stewart Inquiry's response to mobile phone fears in 2000, had actually begun almost two decades earlier in the United States.

Following publication of the Wertheimer and Leeper study in the late 1970s, controversy about electromagnetic radiation shifted to high-voltage electrical power lines, and in this case a possible cancer link was raised immediately. The power line controversy was begun by psychologist Nancy Wertheimer, who claimed a link between childhood leukemia and power transformers based on a cluster she identified in Denver. She eventually published a paper in 1979, with Ed Leeper, linking EMF to cancer. The Wertheimer and Leeper paper was extremely influential and created the basis for a popularization of power line cancer fears throughout the 1980s (Park 2000). From June 1989, Brodeur produced a series of articles in the *New Yorker* on power lines (later published under the title *Currents of Death)*, beginning with the personal story of Wertheimer's discovery. Brodeur's work made a big media impact, particularly in relation to the specter of childhood cancer. Park describes how "a new generation of environmental activists, led by mothers who feared for their children's lives, demanded government action" (ibid.: 153). In a defensive response, the Environmental Protection Agency (EPA) established "safe limits" of exposure. Parents then insisted that EMF levels near schools be measured; when these proved to be above Brodeur's "safe levels," there were demands for children to be transferred to a different school. Campaigners complained that Wertheimer's findings, as well as a 1990 EPA report on links between cancer and EMF and a cluster of illnesses discovered near power lines in Guilford, Connecticut, were not being taken seriously. This led to another Brodeur book, *The Great Power Line Cover Up* (1990).

An association between ill health and living near power lines or electrical substations became established and culturally illustrated by the film, *The Distinguished Gentleman,* in which the actor Eddie Murphy becomes a dedicated environmentalist after meeting a child struck down with cancer from power lines. These microwave anxieties became consolidated as the scientific community pursued the microwave agenda. Park describes how "[a]n entire industry had grown up around the power-line controversy," as "[a]rmies of epidemiologists conducted ever larger studies" (Park 2000: 158).

The Bioelectromagnetic Society was created following the power line controversy, institutionalizing scientific discussion of nonthermal radiofrequency effects. More popularly, *Microwave News* became an authoritative publicizer of microwave doubts, under the entrepreneurial leadership of Louis Slesin. Inspired by Brodeur, Slesin continued the promotion of microwave concerns, albeit in a less sensationalist fashion through the pages of his periodic newsletter. To little effect, in 1995, the American Physical Society took the unusual step of undertaking their own review and publicly announced that the claims of *Microwave News* and Brodeur could not be substantiated. The law became the focus for claims of harm from microwaves, even though most of the numerous legal actions involving radio-frequency bio-effects were either dismissed or settled out of court from the mid-1970s onward (Steneck 1984). These failures did not put a stop to claims maker–driven legal actions, however. For example, in

1990, the mother of a child with a rare kidney cancer met Brodeur while he was promoting *Currents of Death* and filed a suit alleging EMF to be the cause of complaint the following year (Park 2000).

Mobile Phones, Cancer, and Lawsuits

It became evident from the early 1990s that a new focus for EMF concern was emerging. Clearly reflected in the research foci of those working in bioelectromagnetics, concern with the effects of EMF shifted toward low-level outputs from mobile phones. Although mobile phone health fears were subsequently to become politicized in Australia and Europe, concern first developed in the United States with allegations of a causal link to cancer. American *Consumer Reports* eventually covered health issues in its recommendations on mobile phones because the "scary stories in 1993" raised the cancer question (*Microwave News*, November/December 1997). *The* "scary story" of 1993 was generated by long-time mobile phone user David Reynard.

The Reynard lawsuit was an important moment that began the global health fears about mobile phones. The case was instigated after Reynard's wife, Susan, was diagnosed with a malignant left parietal tumor in May 1990. She had used an NEC hand cellular phone for two years prior to the discovery of the cancer. In a complaint filed on 8 April 1992 in a Florida circuit court, the dying Susan Reynard charged: "The tumor was the result of radiation emitted by a cellular telephone [or] the course of the tumor was accelerated and aggravated by the emissions from the telephone..." (*Microwave News*, May/June 1992).

This was the first litigation in relation to a cellular phone, although there had been EMF-related cases over broadcast towers and microwaves from military and police radar. Testimony for Reynard was provided by an Australian, Dr. John Holt of the Microwave Therapy Center in Perth, together with neurologist David Perlmutter, who ran an alternative and complementary medicine clinic in Florida. Initially covered only by local news, the story eventually broke nationally in January 1993 following coverage by the Fort Lauderdale, Florida, *Sun-Sentinel* on 3 January. Every major newspaper ran at least one item over the fortnight following the breaking of the Reynard story. The *Wall Street Journal* featured six stories, *U.S. Today* even more. Republican Senator Edward Markey made the issue his own, with demands for further investigation. An industry poll conducted shortly after the Reynards appeared on *Larry King Live* found that half of all Americans knew about the Reynard lawsuit (*Microwave*

News, January/Feburary 1993), and shares in mobile phone companies plummeted.

In the absence of any compelling proof of a cancer link with EMF, the Reynard case was eventually unsuccessful, being dismissed in 1995 for lack of valid scientific evidence. The Reynard case was unfortunately timed (from the Reynards' perspective), as it came shortly after the establishment of the so-called Daubert standard for the admissability of scientific evidence, which followed the landmark 1993 Supreme Court ruling *Daubert v. Merrell Dow Pharmaceuticals*. Since that time courts have been under increasing pressure to screen cases for merit and keep "junk science" from going before a jury. During pretrial maneuver in Reynard's case, it became clear that there was little substantial basis to his claims, as his expert witness David Perlmutter admitted that no studies had shown any adverse biological effects from cell phones.

Numerous other lawsuits have followed, however. In December 1993 a veteran Motorola research engineer, Robert Kane, filed suit alleging that his brain tumor was caused by radio-frequency radiation. His claims were first reported by the influential CBS program *Eye to Eye*, which portrayed the story as "an industry insider" warning of the dangers (*Microwave News*, January/February 1994). A fifth lawsuit was filed in August 1994 in Tampa, Florida, against Nokia by the widow of a brain tumor victim, through the same lawyers that had taken up the Reynard case. The number of suits continued to grow. In August 2000, a Maryland doctor filed suit with a claim for $800 million against Motorola and Verizon, alleging that a Motorola phone caused his brain tumor. Although the case is unlikely to succeed, based on precedent, it has generated international newspaper reports. The industry has yet to lose a lawsuit, but it has been concerned about adverse publicity. One recent response has been to agree to make information about levels of radiation from cell phones available in 2001.

The principal longer term response of the American mobile industry to the health fears initiated by the Reynard case has been to commit significant funds to research into health effects, and this has been copied by the industry internationally. Motorola developed its own extensive research program, which had the highest funding in the world in 1997 at a time when neither the European Commission's proposed $20 million scheme nor the U.S. industry association's (CTIA) Wireless Technology Research had begun work. The latter, industry-wide effort was unveiled in 1992 and confirmed in July 1993, and was intended to be overseen by the most authoritative scientists and government representatives. Coordinated by the now controversial figure of Dr. George Carlo, however, the program conspicuously failed to generate authoritative research, despite its large budget. This has led to recriminations within the scientific community and mobile phone industry, and Carlo was eventually removed from his position. He now argues that negative health effects were concealed by the industry, and is establishing his reputation as a courageous whistle-blower with the publication of a sensational account of his experiences (Carlo and Schram 2001).

Despite the best efforts of Carlo, however, in the United States the cell phone issue has been contained. Internationally, local campaigning against cell towers has failed to make the impact that it has in countries such as the United Kingdom and Italy. However, the latest legal action and threatened class actions on the cell phone issue appears to have the industry worried and certainly represents an escalation in the battle over claims of health risks from cell phones. A suit against Motorola was filed by Christopher Newman, a Baltimore neurologist, and is being organized by Baltimore "superlawyer" Peter Angelos, who has enjoyed significant success in pursuing asbestos and tobacco litigation. The plaintiff lawyers are attempting to pursue their claims through state courts where the science-based Daubert standard might not be rigorously applied. Perhaps more significant, a new wave of class-action lawsuits filed in late 2001 does not claim, unlike the Newman or earlier Reynard case, that anyone actually developed cancer from a cell phone. Instead, the lawsuits allege a pattern of "fraudulent and conspiratorial conduct" and "deceitful and misleading statements." The essence of the upcoming legal challenges is essentially precautionary, and therefore potentially more effective. They will allege that the mobile industry failed to test its products properly before putting them on the market and failed to warn customers about potential health risks. Although in theory these new challenges should be subject to strict science-based standards, the current allegations might prove successful in shifting the ground away from any need to prove direct harm.

Declining Impact, Increased Reaction

The very different reactions to x-rays, radar, and other forms of radiation show a discernible trend toward emphasizing negative effects and consequences. Looking back at the past in the light of contemporary sensibilities, it is easy to be amused and horrified in equal measure. It now appears difficult to imagine that society did not anticipate the harm that x-rays might cause, for example, and this is the message of recent European writing on such "late lessons from early warnings" (Harremoës et al. 2002). In retrospect, classical modernity appears to have uncritically embraced change and innovation in a way that now seems naive, even irresponsible. Partly in response, we have shifted from an expectation of positive possibilities and improvement to an expectation of the worst possible outcomes. However, the latter is not simply a balanced response to experience but is also one-sided. A simple counterposition between an ignorant past and enlightened present regarding attitudes toward science and technology flatters contemporary assumptions with an "awareness" that is evidently lacking in many instances. There is little more evidential basis to imagining "organic" food must be "healthy," and genetically modified food harmful, for example, than there was in Thurber's grandmother imagining electricity was leaking all over the house. Insisting on the possibility of harm, regardless of scale or context, is not an informed position, particularly given that there is a possibility of harm from countless physical phenomena that surround us. It could even be argued that suspicion of natural physical forces is more rational than the cynical mistrust of the man-made that characterizes contemporary feelings.

Considered historically, it is peculiar that the heightened reaction to risk appears inversely proportional to the extent of proven harm. A number of authors have noted this contrast of greater reaction to diminished effect (Bauer 1995a; Kepplinger 1995; Nelkin 1995). In her analysis of American resistance to technologies, Dorothy Nelkin describes how "one is immediately struck with a paradox. Some technologies provoke organized opposition; others, no less invasive, no more benign, are welcomed, or at least, they are accepted with comparatively little debate" (Nelkin 1995: 379).

Kepplinger usefully situates the elevation of potential problems with technology in the context of a wider tendency toward criticism in the post-1960s world. Discussing media coverage of nuclear power and biotechnology, he notes a massive shift in both Germany and Sweden toward negative events, in general, and criticism of persons, organizations, and conditions, in particular. He notes how the percentage of coverage criticizing technology rose between 1965 and 1986 from 15 to 20 percent to 30 to 50 percent (Kepplinger 1995: 362). Undoubtedly part of a generally more critical and enlivened political culture, it also carries with it a more specific attack on technology. His explanation is to suggest that there are now two cultures, where the scientific and technological elite confronts a "reflective elite" of literary and social scientific provenance. The mentality of the reflective elite changes the culture of journalism to a focus on negative events. Such an impression is confirmed by the

American and British examples, where the media betray an almost obsessive preoccupation with possible negative outcomes. In the cell phone case, the promotion by the British media of anything that pointed toward the possibility of harm from EMF has already been documented.

A common explanation for this development is the idea of "technophobia." This might appear as a particularly pertinent concept for understanding the reaction to the popular technology of recent times, the cell phone. There is perhaps some truth to popular prejudice that some *cultures* such as the Japanese are fascinated with technology, and others like the British are more reticent. Yet culturally bound technophobia explains little, given the rates of cell phone usage among Britons, for example. We live in a common and global age of consumption of new electrical and electronic goods.

Bauer (1995b) illustrates how what is presented as a generalized public "phobia" is in fact socially or, rather, intellectually constructed. Taking the specific example of "cyberphobia," he describes how it was largely created by the popular press and then academics. The first wave of discussion on the subject, between 1984 and 1986, was essentially an anticipation in popular writing of problems that users would experience with mastering computers. The second peak in 1991 was driven by academic commentary, itself influenced by popular discussion. Cyberphobia was promoted by the Department of Psychology at California State University, San Dominguez, which warned that 25 percent of the U.S. public would be "at risk" by the end of the 1980s. Interestingly, European researchers were more interested in the attitudinal opposite: computer addiction and hacking. Cyberphobia appeared not only to have little substantial basis but betrayed different intellectual preoccupations; notably, American bias toward individual reactions and a growing European obsession with crime and fraud. But whatever elite preoccupations prevailed, their basis is called into question by the phenomenal success of the computer in both the workplace and the home since the 1980s. Evidently, an academic and media elite wrongly anticipated, or, rather, imposed an apprehension on, the public that had little foundation.

The notion of technophobia is hardly consistent with what we know about the world around us. Whatever the extent of hostility toward "meddling with nature," information technology has been readily, if not always enthusiastically, embraced. During the course of interviewing for this book, cell phone health risk campaigners invariably began their explanations with the proviso: "I'm not opposed to technology itself, or even mobile phones...." This returns us to the paradox that the utilization of technology remains consistent with a pervasive suspicion of its possible implications. Other recent research uses the more specific notion of "technological stigma" rather than simple technophobia as an explanatory concept. It points to the way that high expectations of new technologies are tainted by media-driven association with risk or danger, leading to a situation where "prestige is replaced by fear and disappointment . . . the benign suddenly turns menacing" (Flynn, Slovic, and Kunreuther 2001: 4). Yet as many questions are raised by this explanation as are answered; not least, Why is this occurring now? As has been indicated, such "technological stigma" hardly seems to have existed at the turn of the century; rather, it appears specific to the post-1960s. A more general and useful contribution is to highlight how a qualified acceptance of the technology that science can deliver coexists with an increasing rejection of social progress (Gillott and Kumar 1995). In circumstances where human progress and achievement are looked on with suspicion, a more fragile and imperfect humanity appears permanently vulnerable to its own creations.

It is quite clear that perceptions of danger, in general, are contextual. A clear example is that of radar. Given the overriding priorities of war, radar was looked on as a something of a miracle. Under these circumstances relatively minor problems are overwhelmed by more pressing priorities. It is unlikely that a device such as radar that played a crucial role in securing the success of society's singular objectives would come under scrutiny; even if it did, its record in demonstrably saving lives clearly outweighs any lesser and more intangible hazards it might pose. Conditions such as war impose a severe, arguably more realistic balance between real and only possible risks. It is difficult to imagine that hypothetical fears about everyday technologies could have acquired momentum in the 1940s.

By equal measure, it is perhaps not surprising that in a society that is not overwhelmed by social and political conflict, we are susceptible to concern about possible problems that are evidently trivial by historical standards. In the abstract, at least, contemporary circumstances in and of themselves suggest a preoccupation with the most minor risks, in a way that extreme social conditions determine a prioritizing of only the most severe. Not only is society no longer gripped by military conflict or its threat, but there is a relative absence of any major social contestation. In short, in an affluent society at the "end of history" is it not inevitable that we have become increasingly susceptible to an anxiety such as that with microwaves? There is undoubtedly some truth to this proposition. As we now live longer and are aware of ways in which we can ensure that we do so, an obsession with health follows relatively naturally. With a heightened sense of the importance of health, we are liable at least to consider any claim that harm might be posed, from even the most apparently innocuous source.

At the same time, fears such as that from microwaves cannot be "read" from social and political circumstances so easily, as society earlier had little choice but to consider only the most pressing priorities and problems. We do now have a choice, not least because we must choose from thousands of competing claims for our attention and concern. These choices do not take place simply at the individual level but are determined by the wider social construction of issues. Alongside authoritative individuals pressing these claims, the role of the media, and our own experience, the most important influence in whether any given society does take an issue such as microwaves seriously is the response of state authority itself. These reactions are the subject of Chapters 5 and 6, where it is suggested that it is not simply given that the "post-political" world should be one dominated by "phantom" risk or technological stigma. Before that, however, it is necessary to examine in closer detail the specific claims that radiation at the "harmless" end of the electromagnetic spectrum might actually cause harm.

4

Radiating Uncertainty

Misconceptions and Misunderstandings

The very word "radiation" induces fear and betrays ignorance. Among other misconceptions about radiation are that the term denotes only its dangerous, ionizing form. Second, it is believed that radiation from man-made sources, be they atomic bombs or cell phones, must necessarily be worse than from naturally occurring forms. A third misconception is that if "a lot" of radiation is very harmful to human well-being, then a little must also have some negative effect. These misconceptions seem to be largely the result of the ways in which radiation has entered public consciousness, particularly with the imagery of nuclear destruction. But misconceptions are also encouraged by some of the more "scientific" claims about the risks of radiation, which appeal to the popular imagination precisely because of the association of radiation only with extreme effects and the lack of wider knowledge about it.

Radiation can be dangerous in particular forms and sufficient quantities, and we are now only too aware of the perils of its ionizing variety. Radiation occurs across a wide spectrum from the directly damaging (ionizing) to the benign (nonionizing; see Fig. 16). The major man-made source of radiation we encounter is from medical x-rays. These have a character quite different from radiation generated by sources such as cell phones; they are not simply "less of the same", and therefore they are not likely to create a similar effect on a smaller scale. Insofar as harm from cell phone EMF is considered possible, it can be only from some as yet unknown process of interaction with the body.

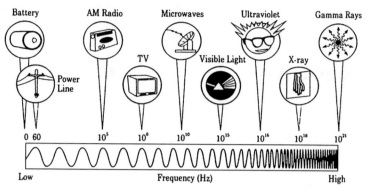

FIGURE 16. Simple representation of the electromagnetic spectrum. Courtesy of Gordon and Breach: Leonard Sagan, "Electric and Magnetic Fields."

We forget or perhaps are not aware that radiation is both commonplace and naturally occurring. Microwaves pervade the entire universe; they are an afterglow of its hot, dense initial state. Since the dawn of life, about 55 percent of radiation to which Earth's inhabitants are exposed comes from the naturally occurring gas radon, about 8 percent from cosmic rays, 11 percent from naturally occurring radioactive isotopes in our food, and so on (Silver 1998: 487). Electric fields are produced by the local build-up of electric charges in the atmosphere associated with thunderstorms. The earth's magnetic field causes a compass needle to orient in a north-south direction and is used by birds and fish for navigation. Some forms of naturally occurring radiation are damaging to health, as illustrated by the illnesses that afflicted underground miners in the nineteenth century because of exposure to radon gas (Cole 1993).

Where radiation causes biological effects, dosage is all important. As one survey of low-level EMF emissions points out, because placing one's fingers on a hot stove will obviously burn them, this does not in any sense suggest that they might burn "a little" if held at a distance of half a meter from the stove (Brauner 1996: 13). Because intense exposure to some forms of radiation impairs health, it does not follow that a fraction of this radiation will impair health proportionately: "In fact... energy processes always proceed in quanta, that is, in graduated stages" (ibid.: 14). Thus sunlight continually heats an exposed skin cell, but the cell becomes damaged only when its internal temperature rises above 47 degrees Celsius. This is similar to the way that organisms respond to many types of exposure. While taking an aspirin each day can produce long-term medical benefits for some conditions, a hundred aspirin at once are obviously extremely harmful. In other words, different doses often result in qualitatively distinct consequences, rather than along a scale of the same phenomenon.

The issue of cell phone EMF effects is shaped not only by misconceptions of radiation, but also by the more general problem of the statistical interpretation of relative risk issues. There are many ways of presenting the same information. Angell illustrates the problem, discussing the relative risk factor of 1.3 that connects postmenopausal estrogen with breast cancer:

For every 10 women who do not take estrogen and get breast cancer, 13 estrogen users will. . . . Instead of saying a relative risk of 1.3, we could say that postmenopausal estrogen is associated with a 30 per cent increase in the risk of breast cancer. Alternatively, since we already know that 3 or 4 of every 100 postmenopausal women will get breast cancer in the next 10 years, we could say that this study shows that estrogen increases the risk to 5 in 100. Or to put it another way, this study shows that your chances of remaining free of breast cancer for 10 years would decrease from over 96 per cent to about 95 per cent. (Angell 1997: 165)

Clearly, very different conclusions about the scale of the purported problem and urgency of a solution are suggested by different presentations of information. A common way that researchers and commentators dramatize the scale of a problem is to present percentage increases in the incidence of a disease without reference to absolute numbers. A rare disease obviously requires only a few new cases in order to create an apparently alarming percentage rise in its incidence: a condition with only two victims rises 50 percent with the next case, for example. In an age where it has become routine to gain attention for relatively minor problems through a dramatic presentation of data, such statistical sleight of hand is not unusual and is highlighted by a number of authors (LeFanu 1999; Best 2001a; Fitzpatrick 2001; Brignell 2002).

A relative risk factor merely indicates how high the risk is above the general background level. As percentage increases acquire greater meaning when we consider the absolute scale they represent, it is perhaps only when set in the context of a familiar risk that more meaningful perspective can be established. No matter how significant it might sound, a risk factor of 1.2 means only a slight elevation, that "for every 10 women without implants who develop connective tissue disease, 12 women with implants in an equal population develop it." By comparison, Angell points out that the relative risk of lung cancer is about 15, that is, for every

10 nonsmokers who develop the disease, 150 smokers do. The relationship between such statistics and the consequences for our actions are even more unclear, as even well established risk factors may have little importance for individuals. Angell contrasts the risk of death from cardiovascular disease for men with high as opposed to lower cholesterol levels. The difference of 3 percent "may not be enough to induce an otherwise healthy man to try and lower his cholesterol levels" (Angell 1997: 172–3).

Underlying these issues is perhaps the most central problem of all, particularly in relation to epidemiology. This is the challenge of establishing *causality* rather than mere *association*. Many phenomena in both the natural and social worlds are associated, but this by no means suggests that one causes the other. We can find any number of associations between underachieving children and their parents in certain societies, for example: the parents might be single mothers, nonwhite, ill-educated themselves, or simply poor. Extreme caution is clearly required before identifying any of these as causes. In relation to mapping incidents of leukemia with power lines, we similarly need to consider the fact that high concentrations of power lines are likely to be in poorer neighborhoods, the more likely correlation being between cancer and socio-economic status, rather than low-frequency fields. Only when associations are overwhelming, such as in cases like smoking and lung cancer, can we more confidently suggest causality, even if we do not yet fully understand the mechanisms or processes involved.

An important part of the reason for people accepting that there might be a health problem with cell phones is that they simply do not understand the scientific issues involved. The author is not a scientist, and this book is not the place where misconceptions about radio-frequency radiation can be definitively laid to rest. A review of the hundreds of studies into electromagnetic fields in general, or the many now being undertaken into the type emitted by cell phones, in particular, would take a book in itself. There are more exhaustive accounts of the scientific evidence to which readers can turn, not least the extensive web resource provided by the World Health Organization (WHO).[1] For an account interpreting the evidence as a cause for health alarm, Carlo and Schram (2001) is the most easily available, if regarded even by other proponents of EMF risk such as *Microwave News* as self-serving. The latter

[1] See http://www.who.int/peh-emf/index.htm.

is a useful, if pro-risk–biased, source for developments within the EMF field.[2]

But it is not only because of a lack of expertise or space that this book is not principally concerned with the actual science of EMF. The cell phone controversy, like earlier comparable moments over VDTs, is a social more than a strictly scientific story. Evidence has only a "walk on" part into a drama that is actually propelled by feelings and beliefs derived from experience of society, rather than newfound scientific knowledge about biological processes. Science has invariably been marshaled after the fact or, rather, assertion, of harm from cell phones. The Reynard case with which the controversy began arose from the coincidence of an individual's death with a history of cell phone use, not from new scientific investigation. As was suggested in the previous chapter, in a different social and political climate it is difficult to imagine heightened anxiety about what, if it is one at all, can be a threat of only very limited proportions. Uncertainty and a consequent need for precaution in the cell phone case draws its authority from a wider precautionary climate, rather than anything particular to the phenomenon of cell phone EMF. As is indicated below, the principal fragments of evidence suggesting concern about cell phone EMF are hardly compelling grounds for precautionary action.

At the same time, the scientific issues involved in the cell phone controversy cannot be ignored in this account. The media reports were based on scientific claims that unexpected effects had been found in experiments approximating cell phone exposure. Without the uncertainties suggested by these experiments, there would not have been any focused concern whatsoever. The limits of the scientific cause for alarm also play a role, in restricting the scope and impact of a controversy that never reached the heights of comparable "panics" such as over breast implants, the MMR triple jab, or genetically modified food. The lack of any substantial basis in these cases, also, however, suggests a more generally limited role for scientific evidence. It is appropriate therefore to review some of the issues around the science of radio-frequency radiation, if only in a highly abbreviated form. Perhaps the principal issue with this, and so many other comparable issues, is what is to be made of possible risk factors. In our precautionary culture, it has become the responsible position to see no risk as too small to take seriously and act on. "Taking action," in a scientific

[2] See www.microwavenews.com.

sense, is problematic, however, certainly if it is with a view to coming up with the definitive resolution demanded in some quarters. In the best of circumstances, science is singularly unsuited to "yes" and "no" answers; where the effects of phenomena are very difficult to isolate, it is especially inappropriate.

A Partisan Debate

As the story cannot be told without some consideration of the science, so the science itself is bound up with the dynamics of the (social) controversy. It is useful to recognize the extent to which the world of the science and scientists involved in this controversy are also subject to social influences and differences of values and belief. Certainly, it is difficult for the science to remain immune from the socially driven controversy, as one recent incident revealed. In the January 2001 edition of the prestigious journal *Epidemiology*, two German scientists at the University of Essen described the possible role of radio-frequency radiation from mobile phones in the development of uveal melanoma. Before publication they presented their results at several scientific meetings where the limitations of their case studies were clearly stated. Following publication they were greeted with what the scientists described as an "unprecedented media rush." The scientists subsequently delivered a paper on what they found to be a sobering experience. They encountered media intent on simplifying their research and attempting to draw unwarranted conclusions. They found that television channels did not broadcast the sections of their interviews where the limitations of the study were emphasized. And they suggested that the "media campaign" was triggered in the first place by a British company that produces EMF shields, "and therefore was most likely driven by commercial interests" (Stang and Jockel 2001). Another German scientist, Dr. Stefan Braune, withdrew an earlier report suggesting cell phone radiation can raise blood pressure, after it had been reported by the world's media (*Microwave News*, July/August 2001). He now believes other factors were to blame for the results, but, needless to say, this later finding did not attract media attention.

Such episodes might not appear worthy of particular interest or surprise. The media can hardly be expected to accurately report, even understand complex scientific issues. Yet, standing back, it is curious that the media should be so interested in what is essentially an esoteric subject, particularly with regard to the small subfields of EMF research in which studies typically take place. In addition, the problem is not simply a general one related to the reporting of scientific inquiry. It is also because of the inherent difficulties in researching and reporting the possible effects on humans of evidently miniscule phenomena that the problem arises so acutely. There is so much room for misinterpretation because, in the absence of a phenomenon with an observable and comprehensible effect (as with ionizing radiation), the world of nonthermal radiation effects is necessarily one of speculation, hypothesis, and disagreement.

At a workshop entitled "EMFs, Mobile Telephones and Health," held in Brussels in October 2001, for example, there were starkly contrasting views. "Radiation effects cannot be denied," said one scientist coordinating the European Commission's REFLEX project into EMF, using in vitro experiments. Meanwhile, a French and a Finnish scientist, both in charge of two of the commission's other EMF projects, insisted that no case has yet been made for significant effects from EMF (*Microwave News*, November/December 2001). While official British and French scientific reviews of the evidence for EMF health effects has concluded there are grounds for precaution, a recent Dutch expert group concluded decisively that there was no health hazard and no grounds for a precautionary approach (Health Council of the Netherlands 2002). The Dutch Health Council's report for Parliament insisted that the effects on biological systems found in a few studies do not equate to human health hazards, and there are no grounds for recommending restrictions even for children.

Inquiry into EMF effects is not simply an accumulating body of knowledge over which scholars disinterestedly debate in their proverbial "ivory towers." It is not necessarily to be regretted, but evidence from particular studies is interpreted and used instrumentally to substantiate predetermined positions of relative danger or relative safety and wider views on what the relationship should be between science, rationality, and society. Even within the scientific community there are very different interpretations of what is essentially the same evidence. To some extent this reflects the particular field within which individuals operate. Physics, for example, is long regarded as the "highest" of the natural sciences, and its practitioners often associated with the most strictly scientific, "ultra-rational" perspectives. The eminent American physicist Robert Park is a determined debunker of what he regards as now pervasive "voodoo science" and regards the search for possible harm from electromagnetism as a prime example (Park 2000). Other scientists, most obviously those working more directly within the field of biological effects from radiation, would vigorously contest Park's prognosis. Recalling Park's views on the issue to James Lin, a prominent scientist working in the field of biological effects from electromagnetism, the author was told: "Well, a physicist like Park would say that, wouldn't he?"[3] No doubt Park would say something similar of scientists whose field of work, and living, is at least partially dependent on continued uncertainty about radio-frequency fields.

There is more to scientific disagreements than different fields of study, or even general assessments about scientific and social priorities. This is a heated world where different scientists are identified with positions not entirely based on the result of scientific findings. Henry Lai, author of the study that generated the most publicized early health concerns connected to cell phones, has continued to assert the relevance of his original studies despite the crucial failure of others to reproduce and confirm his results. He appears convinced there is a significant risk, to some extent regardless of the mass of accumulated findings. Evidence is interpreted very selectively in many instances. For anti-EMF campaigners, the failure to reproduce results does not necessarily invalidate conclusions that EMF is harmful. If others fail to reproduce findings, it is sometimes seen to be further evidence of a scientific establishment closed to the possibility that there is a risk, in the conspiratorial style of thinking promoted by Paul Brodeur.

The different assessments of potential risk lead to conflicting advice about how to behave. Lai argues that mobiles should sometimes be switched off as a precaution by aircraft technicians performing safety-critical maintenance work, for instance. George Carlo has demonstratively used a cell phone only with a hands-free kit, illustrating very clearly his own, very personal position. Quoted in a U.K. newspaper, he declared it to be "very scary that so many children in Britain are using mobiles. We have no idea of the effect. I won't let my 7 year old child use a mobile phone" (*Sunday Mirror*, 16 January 2000). William Stewart has adopted the same position with regard to his grandchildren and aggressively criticized the irresponsibility of marketing mobiles to children.

This is a partisan debate where, to some extent, battle lines have been drawn. In the conference circuit of EMF risk one is quickly initiated into hushed rumors about who is on whose side, and therefore whether they are

---

[3] During conversation at a conference, "Mobile Phones: Is There a Health Risk?," London, 7–8 December 2000.

worth listening to or not. Scientists who have in any way been associated with the cell phone industry, or even simply come to conclusions to which the industry would not object, are regarded by some risk claims makers as irredeemably tainted. Even Michael Repacholi, the coordinator of the current WHO research program into EMF, and author of a famous study that suggested a biological effect from cell phone radiation, is not immune to such rumors. In evidence to the Stewart Inquiry, former leading U.K. activist Margaret Dean stated:

> We are concerned by the presence of a number of individuals on the Independent Group – particularly the participation of Dr. Michael Repacholi. As Head of the EMF WHO project it should not be necessary to call into question his indepen-dence. However, we have been made aware that Dr. Repacholi has, in the recent past, given evidence in support of the Telecommunications Industry.[4]

While it is unclear why scientific opinion must be viewed as for or against an industry, in the outlook of those convinced that there is a significant cell phone risk, there appears to be virtually nobody who stands neutrally "in the middle" whose findings can be assessed purely on their own merits.

Despite the contestation in this fringe area of science, however, at least publicly this is a usually polite debate where the substance of the issues or extent of disagreement rarely emerges. Perhaps regrettably, it is rare for the mainstream science "camp" to more vigorously contest the elevation of microwave concerns, which would enable the very different perspec-tives to emerge and be clarified. In an unusual step, the prestigious *New England Journal of Medicine* has argued that mobile phone health concerns are "something manufactured by activists and the media," as *Microwave News* complained (July/August 1997). The iconoclastic Robert Park is a rare exception in a scientific world apparently reluctant to compromise the impartiality of their reputations by presenting a more focused argu-ment. While "sticking to the science" might be a laudable objective, this is also one of the reasons that the different approaches rarely properly engage with each other. It is only when confronted with the many shield-ing devices marketed as blocks on EMF fields that some scientists have been more publicly skeptical. Following the launch of a new device, the Aulterra Neutraliser, in October 2001, David Land, an applied physicist at Glasgow University, declared it "absolute rubbish." He argued that screening radiation would require putting a sheet of aluminum around

---

[4] Letter accompanying submitted recommendations to William Stewart from Margaret Dean, dated 14 October 1999.

the phone, which would effectively also mean that the phone wouldn't work, as there would be no signal (*Mobilex Environment Monthly*, October 2001). As with precautionary measures more generally, providing "protection" from a source that has not been demonstrated to cause harm is a curious project in the first place.

The continued lack of consensus in the scientific debate is not because there have been no attempts at joint forums where debate can take place, or that those arguing for significant risk have been denied a platform for their ideas. The precautionary proponents of cell phone risk have been given prominent positions from which to argue their case. The international cell phone industry has held frequent "Is there a health risk?" conferences since the early 1990s in Europe, at which the voices of cell phone risk have been given space alongside more established scientific authorities. One of these events, held in Sweden in September 1999, was chaired on the first day by Alasdair Phillips, the first and hardest working proponent of electromagnetic health concerns in the United Kingdom.[5] The second day of the conference was presided over by Louis Slesin, editor of *Microwave News* and Phillips's American equivalent. The chief scientific voices of EMF alarm have been given platforms at this later event from which to present their case: Henry Lai from the University of Washington, Alan Preece from the University of Bristol, George Carlo, Stan Barnett from Australia, and others. For whatever reason individuals connected to the cell phone industry have decided to do so, even sometimes previously obscure and isolated individuals such as British safety device entrepreneur Roger Coghill have been invited to expound their views at corporate conferences and draw on the consequent publicity and authority. The most recent event at the time of writing was also co-chaired by Alasdair Phillips.[6] But whatever the expectations, as Phillips's co-chair, risk expert Professor Ray Kemp, commented, the impasse evident between the two sides was, if anything, more entrenched at this last event than ever before.[7] No evident middle ground has been created through this dialogue, indicating the extent to which this is a very divided field; rather, there is a vocal minority of risk proponents ranged against a mainstream bloc.

Obviously, reputations and careers are at stake, even very direct economic interests in the case of those promoting safety devices on the basis of

---

[5] "Mobile Telephones and Health: An Update on the Latest Research," Gothenburg, Sweden, 16–17 September.
[6] "Mobile Phones and Health – The Latest Developments," London, June 2001.
[7] Correspondence, 21 June 2001.

health fears. In Britain, Dr. Gerard Hyland from the University of Warwick has become well known exclusively because of his outspoken stand. It can be argued, in the style of Robert Park, that the more mainstream scientific authorities in the field also, in their own indirect way, have no interest in definitively resolving the issue, even if it were possible. Scientific priorities and funding inevitably depend on the degree of institutional concern about a particular field, and that is in turn dependent on whether uncertainty persists. That personal interests play their part is hardly surprising or regrettable in their own terms, however, even if they should be properly recognized. Self-interest and advancement is an inevitable and accepted part of most professional fields, no matter how elevated they might appear. People fight for their beliefs and their validity in the most obscure academic disciplines, and their own personal fortunes are unavoidably bound up with how successfully they do so. Because someone has a personal stake in advancing a particular position does not mean the enterprise should be regarded cynically. There seems little doubt that the individuals involved believe themselves to be right, no matter how they stand to gain personally. Alasdair Phillips is a good example, a man who freely dedicates much of his time to helping members of the public concerned about electromagnetism through his Powerwatch website and beyond. At the same time, moral convictions should not preclude more sober judgment; indeed, they are often a barrier to it. The question remains: What basis is there for serious concern and precautionary measures? First of all, what is EMF?

EMF and the Power Line Controversy

Electromagnetic fields are the invisible fields carrying energy through space. Sometimes these waves can be physically experienced, as in the slight tingling of the skin sometimes felt when walking under high-voltage power transmission lines (Sagan 1996: xvi–xvii). Radio interference is a more common evidence of these invisible fields. Less intense fields are generated by all electrical equipment, from hair dryers to televisions.

The waves within different electromagnetic fields have different frequencies, ranging between frequencies from 0 to 300 GHz (see Fig. 16).[8] As the frequency increases, so does their energy. At the highest

---

[8] The unit for frequency is hertz (Hz), which measures the number of complete cycles of a waveform per second (cycles per second).

frequencies the energy of the waves is sufficient to break chemical bonds, separating electrons from their atoms and producing charged ions. For this reason, high-frequency fields are known as "ionizing," while those at frequencies insufficient to do so such as visible light, heat, microwaves, and radio waves are termed "nonionizing." The distinction is important, as nonionizing waves such as those generated by cell phones effectively cannot cause direct human harm through a heating effect.

The lowest end of the electromagnetic spectrum is electrical power, which is referred to as power frequency. The energy is here insufficient even to heat tissue. At this frequency the wave crests are thousands of miles apart, whereas the space separating crests of x-rays is smaller than an atom. There is some terminological difficulty over the different forms of electromagnetism. At higher frequencies the waves are always associated with both electric and magnetic fields that cannot be separated. Thus some scientists use the abbreviation E/MF, where the slash denotes "and." At the lower frequencies, such as from power lines, the electric and magnetic fields can exist separately. Scientists therefore use the term electric and magnetic fields (EMF). Although the strict accuracy of the term can be disputed (in the case of the sometimes separate fields in power frequencies), EMF has become the widely used expression for nonionizing electromagnetic fields.

Before looking in more detail at the specific studies on cell phone EMF, it is useful to note the continued controversy about extremely low-frequency fields (commonly referred to as ELF), especially power lines. The confusing character of the cell phone debate is by no means surprising; the earlier and continuing discussion of power line effects is very similar and still unresolved.

There has been an extraordinary amount of research into radio-frequency and ELF fields, largely in response the emergence of public microwave fears outlined in Chapter 3. Until the 1980s this research was mainly concerned with radio-frequency fields from broadcast transmitters and other sources. It then shifted to power lines in the 1980s, following the Leeper and Wertheimer study that suggested an association with leukemia, subsequently moving back to radio-frequency fields with the emergence of the cell phone issue.

Oddly, at each stage the proposition that unknown effects from power frequency fields might exist has been presented as a new discovery. "High-voltage power cables have been officially linked to cancer for the first time," reported the *Sunday Times* (4 March 2001). The report, identified with renowned British scientist Richard Doll, claims that the overall risk of leukemia, which in all children is one in 1400, becomes elevated to one in 700 for those exposed to magnetic fields of 0.4 microTesla or more (about 0.5 percent of children). One critic pointed out that, typically, the risk ratios involved were too small to be taken seriously, even if they made good headlines (Brignell 2001). If it turned out to be true, and putting issues such as the amount and duration of exposure in actual numbers, the risk represents about one extra case of leukemia every two years as a result of exposure to magnetic fields, out of a total number of 500 cases per year.

Confusion is the most striking characteristic of studies of power lines. A few unexpected results created concern, but then these studies typically proved impossible to reproduce. One authority and author of *Biological Effects of Transmission Line Fields* (Carstensen 1987) concludes: "If you look at the scientific basis for the whole thing, there's nothing there. A few studies seem to give a borderline indication of an effect, someone else tries it, and it disappears" (cited in Fumento 1993: 222). Paul Brodeur claimed there were thirty-two published studies that demonstrated ELF effects. Even on these terms Fumento notes that he failed to point out the hundreds of studies that showed the contrary. Typically, the latter were large-scale surveys. In 1994, a four-year study of the health of 223,000 Canadian and French electrical workers found no increased cancer risk, and an even larger U.S. study the following year found a lower rate than among the general population, which was attributed to them having good jobs (Park 2000: 156–7).

A 1996 American report by a National Research Council panel of scientists reviewed 500 studies of the health effects of high-voltage power lines and found "no conclusive and consistent evidence" that electric and magnetic fields cause any human disease. They noted that some studies indicated a slightly higher incidence of childhood leukemia among children whose homes are near power lines. But in such studies, other complex factors make it difficult to find relationships of statistical significance. In a major 1996 survey into power lines, for example, the only evidence was of a weak statistical association between living near power lines and childhood leukemia. The researchers could not confirm any relationship, but they did explain that neighborhoods with large amounts of power lines "are usually poor, congested and polluted – all of which are risk factors for cancer" (ibid.: 142). The survey also found an increase of chronic leukemia among adults working in industries where they are exposed to intensive electric fields. It is important to reiterate here that a small statistical correlation can suggest all sorts of potential connections.

A definitive, seven-year study by the American National Cancer Institute (NCI) into any connection between power lines and cancer was seen as "exhaustive" and "unimpeachable" with every possible research bias investigated. Its conclusion, announced in 1997, was that there was no significant association. Since concern about EMF first publicly surfaced, any claimed health effects became smaller with better research, to the point where the NCI study found no effect at all. An editorial in the *New England Journal of Medicine*, which accompanied the publication of the NCI findings, expressed regret at the hundreds of millions of dollars that had only increased paranoia and done nothing to prevent the tragedy of childhood cancer (ibid.: 160).

There remains considerable disagreement on the bigger issue of power line ELF, which hinges principally on whether a very small increase in risk found in some studies justifies citing ELF as a "significant risk." The power line controversy was founded on precisely the issue that risk could not be ruled out, and that it was no longer acceptable to proclaim that there was actually no risk. An important landmark emerged in a U.S. Office of Technology assessment in 1989, carried out by three Carnegie Mellon researchers. One of these was Granger Morgan, a subsequently influential figure who coined the American equivalent of the precautionary principle, so-called prudent avoidance. Their often quoted statement is similar to every other that has fueled EMF controversy up to the British Stewart committee report. They said: "As recently as a few years ago, scientists were making categorical statements that on the basis of all available evidence there are no health risks from human exposure to power-frequency fields. In our view, the emerging evidence no longer allows one to categorically assert that there are no risks." Although the researchers then state that this is not a basis for suggesting significant risk, their presentation reflects a tendency of officially appointed bodies to err on the side of caution. A U.S. National Institutes of Health panel in 1998 reported some risk but "probably quite small compared to many other public health risks" (EEA 1999: 275). The panel voted 19 to 9 that electromagnetic fields should be regarded as a potential cause of cancer, using the International Agency for Research on Cancer criteria for carcinogenicity. Eight members said that because of conflicting studies they could not decide, another eight that they probably were not a potential cancer cause. An IARC review in the summer of 2001 concluded that power-frequency magnetic fields are a "possible" human carcinogen, putting power lines in the same category as coffee and tea.

No Harm, But Some "Effects"

Whatever the confusions generated by scientific disagreement, the extent of possible risk from cell phone EMF is not simply a matter of opinion. Nor is it only contingent on whose was the last study to swing the debate in one direction or another, or who has managed to build his or her career and profile most successfully. The WHO fact sheet (June 2000) tells us that there is no consistent evidence of harm from cellular type radiation. Therefore, "present scientific information does not indicate the need for any special precautions for use of mobile phones." In any tangible way, there is not only an absence of evidence that harm has been caused by cell phone EMF, but there is no recognized way in which it could happen. The Institute of Electrical Engineers in London explained recently: "As with power frequencies, scientists have been unable to propose plausible biophysical mechanisms for the fields to cause cancer" (IEE 2001: 4).

The main focus of concern about cell phone EMF is the possible link to cancer first raised by the Reynard case. The most recent and authoritative research continues to confirm the absence of any proven harm in relation to this most dreaded of associations. Two studies published in the *Journal of the American Medical Association* and the *New England Journal of Medicine* conclude that prolonged cell phone use does not cause cancer (Muscat et al. 2000; Inskip et al. 2001). The *Journal of the American Medical Association* report, carried out by the American Health Foundation, compared the cell phone use of 422 control subjects with 469 brain-cancer patients and found no greater risk of tumors in cell phone users. The *New England Journal of Medicine* study, carried out by the National Cancer Institute, came to the same conclusions. "In all of the available scientific literature, there is nothing that indicates any adverse health effects from using cell phones," added Russell Owen, chief of the Food and Drug Administration (FDA)'s radiation biology branch.[9]

These conclusions are important, despite what the layman might regard as an inverted and evasive scientific presentation that asserts only that there is "no evidence to prove harm," not that there is definite safety. The continued absence of proof of harm from low-level electromagnetism is not simply due to a general difficulty in establishing relationships between

---

[9] Cited in Steven Milloy, "Studies Steal Cell Phone Lawyer's Christmas," 22 December 2000, junkscience.com.

ill health and invisible physical forces. The absence of a clear causal link stands in contrast to the proven dangers of ionizing radiation. We are concerned here with its nonionizing relative, which is harmless in any conventional sense. There is no concern about electric fields because it is well understood that the body's skin is a barrier to them; the health concerns about mobile phones relate to their magnetic fields. The only established effect on the body of radio-frequency exposure is a heating effect. Radio-frequency fields do penetrate the body (nearly a centimeter at the frequencies used by mobiles), but this heat is carried away, and is similar in effect to exposing the skin to the sun for short periods. While some small effects from using mobile phones, such as changes in brain activity, have been detected, they "have no apparent health significance" (WHO 2000).

There is an important distinction to be made about the focus of the research programs into EMF. They are essentially aimed at investigating the possibility of effects from the cell phone itself, not from the base stations that relay the signals. While far too weak to cause direct harm, radiation emitted by a phone is directly against the head and often involves prolonged exposure, and this prompts some to see harm as a possibility. By comparison, any impact from towers is even harder to countenance. However, subjectively, cell tower radiation is often regarded as more problematic for the simple reason that while using a cell phone is voluntary, exposure from towers is, in a certain sense, not. Although radiation from towers is more powerful, it is both more irregular and, in practice, distant from (passing) human beings. The searchlight-like beam from a tower typically reaches the ground 100 yards or more away from the structure. As its intensity diminishes rapidly with distance, the maximum exposure at ground level is hundreds of times lower than that from a cell phone. Precaution and the issue of "safety" under such circumstances becomes rather strange, even counterintuitive. If we accepted the possibility of a threat from digital mobile signals, it would be better to be nearer to a tower, as being further away forces the phone to "work harder" and increase signal strength.

Can cell phones then be pronounced "safe"? Certainly not, and for a number of reasons. The distinction between an absence of proven harm and "safety" is an important one. Following press reports in Spain and Australia that they were suggesting cell phones were "safe," the WHO issued a press release on 10 October 2001 insisting: "Such statements are a distortion of WHO's position on the possible health effects of mobile phone use." They reminded readers that while none of the reviews have concluded that radio-frequency exposure caused adverse health consequences, there are identifiable gaps in knowledge and research is under way. There have been signs that the WHO is modifying its previously clear position in a precautionary direction, advising that means are considered to reduce people's exposure, in an updated fact sheet in October 2001 (*Microwave News*, September/October 2001). By early 2003 it was clear that the WHO was intent on establishing an explicitly precautionary approach to EMF, whatever their previous stance.

Besides the gaps in EMF research, there are some distinctive aspects of the cell phone that are seen to justify further study. Because cell phones are held against the head for prolonged periods of time (unlike the far more occasional use of hair dryers, for example), many suggest there is a need for more careful examination than for devices used less frequently in human activity. The second fact is that more than half a billion people own a mobile phone. On this basis, simple mathematics suggests that even if we are talking about a very small risk, many people would be affected. These are the reasons why mainstream scientific opinion believes there are some grounds for considering further investigation. On the same grounds, this rationale for research into handset exposure clarifies the far more limited case for research into cell tower emissions. Still less is there any basis for precautionary measures in relation to towers. Cell towers are obviously not in close physical contact with millions of people worldwide for prolonged periods. While their output is higher, exposure is much more limited.

Beyond this basic proposition that handset exposure should be investigated, there are some more particular refinements to the issue. Critical scientists in the field do argue that there is a case to be answered or at least grounds for continued research. It is useful to recognize from the outset that even those few scientists directly contesting the need for precautionary measures over cell phones do not dismiss a possible health threat out of hand, nor argue that more research should not be carried out. Authorities such as Ken Foster and John Moulder are dismissive of "phantom risk," but they certainly do not argue that more research is unnecessary. In addition, nobody is arguing that if an individual feels sufficiently worried and wants to take precautionary action for his or her own peace of mind by avoiding or limiting cell phone use, then that is that individual's prerogative. Such is the advice of Foster and Moulder and the WHO, even though in both cases they do not recommend or take such measures themselves.

Foster doubts whether there is any real hazard posed by electric and magnetic fields from household appliances and power lines, but views cell phone radiation in a somewhat different light (Foster 1999a: 47). Comparatively little research has been conducted on exposure to microwaves specifically at cellular phone frequencies, and the scientific issues have not been resolved to many scientists' satisfaction. Foster and Moulder note that few of the existing studies involved standard toxicology studies, "the sort that a chemical or a pharmaceutical company would to do to gain regulatory approval for a new product" (Foster and Moulder 2000: 17). They add that there is a particular absence of studies into the kind of pulse-modulated energy transmitted by digital phones, an absence thought especially significant by scientific risk campaigners (Hyland 2000). On the other hand, the lack of harmful effects from other microwave research does have a bearing on this more particular field. One authority argues that "the general lack of hazardous effects at other frequencies must be considered" in relation to cell phone EMF (Jauchem 1998: 269).

The most important issue, however, is that some unexplained effects were thrown up by a number of early research projects. No negative health effect from cell phone radiation has been proven, but subtle biological effects in a few studies invite further research. Others go further, and extrapolate from these effects the need for a precautionary approach to cell phone use. It is certain that cell phone radiation cannot cause direct harm through "conventional" means of heating, as it is simply too weak. What is at issue is the possibility of a "nonthermal" effect, whereby weak magnetic fields somehow interact with tissue. Members of the British Stewart Inquiry noted that this "is a controversial field of science" (Maier, Blakemore, and Koivisto 2000). Yet some recent research does suggest that there are nonthermal effects on living tissue, ranging from immediate early gene expression and micronucleus formation to changes in the excitability of nerve cells, permeability of the blood-brain barrier, and the ability of rats to learn mazes. Neatly summarizing this consensus, an editorial for the *New Scientist* was headlined: "Forget the hype – there's still no evidence that mobile phones will mangle your memories or give you cancer. But the microwaves they emit may be up to something." It described a "variety of strange effects on living tissue that can't be reconciled with conventional radiation biology" (*New Scientist*, 10 April 1999).

The "strange effects" include a "memory loss" study that showed a decrease in the amount of time subjects took to react to words flashed onto a screen and a study of worm larvae exposed to an overnight dose of microwaves that found they wriggled less and grew 5 percent faster than larvae that were not exposed, suggesting that the microwaves were speeding up cell division. Some of Henry Lai's research also suggests that low-energy microwaves can trigger biochemical stress in rats on the basis, for example, that they took longer to perform tasks afterward. General symptoms of memory loss, sleep disturbance, headaches, and so on have been found (Hermann and Hossmann 1997), and changes in the permeability of the blood brain barrier, electroencephalographic activity, and blood pressure are suggested by a few studies (Braune et al. 1998). Another study from 1997 suggested that slices of rat tissue from the hippocampus part of the brain exposed to microwave radiation revealed blunted electrical activity and weakened responses to stimulation, suggesting an impact on memory. But generalizing from these results is immensely problematic. The hippocampus is buried too deep in the brain to be influenced by emissions from mobile phones, as the researcher himself pointed out (*New Scientist*, 10 April 1999). In other research, the work of Adey and his colleagues found that cell phone pulse–modulated energy did not promote brain cancer in rats (Adey et al. 2000). Nonetheless, any study that appears to indicate an *effect* on cells, such as Finnish research led by Professor Dariusz Leszczynski, continues to make front-page news in the United Kingdom, at least, regardless of its extremely limited implications (*Evening Standard*, 19 June 2002).

There is more than a collection of fragments to the case for uncertainty about cell phone radiation. There are certain studies that have provided the scientific basis for the whole controversy and subsequent media campaign, in the manner that certain landmark findings initiated other microwave fears. Foremost among these was an experiment by Henry Lai, comparable in influence to the famous study of Wertheimer and Leeper that initiated the power line controversy. In 1995, Lai claimed that the DNA from the brains of rats exposed to microwaves suffered numerous strand breaks, a type of damage often seen in cells exposed to cancer-causing chemicals or powerful x-rays (Lai and Singh 1996). Such DNA breaks are associated with illnesses such as Alzheimer's and cancer. Another of the key studies that effectively form the basis for the scientific controversy was the 1997 study by Repacholi, now head of the WHO's EMF research program, and his colleagues in Australia. Using mice genetically engineered to be susceptible to lymphoma, the Repacholi team at Royal Adelaide hospital exposed mice to microwave emissions comparable to those from a digital cell phone over a year and a half, and found, to his surprise, that twice as many mice developed lymphomas as those not exposed to the radiation.

Repacholi, among others, insists that risks to health cannot be established on the basis of one set of results (WHO 2000). Many of the studies that have made newspaper headlines are preliminary and not peer-reviewed. In a sense equally surprising as unexplained effects is that they have rarely been successfully replicated. This is very significant. *New Scientist*'s review concluded that this was "perhaps the best reason for remaining skeptical." The studies that suggest increased DNA strand breaks have also not been confirmed (Chou et al. 1992; Lai and Singh 1996; Malyapa et al. 1997). So far, the Motorola-funded team led by radiation oncologist Joseph Roti Roti at Washington University in St. Louis, Missouri, has been unable to repeat the mice impacts. Neither has a Belgian government–funded study by Luc Verschaeve at the Flemish Institute for Technological Research in Boeretang, which exposed white blood cells to microwaves. Another team of microwave experts at the Brooks Air Force Base in San Antonio, Texas, used mice genetically engineered to be susceptible to breast tumors. They exposed the animals to microwaves for twenty hours a day for eighteen months, yet saw no increases in tumor rates. Whatever the difficulties of interpreting animal studies, such results are significant. Moulder argues: "If it doesn't reliably cause cancer in animals and cells at high doses, then it probably isn't going to cause cancer in humans" (*New Scientist*, 10 April 1999). He and Foster point out not only that Lai's results have not been reproduced, but that Roti Roti's research team has identified a possible experimental artifact that might explain his results (Foster and Moulder 2000). The failure to confirm Lai's findings was actually not surprising in scientific terms. "If it was right, it would completely change the way we think about radiation," said Roti Roti (*New Scientist*, 10 April 1999). The inability of researchers to advance beyond preliminary results or hypothetical causes over several years indicates weaknesses in the conceived relationship between cell phone EMF and significant biological effects.

There is a very consistent pattern of studies that demonstrate no cancer connection, in particular. Brain cancer allegations have stimulated a number of follow-up studies, particularly in the United States, where the cancer connection has made the greatest impression. The study by Rothman et al. (1996) was based on a review of health records for more than 250,000 cell phone users and found no difference between those hand-held portable and mobile cellular phones. The Rothman team looked at the causes of death of cell phone users and concluded that increased risk was evident only in relation to car crashes (Foster and

Moulder 2000). Further large-scale epidemiological studies discovered no increase in cell phone–related death rates (Dreyer, Loughlin, and Rothman 1999). Results from a study of 200,000 Motorola employees did not support a cell phone cancer link (Morgan et al. 2000), and neither do more recent studies (Muscat et al. 2000; Inskip et al. 2001).

Minor *beneficial* effects have also been identified, but remain similarly unexplained and unreplicated. Research led by William Ross Adey at the Veterans Affairs Medical Center in Loma Linda, California, found that mice exposed to microwaves for two hours a day were less likely to develop brain tumors when given a cancer-causing chemical. This finding has not been reproduced, like contrasting negative effects, and Moulder suggests it is unlikely that it ever will be. He believes that what we're seeing is the variation from laboratory to laboratory that one would expect from technically demanding experiments that are trying to pick up tiny effects: "Study something enough times and by the laws of statistics you'll occasionally see something," he explained. At the same time, "if microwaves beamed onto mice month in month out for 18 hours a day don't cause cancer, it would be astonishing if mobile phones do" (*New Scientist*, 10 April 1999). Roti Roti repeats the scientific consensus that despite some curious effects, "the fairly simple bottom line is, in the work that I've done, I've found nothing that would alarm me, or alert me to possible hazardous health effects," repeating that the driving risk associated with cell phones is key (*Washington Post*, 22 May 1999).

Even if the cell phone does induce some temporary biological effects, it is an interesting comment on the apparently malign assumptions of contemporary society that "effect" appears to be synonymous with harm. Arguably underlying this view is a conception of the human body as being unnaturally fragile. In fact, it is an extremely adaptive instrument. As one authority points out, "an observable biological effect from exposure to a particular condition does not necessarily imply any health consequence; the body may simply adjust to the new condition" (Fumento 1993: 228). An effect demonstrated in the laboratory may have no significant impact on the body and its interactive defenses. Nevertheless, it is these uncorroborated effects that are the principal justification for further research into cell phone EMF. The proposition that cell phone risk is significant and demands precautionary action is a very different matter, however. Ultimately it is a case that rests on a rejection of the basic causal assumptions of modern science and society. This is because "[s]tarting from the classical concept of causality, it is practically impossible to prove that electromagnetic fields can be a cause of disease" (Brauner 1996: 27).

The Rejection of Causal Thinking and the Nonscientific Case for Precaution

Attempts to construct a conventional case that cell phones or power lines pose a significant risk are invariably weak, often relying on a narrow and selective presentation of evidence. This is highlighted in Fumento's description of Paul Brodeur's use of evidence in the power line controversy. In addition to the earlier study by Wertheimer and Leeper, Brodeur singled out the work of David Savitz of the University of North Carolina as most significant: "Far and away the greatest blow to the effort of the electricity industry to deny that 60 hertz fields . . . could pose a health hazard came on November 20, 1986 . . ." (Fumento 1993: 233). Fumento notes that Savitz himself radically disagreed with the implications drawn from his study by Brodeur. He argued that the possibility of risk from power lines did not justify what would be very expensive measures to limit exposure (ibid.: 236–7).

Studies the results of which are seized on as evidence of harm on closer scrutiny sometimes suggest no such thing. Foster and Moulder (2000) note that the Swedish epidemiological study by Hardell et al. (1999) found no harmful associations overall. This general finding was eclipsed by media interest in the finding that cell phone users who did develop certain kinds of brain tumors were more likely to get them on the side of the head that they used for telephone conversation. This was not a statistically significant result, however. Similarly, a study by Joshua Muscat at the American Health Foundation was publicly highlighted by George Carlo following preliminary discussion of his findings at a scientific meeting in 1999. Before these results were even published, let alone properly assessed, Carlo issued alarmist warnings to television reporters of a cell phone/brain cancer connection. Strikingly, Muscat states categorically in his abstract that he "did not find evidence that cell phone use increases the risk of brain cancer," although he was uncertain how to understand an apparent increase in one of its varieties (cited in Foster and Moulder 2000).

In its own strictly scientific terms, the case for a serious health risk from cell phone EMF is largely theoretical; it remains a "phantom risk." It requires a great effort of will to see the fragments of research suggesting some sort of nonthermal effect as a compelling case. The alleged cancer connection is the centerpiece of Carlo's book: "In the puzzle of cell phone radiation research, the pieces of scientific evidence we have now do fit together. Although many pieces are still missing, those that are in place indicate a big picture of cancer and health risk," he says with confidence (Carlo and Schram 2001: 241). He takes the unexpected results from Rothman's, Muscat's, and Hardell's studies as evidence of sufficient consistency to satisfy the demanding Koch-Henle postulates that confirm scientific rigor (biological plausibility, consistency, temporality, significance, dose-response upward, dose-response downward, concordance). All seven of the postulates have been met, according to Carlo. His assertion is difficult to entertain seriously, as it rests on emphasizing parts of studies that otherwise prove the opposite. Those responsible for the studies, such as Muscat, Hardell, and Repacholi, have themselves rejected Carlo's interpretation.

There is a common tendency to leap from finding a biological effect to demanding precaution. Thus in a 1993 paper, Dr. Ivan Beale from the University of Auckland argued: "The operation of cell sites on or near kindergartens or school properties is likely to result in large increases in radiofrequency exposure for groups of children. This is contrary to the principle of prudent avoidance consistent with good health protection policy" (cited in Ashwood 1999: 41). It is not unusual to find an almost random list of studies, with little regard even for whether they have been peer-reviewed and subsequently confirmed, posted on the Internet as compelling evidence of risk. Enough tiny doubts amount to one big doubt, according to this thinking. The American environmentalist group Earthwatch outlines a long list of materials related to EMF, for example (Begich and Roderick 2000). These are listed together with anecdotal evidence culled from British newspapers of people reporting headaches, and so on, and followed by a demand that "something must surely be done." What is also evident from Earthwatch is an ecological approach that determines a very different way of thinking about life. For them, these are "impacts of new technology on both human health and the planet's operating systems. The idea that both could have impacted in profound ways through the introduction of new energetic factors may well prove to be the environmental story of the 21st century." From this perspective the surprising fragments of scientific results amount to a discovery "that small amounts of energy when delivered in the right way can have the same effects as a massive dose of chemicals. The complexity of living creatures is being found to be influenced by the most delicate fields of electromagnetic energy" (ibid.). Earthwatch advertises a special device, the Cell/Wave Guard, to provide protection from these "small amounts of energy."

Many anti-EMF activists attribute a wide range of powers to electromagnetism.[10] Perhaps most influential in this field is Robert Becker, author of works such as *The Body Electric: Electromagnetism and the Foundation of Life* (1991). Although a "foundation of life," electromagnetism is at other times far less benign, according to this school of thought or, rather, belief. In *Cross Currents: The Promise of Electromedicine, the Perils of Electropollution* (1991), Becker argues that the body is adversely affected by power lines, computers, microwaves, and satellite dishes. Perhaps the strangest phenomenon associated with electromagnetism and advocates of its power is "remote viewing." Proposed by Tim Rifat, who claims to have studied its "biophysical basis," remote viewing is the "ability to travel out of our bodies to remote locations to inspect other environments" (Rifat 1999). In his book he claims to explain this extraordinary "ability" and its use in the Cold War.

At the same time as recognizing that EMF activism is based on thinking at odds with conventional science, it should be borne in mind that there certainly are some unusual effects associated with electrical currents, even electromagnetic stimulation. The basis for this are observations such as that electrical current helps heal bones. Some credence is given to electromagnetic therapeutic effects. Begun in the 1980s, transcranial magnetic stimulation involves holding a small electromagnetic net with metal coils against the skull. It produces magnetic pulses that in turn induce a local electrical current in the brain. A gentler alternative to electroconvulsive therapy, trials have suggested that it can relieve severe depression. While it has generally been restricted to clinical trials, the Canadian authorities have cleared it for limited use in treating depressives.

The contesting of conventional scientific assumptions has long been central to the case for significant biological microwave effects. Scientists involved in the original microwave debate are criticized for their refusal to move away from old causal thinking and its insistence on investigating only thermal effects. Steneck's account of the microwave debate describes "the tyranny of thermal thinking," which involves a "callousness that could have been motivated only by some conspiratorial design" (Steneck 1984: 89). In his interpretation, the optimism of the immediate post-war years conditioned a simplistic method of investigating the known dangers

---

[10] Alasdair Phillips, referred to above as the chair of several international meetings on cell phone health issues, is one such believer. He recommended the author read the work of Robert Becker and Tim Rifat in order properly to understand the issues. American activists such as Libby Kelley similarly recommend the work of Becker.

of microwaves (ibid.: 24–5). According to Gerard Hyland, causal thinking is at the root of misplaced assurances that existing safety guidelines are adequate. For him, "the traditional understanding of 'cause and effect' is thus no longer appropriate..." (Hyland 1999c: 1). In its place, Hyland suggests a "signals and responses" framework, which he attributes to sociology.

Hypotheses about complex interactions between nonthermal effects of EMF continue to be put forward. Professor Denis Henshaw of Bristol University, a well-known investigator of concerns about electromagnetism and health, argues that computers are also a danger because the electrical charge produced makes the user a magnet for every germ and pollutant in the office.[11] Low-level radiation is here identified not as a problem in itself but as a facilitator of other agents of biochemical disruption and damage. Useful reviews suggest that the link between EMF and health is better understood as a hypothetical one, derived from this framework (Brauner 1996). This signal and response effect suggests that the important issue is not only the amount of energy absorbed, but also the possible response of the living organism: organisms can amplify the signals; the signal is merely a trigger. This approach is predicated on the recognition that, in life generally, the impact of the same "signal" varies with different people.

Hyland's method for deducing a risk from EMF is principally based on inference and analogy from related fields, rather than reviewed studies and research. Building on the example of the stroboscope, he notes with a sense of discovery that the regular flashing of mobile telephony signals "happens to lie in the range of the important alpha brainwaves!" (Hyland 1999c: 2). Such potential "electromagnetic aggression" is derived from the example of mobiles being banned on airplanes. If electromagnetism can interfere with control systems, then why not the far more sensitive human brain? he reasons. The particularly low frequency emitted when handsets are in listening mode is suggested to be especially dangerous because it falls within the range of delta brain-waves. These are associated with neural pathology and deep sleep, "so that reports of tiredness experienced during the day are perhaps not surprising" (ibid.: 3). This is the closest Hyland comes to suggesting a specific symptom caused by emissions in this account, although he does not elaborate on either the source or number of such reports of tiredness.

---

[11] See, e.g., Simon Crompton, "Computers and Toxic Chemicals," *The Times* (Health), 31 October 2000.

There is a range of factors involved in whether a signal produces a particular response, in Hyland's hypothesis, but they certainly alter the way in which we should consider what is a "safe" level of EMF. Existing assessments of the impact of mobile phones are restricted to the level of emissions, a largely irrelevant dimension in his estimation, whereas the coherence, frequency, and purity of emissions are far more important in this understanding (ibid.). The impact of a laser compared with general light (no matter how bright), for example, is attributable to its "in step" and pure character, rather than simple intensity. Hyland uses this comparison with light to illustrate the idea that the intensity is less significant than the character of low-level radiation. We are familiar with the potential for light to become harmful, as, for example, when stroboscopes induce fits in epileptics. Such interference is possible because the information transmitted by the regular flashing of the light is recognized by the brain as it "matches, or is close to one utilized by the brain itself" (ibid.: 1–2). Hyland is basically suggesting that the limits on EMF emissions should reflect the hypothetical possibility that they might affect certain individuals, as stroboscopes also affect only a minority.

According to the "signal and response" approach, even a tiny amount of energy might trigger a reaction. However, the difficulties involved in isolating the specific effects of weak EMF, particularly because of the very low levels at which EMF is being measured, remain the same. The random character of the signal and response approach tends only to confirm rather than to disprove any assertion of harm. As its effects are dependent on numerous factors in and around the particular human organism, if there is no obvious negative effect this does not dissuade us from assuming there might be one. It is given by this approach that the majority of humans (those with strong immune systems) will remain unaffected. On the other hand, any harm that does develop (but that may not be attributable to microwaves) can confirm a problem, even though there are no identifiable symptoms. Again, given the very random impact of signal and response, we can assume that it will have different impacts on different organisms. It is difficult to imagine how any proof could be provided. Further complicating the case for a signal and response approach, many campaigners insist that effects simply need to be measured over a longer time period, suggesting that the difference is less one of paradigms and more of time scale.

It is not unreasonable to assume that if EMF can somehow interact with human beings, then it might be only with certain individuals. Many of the medical conditions that confront us today are plainly difficult to isolate to one cause, and can be explained only through a combination of factors. This transforms diagnosis into a descriptive process and makes it difficult to find treatable causes. Hyland's theory of bio-effects is an interesting idea, but nothing more than that. As a proposition it can never be completely discounted, particularly as it positively expects there to be no effect among most individuals. The signal and response approach takes us out of the bounds where anything can be reasonably concluded. One scientist considering this thesis asks, How can experiments be designed to investigate something when the possible methods of likely interaction are not known? (Dendy 2000)

In the absence of being able to take things further experimentally, the claims of people associating their problems with EMF stand as evidence alone. Hyland begins one of his papers by noting the "remarkable consistency worldwide in the symptoms of adverse health disorders...reported by people who are resident in the vicinity of mobile phone base stations...these include tiredness, sleeping disorders, impairment of short term memory, and anxiety states" (Hyland 1999b: 1). It is, first, unclear on what data he is basing his assertions of a global phenomenon. Second, the statement in itself is empty. He is essentially describing reports of people feeling unwell. Similar, impossibly vague reports could describe countless conditions.

It is interesting that scientific findings suggesting there to be no significant risk have made little impact on concerns about harm from mobile phone EMF. Concerns and demands for further research have escalated rather than subsided in the light of reassurance from the most prominent bodies for science and health such as the WHO. As the demand for research has increasingly stemmed from the perception of danger rather than evidence, an important strand of argument has now dispensed with the issue of establishing causality altogether. Leading New Zealand anti-mobile campaigner and psychologist Ivan Beale has argued that courts should not rely on physical evidence, as the very presence of sources of radiation can constitute a health risk, regardless. Particularly because they are invisible, the simple awareness that (unnecessary) sources of EMF are close can induce fear, and fear leads to illness. Journalist James Chapman notes, "the theory that stress rather than any radiation effect could be to blame is gaining increasing currency" (*Daily Mail*, 30 June 2000).

Self-perpetuating concerns with stress indicate that there is little scope for the issue of cell phones and health to be addressed in purely scientific terms. Indeed, institutional responses to the issue, such as the Stewart Inquiry, have emphasized the management of public perception as much as the discovery of specific risk levels through scientific inquiry. The possibility of damage to health from fearing the unknown is not only an attractive argument for campaigners; the psychosocial approach reflects a reality increasingly evident in personal injury litigation (Foster et al. 1999). More than just suggesting the fear to be understandable but misplaced, the trajectory of institutional responses is to more fully recognize and thereby legitimize such fears.

From the perspective of the sociology of risk, it is self-evident why mobile telephony has become a major source of complaint and reaction. The explanation lies in the "invisible" and "incalculable" character of the risk. For the original proponent of the idea that we now live in a "risk society," the German sociologist Ulrich Beck, radioactivity is central to the definition of risk:

> By risks I mean above all radioactivity, which completely evades human perceptive abilities, but also toxins and pollutants in the air, the water and foodstuffs, together with the accompanying short and long term effects on plants, animals and people.

The effects are asserted to be devastating; as he continues: "They induce systematic and often irreversible harm, generally remain invisible, are based upon causal interpretation and thus exist only in terms of the (scientific or anti-scientific) knowledge about them" (Beck 1992: 22–3).

Beck's perspective was shaped by the defining experience of the nuclear accident at Chernobyl in 1985 (Mol and Spaargaren 1993). Empirically based accounts of the meltdown of the Ukrainian reactor argue that the consequences of Chernobyl were very limited, and that the most important human consequences were the forced and unnecessary relocations of people in its aftermath.[12] Regardless of these more complex realities, Chernobyl remains a parable for Beck. What remains important is that risk is now invisible and thereby infinitely more threatening, ultimately driven by the impact of nature back on a destructive humanity. More recently, British-based sociologist Barbara Adam has elaborated the thesis, arguing that the experience challenged the very nature of knowledge and objectivity. Radiation, in her reading, takes on a life of its own, as it

---

[12] Casualties are far fewer than originally anticipated, seemingly confined to the hundreds of people working at the plant. According to the U.N. Committee on the Effects of Radiation, the death toll from the accident and related effects is thirty-one. Swedish radiologist Professor Gunnar Walinder argues that the psychological and social problems caused by the disproportionate, forced evacuations of some 400,000 people had a far more significant impact. See Bate (2000).

" ... disregards the boundaries of bodies, locality, nation and species ... it both affects and is transferred to an unknown number of future generations" (Adam 1998: 208). These propositions, while attempting to incorporate emotional and psychological dimensions to the perception of radiation risk, take the causal origin of the hazard as given and do not investigate the elevation of some concerns about radiation above other, proven risks from (ionizing) radiation. In the absence of any account of what radiation actually is, it forms a seamless and threatening whole.

Committed campaigners against cell phone EMF closely echo Beck's sense of the problem. A leading Australian campaigner, the researcher for the most influential political proponent of EMF risk in the country, Senator Lynn Allison, explains:

This issue is quite profound in its implications because it concerns an environmental problem that cannot be seen, heard, smelt, or touched (although there are some who can feel or are sensitive to EM fields or VHFs). This means that science is on the edge of having to change certain paradigms in order to fully understand not only the nature of electricity but also the nature of what it means to be human, how human beings are constituted, how life functions generally.[13]

EMF remains invisible not simply through its own qualities, but because of a belief that there are inadequacies in our understanding, according to the risk society approach. Restricted to causal terms of reference, radioactivity manages to evade our powers of detection. Unlike the all too visible risks of classical modernity such as smog, contemporary risks are said to be on an unprecedented scale, extremely complex, difficult to calculate, and therefore not susceptible to "instrumental rationality" (Beck 1992, 1995). While even the most dramatic arguments against cell towers do not suggest that they are likely to constitute a major danger, the arguments for the scale of *complexity* of the risk of EMF, as it interacts with other triggers to biological mechanisms, concur with this thesis. Adding to the "incalculability" of impact is the projection of problems into the future. Beck cites the example of Chernobyl, where "the injured are ... not even born yet" (Beck 1995: 31). Traditional concepts of blame, injury, and causality mean little in relation to such future prognoses, as it is not possible to identify or prioritize the source of the problem. According to campaigners against mobile phone EMF, the essence of the potential health risk is also this possibility of long-term harm.

---

[13] Correspondence from Sarah Benson, researcher to Australian Democrat Senator Lynn Allison, 31 August 2000.

It is perhaps not surprising that, when one contemplates possible long-term harm that will become evident only in the future and cannot be approached with any contemporary scientific instruments, the scale of the problem appears overwhelming. Beck has acknowledged that essentially moral judgments on the naive optimism of the past are presented in the form of fact-based objections to specific developments (Beck 1992: 176). This appears to be true of many of the objections against mobile phone EMF, which have shifted pragmatically (from targeting phones to now contesting towers), while retaining a broad suspicion of reassurances about safety and claims that no danger is evident. The idea that today's and tomorrow's risks are invisible, incalculable, and complex is deployed as both a campaigning issue and the psychological explanation for why some people are reacting against specific technologies. In criticism, in and of itself, the belief that invisibility is especially threatening and coterminous with large-scale threats is comparable to the childish fear of the dark.

In a sense the most successful argument for cell phone risk is the simplest. If the very perception of risk induces stress, irrespective of whether it has any real basis (which can, after all, be neither proved or disproved), then surely this in itself should be sufficient to warrant precaution. The problem remains, as explained in Chapter 1, that cell towers do actually have to be sited near population centers. There remains scope for more sensitive relocation and better design of towers. Yet particularly because we live in a society shaped by health anxieties, there also remains the potential for reaction regardless of how sensitive their siting and design. Acknowledging the legitimacy of stress as a factor in itself does not resolve the problem, and there are considerable implications to the basing of decision making on perceptions divorced from any more concrete assessment of possible problems. Ultimately, society cannot be organized around the subjective anxieties of individuals, no matter how much stress the advance of society is causing them.

More Research, No Resolution

The implication of lobbying and campaigning for further research and a precautionary approach to cell phone risk is that there is official and mainstream complacency about a possible risk. Such a view is not justified. The World Health Organization estimates that some 200 studies are under way involving $100 million of funding. These are principally cancer-related animal studies and biological cellular studies, plus around a dozen epidemiological investigations. There is general support for carry-ing out further research. Cell phone operators themselves suggest further research is justified, first on the general grounds that "it would be com-placent to assume that there is nothing else to learn about the effects of electromagnetic fields on health." A second basis cited by one operator is that "[w]hile human health studies are good at distinguishing large effects from small, historically they are less able to distinguish small effects from no effect at all" (cited in Vodafone 1999: 5). The WHO itself has declared that research into possible adverse effects of EMF should be a priority for the next four years and is coordinating research into possible asso-ciations between low-frequency EMF (less than 300 Hz) and childhood leukemia, breast cancer, and diseases of the central nervous system. It has also recommended research into possible associations between exposure to radio-frequency fields (300 Hz to 300Ghz) and leukemia/lymphoma and cancers. Dr. Paul Kleihues, director of WHO's International Agency for Research on Cancer, says that "with an estimated 15 million new can-cer cases each year, we must know if exposure to EMF is contributing to any significant extent to the incidence of disease" (EEA 1999: 275). Major epidemiological studies are being conducted, orchestrated by the WHO program, to compare the cell phone use of thousands of individuals suffering brain tumors with a control group, for example.

Such studies face enormous problems in coming to any reliable con-clusion. People who use mobiles a lot may be more susceptible to cancer because of some other factor linked to their lifestyles. Brain tumors can also take years to develop, suggesting that it is important to find out the extent and character of cell phone use years ago, rather than only recently. Even then, studies rely on the perceptions of individuals with cancer who may be inclined to exaggerate their cell phone usage, having perhaps al-ready decided for themselves that there is some relationship between their disease and cell phone EMF. In addition, there is a more general problem: the need for a prior understanding of cancer's triggers and mechanisms. In a useful reformulation, one account explains: "Should we some day know what role weak magnetic fields play in cancer, then it will only be because we will also know about what causes cancer" (Brauner 1996: 16). What we do know is that the key factor in the development of cancer is age, not electromagnetism.

Angell (1997), in her study of similarly imperceptible risks from breast implants, suggests that more research is needed in such circumstances, be-cause it is only through this process that knowledge accumulates and the balance of probabilities can shift. A recent contribution chose to present the state of knowledge in the field as one where "[e]vidence grows for the safety of mobile phones" (Gottlieb 2001). Yet there are numerous issues to consider that complicate the attractive prospect of increasing certainty in this field. The whole field of carcinogen risk assessment is fraught with problems. Risk assessment requires identification of a demonstrable hazard in the first place, something evidently lacking in the cell phone case. Without a clearly identified problem, such as a discernible increase of disease among an exposed community, even the design of suitable experiments is difficult. Foster concludes that it is difficult to reduce risk in this case, according to accepted models of risk management, because no clear understanding exists regarding the nature of the purported risk. Further, in investigating such subtle effects, it is very difficult to eliminate unintended artifact. The bottom line with risk research, as for science in general, is that "a hazard can be proven, the absence of hazard cannot" (Foster 1999a: 78). It is easy to raise questions, in other words, but we are then left with the difficulties of providing answers in conditions where they cannot prove satisfactory.

Previous epidemiological studies, in particular, have proven difficult to interpret, and similar difficulties will dog further research. Epidemiological studies have difficulty picking up small effects and indeed are seen by some as being totally misleading in these cases. It is for this reason that some argue that "epidemiological studies are, in the final analysis, an unsuitable instrument for researching EMF" (Brauner 1996: 17). Others insist that the whole approach of epidemiology is fraught with problems, particularly as it tends to accept risk ratios considered unacceptable in other branches of science, and often starts from small cluster effects rather than a demonstrable hazard. British medical writer James Le Fanu puts the case against epidemiological studies of small hazards more brutally, concluding: "The simple expedient of closing down most university departments of epidemiology could both extinguish this endlessly fertile source of anxiety-mongering while simultaneously releasing funds for serious research" (Le Fanu 1999: 3). On a more practical level, the difficulty of extrapolating animal experiments to humans is a particular problem because studies have – understandably – not managed to replicate the way in which radiation is experienced from cell phones, for example, and instead radiate the whole of the animal's head.

To an extent, the increasing number of studies concluding there is no cancer link does undermine the authority of claims for harm. Certainly, the continuing legal challenge in U.S. courts at the end of 2001 appeared to have been weakened by further research confirming the absence of a causal connection to cancer. Yet there is a limit to the role of further research in quelling public concerns. The International Agency for Research on Cancer (IARC) has been given 8 million Euros by the European Union to conduct large pilot epidemiological studies into a cell phone cancer link. As Foster and Moulder noted, "even with this extensive data, IARC virtually never pronounces an agent to be a 'non-carcinogen,' and therefore is unlikely to do so with RF energy" (Foster and Moulder 2000). Unsurprisingly, in June 2000, IARC duly declared EMF a "possible carcinogen" on the basis of an association between childhood leukemia and residential EMF exposure, in a move that apparently stimulated a more precautionary stance by IARC's parent body, WHO (*Microwave News*, July/August 2001).

Already, in the mid-1980s, it was pointed out that "microwave radiation is one of the most thoroughly studied of all potential environmental hazards" (Foster and Pickard 1987: 531). These authorities shed considerable light on the apparent contradiction of demands for further research into weak magnetic fields, when so much has already been carried out. It seems that more research into low-level EMF creates an apparently inexhaustible "need" for further research. Because there is no demonstrable health effect to investigate in the first place, much of the research simply throws up speculative links left for others to pursue. They note:

how easy it is to collect evidence which neither demonstrates a hazard nor provides assurance that no hazard is present. The problem is not (as is frequently asserted) that too little is known about the biological effects of microwave energy. Rather, endless exploratory research has yielded many observations the importance of which cannot be reliably judged.... This is because: "an "effect" might be reported by an exploratory study that took weeks to carry out, whereas it might require years to confirm the existence of the phenomenon and to judge its significance, there can be no end to controversy save by exhaustion, or by taking the conscious decision to leave some questions unanswered. (ibid.: 531)

More simply, perhaps, it is important to assert that safety cannot be proven. It is not possible to prove a negative; in this case that something cannot do "harm." The very question has no meaning in the scientific world. Modern science thinks in terms of probabilities rather than absolute certainties, an approach which better captures the complexities of physical processes. Science is not so much engaged in explaining "why a particular thing must necessarily occur, but instead the conditions under which it can occur" (Brauner 1996: 24–5). Simple logic tells us that just because something has failed to happen 1,000 times, we cannot absolutely guarantee that it will not happen on the 1,001st occasion. It is in this sense that a scientist recently pointed out with regard to the demand for mobile phone safety that "[a] Nobel prize awaits the person who first designs an experiment to show that anything is "safe" (Dendy 2000). Fumento is more dramatic, writing that Paul Brodeur's demand that safety be proven is comparable to disproving accusations that someone is a witch (Fumento 1993: 253). The refusal to declare safety might seem almost pedantic to the layman, but it is important to recognize that the whole ethos and authority of the scientist is founded precisely on such otherwise elementary propositions. In a sense, the scientist who declares something strictly "safe" no longer deserves to be taken seriously.

Safety is evidently more a social than a scientific concept. Society recognizes this in other contexts. Even in our increasingly precautionary culture, we make certain pragmatic decisions with regard to safety. Electricity kills hundreds of Americans each year through accidental electrocution, but this does not in itself justify special precautionary measures. Accidents happen, and the assumption of personal responsibility is essential to any modern society. Just about all vegetables we eat are "unsafe," full as they are of potentially dangerous elements. Around 99.9 percent of all pesticides in the human diet are natural pesticides from plants. Who would declare coffee "safe" in the light of the 1,000 chemicals it contains, of which only 26 have been tested, and of these 19 cause cancer in rodents? (Ames and Gold 1999: 157–61). If coffee is not "safe," there seems little prospect of cell phones being declared so. Ultimately, as Angell points out with regard to breast implants, the notion that they "cause an undefined set of symptoms is neither provable nor falsifiable – it is simply an assertion" (Angell 1997: 104). Alternatively, we can say it is a possibility, but only in the most abstract, perhaps ultimately banal, sense.

The Precautionary Principle

Ensuring safety, no matter how hard it might be to define, suggests caution, better still a more anticipatory "precaution." The demand for precaution has become compelling, particularly in contemporary Europe, and is now enshrined as a guiding principle for many areas of policy making. The "precautionary principle" is invoked to legitimize measures such as product bans where there may be no large-scale immediate hazard, but where there is thought to be a possibility of one emerging in the future. The majority of discussions of the precautionary principle focus on environmental or health risks, and the problem of allowing or not allowing a certain activity or product (Shepherd 2000). Precautionary measures have been implemented with regard to cell phone EMF specifically, and radio-frequency fields in general. Italy established "cautionary" limits for radio-frequency fields in 1998 that are as low as one hundredth of international guidelines, and Switzerland followed suit the following year with regard to "sensitive-use areas" such as schools. The Stewart Inquiry found no health threat to the population posed by cell phones, yet recommended a range of precautionary advice. British scientists associated with the Stewart Inquiry conclude that "there is sufficient anecdotal evidence to justify further research and taking a precautionary approach to the use of mobile phones" (Maier et al. 2000). They highlight recommendations to reduce exposure levels for the general public to provide extra protection, to minimize power output, and to print power ratings on cell phones.

So what is the precautionary principle, and what are its origins? The merit and implications of applying it to cell phones and radio-frequency fields warrants some consideration of its character and history.

In December 2000, an annex to the Treaty of Nice declared that all areas of European Union policy making, particularly health and consumer protection but also including international trade, should embrace the precautionary principle. This, the latest step in the institutional consolidation of the principle, affirms its remarkably rapid rise through the course of the 1990s. In the process, the precautionary principle's remit has expanded from environmental impacts to science policy and beyond. The most important example of applying an explicitly precautionary approach, and the one that has most decisively consolidated its influence internationally, is global warming.

Developments such as drought in India are cited as examples of a demonstrable hazard with regard to global warming. More generally, however, it is the worst-case projection of climate change and its consequences into the future that is the key to the debate. About this there is much conjecture and very little scientific agreement or certainty. Taking action in the face of the vast uncertainties in understanding climate change and the potential of human societies to develop and manage environmental change is essentially precautionary. The measures introduced at the "Earth Summit" at Rio de Janeiro to reduce global warming capture the essence of the precautionary principle. Given potentially disastrous consequences, we cannot wait for scientific certainty before acting, even if those measures are at considerable cost and bring about only a tiny, effectively token, reduction in temperatures (Lomborg 2001). The alleged scale of the possible problem in the future compels us to put uncertainty to one side, and perhaps more generally question the need for "proof," according to precautionary thinking. In this sense, we can understand that cell phone risk might also qualify for a precautionary approach, despite its lack of any substantial basis. The fact that so many people use these devices and for prolonged periods suggests that "if there were" a problem the consequences would be devastating, and a "better safe than sorry" approach is justified.

The most widely used definition of the precautionary principle is that from the 1992 Framework Convention on Climate Change signed at the Rio summit, which states in section 15 that

parties should take precautionary measures to anticipate, prevent or minimize the causes of climate change and mitigate its adverse effects. Where there are threats of serious or irreversible damage, lack of full scientific certainty should not be used as a reason for postponing such measures. (Raffensperger and Tickner 1999: 2)

Yet it is widely acknowledged that there is no clear definition to which authoritative reference can be made. In one estimation there are at least fourteen definitions, ranging from the loosest conception of precaution to the most stringent (Vanderzwaag 1999). The main focus of differences is on the extent to which application should be based on at least some demonstrable scientific evidence of hazardous effect; in this sense differences fall between a "scientific" and "nonscientific" precaution (Foster, Vecchia, and Repacholi 2000). Whatever the differences of interpretation, however, the basic contours of the precautionary principle are not difficult to identify. British academic Timothy O'Riordan, the author of the original work that elaborated the principle, *Interpreting the Precautionary Principle*, describes a number of components to his own "nonscientific" understanding:

– Willingness to take action in advance of formal justification or proof
– Proportionality of response
– Preparedness to provide ecological space and margins for error
– Recognition of the well being interests of non human entities
– Shift in onus of proof onto those proposing change
– Greater concern for intergenerational impacts on future generations
– Recognition of need to address ecological debts. (Jordan and O'Riordan 1999: 24)

In the face of scientific uncertainties, parties should refrain from actions that might harm the environment, and the burden of proof should fall on those who propose change. To foresee and forestall is the basis of the precautionary principle; in other words, the "elemental concepts of 'first

do no harm' and 'an ounce of prevention is worth a pound of cure'"
(Raffensperger and Tickner 1999: 1). Assuming that there are growing
areas of scientific uncertainty, and that the consequences of proceeding
with innovation might be devastating for both the environment and humanity, the precautionary principle is a form of systematic risk avoidance.
Where there is "reasonable uncertainty," precaution should act as a decision norm, the onus being on those proposing innovation to disprove
the need for precaution, rather than the other way around. "Reasonable"
uncertainty is here unlikely to be the same as scientific uncertainty. The
need for precaution is justified in the first place precisely because science is
seen to be not yet in a position to judge with real certainty whether developments may have unintended, potentially disastrous consequences. The
example of innovation in biotechnology suggests itself as a prime arena
for precaution in this respect, given its tampering with the very "stuff
of life."

The acknowledged roots of the precautionary principle as a basis
for policy making lie in the so-called foresight legislation introduced in
Germany during the early 1970s, in the context of the wider implementation of social democratic planning. An early example was water quality protection, where the state aimed to avoid future ecological damage
through "forward looking" measures.

"Foresight" involved a distinction between human actions that could
cause danger (and which governments had to prevent at all costs) and
those that could cause risk and required "only" preventative or miti-
gating action. The principle of foresight was used by the German state
to inform its policies on acid rain, North Sea pollution, and other environmental issues. Innovation gave rise to a globally competitive industry in environmental technology and pollution prevention in Germany
(ibid.: 4).

An important influence in "foresight" becoming established more
widely, and in the process being redefined as the precautionary principle,
was German pressure to ensure the adoption of similar principles throughout Europe. This was driven by a determination to "prevent its own industry being placed at a competitive disadvantage. This was not enlightened
environmentalism at work but the dictates of a competitive market of
member states." The decisive weight of German influence in European
Union affairs assured success, as "[t]hroughout the 1980s, Germany continued to use its political and economic power in the EU to multilateralize
precautionary-based environmental policies across Europe" (Jordan and
O'Riordan 1999: 21). What was, in a sense, German foreign economic

policy then generalized "with remarkable speed and stealth" (ibid.: 21). An early landmark was the First International Convention on Protection of the North Sea in 1984. A ministerial declaration from the second North Sea conference codified the new perspective, arguing that "in order to protect the North Sea from possibly damaging effects of the most dangerous substances . . . a precautionary approach is addressed which may require action to control inputs of such substances even before a causal link has been established by absolutely clear scientific evidence" (Raffensperger and Tickner 1999: 5). The principle was subsequently integrated into numerous conventions and agreements at Maastricht, Barcelona, and the Rio summit. In 1993 it was accepted as the fundamental guiding principle of European Union environmental policy.

As an explicit doctrine, even expression, the precautionary principle remains unusual in the United States. There have been attempts to popularize the notion, notably at the so-called Wingspread Conference of 1998, some participants of which were supported by the Environmental Protection Agency (EPA). However, attendees at this environmental forum conceded that "it will be some years before it reaches the level of prominence held in Europe" (ibid.: 9). The concept lacks formal scientific credibility, a factor of greater significance in the U.S. context than the European. Science remains a more important legitimating factor in American society generally, and as a guiding principle for risk assessment more specifically. It is also now associated with the "global food fight" over attempts to ban American genetically modified imports into Europe, where invoking precaution is seen by U.S. observers as a "cover" for European Union protectionism (Paarlberg 2000). Insofar as there is an American equivalent, it is the notion of "prudent avoidance."

More important, however, there are many ways in which the assumptions behind the principle have become commonplace on both sides of the Atlantic, regardless of the extent of the principle's formal fortunes. Indeed, in less formalized and politicized forms, applying precautionary measures on principle was arguably initiated in the United States, not Europe. Often this took the form of legal and federal agency rulings, such as the precautionary ruling on breast implants implemented by the FDA (Angell 1997). Describing "the rise, fall and rebirth of the precautionary principle in U.S. law," one legal scholar notes that American courts signaled early acceptance of the principle in the ethyl versus EPA case that upheld the banning of lead in gasoline as a policy rather than science-based decision (Elliott and Charnley 2000). While explicitly precautionary policy considerations were then challenged in the Supreme Court ruling on benzene in 1980, the centrality of expert judgment was still challenged with the incorporation of risk management perspectives into legal rulings. Risk management is concerned with the sensitive management of perceived public feelings and is far from a return to a strictly science-based approach. It is now easily forgotten that in relation to issues such as precautionary measures against indoor radon, breast implants, and many other allegedly harmful substances, Europe and the United Kingdom were long regarded before the 1990s as insisting on a more sober and scientific approach by comparison with the United States (Cole 1993).

In "free market" America, regulation in areas such as drugs has long been more rigorous than Europe, effectively compensating for an absence of wide-ranging state control over resources. Stricter regulation has had some positive consequences, such as the refusal of the American authorities to allow sale of the deforming pregnancy drug thalidomide (Sjostrom and Nilsson 1972). It has also led to policy making that is precautionary in a less informed sense than that which led the FDA to refuse a license for thalidomide. The Delaney Clause of the Food, Drug and Cosmetics Act prohibits the incorporation into processed food of any level of a substance that has been found to be carcinogenic in laboratory animal experiments. The clause is not informed by any serious or specific expectation that widespread human harm will be prevented so much as a very public demonstration that even the possibility is to be permanently removed.

A precautionary element is also evident in the environmental policies initiated in the United States during the 1970s, when Congress passed some twenty-three major laws for regulating pollutants and other threats to the environment. These included the National Environmental Protection Act (NEPA) of 1969, which addressed the entire domain of environmental protection. This law initiated the process whereby all projects begun through federal resources undergo an environmental impact assessment. Although bounded by scientific criteria, impact assessments have an anticipatory element that deliberately slows the process of introducing new innovations and shifts the burden of proof in a manner similar to the precautionary principle. The American courts have turned down scientifically reasonable appeals against EPA decisions, such as that to suspend the herbicide 2, 4, 5-T, on the grounds that the precautionary principle gives the benefit of doubt to the authority deciding to implement a precautionary measure (Shepherd 2000: 15). As well as illustrating elements of precaution in American policy making, such examples suggest that precaution is implicit in environmental outlook and policy more generally.

American proponents of precaution note that the Chernobyl disaster encouraged a revival of precautionary thinking in the United States, as elsewhere, and cite the Pollution Prevention Act of 1990 and the signing of the Rio Convention in 1992 as evidence of progress. Pushing for further change, they contest the science-based risk evaluation that characterizes the American approach. The problem with risk assessments for them is that they are "based on the misguided belief that humans could fully understand the impacts of their activities" (Raffensperger and Tickner 1999: 2). They advocate control and remediation, rather than only systematic prevention. Specifically, they seek to formalize as a general duty the implicit obligation to act cautiously when enforcing statutes such as the Clean Air Act, Superfund, and the Endangered Species Act. But the Wingspread advocates of precaution realistically expect victories to continue at the state, rather than national level. They are encouraged by the fact that twenty-five states have established some type of pollution prevention legislation (ibid.: 7). In a manner similar to the Delaney Clause, the policy here is to insist that even if present only in quantities unlikely to cause harm, any substance proven to be toxic (at very high levels in the laboratory) should be dealt with in a precautionary manner.

In the United Kingdom as well as the United States, an increasingly precautionary approach was adopted before the 1990s. As a precautionary measure, the British government kept lead emissions from petrol at a constant level between 1973 and 1983 on the basis of campaigners' claims that it could cause brain damage to children, for example. Policy in this area appeared to be primarily a political response to the considerable public pressure rather than professional reappraisal of the issue. This was driven by the perceived political appeal of the newly emerging environmental discourse, allowing the government to go into the 1983 election with a populist environmental victory to its credit and gain credibility at the European level. In other areas also, the British were becoming increasingly precautionary even before the decisive experience of "mad cow disease" in the later 1990s.

Science-Based Precaution?

A curious feature of the precautionary principle is that it is often presented as little more than "common sense." Prominent advocates of applying a precautionary approach to cell phone risk in the United Kingdom, such as campaign legal coordinator Alan Meyer, insist that it is only the extension of common human practice to the sphere of scientific innovation, in a presentation clearly intended to establish it as an inescapable moral precept.[14] At first sight, the difference between the principle and science-based precaution that accepts "plausible" rather than conclusive evidence of a causal relationships might not be clear. Other accounts emphasize: "The precautionary principle is not new, it stretches back at least to the Hippocratic oath whose injunction is: 'First, Do No Harm.' It is also widespread in our daily lives..." (Raffensperger and Tickner 1999: 1). This raises the obvious question: if it is so self-evident and historically rooted, why is it only at the end of the twentieth century that it has been thought necessary to enshrine precaution as a principle? Belying its presentation as little more than a self-evident human truth, its systematic extension to the scientific and other institutional spheres actually marks a decisive departure from traditional scientific approaches, and even the "common sense" of earlier periods not so dominated by the imperative of safety. The original elaborators of the concept are clear on this point:

In a nutshell, precaution challenges the established scientific method; it tests the application of cost-benefit analysis in those areas where it is undoubtedly weakest... it calls for changes to established legal principles and practices such as liability, compensation, and burden of proof; and it challenges politicians to think through longer time frames than the next election or the immediate economic recession. Precaution also exposes the existing discipline bound and reductionist organization of academic research and raises difficult issues about the quality of life for future generations and other species. It is profoundly radical and potentially very unpopular... a profound challenge to some of the unstated assumptions of modern... societies: material growth, the power and efficacy of scientific reason, and the pre-eminence of human interests over other entities... the human race is a colonizing species without an institutional or intellectual capacity for equilibrium. (Jordan and O'Riordan 1999: 27)

Their version of the precautionary principle is thus a challenge to some of the basic working assumptions of modern society, certainly the science that underpins it. In this sense it seems surprising not only that it has been accepted so readily and quickly established as a guiding policy principle, but that this has occurred with so little controversy. The precautionary principle is also an explicit dogma, demanding precaution *on principle* as it does. This is quite at odds with a relativistic era that generally rejects prescriptive, all-embracing beliefs.

---

[14] At the beginning of his speeches at cell phone risk conferences such as the IBC conference, London, 7–8 December 2000, Meyer asserts that the precautionary principle is basic common sense.

It is important to recognize that the precautionary principle emerges from environmental sensibilities and policy making, rather than scientific discourse. Citing the introduction to Rachel Carson's seminal environmental classic, *Silent Spring*, a recent American account suggests that the principle proceeds from the assumption that "[m]an has lost the capacity to foresee and forestall...he will end up destroying the earth" (Raffensperger and Tickner 1999: 1). This is clear from another explanation of the principle's assumptions: "The environment should not be expected to signal pain upon being hurt; it is up to humanity, as a matter of moral principle, to recognize that pain might be imposed and to adopt appropriate avoidance..." (Jordan and O'Riordan 1999: 23). O'Riordan is quite clear that this is a "moral principle" that has been "culturally framed" and therefore "evolved along different pathways," so that all-encompassing definition remains elusive. His principal concern is that the concept's inherent instability will mean that its profound challenge to the existing organizing principles of society will be blunted, as it ends up being watered down (ibid.: 17). His is a "strong" version of the precautionary principle.

The precautionary principle has been criticized for its poor definition and for being of little use in framing specific precautionary policy. Economists such as Pearce (1994) suggest that it fails the test of marginal utility trade-offs, as it cannot justify its costs. Lomborg documents the enormous and, for him, unjustified expense with regard to essentially precautionary climate control measures and American environmental legislation more generally (Lomborg 2001). A few scientists go further than economic or definitional argument, toward more principled objection. Gray (1990) has rejected the principle, since, by definition, it does not have to rely on scientific evidence. Some argue that it is a prescription for paralysis, as, no matter what the interpretation, the onus of proof is shifted onto those proposing change. Prominent scientist George Poste characterizes the principle as fundamentally reactionary. He asserts that "none of the remarkable advances in agriculture, chemistry, computing, energy, metallurgy and materials, medicine and telecommunications that have transformed living standards over the last two centuries would have overcome the hurdle of the precautionary principle" (*Financial Times*, 28 October 1999). Aspirin is perhaps the most commonly cited example of a scientific breakthrough that might fail contemporary precautionary scrutiny. Professor Sir Colin Berry, professor of morbid anatomy and histopathology at Queen Mary College, University of London, argues that the principle is based on irrational assumptions that belittle the achievements of medicine.[15] French scientific critics judge that it hampers innovation and progress, leads to greater bureaucracy, and squanders funds in the pointless pursuit of "zero risk" (Tubiana 2000). Criticism of precaution as a barrier to progress was more systematically developed in Wildavsky's critique, which suggested that society needed more than the easy "no" of precaution. Without an ability to say "yes" to experimental innovation, society will be paralyzed in his estimation. With regard to more contemporary policy, Morris (2000) challenges the precautionary principle on a range of issues, while Durodie (1996) usefully contests its application by the European Union in the banning of the phthalate group of chemicals.

Beyond this handful of critics, it is striking that there is relatively little open criticism of what is, considered historically, an extraordinary step. Overall, there is a "remarkable consensus" that precaution should frame decisions affecting the environment (Jordan and O'Riordan 1999: 22). The vast majority of scientific opinion has acquiesced to precaution, even if it seeks to ease it onto more scientific terrain by insisting on adherence to scientifically based criteria (Foster et al. 2000). The thinking appears to be that it is futile to offer a principled rejection because the ascendancy of precaution is assured. Scientists, along with the rest of society, sense that whatever its problems and limitations, the principle is a concept "whose time has come." Particularly from scientific quarters there have been attempts to prove that scientific inquiry is compatible with the essentially value-driven demand for precaution. This suggests that science will live to fight another day, and appears to be the reasoning behind the Stewart Report into cell phones in the United Kingdom. Demonstrating that an inquiry can be both scientific in character yet precautionary in its conclusions was the message of the British committee.

From the perspective of a more science-based risk assessment it is difficult to understand how the precautionary principle should be explicitly applied in the cell phone case. The use of the principle in a scientific manner was highlighted in a recent and authoritative European Union statement designed to limit its arbitrariness (Commission of the European Communities 2000). Scientific authorities have drawn attention to the commission's recent guidelines as a means of ensuring appropriate application (Foster et al. 2000; Vecchia 2000b). Drawing on the U.S. National Research Council's renowned "red book" of risk assessment,

---

[15] See "Risk, Science and Society" at www.spiked-online.com (1 November 2001) for an edited version of his speech given at the Royal Institution, London.

the European Commission statement emphasizes the need for "reliable scientific data" and, importantly, argues that a potentially hazardous effect must be identified before implementation of the precautionary principle is triggered. The actual scale of the hazard is central to the European Commission guidelines, and it also emphasizes the wide range of possible precautionary actions, including no action at all. In the case of cell phone risk it can be argued that there is a potentially considerable hazard, simply because of the number of users. Yet, as has been explained, no potential hazard has been confirmed. Unexplained subtle "effects" in a few studies do not constitute a hazard. There is too much "uncertainty about the case for uncertainty," so to speak, in the cell phone case to justify science-based precautionary measures.

The recent European Commission guidelines remain only one of many interpretations of implementing the principle. They cannot be regarded as intellectually representative, even if they are authoritative because of the commission's influence and importance. The precautionary principle is necessarily elastic, derived as it is from the wider politics of precaution. Elsewhere, the Commission's Consumer Committee proposed its application, "even where there is no known scientific uncertainty." Furthermore, it argued that when the scientific evidence was available, "too great an emphasis on this may be undesirable from the consumer's point of view" (cited in Durodie 1996: 26). But while we might expect that an ecological lobby group or anti-EMF activists would happily endorse precaution under any circumstances, it is more surprising that scientific authorities are effectively endorsing a non-science-based policy without rigorous justification. The "anecdotal evidence suggesting a hazard" cited by Stewart Committee scientists Maier, Blakemore, and Koivisto above (2000) should not be sufficient to invoke the principle, if it is to be claimed that a science-based policy is being pursued.

Implementing policy against a "phantom risk" has confusing consequences. There is a significant problem with introducing "scientific" precautionary measures on the basis of speculation about negative health effects, illustrated by the demand that specific absorption rate (SAR) levels be printed on mobile handsets, SAR being a measure of how much radio-wave energy the body receives.[16] Measuring SAR is controversial. The technical methodology by which SAR is measured was not agreed internationally until the European Commission published an agreed standard on

---

[16] For a fuller technical explanation of SAR, see, e.g., "Radio Frequency Investigation Limited" at http://www.rfi-wireless.com.

SAR test protocol in August 2001. The American FCC and the European Commission have averaged the rate of absorption into the head over different masses, 1 gram and 10 grams, respectively. A measure of the confusion is that the British Consumers Association claimed, with their testing methods, that cell phones equipped with hands-free kits designed to reduce radiation exposure actually did the opposite, as they redirected radiation to the rest of the body.

Consumer groups are in favor of SAR levels being printed on handsets and their relationship to health concerns explained, much as they have successfully lobbied the European Union for the labeling of any food product that has in any way come into contact with genetically modified products. The Stewart Inquiry called for public access to SAR values, recommending that they be printed on handset packaging, in leaflets at the point of purchase, on labels on the handset and accessible to the LCD screen, and on a dedicated website. The cell phone industry, on the other hand, has long been reluctant on the basis that it would not be possible to represent the information to consumers in any useful way, and would lead to safety comparisons between different handsets that were without meaning.

Acceding to the demand for the publication of SAR levels in the summer of 2000, the cell phone industry has been attempting to establish a suitable wording for consumer explanation, but this is more than a linguistic problem. What might seem a sensible move in printing SAR levels on phones (or their packaging) actually illustrates the difficulty of matching precautionary appeasement of anxiety with any scientific or social meaning. SAR values for a handset are maximum values that do not reflect exposure in everyday use because they constantly adapt to the minimum power required to make a call. Furthermore, we should recall that the entire basis for continued uncertainty concerns the possibility of unexplained nonthermal effects that defy conventional thinking. In this context, precautionary measures based on the SAR of cell phones make little sense. If there were such a nonthermal effect, it would evidently be related to frequency, rather than the intensity of radiation measured by the SAR. In other words, the SAR bears no relationship to the problem, a problem that is only a hypothetical possibility in the first place. Beyond an insistence that no significance be attached to the SAR levels of individual handsets, it is difficult to imagine what explanation can be provided for consumers. Precautionary leaflets explain that "[u]sers may wish to take account of these relative SAR values when choosing a mobile phone" (Department of Health 2000). Exactly how they might "take account" of this highly contested measure of radio signals remains unclear.

More curious than the SAR example is the promotion of precautionary measures in relation to cell tower emissions. Such measures rest on the realm of perception, rather than anything scientific or even simply rational. If people feel threatened or stressed by the presence of something, then a precautionary response now appears to be deemed appropriate, in the British case, at least. Meanwhile, misconceptions and misunderstandings, such as the confusion between the possible effect from cell phones and from cell towers, remain unclarified in the public domain. There have been many different national responses to cell phone risk besides the British, and this is the subject of the next chapter.

5

Diffusing Anxiety

International Dissemination and National Responses to Mobile Fears

Activism, Diffusion and European Responses to EMF Risk

There are substantial differences in the way that different societies have responded to cell phone EMF. Such differences are not unique to this issue, but are evident in relation to radiation concerns more generally, as illustrated by the case of the naturally occurring gas radon. The need for a general household radon policy is highly contested, as there is little evidence to confirm that radon at ground levels represents a significant cancer risk independently of other factors, notably, smoking (Cole 1993).

Ernest Letourneau, director of Canada's Radiation Protection Bureau, showed a world map to an audience in 1991. Seven countries were highlighted, the only ones with proposed or adopted radon standards: Canada, Finland, Germany, Norway, Sweden, the United Kingdom, and the United States. The levels of "protection" differed significantly, even among those taking precautionary measures. The level for U.S. action was 4 picocuries, for Sweden it was 10, and Finland 20. Most ignored a recommendation from the European Commission to adopt a 10 picocurie (per litre of air) standard.[1] Somewhat sardonically, Letourneau commented: "As you see, radon is a disease that spreads North." He dismissed the possibility that variations in radon concentration could account for the differences. Hazarding an explanation, Letourneau suggested that "[t]he geographic configuration is related to luxury ... the luxury of worrying about risk that most countries don't feel is worth

---

[1] A curie, named after the French physicists, is the amount of radioactivity emitted by the decay of a gram of radium. A picocurie is one-trillionth of a curie.

worrying about." He added that only with a sense of the absurd could it be imagined that countries such as Bangladesh or Ethiopia might be considering radon policies, given the expense of acting against an uncertain problem. More specifically in Letourneau's view, the Nordic, Anglo-Saxon, and German societies have more activist environmental values than the French, Latins, and others (ibid.: 141).

Besides wealth and environmental values, wider issues of trust and anxiety were also put forward to explain the dramatically different reactions to radon. A Swedish expert suggested that they were "less neurotic" than in the United States (ibid.: 176). Neighboring Finland demonstrated markedly less concern than even the Swedes: "Finnish people are not very hysterical. They trust authority, and so they assume there is no big problem" (ibid.: 183). Finland is one country positively disinclined to elevate cell phone EMF concerns, as well as the earlier radon issue. Besides the possibility of greater trust within Finnish society, this reflects the crucial importance of the cell phone manufacturer Nokia to the economy, and a still positive attitude toward science and technology more generally (see Chapter 6). Other societies such as Ireland have not systematically engaged with the issue, despite the early appearance of some localized reactions. By contrast, in Italy, Switzerland, and Australia, mobile EMF risk has acquired a high profile and led to restrictions on EMF that are at odds with the international community.

Cell phone EMF concerns have spread from their original appearance, in the Reynard lawsuit in the United States, to many other societies. This is partly the result of the determined efforts of activists, who have set up websites to circulate speculation about negative health effects. As well as *Microwave News*, the *EMF Guru* website has become an influential source for those interested in negative health effects from electromagnetism, among several others. National campaigning bodies such the EMR Alliance in the United States and the British-based Mast Action U.K. have their own websites, as do many more localized anti-tower groups.[2] These websites provide an important focus for not only the distribution of materials but establishing international networks. The website for CARE, for example, a local American campaign group, provides links to the websites of British campaigners Roger Coghill and Alasdair Philips and to Australian opposition sites such as the Electromagnetic Radiation Alliance.[3] In representing

---

[2] EMR Alliance at http://www2.cruzio.com/~rbedard/emrall.html and Mast Action U.K. at http://freespace.virginnet.co.uk/mast.action.

[3] http://www.c-a-r-e.org.

local claims it is very common for protesters to cite information drawn from such international sources, particularly the existence of more precautionary measures in other countries. The adoption of more restrictive standards in another country or even region is, for activists, compelling proof of the legitimacy of their own demands for action.

A number of what might be termed "risk entrepreneurs" have traveled internationally, disseminating arguments about health concerns from societies where fears are more developed to those where they are less known.[4] Many conferences have been held on the issue of EMF, mobile phones, towers, and health, and it is also through this "conference circuit" that an, albeit limited, international network has cohered. American activist Libby Kelly from the Council on Wireless Technology Impacts (CWTI) established links with key U.K. campaigner Margaret Dean through the Internet and e-mail. As a result, Kelly flew to the United Kingdom and addressed the meeting at the British House of Commons in June 1999 that first raised the political profile of British anti-tower activism. The British science lecturer Dr. Gerard Hyland, himself a key speaker at the Westminster event, has subsequently become increasingly prominent at European conferences on the issue, as well as continuing to advise local anti-tower campaigns in the United Kingdom.[5]

The most ubiquitous campaigner in these international forums has been Neil Cherry from New Zealand, described as a "bio-meteorologist and elected official" in publicity. Cherry has spoken at a series of anti-EMF meetings in the United States and has also addressed many other international events. In March 1998, Cherry went on a speaking tour in California, Colorado, and Massachusetts organized by the CWTI. After explaining, "I am not an expert," he justified his activities during the tour on the basis that "[p]eople are thirsty for information, and I am able to confirm that their fears are based on science, not mere innuendo" (*Microwave News*, March/April 1998). Back in Australasia he also conducted speaking tours, but has attracted pointed criticism in the more charged political environment with regard to EMF in Australia (see below). He has been denounced by Australian Communications Minister Senator Richard Alston as a "shameless charlatan" (*Sunday Mail* – Queensland, 16 March 1997).

---

4 Following the category of "moral entrepreneurs," denoting those central to the construction of moral panics, in the work of Cohen (1972), among others.
5 Hyland addressed European MEPs at the European Technology Symposium in Brussels in April 1999, for example.

Many of these activists were brought together at a forum in Austria during June 2000 that questioned existing EMF exposure limits for base stations from a public health perspective. The event was the most focused event to date, attempting to pressure international authorities into a non-scientific precautionary stance on mobile EMF, and was publicized as an exemplary approach by activists as far afield as Australia.[6]

The conference was presented in dramatic terms, reminiscent of a fully fledged political movement. The conference website declares the Salzburg event a "turning point" and "an information offensive with historical significance."[7] The principal focus of attack was the international guidelines of the International Commission on Non-Ionizing Radiation Protection (ICNIRP), dismissed as "scientifically untenable and on the other hand not able to protect human health." An official from Salzburg's Public Health Department welcomed the participants with a description of WHO as "blind in one eye or deaf in one ear" for its reliance on the ICNIRP's recommendations. Berating the absence at the conference of recognized authorities from these bodies, the official identified an "arrogance and disdain for those who think differently; we should not leave the public in the dark about it." Arguably, such strident language only underlined their isolation from mainstream scientific opinion and wider influence, however. The wider irony is that ICNIRP's exposure levels are already precautionary, with an additional safety factor of five above established limits such as those of the United Kingdom, and WHO can hardly be accused of ignoring the alleged risk of cell phone EMF given its large-scale ongoing research program.

It is revealing to note the list of speakers at the Austrian event. Along with Neil Cherry, and Louis Slesin from *Microwave News*, there was a regional EPA official and two American EMF "consultants," as well as other American EMF activists. An official from the Health Promotion and Environmental Protection Office of Toronto Public Health was on the speaker panel. While cell phone fears have not become prominent in Canada, there has been some publicity and campaigning in Toronto, the city where the possible link between miscarriage and VDTs was first aired. Significantly, with regard to the contemporary story of cell phone fears, other speakers were Livio Guiliani from the Italian National Institute of

---

[6] Letter to *Courier Mail* (Brisbane) from Landborough/Mount Mellum Action Group, 15 November 2000.

[7] International Conference on Celltower Siting, Salzburg, Austria, 7–8 June 2000. See www.land-sbg.gv.at/celltower.

Occupational Safety and Prevention (ISPESL) and another Italian scientist, reflecting the importance of Italy to anti-EMF campaigning in Europe and the specific role of the ISPESL in determining Italy's distinctive position. It is also revealing that a public health official from Scotland and another Scottish expert addressed the Salzburg event. The adoption of precautionary measures by local Scottish councils established the momentum for campaigning across the United Kingdom, and Scotland remains an important center for local U.K. campaigning. More significant, the new national Parliament has argued for the legitimacy of health concerns despite the difficulties this presents for decisions in planning controls. A report of the Scottish Parliament in 2000, for example, "clearly states that health is a factor that should be taken into account," to some consternation from the cell phone industry.[8]

Yet typically localized reaction against towers is not readily generalized into a wider campaign simply through the intervention of activist claims makers. In an episode characteristic of reactions against cell towers throughout Europe, two men whose houses were closest to cell transmitters sited on a water tower in the Belgian village of Hoeilaart began a lobbying campaign. A petition was signed by eighty inhabitants, and, by order of the Telecommunications Minister, radiation levels were measured. Although the village mayor announced that the results showed levels too low to cause harm, the inhabitants of the community were reportedly not reassured and still preferred the transmitters to be relocated. One of the lobbyists, Peter Vanhove, was then contacted by the founder of a new organization against masts, asking him whether he would formally establish a group locally. But Vanhove refused, explaining that he wasn't a "fanatic" (*De Standaard*, 10 August 2000). His objections were very practically based, driven by a desire for more discrete tower siting, rather than the fervent beliefs of anti-EMF activism. The Belgian case is also revealing and symptomatic in that, despite the failure to generalize anti-mast activism, some momentum had subsequently been established to restricting tower erection by the precautionary response of local and national authorities. Belgian cell phone operators are claiming that regional and federal intransigence is preventing them from catering for exploding cell phone demand, with approximately 1,000 planning decisions undecided. In a press release, the Belgian operators' association, Mobistar, issued an

---

[8] Scottish Transport and the Environment Committee, "Report on Inquiry into the Proposals to Introduce New Planning Procedures for Telecommunications Developments" (3rd Report 2000).

ultimatum to the regional and federal authorities, insisting that unless the situation with planning consents improves they will be forced to commence court action for compensation. Mobistar argued that having paid a high price to operate the system, "licenses are . . . in effect, becoming useless" (cited in *Mobilex Environment Monthly*, November 2001).

The process of diffusion has been facilitated not only by lone individuals attempting to set up national campaigns and the efforts of international EMF activists, but also by institutionalized responses to health concerns from some organizations and nations that have invited others to follow suit. The publicizing of alleged dangers from hands-free kits by the British Consumers Association led to its sister organization in Australia promoting the same issue in August 2000, for example. Despite the lack of the high-profile media campaign on the issue that characterized U.K. anti-EMF responses, the French authorities produced their own report in direct response to the British Stewart Inquiry. Gathering together a group of experts in exactly the same manner, the *Rapport Zmirou* came to the same precautionary conclusions two years later, while similarly acknowledging the lack of evidence for harm from mobile EMF (Directeur General de la Sante 2001). The French initiative was interesting because there was no evidence to suggest it was a response to determined media pressure, indeed, any direct pressures related specifically to cell phones at all. Neither cell phones nor towers have been the subject of significant concern in France.

The origins of the French expert inquiry appear to emanate from a wider problem of political legitimacy. In an even more aggravated fashion than in other European nations, the French political class has sought to demonstrate very publicly its commitment to consumer safety, regardless of the extent of specific concern about particular issues. This dynamic was evident in the row between the United Kingdom and France that dominated European affairs at the end of 1999 over the refusal of the latter to lift the ban on British beef because of continued suspicions about "mad cow disease." Significantly, the French explained their refusal as an absolute commitment to the safety of the consumer, a commitment said to be so binding as to take precedence over the European Union law that compelled a lifting of restrictions. In an official communiqué, the government insisted that "France cannot lift the ban on British beef . . . [because] the government is driven as a priority by a concern for public health and consumer safety" (cited in Burgess 2001: 95). As was widely acknowledged, French obduracy had its roots in French politicians' extreme sensitivity toward consumer health issues since the HIV-infected blood affair in the

1980s.[9] The resignations that followed led to a wider collapse of authority that was intimately bound up with issues of consumer safety. *Le Monde* explained that the infected blood scandal had left the French political class "traumatized.... They see in it a major reason for the loss of legitimacy from which politics is suffering in France" (cited in ibid.: 95). It is unsurprising, in the context of attempting to recover the lost legitimacy through the same sphere of consumer safety, that the French authorities felt compelled to stage their own cell phone inquiry, and thereby further affirm their newfound identity as guardians of consumer health and safety.

The establishment of ultra-precautionary standards in some nations also invites others to follow, in a more compelling manner than the campaigning actions of a few individuals. In Toronto, one report described how "residents...hardly seemed to notice" the city's 7,000 cell phone transmitters, even if the city did have one elderly activist known as the "tower lady" who traveled around municipalities trying to generate opposition (Garrison 2001). Toronto's Board of Health certainly did notice and respond to the issue, however. Following complaints from one group of residents, an inquiry was launched. One of the scientists brought in by the Health Department was Henry Lai, who argued that exposure should be kept to a minimum on the basis of his experimental conclusions. The Public Health Department then called for the EMF standard to be tightened by a factor of 100, "to bring Canada in line with Italy and Switzerland." Attempts to bring guidelines for radiation levels down to more universally recognized limits also invite alarm. Australian federal proposals to bring limits into line with European standards led to fierce reaction from campaigners and headlines about a "doubling" of radiation levels (*Courier-Mail*, 21 April 2001).

Initiatives from European Union institutions are especially influential in the diffusion of health concerns because of their Europe-wide authority. Following the 1992 Reynard lawsuit in the United States, it was through the European Union that mobile concerns were next reported internationally, through the news agency Reuters (3 October 1995), and then in the United Kingdom (*Financial Times*, 4 October 1995). In October 1995, under political pressure from the European Parliament, the European Commission publicly announced a special investigation into

[9] More than 1,200 people died and some 3,600 were diagnosed HIV positive after the transfusion service, ignoring medical warnings, used blood contaminated with the virus. The scandal led to the defeat of the previous Socialist government and criminal charges against a former prime minister and two of his cabinet colleagues.

the effects of radioactivity on the health of mobile phone users. Several members of the European Parliament (MEPs) have subsequently promoted the issue of cell phone dangers, and these initiatives have figured prominently in substantiating activists' demands for government action in their own countries.[10] U.K. MEP Stephen Hughes urged the European Parliament to impose more restrictive radiation limits in 1996, while Italian MEP Gianni Tamino put forward a motion on health concerns in 1999 with support from U.K. anti-EMF activists. In March 1999 the European Parliament stated that "it is imperative to protect members of the general public in the community against established adverse health or potentially harmful long term effects that may result as a consequence of exposure to EMF fields." Influential activist Graeme McAlister from Friends of the Earth (FoE) Scotland, declared in a press release that the European Commission statement demonstrated official recognition for nonthermal effects.[11] McAlister's publicity and lobbying was the most important influence in pushing Scottish local councils to adopt precautionary policies, moves that were then imitated in the rest of the United Kingdom. If McAlister might have overstated the scientific significance of the European Commission declaration, the authority it provided certainly proved important to campaigning success in Scotland and the rest of the United Kingdom.

The setting of differential standards and political interventions around cell phone fears have been important factors in pushing the profile and diffusion of concerns internationally. Conversely, where official responses have principally confined themselves to funding further research, the impact of the issue has been more limited. The precautionary approach toward environmental affairs was innovated in Germany, where environmentalism is a vital part of the contemporary national identity and consciousness (see Chapter 4). There is considerable media interest in the cell phone issue, as demonstrated by German scientists' concern about media interpretation of experiments, described in Chapter 4. Some reports even suggest a comparatively high level of public concern about cell phone EMF among the country's 48 million subscribers.[12] Yet by comparison with the

---

[10] In the early 1999, MEPs Gianni Tamino, Charles Tannock, and Philip Whitehead (on behalf of the Environment Committee of the European Parliament), for example, urged precaution and continuous monitoring of low-level radiation.

[11] Press release from Graeme McAlister of FoE Scotland, 30 March 1999.

[12] In conversation with the author, Hans Kastenholz at the Center for Technology Assessment in Baden-Württemburg indicated a high number of telephone inquiries from the public about cell phone and tower safety.

United Kingdom, the German reaction has been restrained. The German authorities were quick to acknowledge the issue when it first emerged in the early 1990s, but their response was very clearly concentrated on a demonstrated commitment to initiating scientific investigation.

Reflecting the country's heightened environmental regulatory framework, the German Radiological Protection Commission announced in December 1991 that cell phones could no longer be exempt from health standards on the basis of their low emissions, and that companies would now have to prove that phones complied with safety limits. The industry responded quite early to emerging concern. German Telekom allocated $3 million for health research at a number of institutes in 1993, for example. Manufacturers, network operators, and governmental authorities have subsequently funded a dedicated institute, the Forschungsgemeinschaft Funk. Research projects into possible health effects have been carried out throughout the 1990s. As recently as July 2001 the Environment Ministry announced a further 1 million Euros to be spent on wireless health concerns. There was also a ready-made infrastructure in Germany through which such issues could be dealt with in a technical, rather than politicized, form. The practice of technology assessment is an established and influential practice carried out at a number of regional centers. More important, the government is not so responsive to media-generated concerns as it is in the United Kingdom, nor so newly intent on demonstrating its commitment to consumer safety as in France. Before the results were known, politicians generally refused to be further drawn on the issue. Even the influential Green Party did not fundamentally break from a consensus that restricted the German response to the funding of research. While continued research ensures periodic bursts of publicity around their findings, the issue has not acquired any sustained momentum.

German discussion remains focused on whether evidence suggests any harm. As a consequence, cell phone EMF is a localized issue in Germany, focused on towers rather than handsets, and with no national focus to cohere responses. One German expert explains: "There have been no significant events in Germany which influenced the mobile phone issue on a national level. In fact, the controversy about mobile phones and masts is very much a local issue which is usually triggered by the siting of transmitter stations."[13] Local campaigning is particularly strong in southern Germany, and there is also an Internet-based environmentalist

[13] Electronic correspondence with Holger Schuetz, 12 January 2001.

campaign against "electrosmog" that has managed to generate some publicity.[14]

There were signs from late 2000 that long after the controversy had abated in the United Kingdom, in Germany greater prominence is being devoted to health fears by prominent officials and politicians. During a recent media interview, the head of the German radiological protection agency criticized phone companies for disregarding concern about the siting of masts and urged parents to stop children from using mobile phones, for example (*Berliner Zeitung*, 11 August 2001). In December 2001, German operators acceded to federal pressures to a set of precautionary measures, including handset labeling, in a bid to fend off any proposals for extreme precautionary Swiss-style exposure limits. Yet overall, the German experience to date is interesting in suggesting that even in a society readily susceptible to risk concerns, political restraint and consensus limit the potential for controversy. As more generally, the indispensability of the cell phone is the most important factor in limiting the potential for the issue to impinge on public and political consciousness.

The Marginalization of Mobile Tower Health Concerns in the United States

The reaction of state authority appears to play a crucial role in determining the extent to which cell phone concerns make a wider impact. A closer examination of the issue's evolution in particular national contexts demonstrates this role. The starting point is the development of cell phone anxieties in the United States subsequent to the Reynard lawsuit, which illustrates the limits of cell phone concerns under circumstances where the state does not publicize or endorse precautionary health concerns. The most important examples where concerns have become more prominent are Italy, Switzerland, and Australia, and these cases are examined at some length. Australia is important because it was there that "mobile fears" first became apparent after the United States, and led to an innovative state strategy based on dealing with earlier concerns about power lines. The Italian experience is similarly central in the international story of mobile EMF, because the state adopted an explicitly nonscientific response, which, alongside Swiss standards, is uniquely precautionary.

---

[14] This campaign organized the circulation of a letter to U.N. Secretary General Kofi Annan, asking for a moratorium on all telecommunications until the health issue is resolved. See their website at http://www.buergerwelle.de/d/dindex.html.

At the beginning of 1999, *Microwave News* ran the headline, "The Action Moves to Europe." Slesin regretted that while in Europe, "the issue of EMF health effects has been placed in a public health context. In America, it has more often been treated as a battle best left to individuals and their lawyers." Slesin added that attitudes toward business were too favorable in the United States compared with Europe; the United States remains averse to business regulation, and "industry is generally given the benefit of the doubt." As a consequence, although the idea of "prudent avoidance" was an American one, "it seems to have taken firmer root across the Atlantic" (*Microwave News*, January/February 1999). An interesting cultural reflection of this contrast is that although a cell tower was central to an episode of the American animated TV show *The Simpsons*, the issue of health risks was entirely absent. The principal consequence of the transmitter being placed on the Simpsons' roof was that the mother, Marge, was able to listen in on other people's conversations! At a more serious level, a congressional review of cell phones and health commissioned by Senators Joseph Lieberman and Edward Markey reiterated the scientific consensus that despite no proven health effect, there was not, as yet, sufficient information to conclude that there is no risk. The review, an update of an earlier report, was factual rather than precautionary, leading the industry body the CTIA to describe it as "both balanced and fair" (cited in *Mobilex Environment Monthly*, May 2001).[15]

Compared with many European countries, local protest and media coverage of cell phone health risks is relatively subdued in the United States. This is despite the issue's early emergence and the continuing legal actions subsequent to the Reynard case. It is also despite the campaign having had the support of a well-known figure from the world of entertainment, the former *Dallas* star Linda Evans.[16] The failure to find a celebrity "front" for the campaign against cell phones was felt to be the key limitation of the British campaign by its most consistent journalistic champion.[17] Yet

---

[15] *Research and Regulatory Efforts on Mobile Phone and Health Issues* was released by the General Accounting Office on 22 May 2001, and is available at http://www.gao.gov./new.items/do1545.pdf.

[16] Alongside Henry Lai and Neil Cherry, Linda Evans was a speaker at a public forum staged by the CWTI in April 1999 at Tiburon, California.

[17] Interview with Cathy Moran of the *Express* newspaper, 23 August 2000. Television presenter Gloria Hunniford and model Jerry Hall, among others, have lent their names to specific U.K. protests, but only pop music promoter and son-in-law of Hunniford's, Russ Lindsay, became anything like a more consistent "face" for the campaign.

the far greater impact made by cell phone fears in the United Kingdom, in the absence of a famous supporter, suggests that even in a celebrity-obsessed age this factor is not decisive.

The cell phone is now even associated with safety, rather than hazards in the United States. Several West Coast states were considering repealing bans on cell phones on school grounds in late September 2001, for example. The ban existed because of their association with drug dealing in the 1980s. Now, in the wake of the Columbine shootings, when students raised the alarm via mobiles, sponsors of the original legislation are proposing its repeal. The cell phone perhaps also demonstrated its potential with the pitiful calls from on board the doomed airliners on September 11. Mary Flowers, who introduced legislation banning mobiles in Illinois in 1985, now says: "We know that these are not safe times. Our safety net is gone, and the security of a cell phone can help restore it" (*Mobilex Environment Monthly*, October 2001).

With continuing legal action, the mobile phone handset issue in the United States is not resolved, but it is contained. At the same time, there is evidence to suggest that, as in Europe, towers rather than handsets are now at the center of concern. One of the foremost American authorities on nonionizing radiation, who maintains a highly influential website for advice, reports five to six calls per day for advice on base station issues, compared with only one for handsets since late 2000.[18] In May 1999 there were estimated to be at least seventy community groups across the United States to combat local construction of towers and antennae.[19] The campaign focuses on specific cell tower confrontations, notably the Sutro tower in San Francisco, and the Canyon Area Residents for the Environment (CARE) campaign against the "antenna farm" in Golden, Colorado. It is important to recognize, however, that campaigning in the United States is not specific to emissions from cellular base stations. It concerns a wider range of facilities, reflecting the much longer period over which various forms of electromagnetism have been successively problematized. The high-profile CARE campaign, for example, is directed against TV/FM broadcast antennas and radar, and is now focused on stopping a high-powered "supertower" being erected on Lookout Mountain in their area of Colorado. Campaigns are localized, although there have been some

[18] John Moulder of the University of Wisconsin in a speech to IBC conference, London, 7–8 December 2000.
[19] Alison Sloan, "The Cellular Tower Wars," *Green Guide, Mothers and Others*, May 1999.

well-organized events on the issue.[20] The most influential groups are the Council on Wireless Technology Impacts (CWTI), founded in 1996, and the EMR network, based in Vermont and launched in 1998.

Without making any sort of wider impact, opposition to cell towers began in the early 1990s, as *Microwave News* documented throughout that period. In Morelands Hill, Ohio, a local elementary school agreed to host a tower in November 1990 but encountered opposition led by a local businessman. In January 1992 at Fisher Middle School in Los Gatos, California, local activists, led by attorney Mark Portman, opposed tower planning permission. An environmental impact report was submitted in May 1993, which reported no problems, but local activists complained that the authors of the report had shown bias. On the basis of a study by Dr. Bill Guy, the planning commission rejected the environmental assessment and refused permission, provoking the company, Mobilnet, to threaten legal action and look for another site. By the end of 1993, in the wake of the Reynard case, local opposition to mobile towers began to be more systematically reported. In Merton, Wisconsin, opponents of Ameritech's plans for a tower on a high school football field claimed victory. The planning commission refused the application after submissions from community activists. In Sarasota, Florida, opponents of a Cellular One tower to be sited near an elementary school were also successful. In Lincoln Park, New Jersey, a tower was rejected by the town council. Another site was opposed at nearby Boonton because of its proximity to a children's playground. The mobile operator sued the town, but lost. In November 1995, New York's Supreme Court affirmed the right of the town of Harrison in Westchester County to impose a ninety-day moratorium on mast erection, although the decision rejected any health grounds for the move. However, a similar moratorium in nearby Tarrytown on towers, based on public perception of a health risk, had earlier been overturned. There were also numerous attempts to block mast construction in Washington State (*Microwave News*, November/December 1995).

At the state level, the issue of mobile towers centered on the desirability of siting them near schools. San Francisco became the first major city to ban towers from school property in late 1993. The decision was based on the views of an official from the Department of Health Services that there was no need to expose children to something that "was not yet

---

[20] The EMR Network held a Cell Tower Forum on 2 December 2000, in Litchfield, Connecticut, for example. There were many prestigious speakers, including several senators. See http://www.emrnetwork.org/conference/conferences.htm.

thoroughly studied" (*Microwave News*, November/December 1993). On 8 November 1995, the California Public Utilities Commission urged cellular companies to avoid building masts on schools or hospitals, using them only as a last resort. The decision explicitly referred to unanswered scientific questions, arguing that "public perception about potential health problems will continue to exist as long as there remain unanswered and unexplored questions in the scientific community on the EMF and RF radiation issue." The Connecticut state Parent Teacher Association passed a resolution in May 1994 seeking legislation on the issue of EMF safety and suggesting that towers should be at least 200 yards away from schools "until scientific evidence...conclusively determined them to be safe" (*Microwave News*, November/December 1995). Palm Beach County in Florida also banned masts from schools in late 1997, following the advice of the California Public Utilities Commission to keep antennas away from schools.

The mobile phone industry was becoming frustrated at local decisions attempting to prevent or slow down the roll-out of the system. The industry complained that some localities were setting exposure standards more stringent than those used by the official federal body, the FCC. They vigorously petitioned Congress and won a tactical victory in August 1995 when President Clinton ordered federal facilities to be made available for mobile tower siting. Industry pressure eventually led to the Telecommunications Act of 1996, which sought to establish a standard over more than 30,000 zoning jurisdictions in the United States. It explicitly sought to "encourage the rapid deployment of new telecommunications technologies and minimize potential hindrances" (Tuesley 1999: 892). At the same time, the act called for cooperation, co-location of towers and education to narrow any gaps between the views of industry and local residents, arguing that "the spur of the 1996 Act is necessary to bring otherwise disinterested parties to the table with providers" (ibid.: 911). The chairman of the FCC explained that "the goal here is to find a way to make sure that local zoning authorities can work with the wireless industry to make sure that their tower siting needs are accommodated" (ibid.: 906).

The Telecommunications Act did not mean that towers could be put up anywhere without local consultation. In Greenburgh, New York, the local ordinance developed on the basis of the act compelled companies first to consider commercial sites. If the phone companies rejected the commercial site possibilities, a public hearing was necessary before other sites could be considered (*Microwave News*, September/October 1996). At the same time, in a significant test case, the new telecommunications law made an immediate impact in three California siting decisions in early 1996. What *Microwave News* termed the "federal preemption of safety issues" made it possible for contested antennae to be erected by Pacific Bell in San Diego, San Francisco, and San Jose. Opposition to rooftop towers in San Francisco appealed to the earlier decision by the Public Utilities Commission that towers should be kept away from schools and hospitals. Members of the San Francisco planning commission reportedly expressed sympathy for public health concerns but were forbidden by the new federal law from applying safety standards below established federal limits. Much to the irritation of the industry, the San Francisco planning department passed an eighteen-month moratorium on new transmitter sitings in September 1996.

Vermont senators attempted to amend the 1996 act in the following year, but failed to restrict federal pre-emption of local decision making. Siting disputes were not entirely removed by the act, however. Most commonly, city councils attempted to stall the planning process by establishing moratoria on tower erection. On a number of occasions phone companies retaliated with lawsuits and lobbied the FCC to stop the moratoria from being imposed. At the beginning of 1997, the industry association CTIA sent a list of 150 communities with moratoria in place to the FCC requesting action to prevent these local stalling tactics. In response, a group of 160 local authorities dubbing themselves "Concerned Communities" asked the FCC to deny industry's petition. Senator Patrick Leahy introduced a bill in October 1997 to change the federal law, which challenged the exemption of health considerations provided emissions were within FCC limits. Republican Bernie Sanders (also from Vermont) backed similar legislation in the House of Representatives, as activists and unions mounted legal challenges to the FCC's regulation in 1997 (*Microwave News*, November/December 1997). A truce was subsequently brokered between industry and local officials, whereby moratoria were to be recognized as legitimate, but federal control of the overall process remained. In August 1999, Senator Leahy, again unsuccessfully, called for the weakening of the federal control over local siting and also for federally funded research into EMF effects.

The federal regulation of the cell tower issue prevented the setting of local standards and effectively contained the issue within debates about local versus national control. This seems to have been important in preventing health from emerging as a campaigning focus, and health claims were rendered marginal to mobilization for community control of siting decisions. Instead, issues of local control and esthetics have been at the fore in the United States. After the Telecommunications Act, esthetic objections became one of the few bases on which local governments could object to cell towers. It is therefore not surprising that the most influential and well-organized protests are in areas of natural beauty, particularly mountains where towers are very prominent, including Buffalo Mountain in Vermont and Lookout Mountain in Colorado. Most of the political influence in Congress and the House of Representatives comes from the scenic state of Vermont. Esthetic concerns are not at the fore among EMF activists entirely as a preference, however. This is made clear by Libby Kelly of the CWTI, a highly influential activist. Being explicitly denied by the 1996 federal law from opposition on health grounds, "town leaders and planners are becoming cleverer at basing their decisions on visual appeal or character of the neighborhood," she explains. "People learn they should not use the health issue as their lead concern."[21] Even more direct is the financial issue of property prices falling as a result of a nearby tower. A lawsuit in Illinois in the spring of 2001 tried to force Ameritech to take down a tower because of the impact it had on property prices. In a rare victory, compensation was awarded to a Texan couple in 1999 for the ill-defined "nuisance" caused by a cell tower.

The discouraging of specifically health-based complaints not only has shaped the character of neighborhood opposition to cell tower sitings, but also has influenced the forms through which more professionalized opposition has presented its case. Whatever their private convictions about microwave dangers, American anti-EMF campaigners do not exclusively emphasize health issues even in their publicity. In October 1996, the Communications Workers of America (CWA) and EMR Alliance prepared a manual on how communities could best oppose mast erection, for example. The handbook did not dwell on health concerns alone, but aimed "to help communities mobilize against the placement of cell sites or facilities where they believe placement would adversely affect their health, safety, property values and aesthetics of their community."[22] Restoring local control against the federal authorities and limiting commercial encroachment is the priority among activists in the state of New Hampshire. Their website declares that their objective is to

[s]top the further expansion of big government by getting involved. Citizens from around the state appeared at a public hearing with the state to hear why the

---

[21] Cited in correspondence with Libby Kelly, 30 November 2000.
[22] EMR Alliance and Communications Workers of America (CWA), *Your Community Guide to Cellular Phone Towers*, booklet, 1996.

public lands on their mountains are being polluted with commercial enterprises. The state can hear our voice.[23]

The terms of opposition in the United States have been set by the federal response and are expressed principally through law. The chief priority of the CWTI has been to oversee and support a federal court case against the Telecommunications Act. In September 2000, it submitted an appeal to the U.S. Supreme Court "to safeguard public health and restore local control of siting of cellular towers." The key focus was to declare the act "unconstitutional because it violates the rights of local control set forth in the Tenth Amendment."[24]

When EMF health risks are discussed in American campaigners' sometimes vigorous Internet debates, towers are mentioned far less than in their European equivalents. In the United States, mobile phones are much more prominent in public awareness because of lawsuits against manufacturers. This relative lack of concern about tower health issues is reflected in the accounts of the two women who are effectively spokespeople for the campaigning and the industry perspectives. Jo-Ann Basile, vice president of the Telecommunications Industry Association, is the most senior American mobile phone industry spokesperson. Unlike many of her British equivalents, she has a relaxed attitude toward tower siting, reflected in the fact that the industry does not monitor press reactions (as it does in the United Kingdom).[25] Siting is already very sensitively handled by U.S. operators, in her view. Although in conversation she conceded that there are still occasional cases of local "outrage," this can be partly explained by the influence of the Internet. Activists, somewhat ironically, complain of the "army" of industry "communicators" who negotiate with local communities. There is a longer history of engaging "NIMBY" concerns more generally in the United States, such as over toxic waste dumps, and operators were sensitive to potential community opposition from the beginning. The most developed example of the consultative approach employed by the cell phone industry to minimize local opposition is the risk communication strategy of "negotiated rule making" used in Massachusetts (Massachusetts Municipal Association 2000). In an effort to reduce conflict with local municipalities, wireless operators established collaborative forums where local officials and industry representatives

[23] http://www.isga.com/nhtower.
[24] CWTI campaign press release, September 2000.
[25] Informal interview, 8 December 2000.

established uniform standards over mast siting and more generally built greater trust and cooperation.

In a different way, activist Libby Kelly also expresses the low profile of the health issue. She is sure that "people are much more active in opposing antennas and the press covers the stories better in the U.K.," and regrets that only "foreign papers abound with controversies" over studies linking cell phone use to ill health.[26] American campaigners are now quite reliant on the diffusion of reports from abroad, particularly the United Kingdom. BBC *Panorama* documentaries on reported ill effects have been discussed in the United States, and the Stewart Inquiry has proven an important reference point, as it has in other countries. Kelly bemoans insularity and a lack of engagement on the issue among Americans and contrasts it to the greater engagement that she imagines animates Europeans and Australians.

Contrary to Kelly's impression, our research suggests that "public" reaction has actually been quite limited, even in Europe and Australia, and cannot account for the higher profile of the issue. There are a number of other reasons, besides the character of state responses, as to why mobile phone EMF issues appear to have become more prominent in Europe and Australia, having originally emerged in the United States. The less-developed public and media profiles are also related to the fact that mobile phone market penetration in the United States is lower than in much of Europe: 37 percent of the American population in 2000, compared with up to two-thirds of the population in some European countries. There are far fewer cell towers in the United States, particularly relative to population density. American anti-EMF campaigners have not been able to draw on the support of environmental organizations, as has been done in Europe. Kelly points out that the "natural environmental community" of groups such as the Sierra Club have kept out of the issue in the United States. FoE and the Greens have been critical to promoting mobile EMF concerns in Scotland and Italy, by contrast. The absence of a wider campaign also appears to be related to the weakness of the evidence of harm from EMF, a factor apparently more important in the United States than in Europe. As Kelly explains, "some old-timers from other movements are waiting for the RF science to be more conclusive before jumping in." Instead, their "chief allies" are what she terms the "health environmentalists": breast cancer activists, those with "environmental illnesses," alternative health practitioners, and "independent" scientists and

[26] Correspondence with Libby Kelly, 30 November 2000.

engineers.[27] A more straightforward factor is simply the size and complexity of American society. Where it is relatively easy to make an impact with a single issue in the United Kingdom, it is far more difficult in the United States. There could not have been the sort of newspaper campaign against mobiles seen in the United Kingdom for the simple reason that America lacks a widely read national press.

Politicization and State Assimilation of EMF Concerns in Australia

Australian mobile EMF concerns exploded into the public arena after the conclusion of the Reynard lawsuit in 1994, following extensive campaigning around power line ELF. While the issue more slowly evolved over a period of time in the United Kingdom and elsewhere, the community backlash was sudden in Australia, and operators felt forced to evolve an innovative strategic response. Since that time, the mobile industry and the state have attempted to limit concerns through accommodation. Despite or partly because of this, anti-tower protests emerged again in 1999, and the issue continues to be controversial more generally. There is evidence of relatively pronounced public concern having been consolidated. The New South Wales Cancer Council Helpline has its own spokesperson on mobile phones, for example, and indicated in a press release that it perceived "widespread anxiety within the community" regarding cell phones (cited in *Mobilex Environment Monthly*, August 2001). Partially because of the accommodation of anti-EMF activism, Australia has EMF exposure limits significantly below those of ICNIRP, and there is concerted opposition to bringing them into line with international standards. Australian incidents and campaigners figure prominently in the anti–cell phone EMF circuit internationally, reflecting the fact that the issue arose, and industry and the state evolved a response, at a slightly earlier stage than in Europe.[28] Campaigners in many countries draw on the Australian example. The "international perspective" for U.K. activist Roy Ashwood's media publicity was drawn from the Australian experience, for example (Ashwood 1999).

The accommodation of anti-EMF activism has had some chaotic political consequences. Unusually in comparison with other nations, Australian

---

[27] Ibid.
[28] Many key individuals in the mobile health story are Australasian, including the coordinator of the U.K. mobile industry's response, Mike Dolan of the Federation of Electronic Industries; the New Zealand campaigner Neil Cherry; and Michael Repacholi, coordinator of the WHO EMF program.

controversies have been centrally driven by a key political figure. Democrat Senator Lyn Allison is an uncompromising anti-EMF campaigner who draws on the scientific authority of George Carlo. Allison demanded a moratorium on tower construction, politically linking the issue of towers and handsets in a way that did not occur in the United States (*The Australian*, 25 October 1996). Her researcher, Sarah Benson, is a highly focused EMF campaigner who has philosophical belief in the effect of electromagnetism on the body. Having established a high profile on the issue from the mid-1990s, Allison was one of six senators placed on the official Inquiry into Electromagnetic Radiation, which produced its findings in May 2001.[29] Allison's report, as chairperson, called for a freeze on any relaxation of radiation standards, enforcement of wide "buffer zones" around all new power lines, and federal government warnings to parents about possible increased risks to children. Most controversially, the report called for a $5 dollar levy on all mobile users to pay for research into health effects.

In effect, however, the report was Allison's own, as the other five senators denounced its recommendations in their own minority commentary and remain opposed even to any increase in research funding. Liberal Senator John Tierney, the inquiry's deputy chairman, dismissed the entire inquiry as a "waste of time" in his six-page commentary, as research has found no negative health effect. He dismissed what he regarded as needless scaring of the community, and even suggested that it made sense for children to carry cell phones in case of emergency (*Courier Mail* – Brisbane, 8 May 2001). An equally animated response to denunciations came from Allison, who attacked the process of setting mobile health and safety standards as a "sham" that reflected government bias in favor of the cell phone industry.

The context for widespread reaction against the large numbers of towers in urban centers, which so suddenly appeared in the early 1990s, was the earlier reaction against power lines. Public concern about power line EMF was already well established, beginning in Victoria in the early to mid-1980s, and then becoming a public issue in New South Wales around 1989. The power line experience also provided a model for an accommodatory cell phone industry response.[30] The anti–power line campaigns

---

[29] The report is available at http://www.aph.gov.au/senate/committee/ecitactte/Emr/index.htm.

[30] Mike Dolan, who coordinated the electricity industry response, organized a half-day seminar in the mid-1990s with American risk communication authority Peter Sandman,

led to government inquiries. In New South Wales there were five different projects, leading to the establishment of the Gibbs Inquiry, which reported to the regional government in 1991. This was a landmark report by a former Chief Justice of the High Court of Australia. A high-voltage transmission line in Melbourne became the focus of public attention and led to the Peach Panel Report in 1992. Finally, the Australian Senate conducted an inquiry in the late 1990s on the 330-kV connector between New South Wales and Queensland, and this was also the subject of a report. A number of organized activist groupings emerged and were consolidated through the politicization of reactions to power lines, principally in Victoria (Powerline Action Group) and New South Wales (Electromagnetic Radiation Alliance of Australia). EMRAA is today the most important center for opposition to mobile phone masts. Low-level radiation health concerns were also aired in relation to television towers in the Australian context, with an explicit link to cancer.

Australia's 18 million inhabitants are mainly grouped in a small number of cities and urban centers, suggesting the need for a concentrated network of towers. The mobile phone and tower network was constructed comparatively early, at the beginning of the 1990s. The system was "rolled out" very quickly, initially, at least, with little regard for local sensibilities, according to prominent industry representative Brent Gerstle.[31] The three main operators were given some exemption from planning restrictions, and this appears to have played some part in de-sensitizing them to the need for considerate siting.

While the rapid and concentrated creation of a mobile phone infrastructure in Australia provided the opportunity for widespread reaction, there are other conjunctural factors involved. One reason (in addition to Internet and e-mail communication) for the relative success of Australian campaigning, according to Lyn Allison's researcher Sarah Benson, is what she terms "scientists who work in an open fashion – doing research and staying in touch with community groups."[32] Certainly, there has been a proliferation of Australian experts claiming knowledge of health effects from EMF, some of whom were influential from an early stage. Bruce

attended by forty electronic industry representatives and twenty-five mobile phone operators. This attempt to make industry aware of the need for an accommodatory response was unprecedented at this time. Mike Dolan, coordinator of the operator response to the Australian power line controversy, was subsequently recruited by the British Federation of Electronic Industries to respond to mobile phone fears.

[31] Correspondence, 3 February 2001.
[32] Correspondence with Sarah Benson, 20 September 2000.

Hocking, an occupational health consultant and formerly chief medical officer for the main wireless operator, Telstra, tracked down cases of complaints against digital mobile technology from 1997 and insisted that there were dangers to exposing children (*Microwave News*, May/June 1997). Technology journalist Stewart Fist is a well-known proponent of cell phone risk among Internet campaigners. Anti-EMF scientist Stan Barnett has also been influential internationally. Most important, Don Maisch, a journalist based in Tasmania, collected a series of papers and published them under the title *Fields of Conflict* in 1996. Sarah Benson and others cite his work as inspiring their involvement. Maisch is widely known and his website (and consultancy) claims to have received almost 50,000 hits since 1997.[33] New Zealander Neil Cherry, referred to above, subsequently became the most widely influential figure, inspiring the animosity of government ministers and undertaking speaking tours both in Australia and internationally.

In New Zealand early state responses to cell towers from 1994 were driven by environmentalism (comparable to Switzerland, below). Environment Commissioner Helen Hughes explicitly called for a "prudent approach" to the setting of exposure limits, and the country's Environmental Court, while accepting that nothing was proven, decided that the current safety standards should be increased twenty-fold as previous standards had been based on the analog system. The Ministry of Education ruled that transmitters could not be placed on Crown-owned schools.

In Australia, the tower issue was brought to prominence almost overnight by a confrontation in Harbord, Sydney, in 1994. There were protests against a high bank of transmitters, owned by Telstra, located next to a kindergarten and other children's' facilities in suburban Sydney. The protesters chained themselves to the surrounding fence, some with their children. Telstra initially tried to respond to their concerns with scientific argument, comparing emissions to everyday items such as light bulbs. However, industry representatives report an early recognition that they were dealing with perceptions that had little basis in science, but that had to be negotiated nonetheless. Formally, Telstra continued with "maintaining its position on negligible risk but acknowledging the community's outrage." But in their press release, Telstra "concluded that the community had rejected the scientific evidence provided by government instrumentalities" (Chapman 1995). Within two weeks of media pressure, Telstra switched off the transmitter. Two television crews described the protests

---

[33] http://www.tassie.net.au/emfacts.

as "people's power." Member of Parliament Tony Abbott declared it a "sign that people can beat big business . . . that battlers, the little people, mums and dads, can win" (cited in Chapman and Wutzke 1998: 619).

More local protests began to develop in Australia through 1995 and into 1996, but with little publicity. The EMRAA was formed in 1996, as leaders Lyn Maclean and John Lincoln began addressing local meetings. Health effects were a "hot issue" in Australia throughout 1997 (*Microwave News*, July/August 1997). In early July, residents in a town south of Sydney claimed victory against an attempt to erect a Vodafone mast near schools. An insurance company claimed to be siding with local residents' fears when it refused Vodafone entry to their building in Sydney. On 21 July 1997, the *Herald Sun* reported that 500 protesters marched through a Sydney suburb calling for the removal of towers, carrying a burning effigy of Australian Senator Richard Alston, the chief minister responsible for dealing with the issue and regarded by campaigners as a forthright opponent of the idea of EMF health risks. While anti-tower protest subsequently died down, it emerged once again a few years later.

Australian operators' approach to base station siting is inherently precautionary, adopting a "least community impact" approach to ameliorate possible community concern. Operators such as Vodafone Australia are self-consciously proud of their developed community relations practices, yet this has not prevented a new wave of community opposition to base station deployment in 1999 and 2000.[34] The Australian Telecommunications Industry Ombudsman reported a "significant" increase in complaints about tower siting during the first half of 2000 (*Courier Mail* – Brisbane, 13 May 2000). In part this was because the new operator, OneTel, was less practiced in anticipating and negotiating community opposition. Campaign coordinator Lyn MacLean argues that One Tel's activities reignited reactions.[35] In just five weeks in early 2000, some sixteen action groups were established in Brisbane alone, generating widespread media exposure. Recognition of health concerns and regard for public sensibilities had become the norm for the three established operators, and communities were "shocked" by OneTel's failure to behave in a similar way.

[34] Queensland has been at the center of media reaction, and the *Courier Mail* – Brisbane is most influential in the state. Scanning all articles in the paper linking mobile phones and towers to health up until August 2000 confirms a pattern of a spate of early stories at the end of 1996 and into 1997, then a reigniting of the issue toward the end of 1999 and at the beginning of 2000.

[35] Correspondence with Lyn Maclean, 25 September 2000.

The other prompt for renewed anti-tower campaigning was the grow-ing support among national politicians and local councils for local anti-tower campaigns. By 2000 campaigning had de facto official political support. Driven by Lyn Allison, the Australian Democrats had advo-cated the transfer of authority of mobile phone policy decisions from the Department of Communications and the Arts to the Department of Health. They also pushed for requirements that manufacturers and doc-tors record health complaints related to cell phone use, for restrictions on marketing to young people, and for a ban on towers near school prop-erty. At the state level, the Greens promoted the issue, and the opposition Minister for Labour has demanded legislative changes. Unions and state council bodies have similarly embraced cell phone health concerns. Fund-ing for research in Australia has not been confined to industry sources, as it has in the United States. In an implicit admission that this is a national, rather than solely commercial, problem, the Australian government an-nounced a five-year $3.5 million project on potential health effects in November 1996. In the summer of 1998, the Australian government announced further research funding.

Unlike in the United States, it is explicitly health-based worries about EMF that appear to have dominated Australian complaint. A Queensland councilor explained that "they are mostly worried about electromagnetic radiation and, secondly, the visual amenity" (*Courier Mail* – Brisbane, 25 January 2000). Prominent Australian campaigners are not only sus-picious about long-term adverse health consequences from EMF but em-phasize an immediate impact. Allison's researcher, Sarah Benson, says that her health has been severely affected by EMF, and she was consequently "suffering considerably." She "immediately realized that a crisis was at hand and became active."[36] Benson formed an organization called Elec-tromagnetic Radiation Awareness Network, which has been subsumed into EMRAA. There appears to be less of the hard-headed pragmatism and professional lobbying that characterized the American campaign of CWTI. While there are groups claiming real and immediate effects from EMF in the United States (and Ireland and Sweden), they do not have a high level of campaigning influence. The most striking feature of anti-EMF campaigners in Australia, however, is the extent to which they and their concerns have been brought into an influential role with the state.

State accommodation to health concerns in Australia was first local, and then national. One Sydney council proposed its own low exposure

[36] Correspondence with Sarah Benson, 20 September 2000.

limit in 1996, and the Queensland Democrats passed a motion opposing antennas on schools. The first local policy on towers was established by Sydney's Shire Council, stating that towers must not be within 300 meters of sensitive areas. Other policies implemented by Sydney councils imposed special restrictions for schools, children, and workplaces (Chapman and Wutzke 1998: 620). This policy was reproduced by many other councils and the New South Wales Local Government Association (LGA), in an explicitly health-based decision that was advertised by EMF activists internationally. They questioned whether Australian EMF standards were able to protect public health. State accommodation is similarly evident at the national level. Early in 1996, the Ministry of Education declared that antennas would not be allowed near public schools and endorsed a policy of prudent avoidance with regard to children and EMF exposure. The Telecommunications Act of 1997 removed the immunity from regulations previously enjoyed by carriers erecting towers.

A tripartite relationship emerged between carriers, government, and activists in Australia. Such a trajectory was evident since the Harbord confrontation. Faced by determinedly nonscientific, even anti-scientific, public attitudes from the beginning, representatives of science and industry made an early assessment that such attitudes had to be appeased rather than confronted. Even the secretary of the EMRAA concedes that, after the early Sydney protests, the carriers "became much more responsive to community concerns about the location of towers." Local and then national government followed suit, and with the second wave of reaction against towers in 1999, the structures of this tripartite relationship began to emerge. In early 1999 the Government Standards Committee, responsible for establishing a new radiation exposure standard, came to a standstill when community representatives refused to vote for a more lenient standard with no explicit precautionary framework. This was only a temporary setback on the road to a more participatory and precautionary approach, however.

The campaign coordinating group EMRAA has been given a consultative role by the state. In late 1999, the Australian Communications Authority suggested a precautionary code of practice to be devised by the Australian Communications Industry Forum and a numerical standard for exposure to be set by the Australian Radiation Protection and Nuclear Safety Agency. Both of these bodies contained representatives from EMRAA. The new code of practice is explicitly precautionary in its approach to the siting, design, and operation of all telecommunications radio equipment: suppliers must provide information, document decisions, and minimize emissions. Operators are bound to agree with councils on a community-wide consultation process. This consultation with communities can include advertising in local papers, posted notifications, and the door-to-door supply of information to householders. Operators must make the public aware of "health issues," not simply that a tower is to be erected, which is hardly a straightforward task given the contentious nature of any health claims in the first place. They have to provide information about compliance of the facility with radio-frequency limits, its emission levels, and other facts. Operators are also bound to operate at the lowest possible power levels. "Road shows" about EMF toured five major cities as part of this process, at which anti-EMF views and the established scientific consensus were promoted side by side. In August 1999, the Reference Group on EMF was established under the Department of Health to provide a national forum for addressing concerns about EMF. This body has two representatives from EMRAA. The Australian Senate's inquiry into EMF in 2000 canvassed widely for oral submissions from campaigners and the concerned public.

The most refined focus for the assimilation of anti-EMF activism came with the formation of the Mobile Carriers Forum (MCF) in August 2000. Its creation followed the federal government's calling of all carriers to a meeting and giving them two weeks to devise a plan to restore the confidence of politicians, councils, and the community that the industry could manage tower deployment better. Otherwise the cell phone industry faced increased state regulation. The MCF aims to improve consultation and promote site sharing and runs an information campaign with a website and fact sheets.

It could be argued that the cell phone issue, in general, and that of towers, in particular, would have become more inflamed had carriers and state alike not appeased anti-EMF activism to such an extent. Whatever the truth of the claim, unusual views about electromagnetism have been legitimized through official recognition. Accommodatory initiatives have, arguably, afforded the issue a longevity it otherwise would not have enjoyed. Certainly, a political strategy of making concessions to health fears is not without consequence.

Italy and the Emergence of Nonscientific Precaution

In parts of Central and Southern Europe cell phone "electrosmog" has become a significant issue, largely independently of events elsewhere. In April 2001 Italy held the world's first national day against "electromagnetic pollution." At the same time, a dispute came to light between two government ministers on the issue. Particularly during the stewardship of Environment Minister Willer Bordon, Italy has been at the forefront of introducing new laws limiting emissions from radio and telephone antennae. Bordon had already ordered several radio transmitters to be shut down, including those of the Vatican's radio station in Rome on the grounds that childhood leukemia was more frequent in an area 6 kilometers around the Vatican's transmitters compared with the Roman average. This led to a diplomatic incident, as the Vatican claimed sovereign immunity from prosecution (and stated that emissions were, in any case, within guidelines). A trial was set at the beginning of March in Rome to consider charges against Vatican officials of causing "electrosmog." Elsewhere, in a move with remarkable implications, a Turin prosecutor placed Chicco Testa, the chairman of state electricity utility ENEL, under similar criminal charges on the same day.

For Bordon, the childhood leukemia claim added up to "sufficient elements... to claim that it is a problem that needs to be dealt with seriously. The cases are few, but present. Precaution is [therefore] justified" (*Il Giornale*, 21 March 2001). Bordon also introduced a "green hotline" encouraging people to complain about what they deemed "abusive" siting of towers. There was criticism of Bordon's stance from Foreign Minister Lamberto Dini. Health Minister and renowned oncologist Umberto Veronesi insisted that there was no clear evidence linking "electrosmog" with cancer. Responding to outrage from environmentalists, Veronesi further defended his views in an editorial for the Italian daily *La Stampa* (2 April 2001). There is wider scientific concern within Italy about the country's policy on the issue, most notably from Paolo Vecchia, a leading national authority on the issue.[37]

Other developments reflect a distinctive embedding of microwave concerns beyond Minister Bordon. Italians have enthusiastically embraced the mobile phone, with levels of usage comparable to Scandinavian and British populations. Yet anxiety about mobile phone EMF was already evident in the mid-1990s. A government decree proposed in 1995 instructed Italians to keep the antennae of their cell phones at least

---

[37] Paolo Vecchia's unpublished accounts (2000 b–d) of Italian developments are drawn on extensively. Vecchia is the head of Non-Ionizing Radiation at the Italian National Institute of Health (ISS), president of the Italian Radiation Protection Association (AIRP), president of the European BioElectromagnetic Association, and Italian delegate to the EMF Project of WHO.

twenty centimeters away from the body (no explanation was given as to how they were to conduct a conversation at such a distance!). More significantly, a decree on the exposure of the general public to radio-frequency fields was enforced in January 1999 (Decree No. 381/98) that was substantially different from the international guidelines of ICNIRP, as low as one-hundredth of recognized exposure levels, in fact. Italy has found itself isolated in the European Union as a consequence of its unusual position. At a council meeting on 12 July 1999 it was the only country to vote against the European Commission's recommendation that ICNIRP guidelines be followed and a common European standard thereby endorsed. Although the implications of the new Italian legislation may prove too costly actually to implement, there are certainly indications of an attempt to do so. In April 2001 the government announced that it had earmarked L267 trillion (£86 million) from third- generation license auctions to help reduce electromagnetic radiation.

"Elettrosmog" appears to be a routine expression in Italian society, meriting a box of explanation and graphs in a newspaper article actually about the "etiquette of the mobile phone," for example (*Il Giornale*, 30 August 2000). The issue has enjoyed a high media profile since the later 1990s. There is evidence that the politicization of EMF concerns resonates with wider public awareness and concerns. Reflecting increasing preoccupation with safety issues such as health and crime, rather than traditional politics, Italian press commentary describes how "Italians Are Catching the 'Nimby' Syndrome" (*International Daily Herald Tribune*, *Italy Daily*, 10 March 2001). Recent research indicates that anti-EMF campaigning constitutes a large part of this newly emerging, informal campaigning in Rome (Mudu and Pessina 2000).[38] Unsurprisingly, the evolution of anxiety and campaigning against "elettrosmog" is beginning to become the subject of serious academic inquiry (Nocenzi 2000). There is already an earlier, sympathetic account of concern with "suspect waves" (Carra 1994). The United States was the only other country where microwave concerns have been the subject of a similar historical account (Steneck 1984).

Authoritative surveys of Italian life describe the emergence in recent years of a more fearful and isolated society with inadequate representation (Angeli 2000: 40). Alongside a growing fear of crime and "others," an even more individualized anxiety about new technology is evident that

---

[38] The research was based on content analysis of the main Roman newspaper *Il Messaggero* between 1998–99.

"alternates between exultation in its power and anguish at its uncontrol-lability" (ibid.: 37). Alongside this development there is a transformation in perceptions of health and illness, "such that Italians increasingly tend to ascribe medical importance to even minor ailments and complaints, things relating to physical image and personal security not traditionally eligible for medical treatment." Working in tandem with the elevation of relatively minor complaints is the "expectation of treatment for virtually any malady" and the demand for the granting of "recognition to new diseases" (Angeli 1999: 80). It is in this context that analysts locate the growth of concern over both domestic sources of "micro-sources of pollution in the home," such as cell phones, and the more public opposition to the installation of TV and radio masts, electricity pylons, and cell towers (Angeli 2000: 38).

However, Italy is not the only European country to pursue a similar policy of extreme caution with regard to EMF emissions. In 2000, a similar although differently formulated ordinance was enforced in Switzerland, where the expression "electrosmog" is also widely employed. Both the Swiss and Italian regulations not only are at odds with international standards, but also are not derived from scientifically based criteria. The Swiss and Italian EMF guidelines assume effects from long-term exposure. This difference drives Italian opposition to the European Union and ICNIRP guidelines. However, in trying to set guidelines on the basis of "possible long-term effects," no precise numerical values for exposure limits make logical sense. The Swiss limit for base stations does not apply to the far higher emissions from handsets, and it also sets the lowest limit that is considered economically feasible, rather than scientifically necessary. Slovenia is the only other country to suggest that it may introduce similar nonscientifically based limits, arguing for an additional safety factor of ten for new mobile installations, but curiously following ICNIRP guidelines for existing installations (Vecchia 2000b: 261). Interestingly, both Switzerland and Slovenia border Italy, making a small bloc of ultra-precautionary anti-EMF states.

The Swiss standard appears relatively straightforwardly derived from official environmental policies, themselves the product of the long-term influence of environmental ideology and politics. The Swiss Ordinance is justified by the need to comply with the general law of Switzerland, specifically the Environmental Protection Law (EPL) of 1983, which emphasizes precaution and stipulates that EMF emissions are to be kept as low as is technically and economically possible. New emission guidelines by Swiss Environmental agency BUWAL in March 2001 set emission limits significantly more stringent than ICNIRP. These have led to considerable concern among cell phone operators. Andreas Wetter, head of Orange Switzerland, says it will cost Orange $300 million to adjust its existing GSM network to bring it into line with new guidelines, rendering an effective network financially unviable. Swiss operator TDC argues that it will not be possible to build up a network in cities such as Zurich, Basel, or Geneva, leading to a Swiss "mobile free oasis" in Europe (*Mobilex Environment Monthly*, August 2001).

As in the USA, cell phone EMF fears in Italy have their origins in earlier reactions against microwave facilities, such as radar installations, power lines, and the TV transmitters that litter the landscape. There is also a wider backdrop to Italian developments. A chemical contamination at the town of Seveso in 1976 created a heightened sensitivity toward toxic deadly pollution, independent of the extent of actual harm caused. Following an explosion at a chemical reactor, a vaporous cloud of dioxin was released. There were complaints of nausea and other problems among residents, although even years later it was concluded that no fatalities could be attributed to the gas release. Whatever the real impact, however, Seveso became something of a parable about the perils of contamination within the newly emerging environmentalist discourse (Fumento 1993: 112). Immortalized in an influential book as "the poison that fell from the sky," it became a reference point in campaigning against toxic waste in the United States, as well as in Italy itself (Fuller 1977).

The Italian approach to mobile telephony is also bound up with controversy over power line ELF, and the issue retains prominence alongside more recent concern with cell phone EMF. In the early 1980s, when the American Wertheimer study was not yet known outside scientific circles, Italian opposition to power line erection developed on a largely economic and classical environmental basis. Demands for the relocation of power lines were based not on health fears as much as concern about their impact on the value of farming land and general beauty of the landscape. Sporadic local protest was transformed by the involvement of environmental groups. The Green Party, which was then an opposition force in the Italian Parliament, pushed for nonscientifically based exposure limits. The key early turning point came in Tuscany in 1985. In the town of Pietrasanta there was concern about the unexplained appearance of low-flying helicopters. Asked to investigate, the local judge discovered that the helicopters were transporting cables to attach to the masts of a new electricity distribution grid in the hills. As environmentalists became involved, residents argued that the cables could be routed under the ground or sea, rather than ruining local countryside (Carra 1994). The state electricity company ENEL was stopped from installing a power line by a local judge on the basis of "uncertainties" rather than identifiable health risks.

A new environmental association emerged in the course of early reactions against power lines, Legambiente (League for the Environment), as well as numerous citizens' groups and committees. The first, CONACEM, was formed in 1990. Opposition to power lines spread, with the state electricity provider finding that local decisions against it made their construction increasingly difficult, leading even to the abandonment of projects. In 1996 a leftist coalition won the elections and the Green Party assumed control of the Ministry of the Environment, thereby becoming responsible for regulations on EMF exposure. Even though in government, the Greens continued their oppositional radical campaigning activity, attacking the regulations of official bodies such as the European Commission and WHO on environmentalist websites.[39] Green Party anti-EMF sentiments effectively became official government policy. The influence of local judges and differing attitudes taken by parts of the state regulatory machine also contributed to heightened sensitivity about EMF and health within Italian society. As concern has abated over power lines (particularly as ENEL began to construct networks underground), attentions shifted to cell phone transmitters.

As in other countries, individuals with some scientific authority have been important in legitimizing anti-EMF concerns. A number of non-specialist scientists are active and influential in particular regions known for EMF opposition: a toxicologist in Veneto and Emilia Romagna, a famous biologist in Tuscany whose son died of leukemia, and a professor of physics in Puglia (Vecchia 2000c). Perhaps most important, one institution within the state regulatory apparatus has broken the consensus established among other bodies in its field. The National Institute for Prevention and Safety at Work (ISPESL) has struck out on its own, arguing for a safety standard for EMF derived differently from that of other Italian and international authorities. Not restricting itself to occupational exposure, the institute has increasingly been concerned with public exposure. In November 1999, it organized an international symposium with the Minister of the Environment and other politicians. The main invited speaker was New Zealander Neil Cherry. Following his presentation, ISPESL insisted that the government implement stricter guidelines in

---

[39] See http://www.verdinrete.it/livorno/ondakiller.htm.

opposition to the European Commission consensus.[40] The curious consequence of the ISPESL's influence at the wider level is that, as Vecchia
describes, Italy has "rejected at the political level what its representatives had strongly supported at the scientific and technical level" (Vecchia
2000c). The Italian representatives on the European Union scientific
steering committee that called for the Europe-wide standard concurred
with the established scientific approach. Meanwhile, official Italian rejection of this position was driven by the influence of the ISPESL and the
Greens.

There was no major controversy over broadcast towers in Italy until officials from ISPESL certified at a court hearing in Puglia that an
antenna from a local television broadcaster was the cause of a number
of pathologies in the surrounding area. Even greater concern has now
emerged around mobile towers. The campaign against base stations has
intensified since the 1998 decree on exposure to weak EMF fields. Vecchia
suggests that the two are related; the non-science-based precautionary policy appears to have fueled anxiety about EMF. He notes that "the general
public perceives unduly restricted limits as an implicit recognition of severe risks" (ibid.). After the Venetian case, the judge urged citizens from
all around the country to report suspected cases of health problems associated with EMF exposure. Over 10,000 reports were collected in less than
one month, the majority of complaints relating to cellular base stations.
Several local rulings have limited base station operation until such time as
health fears are proven to be unfounded, such as in Bologna and Naples.
Regional authorities are also taking it upon themselves to "educate" the
public about EMF dangers. The administration in Emilia Romagna began
a "communication campaign" in March 2000 in all the cities of the region.
In November, it initiated a more intensive effort with provincial seminars,
an exhibition, a regional conference, and an environmental education
program in schools (ARPA 2001).

Distinctive features of the Italian government system have driven the
stigmatizing of EMF. The twenty Italian regions are permitted local laws
in areas such as health. In January 2000, Veneto set an EMF exposure
limit even lower than the national level. Similar laws are proposed in
Emilia Romagna, Tuscany, Lazio, and Puglia. At the same time, they are
subject to the influence and encouragement of state decrees. A national
decree in 1999 encouraged regional authorities to implement ever more
restrictive EMF standards. The functioning of the law is also distinctive:

[40] See http://www.verdinrete.it/livorno/trento.htm.

a degree of arbitrariness exists that has made prosecutions possible that are difficult to envisage in other societies. A judge dealing with specialized matters chooses his or her own technical adviser; judgment can therefore be based on individual opinion, rather than the consensus of the scientific community. Individual rulings against EMF appear nonetheless to be of considerable significance in a pattern of escalating concern and even punishment. In a ruling on 14 May 1999 in Rimini, after a joint action by people living close to a power line, expert testimony argued a "reasonable probability" that EMF was the main cause of reported symptoms.[41] The executive engineer of ENEL responsible for the project was sentenced to three months' imprisonment, despite the fact that the power line had been built in full compliance with Italian state regulation.

Court rulings preventing the operation of transmitters can be interpreted by the public as proof of danger and can stimulate further reactions. Local restrictions can also form the basis for more restrictive national laws. Parents in Veneto withdrew their children from school near a power line in February 2000. A lawsuit was also launched that pushed for the restrictive Veneto limits to be elevated over national guidelines, and the ruling was in favor of the parents. The Ministry of the Environment subsequently recommended that Italian regulations fall in line with the restrictive Veneto law, and the court gave notice that ENEL was under investigation.

A dynamic was established by the combination of activating factors in the Italian situation. Limits established by regional authorities and local judges are inevitably perceived as hazard thresholds suggesting danger levels, rather than an essentially arbitrary level determined by political and legal considerations. Once such a limit is set in one region or at one level of the state, it immediately implies that higher levels in existence elsewhere are putting the population "at risk." Institutions are under moral pressure to respond, and a potentially limitless escalation of precaution becomes possible. As at the local level, the existence of differential EMF safety standards internationally now invites the accusation that those not following the Italian precautionary stance are paying insufficient regard to the health of their citizens.

The distinctive features of the Italian situation can be seen as symptomatic of a relatively weak and fractured state, where the judiciary has amassed authority and influence at the expense of centralized state control, and the health and safety executive can pursue their own agendas.

[41] The judgment can be found at http://www.lexambiente.com.

There are also important technical reasons for the high profile of microwave issues in Italy. Italy has the highest number of broadcast towers in the world, both in the total number of emitters and in relation to population size, estimated at around 60,000 (compared with less than 10,000 in the United States). This is partly due to a historical absence of state regulation, but it is also due to the unusually mountainous topography of the country. These thousands of towers are often sited near small, rural communities where reactions are likely to be more focused than in more anonymous urbanized settings.

There is no evidence to suggest that specific health-based fears spontaneously dominated early Italian reactions to power line ELF and then to other forms of low-level radiation. When reaction first emerged in the mid-1980s, esthetic and economic issues appear to have been dominant. Farmers, for example, were not enthusiastic about installations appearing on their land and the impact on its value (Carra 1994). Environmentalists often contested new electricity networks on esthetic grounds, based on the Galasso Decrees of the early 1980s that were intended to maintain the natural beauty of the countryside against new developments. The designation "natural beauty" was contested, and it also proved difficult for environmentalists to challenge powerful and influential monopoly service providers. Under these circumstances, and with a changing political and cultural climate, the health argument developed as a potentially more effective way to proceed. The health emphasis appears to have emerged as a more effective means through which ENEL, and later other service providers, could be taken on in the courts, particularly once the sympathy of "the people's" judiciary toward health claims became evident.

Health concerns about nonionizing radiation seen to have elevated concern about all forms of radiation in Italian society. Widespread European alarm over health risks from American depleted uranium-tipped shells in late 2000 originated in Italy. Following the premature deaths of eight Italian soldiers from leukemia it was immediately concluded that exposure to the ammunition during NATO operations against Yugoslavia was to blame. "Balkan war syndrome" became a media phenomenon in Italy and then, to a lesser extent, in other European countries. What is curious, however, is that the distinctive Italian approach to EMF is not well known, even among most campaigners against cell phones and towers in other countries. Italy, Switzerland, and perhaps Slovenia constitute a relatively self-contained "bloc" of EMF-sensitive nations in Central and Southern Europe. It seems partly because of language that Italian reactions have not become more widely influential. The diffusion of EMF concerns from the United States to Australia, Ireland, and the United Kingdom, by contrast, was undoubtedly assisted by shared language, among other factors. Resuming the story of the emergence of anti-EMF campaigning and anxieties in the English-speaking world, we turn first to Ireland, where, principally in the form of anti-tower protests, reactions next made an impact after Australia.

Ireland and Diffusion to the United Kingdom

In the British Isles, it was in Eire that health-related protests against mobile masts were first reported, followed very quickly by opposition in Northern Ireland. Campaigning against towers then spread to the U.K. mainland, first to Scotland and then to the rest of England and Wales, where the media had already devoted considerable attention to fears about the health impact of cell phone handsets.

Ireland figured prominently from 1996 until 1998 as a center of opposition to base stations. As in Australia, protest against electricity pylons had already been taking place, setting a precedent for later anti-tower reactions. In the Irish case the character of reaction was highly localized protest against the masts' impact on rural life and the landscape, and began around 1994. Many of the masts were erected on police property, others on the land of local farmers. Residents later contested the siting of mobile masts after local meetings were held in response to planning issues. Confrontations were often highly charged. In late 1998, for example, it was felt necessary to bring in riot police to seal off the isolated village of Kerrykeel in County Donegal for the erection of a sixty-foot antenna on the police station.

There was a clear articulation of health concerns in the Irish situation. Reflecting this reaction, the Cork newspaper *The Examiner* ran an editorial in January 1998 entitled, "Phone masts raise genuine health fears" (cited in *Microwave News*, January/February 1998). Complaints were made explicitly on health grounds even though esthetic arguments stood a better chance of stalling the siting process. But although articulated through health concerns, the dynamics of local Irish protest were also informed by local politics and feelings. Local meetings reportedly became a focus for the airing of personal resentments, according to mobile operator representatives who attended many of them.[42] Typically, relatively prosperous

---

[42] Interviews with Olivia Dobbs of Eircell and Tom Heffernan of Digifone, 8 December 2000.

farmers accepted money to have base stations placed on their land. Opposition from local people occurred in the context of resentments about the behavior of wealthy farmers and Dublin-based "big business." Towers were a symbol of corporate and state disregard for local feeling and something from which only better-off landowners stood to gain. Irish observers also report that local opposition was often led by non-Irish individuals, often from mainland Europe, who had settled in the area as a rural idyll. While a local farmer might have a more practical view of the surrounding countryside, and accept money to have masts sited on it, it is not difficult to understand that those who have moved to an area precisely to enjoy its "unspoiled" qualities might be most vociferously opposed. Even though originally "outsiders," such a dynamic fits into a wider pattern of apparent "rural unrest" being driven by relatively recent arrivals (Ward and Lowe 1999).

It appears particularly clear in the Irish context that prominent themes and issues within society and politics have informed confrontations over mast erection. The view that government has been "bought out" by business is widely held. A resident of Carrick-on-Shannon objected to a planned site, for example, asking, "[H]ow can the government stand over the siting of these masts in a residential area with children playing nearby? It seems it has facilitated big business over us" (*Irish Independent*, 17 November 1997). The opportunity to give expression to these issues was provided by the planning regulation requirement for a local meeting among the inhabitants if a tower was to be erected. The representatives of cell phone companies were obliged to attend and confront local grievances. They reported intense hostility to the perceived intrusion of "big business" and government's apparent collusion with it. They also reported public hostility to themselves personally, as privileged urban individuals who did not really care about what happens to rural Eire and its people.

By the beginning of 1998, industry and government alike felt compelled to respond to the growing tide of disapproval about the construction of mobile towers. In February 1998, Irish Telecom firm Eircell released a report insisting that families had nothing to fear from cell phone towers. At the state level, three government departments sponsored a conference eventually held at Dublin Castle on 6 March 1998. Initially intended for local authorities and health boards, the industry and members of the public were also allowed to attend. At a packed meeting, the Minister of Public Enterprise opened with the suggestion that this was an issue that was likely to "grow and grow." The conference was addressed by leading scientific authorities and not dominated by minority views about potential dangers from EMF. Beyond the 1998 Dublin Castle meeting, the issue of mobile phone masts and health was not politicized, however. None of the main political parties or individual politicians identified themselves with the issue. Mobile phone industry representatives suggest a widespread recognition among government and politicians that Ireland is too small a country to afford to question fundamentally the economic opportunities associated with the expansion of the wireless network. Ireland in the 1990s has been vigorously promoted as the "Celtic tiger": a booming economy driven by technology-based foreign investment. A cross-party consensus appears to have accepted this vision of a modernized and prosperous Ireland, and it is in this context that politics did not orient itself toward largely rural reaction against mobile technology.

Without the engagement of national politicians, localized protest hasn't acquired a wider profile in Ireland. Although there are local forums for discussing planning applications, there is no regional authority that could make it possible for local rulings to define national policy in the way that has happened in Italy, for example. Increasingly, in 1999 and 2000, local environmental protest has come to center on opposition to landfill sites, rather than mobile towers. A renewal of campaigning against these structures cannot be ruled out, however, as protest has also dissipated simply because the cell phone tower network has been substantially completed. At the end of 2000, the new mobile company, Digifone, reportedly experienced problems similar to those encountered earlier by the established networks. Like the British and Australian latecomer operators (Orange and One Tel, respectively), Digifone has been forced to try and catch up with the already established networks of existing operators. Digifone does not appear to have yet reignited protest as One Tel did in Australia, but established network operators are concerned that towers may again become the central focus for rural protest as a new program of mast erection follows the introduction of the third-generation system.

In Ireland, anti–mobile tower protest appears to have been absorbed into an established pattern of local sentiments and relationships. A comparable pattern is evident in the case of Northern Ireland, which became an important focus for tower protest in 1998. As the issue effectively peaked in Eire with the Dublin Castle meeting at the beginning of 1998, reaction became apparent north of the border. Margaret Dean, fulcrum of the highly organized reaction in Northern Ireland, attended the Dublin meeting, having found out about it through *Microwave News* on the Internet. She also became aware of the American discussion of

EMF through Libby Kelly of the CWTI, whom she contacted over the Internet.

Protest in Northern Ireland was galvanized by the Dublin Castle meeting. Dean's witness statement to the Stewart Committee notes that it was immediately following the Dublin seminar that she prepared a report for Northern Ireland Families Against Telecommunications Transmitters (NIFATT) and then led a delegation to meet Lord Dubbs and Tony Worthington (then ministers, respectively, for the Environment and for Health in the Northern Ireland Assembly) to lobby for changes in the legislation regarding the erection of mobile phone masts in "sensitive" areas. Dean was subsequently elected as secretary of NIFATT in June 1998. NIFATT had already been in existence for ten months when Dean came into contact with the campaign through the Social Democratic and Labour Party. She was quickly able to assume leadership of the campaign, along with biologist Hilary Kennedy.

The digital telecoms networks were rolled out in Northern Ireland before any of the other countries of the United Kingdom, but this itself does not entirely explain the earlier coherence of reaction. Rather, urban community campaigning networks were already in place because of the politicized environment of Northern Ireland. Sectarian strife and widespread anti-state feeling had created a uniquely charged environment sensitive particularly to anything associated with the military, whether that connection was real or merely assumed. The decades-long British military presence was organized around imposing military bases and a high-tech "surveillance state" monitoring the population's movements and even conversations. Particularly for those, mainly Catholic, opponents of the military presence, experience suggested that any technology-based structures might serve some military or surveillance purpose; nor would it be surprising if they even caused harm, as public safety was hardly of paramount concern to the British military, in the estimation of much of the Catholic minority.

Some of the long-established themes of anti-EMF campaigners resonated among the Catholic community. Their hostility toward the British military presence conditioned a suspicious attitude toward unfamiliar developments such as the sudden appearance of prominent new transmitters. Local people in areas such as Armagh and Newry were long accustomed to elaborate and extensive covert monitoring and eavesdropping on their activities by the military. Of all the British campaigners, Margaret Dean most readily suggests the sinister military origins of EMF technologies. Associations had already been established by the public between military technology and indirect health effects. In a reputed case around the town of Newry, campaigners argued that a local cancer cluster was related to army transmitters. According to Dean, local campaigner Mary Allen successfully fought to reduce such emissions. The lack of planning regulation also had an impact. Initially, mobile masts were effectively exempt from even the limited planning restrictions applicable in the U.K. mainland. Still conditioned by the priorities of a militarized society, local planning control was particularly weak. It was not necessary to gain the permission of the local authority for tower erection, and the borough councils had no power to deal with planning.

There were organizational links already in place that could readily turn attention to an issue such as telecommunications towers in Northern Ireland. Networks of "concerned mothers" had long campaigned against direct threats to their children, such as drugs and violence within the community. It would not be difficult to shift attention to more imperceptible threats such as microwaves in the Northern Irish context. Leading U.K. campaign coordinators confirm that the strength of community association was particular to the Northern Irish campaign, and this helps to explain its success and prominence.[43] A direct measure of this difference is that, of all the public consultations held by the Stewart Inquiry, only the Belfast meeting was well attended. The NIFATT network ensured that over 100 people turned up to voice their concerns to the committee.

The existence of determined community activism was important to providing the basis for organized anti-tower campaigning. But most significant, the dramatically changing political arrangements in late 1990s Northern Ireland created the opportunity of access to political influence for this new "post-political" movement. The changes in government and local control that were part of the Northern Irish "peace process" appear to have been important in providing the political space for campaigners to be taken seriously by authority. The British government sought new forms of management and control in the province at the end of the 1990s. The "peace process" has led to the incorporation into regional government of representatives from all sections of the community, with particular enthusiasm for those that did not exemplify the political allegiances and preoccupations of the past. Under such fluid circumstances, there appear to have been considerable opportunities for individuals associated with a neutral and depoliticized concern such as with EMF rapidly to assume some influence.

---

[43] Interview with Cathy Moran, 23 August 2000.

NIFATT activists under Dean's leadership successfully canvased local political support and lobbied the newly created Northern Ireland Assembly. A delegation of campaigners was received at the Assembly in December 1998, just before they took a test case on tower siting to judicial review. Notably, the delegation included London-based lawyer Alan Meyer, later the legal representative and activist for Mast Action U.K. Also present was MP Phil Willis, the first British MP to promote cell phone concerns at Westminster, and it was as a result of this experience, he recalls, that his interest in the issue was consolidated.[44] The explanation of cell phone EMF to which Willis was exposed was from Roger Coghill, a fourth member of the delegation to the Assembly. Coghill is a longstanding promoter of beliefs about the powers of electromagnetism and a safety device entrepreneur. In its submission, NIFATT sought "the same protection for citizens of N.I. that is afforded to citizens of Australia, New Zealand, the U.S. and elsewhere – where planning regulations . . . exercise a policy of prudent avoidance within residential areas. . . ." Special thanks were made before the meeting to Jim Shannon of the Democratic Unionist Party, but the chief whips of all parties were thanked for their "help and encouragement" in establishing an audience for the delegates.[45] It is significant that the EMF safety issue clearly demonstrated its capacity to cross the old political divide, as it was a Protestant-based Unionist party representative who was singled out for special praise by an organization whose social roots lay in Catholic-based anti-militarism.

The success of NIFATT's lobbying was remarkably rapid; it is difficult to imagine, without the conditions of political flux and integration, that such an impact could have been made by isolated individuals championing an esoteric concern. In August 1998, new planning procedures were introduced in Northern Ireland bringing them into line with the rest of the United Kingdom. Planning departments now had to go through the prior approvals procedure to decide whether the operator would have to seek full planning permission. The planning service was also required to consult with borough councils, although they still have less power than on the mainland. The judicial review brought in April 1999 instigated by NIFATT activists then gave local councils the powers enjoyed in the mainland United Kingdom. The courts ruled in their favor, declaring that the

---

[44] Interview with Liberal Democrat education spokesman Phil Willis MP, 14 November 2000. His interest was sparked after an anti-mast protest in his Harrogate constituency in 1998.
[45] From account of the meeting distributed among campaigners in December 1998.

planning service acted unlawfully and should have allowed the local council to withdraw "permitted development rights" that allow tower erection without full planning application procedures. Following the review, Margaret Dean requested letters from activists throughout the United Kingdom in May 1999, in the hope of triggering a full-scale public inquiry into mast siting.

The renegotiation of social and political arrangements in late 1990s Northern Ireland appears highly relevant with regard to how easily "ordinary campaigners" were able to gain access to those in power, and thereby legitimize EMF concerns and effect actual legislative change. Dean was able to arrange a meeting at the province's assembly headquarters, Stormont Castle, with what she describes as "ease." Meeting ministers for health and for the environment, Dean brought with her a man from Newry who claimed negative effects from a mobile mast, ranging from his wife's illness to dying pigeons. The claims were reportedly treated very seriously.

Anti-tower protests, particularly in relation to schools, have certainly not abated since the judicial review. Over 1,000 school pupils staged a mass walkout from St. Mary's Grammar School in Belfast in October 1999, for example. One Andersonstown mother had already withdrawn her child from the school. At the more organized level the campaign has fallen away, however. Partly this was because judicial review and a change to planning law was achieved. Equally important, Margaret Dean, the dynamic fulcrum of the campaign, moved to Eire, the tower that originally stimulated her campaigning remaining near her (unsold) home. But before she left the anti-tower networks Margaret Dean was to play an important role in the diffusion and consolidation of campaigning on the U.K. mainland. In completing this survey of the internationalization of campaigning against cell phone facilities, it is to these developments that we now turn.

The British Campaign Against Masts

In the rest of the United Kingdom, protests against tower siting first gained prominence in Scotland. Base stations were sited prominently and near centers of population in Scotland before the rest of the United Kingdom, mainly for topographical reasons, as the digital signal was liable to be blocked by trees, tall buildings, and land formations. While in large towns the industry had been siting masts on top of tower blocks for some time, these had not provoked much concern because these locations already hosted a number of other telecom devices, which meant that the new masts were not particularly obtrusive.

Following two inquiries about towers in Scotland, Graeme McAlister of FoE Scotland began a lobby campaign. After contacting Alasdair Philips at Powerwatch, McAlister compiled information on the attitudes about cell phone towers in different countries, noting that Australia in particular took a precautionary approach. In what turned out to be a very successful tactical move, McAlister then issued a report surveying the thirty-two Scottish councils' attitudes toward towers in December 1998 and January 1999. The survey noted that two Scottish councils had adopted a precautionary policy with regard to what were deemed "sensitive" council properties in early 1999. Others quickly followed, and soon over 50 percent of all councils followed their lead in responding to the FoE report. Pressure to address the issue was quickly felt in the new Scottish Parliament. In May 1999, its Transport and Environment Committee decided to launch an inquiry into mast safety, eventually concluding in March 2000 that all towers should require full planning permission, as there was "reasonable doubt" about health risks. Following this success, FoE Scotland issued a substantial campaign briefing, which was to lead to them taking on an advisory role for activists throughout the United Kingdom, rather than only in Scotland.

The publication of McAlister's research paper had already resulted in a flood of inquiries from the rest of the United Kingdom, as reports by the Scottish press went around on the press wires. Given the go-ahead by the London FoE office, Scottish FoE, and McAlister in particular, then became the focus for campaigning advice for those seeking to oppose masts in the United Kingdom. Having carried out the first research on official responses to towers and planning permission, and having been taken so seriously by Scottish councils and the Parliament, McAlister's authority was considerable. He, along with Margaret Dean and MP Phil Willis, then played a central role in setting up the seminar at the Houses of Parliament that launched the tower issue in England.

Some early opposition to masts in England was, like in the United States, principally esthetic: because they were an "eyesore." This reaction was typified by, and focused around, the agenda of the Council for the Protection of Rural England (CPRE). Its April 1996 briefing on telecommunications (CPRE Policy Position No. 5) noted the towers' "unsightly" character. Independently of Scottish developments, some English councils also began to oppose the siting of specific towers on general planning grounds, typically the result of lobbying by local individuals and councilors.

Individuals' opposition to masts constructed near their homes or children's schools began to consolidate into campaigns in late 1998. Although one campaign had begun as early as 1994, it was not until late 1998 through to the summer of 1999 that the number of groups increased significantly and established regular contact with one another.[46] A small, informal meeting of the group of early activists was held in December 1998.[47] Few of these campaigners had had previous political or campaigning experience. There was a significant degree of secondary expertise with regard to mobile telephony and mast location, however. Some had knowledge of planning issues, and others – professional electrical engineers – were familiar with basic electrical science. As a measure of the importance to the activists of media exposure, part of the meeting was spent watching videos of national television coverage related to handset radiation and local news coverage of their own campaigns. But without any influential backing or connections, these early campaigners were not able to make any significant national impact and refrained from even announcing themselves as a fully fledged campaign.

It would require a combination of individuals with distinctive expertise and political connections to create an organized campaign against cell towers, and even then it has proven difficult to sustain. Following his experience in lobbying over towers with Margaret Dean in Northern Ireland, MP Phil Willis pressed for political action in the British Parliament in late 1998 and 1999 on the basis of a lack of certainty about possible health effects. The combined efforts of Willis in England, Dean from Northern Ireland, and McAlister from Scotland culminated in the launch of a U.K.-wide campaign. The other key figures who emerged, bringing with them some scientific and legal expertise and indirect financial backing, were Alasdair Philips, and Gerard Hyland, and Alan Meyer, who were to become technical, scientific, and legal advisers to the anti-mast campaign, respectively.

Alasdair Philips was effectively the United Kingdom's lone and long-standing campaigner about pulsed radio-frequency signals, through his Powerwatch website. Philips himself recounts a fifteen-year-long effort to raise EMF issues through the media, gaining his first significant media coverage in 1990 (related to stories of strange effects on the women camped out at the famous Greenham Common anti-nuclear protests of the

---

[46] The lone campaign run by Roy Ashwood through his website.
[47] Held in the town of Tamworth on 29 December.

mid-1980s).[48] Much more recently, Philips was joined by physics lecturer Gerard Hyland in promoting scientific uncertainty about mobile EMF in the media. Hyland was even more successful than Philips in generating publicity, boasting that between November 1998 and February 1999, he was featured in two nationally broadcast television programs, numerous radio interviews, and "no less than 16 local and national newspapers and several international magazines."[49]

Besides their media profile, both Hyland and Philips have been crucial to galvanizing local campaigns through speaking at public meetings and organizing new campaigners into e-mail networks. A third individual central to establishing a national profile was solicitor Alan Meyer. His involvement arose through high-profile businessman Mohammed al Fayed, owner of the famous London store Harrods. Al Fayed opposed the construction of a tower near his home in 1997. During the case, many people contacted Meyer, who was his solicitor, wanting to know how to oppose towers successfully. Previously, there had been no coordination among anti-mast campaigners outside the small circle that met in late 1998, but Meyer increasingly took on the role of campaign adviser, providing free legal advice with al Fayed's support. He estimates helping at least sixty to seventy local groups. Meyer was part of the delegation that lobbied the Northern Ireland assembly with Dean and Willis. Through close association with Margaret Dean, he became an important gatherer and distributor of pro-precautionary research. The external organizational drive from McAlister in Scotland and NIFATT in Northern Ireland was now complemented with an organizational fulcrum within England.

The tower issue was put more squarely on the political map on 16 June 1999, when campaigning work by FoE Scotland, NIFATT, and the early English activists culminated in a seminar at the House of Commons. Coffee mornings and garage sales took place to raise the money for the proposed event. The seminar was celebrated by activist Jan Greenroyd as the first ever seminar at the House organized by ordinary members of the public.[50] The event was represented in its accompanying literature as organized with the aim of unifying the U.K. groups; a map shows NIFATT covering Ireland, FoE covering Scotland, and then "the community groups

[48] Correspondence with Alasdair Philips, 2 August 2000.
[49] Cited in Hyland's curriculum vitae, which formed part of the "pack" for the House of Commons seminar.
[50] Interview with Jan Greenroyd, 19 August 2000.

of England and Wales." The seminar was also important with regard to wider diffusion and the cementing of international links. Campaigning scientist Henry Lai and the U.S. campaign coordinator Libby Kelly were flown over to the United Kingdom. The anti-EMF scientist Michael Kundi from Vienna also attended, establishing European links. Ten MPs and three government ministers attended this highly unusual event, a grassroots campaign being launched in the Houses of Parliament itself.

Political awareness of the seminar added to the media-driven dynamic behind the creation of the Stewart Inquiry, a view supported by Phil Willis. The inquiry began only a month after the seminar, in July 1999. The other direct influence and precedent for the Stewart Inquiry was provided by the House of Commons Select Committee on Science and Technology which began its own inquiry, gathering evidence from many sources, including FoE. In September 1999, the Select Committee recommended the adoption of the more precautionary ICNIRP emission guidelines to replace those of the NRPB. It also called for an increase in research and an 80 percent cut in permitted radiation levels from phones. The committee did not restrict itself to technical recommendations. MP Dr. Ian Gibson from the committee later publicized his views in the tabloid press. Avoiding any specific suggestion about how such an objective might be achieved, he suggested that the United Kingdom, as a nation, might have to sacrifice the convenience of the mobile phone for the sake of our health (*Sunday Mirror*, 26 March 2000).

Despite the House of Commons seminar, it continued to prove difficult to sustain any sort of national campaign, even if a legislative momentum within formal political circles had been established. The key individuals involved in establishing a profile for tower concerns subsequently drifted away from the issue. Margaret Dean, Phil Willis, and Graeme McAlister all became inactive, although Willis's interest was revived at a later stage. New individuals emerged to attempt to turn local cell phone tower concerns into a national campaign. A fresh organizational focus was established in the regional authority, the Kent County Council (KCC). Through its Liberal Democrat group, the KCC began the only published voice of the campaign in the form of a widely distributed newsletter and subsequently began responding to national inquiries. Most significant, KCC was advertised in the national daily newspaper, the Express, as a useful source of help and information for those wanting to pursue their grievances. The campaign newsletter reported over 150 phone calls as a result, and continued to receive many other telephone inquiries that it redirected to Alasdair Philips at Powerwatch, Graeme McAlister at FoE, or Alan Meyer.

The other significant new individuals to emerge around the tower issue were working-class mother Julie Matthews, who believes that her child's learning difficulties are related to EMF exposure, and her friend Christine Mangat. Under their leadership, a national campaign, Mast Action U.K. (MAUK) was eventually launched at the House of Commons on 13 December 2000. Sponsored by Conservative MP Marion Roe, some 100 campaigners, press members, and others heard speakers argue for the "sensible siting" of masts.[51] MAUK has struggled to maintain any subsequent activities, let alone profile, however, as the cell phone and tower issue faded in 2001. In a rare appearance, MAUK staged a photo opportunity in London in November 2001 to warn of the dangers of unprotected mobile usage. Claiming that usage without protection leads to "a 50% greater risk of getting cancer," the event promoted safety devices distributed by a Santa Claus, but generated little publicity.[52] While at the local level, campaigning against towers continues with the support of some local authorities, even the British media appears to have tired of the tower issue, as it did with handsets before that.

In one of the most interesting possibilities for the future, the potential to pursue anti-tower complaints through the Human Rights Act, introduced into British law in 2000, has been raised.[53] The need for substantial funding to pursue such an avenue is likely to continue to limit this option, however. Ultimately, in a society where cell phone usage is almost universal, there was always likely to be a limited shelf life for alarmism about handsets and even the siting of towers in communities and near schools. By 2002, the principal profile for the issue is provided by William Stewart, author of the precautionary report from the inquiry into health effects. He generated front-page headlines about the alleged "cynicism of the mobile phone firms" in January 2002 (*Daily Mail*, 26 January 2002), as well as stories in other newspapers and numerous radio interviews.

Unveiling the British government's £7.4 million research program into mobile phone health effects, Stewart repeated his earlier attack on the

---

[51] Health is a longstanding concern of Roe's; she chaired the Select Committee on Health between 1992 and 1997. The more direct connection to the campaign is that Roe is the constituency MP for Julie Matthews.

[52] Press release distributed via TopMark Ltd. from Topmarkltd@hotmail.com.

[53] Alan Meyer and, more recently in November 2000, Liberal Democrat leader Monroe Palmer in the London Borough of Barnet threatened the use of the new Human Rights Act against a mobile operator.

cell phone industry. Although the industry does not advertise to children, he called it "irresponsible" for allegedly targeting youngsters. Stewart suggested that "texting" might be a safer alternative for children, but the inquiry's vice chair, Lawrence Challis, added that this too might cause new problems, and he advised that boys hold phones away from their groins while composing text messages. He also reminded parents of their "responsibilities," although it was unclear how they were to enforce more limited usage on the "mobile world" of British teenagers.

Having made an impact in stimulating a precautionary response from authority, EMF activism has remained, in practice, marginal. By 2002 MAUK had been dissolved into a more established campaign for general planning "sanity," as it failed to make any impact following its launch. Yet even some six years after they made their first appearance, anxieties about cellular phones and towers refuse to be entirely laid to rest in the country where they have been promoted more systematically than any-where else. Studies suggesting uncorroborated possible "effects" from cell phone EMF can still make front-page news in British newspapers, as with research on the blood/brain barrier carried out in Finland by Professor Darius Leszcynski (*Evening Standard*, 19 June 2002). The United Kingdom's distinctively attenuated combination of a health-campaigning media and a political class willing to accommodate and even to champion such concerns has ensured a curious longevity to the mobile EMF issue, at least in the public domain. Nearly four years after its abortive "menace of our mobiles" campaign in the autumn of 1998, Britain's most popu-lar newspaper, The Sun, ran a four-page "special investigation" into the "plague of the mobile phone masts," including an article by prominent Labour Party MP Frank Field explaining his efforts to pass a bill helping local protesters oppose tower sitings (15 July 2002). In the next chapter some of the historical components that have combined to constitute this precautionary culture are explored more comprehensively.

6

The Culture of Precaution

Understanding Patterns of Reaction

In the preceding chapters we have looked at key aspects of the cell phone "revolution," from its rapid assimilation through its peculiarities as an item of technology to the current knowledge about the impact of radio-frequency radiation and the often insensitive way in which towers have been sited in communities. These are important factors in establishing the conditions for a reaction to cell phone EMF and help to account for some of the differences in the profile of cell phone EMF issues between different societies. In themselves, however, these aspects do not offer a satisfactory explanation of the way that health fears about cell phone EMF have evolved and been sustained. For example, as the number of studies showing no adverse health effects from cell phone and tower radio-frequency radiation mounted, so did the number of campaigners worldwide. Nor have suspicions about cell phones abated as mobile communication has become more familiar and popular.

To seek explanation in these aspects of the cell phone itself is to overlook the extent to which concern about the health effects of cell phone EMF has been shaped by the character of institutional reaction. In many cases we can see clearly how the institutions of government have fostered and instigated health fears and demands for protection. As this chapter goes on to discuss, the different types of state response throw light on the prevalence of the health issue in different societies.

But these responses from state institutions themselves demand explanation. We have to explain why, when cell phone EMF has been both accepted in popular consumption and as yet exonerated by scientific study, the official responses to concern, such as the Stewart Inquiry in Britain and the Italian legislators' initiatives against "electrosmog," appear to have treated the issue as of profound significance? There are many other health risks far more tangible and prevalent across even the most advanced societies, which struggle to achieve such a high level of attention. As suggested in earlier chapters, the decision to respond to the issue is determined by social pressures rather than risk statistics or scientific evidence.

However, it is also evident that the institutional responses are not concessions won by *popular* pressure. Anti-tower action is clearly not a popular cause in any way that we might understand that notion from past movements and campaigns. In terms of commitment, size, impact, and the significance of the issue, it is not even really a campaign in any meaningful sense, although individuals may be campaigners. Yet it appears to have been treated as one by a range of state institutions in the countries through which the issue has diffused, particularly in Europe and Australia. In many cases, the degree of policy innovation around cellular phone safety seems to have outstripped the expectations of the campaigners. In Britain, campaigners were surprised and delighted by the outcome of the Stewart Inquiry and said that in a number of points it far exceeded what they hoped for. This is quite unlike issues that provoked far larger popular reactions in the past, when official responses usually represented some sort of *compromise* with popular demands and worked to close them down rather than encourage claims and concerns.

The seeming indifference of state responses to the small size of campaigns and to the lack of evidence of risk points us toward the idea of some states being predisposed to taking action on risk issues. Often this is where there is a legacy of alleged mismanagement of public risk, resulting in an administration being sensitized to the possibility of being "caught out" by the advance of scientific knowledge. This sensitivity was clear in the French blood scandal discussed in the previous chapter. It is most evident of all across institutions in the United Kingdom, where the official response to the cell phone health issue is the most developed and where the legacy of the BSE "crisis" is most intense. Bound up as it was with the political annihilation of the Conservative government, the mishandling of the BSE issue became a potent symbol of failure and humiliation for governments across Europe. This has contributed to a political culture that is highly sensitive to the need for popular legitimacy and motivated by trying to avoid accusations of being out of touch with people's concerns about food and product safety. The British media have become adept at

reminding the authorities of the consequences of not heeding "new scientific findings" and replays the BSE parable through other risk-related
issues, including cell phone EMF.

That the handling of an issue such as BSE could become such an enduring legacy is, arguably, symptomatic of the failure of political nerve
that was already informing institutions and policy. This is explored further on in the chapter in discussions of two broader populist trends aimed
at relegitimizing institutions: the politicization of science and the rise of
consumer protection, which are the context for understanding the official reactions to the cell phone issue. They reveal a pattern of touching
the public through the lowest common denominator of safety, backed
up by the fear of being accused of ignorance of public concerns. In this
wider context, we can see that radio-frequency radiation is just one issue among several that could evoke a response from apparently nervous
authorities.

Which issues merit a response is not particularly obvious in societies
characterized by the decline of participatory politics. It is perhaps unsurprising that the consequence of this is a state prepared to act on even
the most marginal of risks. What is more, the search for points of connection with society invariably means absorbing and attempting to lead
the most conservative impulses: the articulation of individualized concerns that are frequently centered on health, suspicion of technological
progress in mastering nature, and resultant demands for protection and
vigilance.

In the rest of this chapter, then, we schematically identify some of
the principal elements that have combined to constitute the culture of
precaution: the politicization of science, the rise and absorption of the
consumer safety and environmental agendas, and the tendency toward the
"socialization" of medicine. Looking particularly at the United Kingdom,
where scientific and policy institutions have become so defensive that they
now *promote* distrust of themselves and their evidence base, we situate
the cell phone issue in the wider context of institutional responses to
social mistrust of science and authority. It should not be forgotten that
precaution, and the perceived need for such a reflex, lies in social mistrust
rather than the practice of science. As two leading writers on the subject
have argued,

Precaution reflects the mood of distrust over the introduction of risky technologies,
processes and products that are assumed to be forced on the unknowing and
susceptible public by commercial interests, allied to governments, and exerting
manipulative power over consumers. (Jordan and O'Riordan 1999: 17)

Before we begin, it is necessary to return to some of the more straightforward factors that help to explain the patterns of response to cell phone EMF and the siting of cell towers.

As we have seen from the different cases of cell phone risk in the previous chapter, there is a range of essentially given, technical factors that influenced its profile as an issue of public concern across different societies. First, there is some correlation between concern and the visible presence of an operating mobile network, although the extent of concern does not directly correlate to the alleged harm caused. The existence of an extensive mobile network and infrastructure is a prerequisite for any popularization of concerns about mobile technology. The societies that have been at the forefront of cell phone health concerns are frequently those countries and regions where networks were first and/or rapidly constructed. In the United Kingdom, a regional pattern of response has spread from Northern Ireland to Scotland, and then England, roughly coincident with the pattern of the "roll out" of digital infrastructure. The large numbers and prominence of towers in Italy and Scotland due to the mountainous terrain have contributed to a heightened concern about EMF. Many of the countries in which operators are now meeting with negative public reactions are those where an extensive network is being developed for the first time, such as in Armenia and Egypt, and therefore very conspicuous in its sudden appearance.

Conversely, in the absence of a prominent mobile phone infrastructure, and perhaps also without the ubiquitous presence of handsets within society, reaction appears less likely. The comparative lack of organized concern in Canada – a society that shares so much else with the political cultures of countries where concern has become prominent – is partly explained by the undeveloped nature of the mobile network. Cellular phones remain relatively expensive and uncommon in Canada, and radio-frequency radiation from them is not yet a prominent issue. In Holland, not only has there been little controversy, but the official government inquiry contested any need for precautionary measures (Health Council of the Netherlands 2002). A number of factors are at play in this instance, ranging from the relatively small number and prominence of towers in what is a very flat country to a relative absence of risk sensivity within Dutch political culture that sharply contrasts with other European countries such as the United Kingdom, France, Belgium, and Gemany.

The character of the roll-out of digital networks in each country also has some bearing on the ensuing reaction. Obliged by the terms of their licenses, particularly in Europe, to establish an operating system to a tight time scale, companies were concerned more with fulfilling statutory obligations than engaging with public siting concerns. To facilitate the rapid setup of the network infrastructure, companies have been keen to benefit from exemptions from the usual planning restrictions for their towers, and this has contributed considerably to the provocation of local community outrage. Unsurprisingly, the late-coming operators in several societies (such as Orange in the United Kingdom) have borne the brunt of complaints. To catch up with the infrastructures of already established rivals so that they could provide competitive coverage, they have hurried the siting process and consequently been accused of showing less sensitivity toward local concerns and less willingness to engage in time-consuming consultation than their competitors. Hence the often repeated protest among U.K. campaigners that towers appeared "overnight." In Australia, the initial wave of health concerns and protests appeared to be receding when One Tel entered the market as a new competitor, whereupon the community reactions were swiftly reignited.

As the scale and prominence of the mobile network are important in determining the extent of reaction, so too is the extent of comparable anxieties and campaigning over other issues, against which cell phone health concerns must compete. Even considering only health concerns, there are many potential competitors to mobile phone EMF that could otherwise animate and engage individuals and institutions. This seems to be a particularly important factor in the American reaction to mobile phone EMF. There are innumerable citizens' lobby groups in the United States and a highly developed system through which their influence is potentially brought to bear. American campaigners have consequently had to fight particularly hard to gain attention. The campaigners' submission to the Supreme Court in late 2000 involved a level of externalized expertise and professionalism not evident in other national campaigns. Even then their case has gained relatively little national publicity. The problem of establishing a national profile in such a large, diffuse society, not least in the absence of a widely read national press, makes it even more difficult for campaigners to draw attention to marginal concerns. American campaigners envy the ease with which cell phone health stories have dominated the European, particularly British media. However, such problems are not insurmountable. The Reynard case temporarily raised widespread awareness of the issue through the national media publicity it generated. It is probably easier to make a national impact for an issue in a smaller, more homogeneous society like Australia than in the United States, but this factor does not appear to be decisive.

Reactions against cell tower EMF do not follow any straightforward pattern of tower development or the extent of mobile phone usage, nor are they simply an expression of the size of a society or community. Reactions reflect and are absorbed into existing cultural, social, and political patterns. The U.S. response, for example, has been characterized by regular attempts to pursue complaints through the legal system, reflecting the highly developed position of civil law in the regulation of American society. As a result the EMF issue has been modified, in this case largely confined to individual health claims related to mobile handset exposure. In contrast, the discussion about how authorities should respond to public fears is much more a feature of the European concerns. The importance of existing social and political patterns is also evident in the Italian case, where concerns have been absorbed through disorganized state authority and focused on policing EMF emissions, with the threat of legal action against the owners of offending transmitters. The pre-existing suspicion of radiation and the peculiarities of regional power distribution in Italy together appear to have led to unprecedented official endorsement for a nonscientific precautionary approach to mobile phone EMF.

Cell towers seem unwelcome when they are close to homes and schools in all of the societies where there have been reactions. Yet there are a number of factors that limit any form of reaction, one of which is financial compensation. Unsurprisingly, complaints about tower siting are less likely to be articulated by individuals and institutions that are paid by mobile operators to accept a structure on their property. Typically, the individuals most adversely affected and not provided with compensation feel sufficiently strongly about the inappropriate siting of a tower that they are prepared to begin campaigning. Other locals are often sympathetic to their neighbors' plight, but rarely sufficiently so to devote time and resources to fighting for tower removal. Unlike the presence of a nuclear power plant, for example, that can overshadow a whole community and plausibly represent an equal degree of risk to all, mobile phone and tower fears rarely have any wider local or regional impact. It is often only through a common focus, for example, where parents of children at a school feel "threatened" by a tower, that a less individualized reaction emerges. Whether such (still localized) reactions combine to gain a wider profile is usually in the first instance most dependent on the receptivity of the media. The responsiveness of the media itself reflects dominant cultural concerns. British and Italian newspapers have readily responded to the issue, arguably reflecting a wider resonance for sinister health threats. The national media in Holland and Scandinavian countries have proven far less receptive, and the issue has not become so prominent in these societies.

State Reaction, Legacies, and Legitimacy

The different responses of the state and its institutions and representatives (often first at the local or regional level) to the articulation of public concerns through the media seem to determine the subsequent pattern of the issue's development. Put simply, cell phone EMF health fears became an issue in places where regional and national authorities responded. These responses appear to have compensated for the weaknesses of the anti-tower campaigns in other respects: first, the absence of a widespread popular reaction against towers that could sustain an influential campaign; second, the absence of scientific authority associated with health claims. It is only through being taken seriously by state bodies that the allegations about hypothetical risks have been able to command authority and acquire momentum beyond the immediate reactions of some individuals in each locality. In Australia, national politicians immediately seized on the first significant confrontation over a tower siting to align themselves with "the people." This was an important early moment in establishing a route for absorbing EMF activists into a policy-making role with the state, and thereby ensuring a sustained profile for the issue. In Ireland, by contrast, politicians and state bodies remained aloof, despite many heated confrontations over tower siting.

Health concerns require external confirmation and validation in the absence of demonstrable effects. Such confirmation can come about through a number of means. The processes involved in the Italian case of local judges unilaterally declaring towers unsafe, regional authorities setting their own nonscientific standards, and national political parties and authoritative institutions encouraging safety doubts demonstrate the process most clearly. The combination of these different elements has resulted in heightened safety concern and a standard of "public protection" from EMF at odds with the rest of Europe. On the other hand, where the state has either not systematically engaged with EMF concern or acted ostensibly to contain responses, EMF health claims have been less successful in agenda forming. Although allowing a degree of local consultation over tower siting on the basis of visual amenity and potential impact on property values, the U.S. Federal Communication Act of 1996 has been relatively successful in marginalizing health concerns. The government in Ireland provided one national forum for discussion on potential health impacts at Dublin Castle, but steered clear of raising the issue any further. Elsewhere, such as in Germany, government has resolved simply to provide research funds and postpone further response until cause for concern has been established.

In Finland there is a less hospitable reception for health concerns about cell phones partially because of the importance of the cell phone industry to the national economy. Nokia is not only a major employer, but also a national institution that puts Finland on the world map. Such a consideration appears to direct politicians and influential individuals away from accommodating minority fears, and despite the high number of towers and high cell phone usage, there is very little concern about health effects. The high regard for the cell phone industry in Finland is also consistent with a relatively positive public and institutional attitude toward science and technology more widely. Leading the way technologically is "a continuation of the task of constructing the Finnish nation" (Miettinen and Väliverronen 1999: 11).

The other side of this pro-technology coin is lack of public interest in forums for the discussion of new technologies; Finnish environmental interest has remained more old fashioned, focusing on issues such as forest preservation rather than technology assessment. This is seen as indicating that Finland "lacks the civic tradition of underlying democracy, dialogue and participation" (ibid.: 20). But it is important to remember that there is no "tradition" of a democratized science and technology anywhere. Consultation was initiated in the United States in the late 1960s, and has more recently become fashionable in Western Europe. Finnish exceptionalism is more temporal than substantive, although the extent to which precautionary attitudes toward science and technology are now entrenched internationally makes Finland appear strangely accepting of progress and technology.

Elsewhere, the general economic importance of telecommunications development limits the scope for politically entertaining health concerns; this factor is especially important in smaller and more vulnerable economies such as Ireland. More generally, in countries where "postpolitical" concerns such as health have not yet entered the political realm, economic imperatives remain dominant. This would appear to be the case in Japan, for example, where health concerns have been reported but largely ignored by the state.

There is a strong correlation between the extent of legitimacy that state authority enjoys and the alacrity with which claims makers' concerns are entertained. This appears to be an important factor in the rapid response and accommodation to EMF fears in Scotland and Wales. In the language of the Independent Expert Group on Mobile Phones:

Devolved power provides an opportunity for a less centralized approach to planning issues, and this may allow more areas of local and regional concern to be addressed in legislation and guidance. Already the devolved assemblies and parliaments have played a key role in raising public awareness regarding the potential health impact of mobile phone technology. (IEGMP 2000: 37)

The IEGMP report specifically welcomed the report by the Scottish Parliament's Transport and Environment Committee in March 2000 that proved so important in encouraging claims makers. The background to the Scottish Parliament's role in "raising public awareness" was their own very recent creation. They embraced anti-tower campaigners' concerns as a means of distinctively and rapidly demonstrating the responsiveness of the new Parliament to "the people" in circumstances where there are few popular causes, still less mass movements, with which to identify. A similar process is evident in the Welsh and Northern Irish cases. Campaigners indicated that Welsh Assembly members have been especially encouraging and sympathetic to their concerns about radiation from towers.[1] In Northern Ireland anti-EMF campaigners found access to the new government remarkably easy, being invited to present their claims at Stormont with little lobbying on their own part. Arguably, the Welsh and more precarious Northern Irish assemblies have a more limited mandate and lack the credibility even of their Scottish equivalent.[2] Their responsiveness to marginal "public" concerns appears proportional to their need to demonstrate that they are indeed representative and able to effectively address local issues.

While the need to find issues that can function as a source of legitimacy is quite crudely demonstrated in cases of newly formed regional government, the same dynamic has been at work in more established institutions. The sense of crisis triggered by the "mad cow disease" or BSE episode, first in Britain and then across Europe, has become a defining influence in the handling of scientific issues such as cell phone EMF. The British Conservative government was accused of first failing to respond to

---

[1] Interviews with Jan Greenroyd on 19 August 2000, and representative of Gower Residents Against Mobile Masts (GRAMM), 1 November 2000.

[2] Around 60 percent of voters voted for the new Scottish Parliament, while only there was only a 50 percent turnout for the Welsh Assembly. As elections to establish national institutions for the first time, these voting figures are extremely low.

a possible link between BSE in cattle and the horrific illness human variant CJD, and then of reacting in ways that betrayed confusion about the level of public risk. The story has subsequently been rewritten several times, revealing further elements of mismanagement, largely with the benefit of hindsight. Successive cabinets have struggled with the ongoing legacy as the British beef industry all but collapsed, consumers overreacted, deficiencies in the enforcement of food regulation were revealed, and the level of risk and mortality statistics were the subject of ongoing speculation. The issue became the defining justification for European food regulation. Its legacy has been evident in the Belgian crisis over possible dioxins in chicken from contaminated grain in the mid-1990s and also informed the reaction to the French government's confused handling of the Coca-Cola contamination scare in 1999. But nowhere has the legacy been as strongly evident as in Britain, where it now informs the institutional response to all new risk concerns.

The BSE issue not only disposed British government institutions and figures to be highly sensitive to scientific issues of risk factors and causal links. It also elevated a group of critics in the media, in environmental organizations, and in government itself who gained from the credibility lost by the incumbent establishment. The Labour government, elected in 1997, was acutely aware of what the issue had done to its predecessors. Its own struggle to respond to the reaction against genetically modified organisms, which involved many of the same critics and drew on the new concerns about mass production of food, showed that there was a broader applicability. As well as inheriting the same anti-political cynicism and media scorn of government institutions that drove the BSE crisis, the government also assumed control of a political and scientific establishment damaged by the experience and acutely sensitive to the need to regain credibility. The ongoing official inquiry added to this insecurity and resulted in the Philips Report, which condemned the scientific and government responses to BSE (BSE Enquiry 2000). William Stewart was the government's chief scientific adviser from 1990 to 1995, and as such was intimately involved in the defining experience of BSE. The report attacked the whole nature of decision making on scientific and health issues in the United Kingdom, citing an alleged culture of secrecy and propensity to downplay risk and calling for greater openness, transparency, and public accountability.

Stewart's subsequent report on cell phone risk was clearly very directly shaped by these "lessons" of BSE. Had there been no Phillips Inquiry, it can confidently be argued that there would have been no inquiry into cell phones, let alone one that concluded in the explicitly precautionary manner that it did. As many acknowledge, the shadow of BSE hung over the cell phone experience in the United Kingdom. This meant that cell phone risk was judged not in its own terms but in the highly politicized, precautionary environment cast by the inquiry into "mad cow disease." At the same time, although the politics of precaution assume a particularly aggravated form in the United Kingdom, a wider culture of precaution innovated earlier in the United States is now evident internationally. In Australia, Italy, and other European countries, a similarly precautionary approach was taken to the cell phone issue. The imperative of precaution has successfully diffused and is a crucial factor in explaining the impact made by cell phone health concerns.

Attempting to connect with "public concern" is the overriding focus of initiatives to revive political engagement. In the United Kingdom, a recent influential report on the reform of Parliament, for example, recognized that it has lost influence and argued that "crucially, Parliament must reflect and articulate issues of public concern" (Hansard Society 2001: 1–4). Yet in an age of depoliticization, disengagement, and the decline of social and political institutions, it is not clear how this can be done. Effectively, the media appears to act as a surrogate for this "public concern" in the absence of any other aggregation of public feeling. In the parliamentary reform document, responsiveness to the public is translated as becoming "attuned to media requirements" in the way that other government institutions now are.

In fact, on the cell phone issue, state authorities in a number of countries have responded in a precautionary manner to concerns voiced typically by a small number of claims makers through the media. This approach appears to be becoming the norm in those societies through which health fears about cell phone EMF have diffused. It is evident particularly in the ostensibly neutral form of commissioning epidemiological research to investigate new risks and conditions. The historian Ben Shephard has noted how such an approach became established in the United States in dealing with claims associated with "Gulf War Syndrome" in the 1990s. While others were dismissive of claims for this new syndrome, the Clinton administration was accommodating, eventually spending over $115 million on inconclusive epidemiological studies. Explaining this development, Shephard suggests:

The politicians had learned that the most effective way to counter emotional press reports focusing on individual cases was to commission elaborate epidemiological surveys. The scientific community, at first very skeptical about Gulf War Syndrome, took it much more seriously when the scale of research funding became apparent. (Shephard 2000: 383)

There are then particular reasons why some institutions respond to risk issues at a given time: to demonstrate effectiveness and relevance, as a proxy for other tensions, or to escape criticism, for example. But the trajectory of nearly all institutions is toward greater accommodation of nonscientifically based fears and concerns in the management of scientific issues (and exceptions, such as Finland, tend to prove the rule). We can make sense of the political receptivity to the new breed of "risk issues," including cell phone EMF and health, only as part of a broader reorganization of the relationship among science, policy, and society. This has been informed by two historical developments in the postwar period: the politicization of science, which has seen the reorientation of science toward policy; and the rise of consumer politics, which has seen the reorientation of business and politics toward protection of individuals.

The Politicization of Science

The attention devoted to science by government has increased dramatically over the last decades. Jasanoff (1994) describes how the expanding role of scientists in policy making has made them into the "fifth branch" of government. Recent analysis shows that the proportion of questions, motions, and debates in the British Parliament with a scientific content has risen six-fold over the past decade. Biological (medicine and food) and environmental sciences (including energy) accounted for most of the growth (Shepherd 2000: 1). For some analysts of science and technology policy this process is highly problematic. "Science is becoming yet another playing field for power politics, complete with the trappings of media spin and a win-at-all-costs attitude," complains one (Pielke 2002: 368). Some practitioners in particular fields who have to contend with the consequences have also raised concerns. "Toxicology is being shaped by worldwide political agendas, triggered by the public's desire for swift and precautionary solutions to the possible health effects of environmental chemicals," argue two Italian scientists. In their view, "[t]he resulting feedback loop has impoverished the discipline, because its growth has largely been driven by the demand for protocols for regulatory action" (Lotti and Nicoterra 2002: 481).

It has become so commonplace to hear the political authorities of advanced countries making public statements about risk issues that we perhaps do not spontaneously question why issues of science and evidence should have such a profound impact on the policy makers. In the United States, Australia, Britain, and, increasingly, much of the rest of Europe, areas such as the economy and international affairs often are marginalized in political debates, in favor of inquiries and deliberations on disease pathologies, environmental impacts, and health risks. Ministers and authority figures frequently present themselves as more anxious about their accountability for these kinds of issues than they do about sending troops to war or about the decline of economic sectors. In the British Parliament, for example, there is typically more activity and questioning around issues of health and safety such as cell towers than about bipartisan military interventions such as in Yugoslavia or Afghanistan. While this interest in risk issues might accord with our contemporary sensibilities, it is not self-evident why it should be the case. War and economics do, after all, have a significant and tangible impact. To understand this political preoccupation with questions of scientific inquiry and risk, we first need to consider the relationship between policy and science and how they have become increasingly interdependent.

It was principally through the experience of the Second World War that science and technology became both revered and a fully distinct social sphere. Victory would no longer be secured through the "quality" of men; Stafford Cripps, a member of the British war cabinet, proclaimed that "the battle would not be won merely by the physical ascendancy of our race, but by the ingenuity of those who have been trained in our schools, technical colleges and universities" (Rose and Rose 1969: 58). War would be a scientific affair, which not only demonstrated the utility of science but accelerated its development and later application beyond the military arena. We have already noted the example of radar, but the technology that made rockets and computers possible also developed under the circumstances of war.

Scientists themselves were not always entirely comfortable with the transformation of their role and position within society, particularly in relation to war. Sir Frederick Gowland Hopkins and Lord Boyd Orr wrote to *Nature* in 1936 protesting against the "prostitution of science for war purposes" (ibid.: 270). But the prestige acquired by science during the Second World War played a crucial role in assuring its central place in the post-war order. If science had won the war, perhaps it could also "win the peace." To accomplish this task, a scientific community could demand maximum autonomy as a newly distinct constituency within society. Post-war science policy was defined by Vannevar Bush's report,

Science: The Endless Frontier, as a period of "scientistic hegemony" (Bush 1946). Wider engagement in the scientific project was not denied, but, "instead of controlling science, the public was encouraged to make better use of it and to learn more about it..." (Elzinga and Jamison 1995: 587). At the same time, science was drawn into closer embrace with the state and political realm. Scientific priorities were determined to a greater extent than ever by the political imperatives of the day, in this case the demands of the Cold War against the USSR. The Soviet launch of Sputnik prompted a massive expansion of the scientific role, and the emergence of both "policy for science" and "scientific policy."

It is now difficult to appreciate the historical uniqueness of science and technology's place in the authority of modern societies. In the late 1960s this could still be recognized, as its central place in the legitimacy of the post-war West had been established only in the previous two decades. British sociologists could observe:

A hundred years ago a speech by any public figure was incomplete without careful reference to at least one member of the trinity of Church, Queen and Nation. Today a similar speech demands at the least a ritual bow in the direction of that indivisible pair: Science and Technology. No political manifesto, company's chairman's annual report or novelist's reflections on the state of the times can afford to omit from its repertoire some passage aimed at science or the scientist. (Rose and Rose 1969: xi)

As science emerged from the "ivory tower" to the center of society and policy making through the experience of war, we were confronted by "big science" and "technocracy," which quickly became targets for political attack. The unqualified enthusiasm of some scientists for prosecuting mass destruction was hardly helpful. The Hungarian John von Neumann certainly did not regret his work on the Manhattan Project. A leading advocate of first (nuclear) strike, his purported motto was: "If you say why not bomb them tomorrow, I say why not today? If you say at 5 o'clock, I say why not one o'clock?" (cited in Gillott and Kumar 1995: 176). If the description of a blindly technocratic elite pursuing an agenda regardless of social consequences is unconvincing today, it does ring truer for the immediate postwar years. The nuclear program was dominant and led to what Cole describes as a "legacy of distorted institutions," where the usual structures for the regulation and deliberation of science and technology were abandoned. A nuclear future was a part of an American "manifest destiny"; it was "our great sacred trust," as one senator put it (Cole 1981: 125–6). It is from this period that the sense of a sinister science collaborating with government and business in a "military industrial complex" originates. Indeed, Paul Brodeur, the creator of concerns about microwaves and everyday radiation, began his career as a radical critic of Cold War conspiracy. He was very much a product of this period and remained convinced that a veil of secrecy and menace not only lay behind nuclear testing but pervaded other walks of life.

In the United Kingdom, science and technology were never quite so central to political legitimization as in the United States. They were politicized in the 1960s, however, with Harold Wilson's proclamation of British renewal through the "white heat of technology." Where it had been unimaginable before 1964 that the principal issue was harnessing technology, "[n]ow it is hard to imagine an election in which it would not be" (Rose and Rose 1969: xii). In the United States, the reliance on science was more immediate and pronounced; arguably because American society had fewer alternative, historical sources of authority to draw on. In the absence of a national church or royalty, America had always necessarily been more future-oriented.

Like developments in many other spheres, the authority of science and its newfound elevation within society was questioned by the cultural transformation of American society at the end of the 1960s and into the early 1970s. Authoritative accounts describe the development of a "confidence gap," a crisis of authority where "[f]irst students and intellectuals, then leaders, and eventually the public itself became concerned about the gap between the promise and the performance of our major institutions, particularly government and business" (Lipset and Schneider 1983: 1). Science and technology suffered attacks similar to those against the post-Vietnam state itself; more than this its elevated status became a focus for a political class anxious to deflect criticism. President Johnson attacked scientists for not being sufficiently concerned with domestic policy as students turned away from tarnished science toward social science. Technocratic doctrine was not overturned but was now intended to be responsive to wider influences. Science and technology policy moved into a period of "social relevance" and a "new kind of accommodation" in the early 1970s (Elzinga and Jamison 1995: 587).

In the United States, one innovation in response to this new mood was the creation of an office of "technology assessment" in 1972, institutionalizing a more cautious and consultative approach to technological development, and one that has subsequently become enormously influential in continental Europe. A European Union inquiry has noted with some envy that the United States "has by far the longest and most comprehensive tradition of transparency and openness of all the scientific advisory systems." The report locates the origins of this openness in "the dual crises of public confidence in Executive government (in response to the Vietnam war) and in scientific expertise (stemming from American public concerns over the environment, nuclear technology and medical malpractice in the 1960s and early 1970s)" (Stein and Renn 1998: 1). This was confirmed during a recent fact-finding visit to the United States, when authorities at the Kennedy School of Government told members of a British House of Lords committee that the regulatory framework for science and technology in the United States was established as "responses to the mistrust of government, business and science perceived in the 1960s" (House of Lords 2000b: 9–10).

In response to attacks on its closed and elitist character, science-related policy making was opened up to lobby groups on the principle that those affected by science and technology should also have a voice in its operation. The Federal Advisory Committee Act of 1972 (FACA) stipulated that each expert advisory committee serving federal agencies must be made more open through the publicizing of meetings being held publicly, and with advance notice among other innovations. There were already 800 FACAs by 1983, codifying a culture of openness. While in one sense only formalizing advice that agencies might receive by other means, they were also a demonstration of commitment to the public that all views were being considered, limiting accusations of bias and providing some insulation from litigation (Stein and Renn 1998: 16). In the process, policy makers institutionalized a relationship with the new public interest groups, a feature of government that was to become central to the politics of risk issues and that gradually diffused to Europe and beyond as other governments grappled with a loss of confidence in established institutions by seeking new forms of "accountability."

In Britain, where science had never been quite so central to state authority as in post-war America, the loss of confidence in science as a source of social progress was more muted. Interest in the transformative impact of technology had been subsumed under the pressing issues of economic decline in the early 1970s. Science and technology as a policy matter came to the fore again only in the 1980s, when Margaret Thatcher raised the issue of whether public attitudes toward new technology might be impeding technical change and launched the first policy-oriented research on the public acceptability of new technologies. The Royal Society's 1985 report on the public understanding of science then codified its role in "promoting national prosperity," and investment in science was thereby "an investment in the future" (Royal Society 1985). Britain needed a more scientifically literate population if it was to remain competitive; some educationalists, policy makers, and politicians should be better informed, and scientists should learn to communicate better. The outcome of this was the establishment of the Committee on the Public Understanding of Science together with funding for research into the role of science in economic development. The highpoint of this growing belief in the centrality of science to British economic policy was the establishment of an Office of Science and Technology, which brought the chief scientist into the civil service as a permanent secretary. In May 1993, elaborating the thinking behind this new department, the government released a white paper, *Realizing Our Potential*, which has been described as the "fullest expression of . . . the pragmatic instrumental approach to science policy" (Healey 1999: 72).

It was not until the BSE issue reached its height and brought together an accumulating disillusionment with scientific progress with the intensifying hostility to the Conservative government that the authority of scientific institutions was sharply called into question in the United Kingdom. Already at this time, influential sociological perspectives were beginning to challenge the pragmatic model (Irwin and Wynne 1996). This was echoed by the change of political regime in 1997 to the Labour Party, which brought with it a rapid development of interest in science as a subject of public policy. In the light of the BSE experience, Chief Scientific Adviser Sir Robert May argued for more openness, early release of scientific data, and involvement of experts from other disciplines in decision making. As Healey noted, there were still the old elements of communicating science "as a public relations exercise," but "the degree of public involvement in these initiatives, and in particular their degree of interactivity . . . does put them in a qualitatively different sphere" (Healey 1999: 75).

As the loss of confidence in science-based policies has become generalized across many societies, particularly from the United States to Europe, so the scientific and political elite have found it more difficult to sustain a sense of authority. To compensate for their uncertainty about the ability of science to deliver social progress, objective truth, or even publicly acceptable innovation, such as genetic research or cell phones, they have increasingly rejected the scientific frameworks of the past and attempted to reorientate themselves and their institutions toward some kind of broader public engagement. *The irony is that attempts to reform science have extended the role of science in policy much further than the Cold War or nuclear age ever did.* It has been reoriented toward a far wider set of policy demands, not least of which is its involvement in broader political efforts to recover public trust and legitimacy. This has had a profound effect on scientific thinking itself and held up essentially irresolvable controversies for public deliberation.

But before we go on to look at this preoccupation with accountability and responsiveness, we need to consider the social and political trends that have given rise to the new demands being made of science, namely, the rise of consumer and environmental protection. These have held a powerful attraction for policy makers anxious to distance themselves from the traditional authorities of business and politics, which are perceived now to be out of touch with popular needs. Consumer and environmental issues have also spawned new voices and claims makers to fill the gaps left as those older authorities lose their influence and their constituencies. Without the gaps and opportunities created by policy makers seeking out new concerns, it is highly unlikely that an issue such as cell phones and health, like many other risk claims, could have been sustained.

The Rise of Consumer and Environmental Protection

Mayer notes how consumer issues attain a prominent place in a nation's public policy agenda. Occasionally,

consumer safety problems are so dramatic or intense that they attain issue status almost spontaneously. More commonly, issues are either "pushed" by mobilized interest groups or aroused public opinion or they are "pulled" by policy makers who choose particular issues according to the needs of the situation. (Mayer 1988: 94)

His and other studies on the United States and the United Kingdom note that consumer issues are most commonly "pulled" (Flickinger 1983). This means that the issues coming to public attention are not those with the highest objective risk but those, often driven by the media, to which authorities feel disposed to respond. The response to BSE is a clear example of such "pull" (see Fig. 1).

In response to its crisis of legitimacy in the late 1960s, the American state incorporated the concerns of the newly emerging consumer movement, led by Ralph Nader. The politics of consumer protection were to evolve into a driving force of key institutions of the American state, most notably, the Food and Drug Administration (FDA) and the Environmental Protection Agency (EPA). While Europe was much more invulnerable to consumer protection policies in the early 1970s, European countries have, in the last decade, had to confront the same disillusionment with politics and social progress that had been more dramatically expressed in the United States following Vietnam. In doing so, the United States has been a source for Europe of intellectual ammunition for attacks on scientific innovation and its application by "big business" and a source of consumer-based policy ideas. In many areas of concern about health and environmental impacts, Europe now leads the way. This is because attempts to reorientate policy thinking in response to disillusionment were closely bound up with the rapid expansion of a European government, and this meant that in a very short time Europe was able to establish the regulation of consumer and environmental issues as its defining identity. According to a leading commentator on European affairs, "Europe is setting itself up as a super-cop, a global regulator," based on "a stubborn conviction that citizens have to be protected from themselves" (Roger Boyes, *The Times*, 18 July 2001).

When it first emerged in the early twentieth century as a concern of the American state, the rhetoric of consumer protection was accompanied by practical measures to prevent consumers being poisoned, endangered, or cheated by unscrupulous companies. In fact, it was often endorsed by "big business" because compliance with environmental or safety standards invariably weakened the competition from small enterprises. However, as confidence in the effectiveness of post-war politics was shaken, based as it had been on the enmeshing of policy, science, and corporations, the political establishment drew increasingly on the anti–big business and anti–big science sentiments of critics such as Ralph Nader. It sought refuge in the role of protecting society's health and environment, and with each new regulation, the rhetoric of protection became more significant and invited campaigners to identify further risks. An important milestone was the 1964 Surgeon General's report on smoking and health, which established that a popular commercial product caused cancer. The themes established by the smoking example were subsequently repeated many times over, and in relation to risks that lacked the substantial basis of the smoking/lung cancer connection.

Congress took the lead in promoting health, safety, and business accountability, first of all in relation to the issue of auto safety following the success of Nader's defining work, *Unsafe at Any Speed* (1965). Calling attention to the problem of road accidents, Nader argued that individual responsibility in the form of how well we drove was largely irrelevant. The problem was that the American automobile held "designed-in dangers," as his book was subtitled. Holsworth's less well known account of the "public interest liberalism" represented by consumer politics contends that Nader's liberalism was not that of the confident perfectibility synonymous with a classical liberal outlook but a "defensive liberalism which considers the life of man to be one of constant anxiety . . . threatened by the knowledge that the unscrupulous will perpetually seek to take advantage of the unwary" (Holsworth 1980: 4). Nader's approach was to shake up the complacency of society through "describing a series of risks to which consumers were routinely subjected" (ibid.: 25).

Consumer protection initiatives appeared in rapid succession from the 1960s, including hazardous substance labeling, drug competition regulation, fair packaging and labeling, cigarette labeling, and toy safety. According to Nadel, President Lyndon Johnson placed consumer protection high on the presidential policy agenda in order to offset domestic division regarding the Vietnam War without further straining a tight government budget: "To champion an issue as inherently popular as consumer protection was an irresistible opportunity for a President concerned both with getting new programs and with achieving consensus" (Nadel 1971: 41). Even stridently pro-business presidents such as Nixon found the issue irresistible and continued the newly established tradition of a consumer message to Congress, adding a new consumer right, to register dissatisfaction. Carter too included consumer groups in his basic coalition and made their priorities his own.

In effect, government, at least rhetorically, turned on business to shore up its own legitimacy. Identifying the three peaks of consumer protection, Brobeck points out that they "diminished public confidence in business and heightened confidence in government and, by implication, new regulatory controls" (Brobeck 1993: 595). In the process, the public interest became interchangeable with consumer interests. The range of risks proposed for regulation was continually being expanded, both by the new regulatory authorities and by the much more widely entertained critics of business and science. As the authorities sought credibility in the protector role, they went beyond the buyer-seller relationship and became concerned not so much with the consumer as a purchaser of goods but with a more general vigilance about risks, specifically those related to health and the environment. This has also been very much the theme of European risk regulation.

The growing preoccupation with risk protection, which was diffusing from the United States to other societies, led to greater risk sensitivity in general. A combination of defensiveness among the elite and increased awareness in the populations meant that previously marginal concerns about the environment and health found a hearing. The discourse on environmental risk emerged first in the United States on the tails of its consumer protection ethos, and the intimate relationship between environmentalism and consumer protection is well documented in the key works on the rise of the consumer movement (Nadel 1971; Pertshuk 1982; Mayer 1989). Environmentalism proved instrumental to the legitimacy of the state's role as a protector of individuals from risk, arguably even more so in Europe than in the United States. It brought to consumer protection politics the credibility of grass-roots activism, community concerns, and the ideology of the guardianship of the future. Environmentalism has also generated a whole new range of areas for regulatory intervention.

Particularly within Europe, it is forgotten that contemporary environmentalism is an originally American phenomenon (Hays 2000). One European sociologist dates the start of modern environmentalism to 1970, when Earth Day was held in the United States (Therborn 1995). The American-born organization Friends of the Earth subsequently appeared in the United Kingdom and France. Animated by nuclear power and electoral mobilization, environmental politics subsequently made its biggest impact in Germany where, along with the United Kingdom and the Netherlands, elections were first contested in 1979. The now common preoccupation with cancer from environmental hazards was just becoming apparent in the late 1970s, a development that led Douglas and Wildavsky to write their defining work, *Risk and Culture*. They identified the famous, if still contested, Love Canal episode in 1978 as the turning point. The grass-roots environmental movement came together around the discovery of widespread toxic chemical pollution in the Love Canal neighborhood near Niagara Falls, New York.

The uncontested facts of Love Canal were that 21,800 tons of residues, some of which were known to have adverse effects on human health, were buried in a landfill in Niagara Falls, New York. Some of this waste made its way to the surface and also leached into the local canal. While the presence of toxic chemicals had been confirmed on the property of specific homeowners, there was no evidence of a risk of physical harm to residents. Coping with the consequences of earlier dumping of toxic waste was a real problem in the United States, but the Love Canal protestors' claims that it could cause cancer was contested. Senior scientists continue to contest the elevation of the environmental threat of cancer (Ames and Gold 1999). Nevertheless, in August 1978, President Carter proclaimed a national emergency and residents of the neighborhood adjacent to the

Love Canal landfill were notified by state health officials of a "grave and imminent peril" (Fowlkes and Miller 1987: 55).

Carter went on to politicize the issue of waste with the passing of the "Superfund" clean-up legislation in 1979, which committed billions of dollars to cleaning up former waste sites, largely on a precautionary basis. Reactions multiplied and the anti-toxic movement mushroomed. More and more "contaminated communities" protested against invisible "toxicity," said to be harming children in particular (Edelstein 1988). An "antitoxics" movement was created (Capek 1993). There were 242 groups identified by 1981, 600 by late 1984, and 5,000 active groups (now organized through the Citizens Clearinghouse for Hazardous Waste) by 1989 (Masterson-Allen and Brown 1990). By the 1980s, the authorities were prepared to commit billions of dollars on the basis of concerns that might previously have been dismissed as irrational. Particularly to corporate leaders and state officials of an earlier period, "it must appear that the poor have inherited the earth" (Sapolsky 1986: 187).

The political establishment's concern about "toxic communities" was barely diffused to Britain or Germany, where environmentalism was also growing, until relatively recently. In areas such as chemical regulation, "British experts consistently represented the risks as less severe than their counterparts in the U.S." and favored a case-by-case regulatory style (Jasanoff 1995: 326). The United Kingdom was similarly dismissive of what was emerging as a potent issue in the United States, the alleged dangers of pesticides to children (Fumento 1993: 38). Since the time of these studies the gap has narrowed, however. Europe is more explicitly precautionary, at least in relation to new technologies such as genetically modified organisms. However, there is still diversity in the diffusion of many health-related issues to particular countries, as we have seen in the cell phone EMF case. Following controversy over the safety of breast implants, which was so disastrously politicized in the United States, the British Department of Health reviewed all published studies in 1994 and pronounced them "disappointingly poor" (Angell 1997: 108). It never followed the United States in a precautionary ban.

Despite differences in the profile of how subsequent issues diffused, though, the American concern about "toxic communities" preempted a broader pattern of political intervention. As such, the Love Canal incident and the reaction of science and authority to expressions of public anxiety about contamination provides useful context for the contemporary discussion of dangers from cell phones. Here lay the beginnings of a reaction by science and the state that, in spite of the lack of evidence of harm, acted in a precautionary manner and devoted considerable resources to removing the source of grievance. In doing so, public suspicions were recognized and legitimized.

The Growing Preoccupation with Risk and Embracing of Activism

It is difficult to imagine a controversy such as cell phone radiation making the newspaper headlines and spurring government action before the 1970s. As we have seen, there was little assumption that technologies such as x-rays and radar would be harmful. Social consciousness is now very different throughout the Western world. Resonance for the notion that we can be irrevocably harmed by weak, invisible radio frequency waves shows a sense of vulnerability to very minor phenomena. It is as if the very process of harnessing and shaping natural forces – particularly, radiation – is a hazardous enterprise that we are likely to regret. From the experience of discovering the harm that can come from x-rays and radar, even more from large-scale nuclear energy, we have extrapolated the possibility of harm to far more innocuous "radiation." Yet microwave fears are more than simply an extension of the caution born of knowledge and experience. Most of us are largely ignorant of the science of radiation, after all, suggesting "awareness" is more a product of a particular way of understanding the world. At the mention of "radiation," "pesticides," "genetic modification," and the like, we bring to the discussion assumptions and fears that have little direct relationship to the particular technology in question but instead reflect our insecurities and the social messages we pick up about the likely cause of humanity's problems.

People in deprived circumstances or struggling with health problems are, not surprisingly, particularly sensitive to these risk messages. The original alarm at Love Canal had been generated by a small pilot study report on chromosome damage that suggested residents might experience higher incidence of miscarriage and birth defects. This defining moment "encapsulates the mixture of science, publicity and politics, that, by this point had come to dominate events" (Tarr and Jacobson 1987: 338). More amorphous complaints were also claimed, including disorientation, memory loss, and lethargy. One account describes how Lois Gibb, who went on to lead the national movement, heard news reports positing a link between the chemicals in Love Canal and respiratory disorders. With an asthmatic son, these reports "triggered an association in Gibbs' mind between her son's health problems and the polluted canal" (Masterson-Allen and Brown 1990: 486). In an interesting parallel with the most recent complaints about cell phone base stations, Edelstein noted that toxic as opposed to natural disasters were more psychological: "the 'facts' of toxic disaster are often unclear, making the 'perception' of the disaster central to its subsequent effects" (Edelstein 1988: 6). Edelstein observed that members of "toxic communities" typically reassessed their whole environment. His own data suggested that "even conventional health problems are reinterpreted after toxic exposure is announced and patterns of ill health come to light in the affected area" (ibid.: 52).

While the affliction of unexplained or untreatable illness seems to have always disposed people to be concerned about unknown dangers from their surroundings, intellectual support of such fears is more recent. The notion of living in a "toxic environment" became routinely used in academic books (Clarke 1989). Commentators extracted from these local fears and reactions a broader intellectual insight: as we consume the environment around us, there is consequently "no safe place" (Brown and Mikkelsen 1990; Troyer 1977). This spawned the discipline of environmental sociology in the United States, and a whole genre of books that examined "contaminated communities" and their "resistance." The title of Henry Vyner's *Invisible Trauma: The Psychosocial Effects of Invisible Environmental Contaminants* (1987) exemplifies the notion of dramatic, yet invisible effects.

The intellectual reaction to the anti-toxic movement as it developed in the 1980s was quite different from that which developed with the public rejection of fluoridation in the 1950s.[3] Unlike other controversial public health initiatives such as milk pasteurization, immunization, and water purification, fluoridation was subjected to continued voter scrutiny and remains a contested policy. Many American communities voted against the introduction of fluoride compounds to the public water supply when the 1950 Public Health Service called for a national program of fluoridation. Yet public health officials refused to debate anti-fluoridationists because it would only "legitimize their standing as experts by appearing on the same platform" (Sapolsky 1986: 7). Even sociologists at this time felt confident in contesting the "crude suspicion" that informed hostile reactions: "Somehow our chlorinated, sieved and strained water has become 'natural' whilst the addition of fluoride is a grave disturbance of the proper order of events" (Rose and Rose 1969: 150). The reaction was seen as just one example of "a latent tendency toward naturalism"

---

[3] See Crain et al. (1967), and Sapolsky (1969) for authoritative accounts of the fascinating issue of the reaction to fluoridation.

by some social scientists in the journal *Public Opinion Quarterly* (cited in
Sapolsky 1969: 1402). "Alienation" (from "big government" and "mass
society") was used to explain behavior deemed irrational. There was an
accompanying fascination/repulsion with those opposed to fluoridation:
"In America you can get a Ph.D on the study of the lay anti groups"
(Gotzsche 1975: 25). This is not to suggest that criticism of a universal
policy of fluoridation is necessarily of the character suggested above. Some
later critics were well informed, raising the issue of dosage and the fact
that in some areas high levels of fluoride are already present through food
and the "natural" water supply (ibid.).

In stark contrast to the "irrational masses" who alarmed social scientists in the 1950s with their opposition to fluoridation, people reacting to
"contamination" after the Love Canal incident began to be described
in flattering terms. Alienation was now viewed as an understandable
reaction to being marginalized, rather than a disturbing pathology. Sociological studies describe an overwhelming sense of "feeling trapped in
a dangerous location, and unable to trust conflicting reports by outside
agencies" (Capek 1993: 11). Spearheaded by radical writers, reactions
were presented as an exciting form of "people's power." Significant claims
were made, such as that campaigning against contamination empowered
women and sent participants on a steep learning curve whereby they were
actually fighting for the future of the planet. Accounts added only as a
minor qualification that reactions might be based on fear and therefore
an overreaction. To the extent that authority might be frustrated by this
irrationality, the state and its representatives had only their past practice
to blame (Masterson-Allen and Brown 1990: 489).

The anti-toxic movement not only escaped critical analysis, but it was
also endowed with pseudo-scientific insight, an extreme example being
the invention of the term "popular epidemiology" to describe the process
of a layperson becoming aware of toxicity (ibid.: 488). Conventional science, on the other hand, began to be portrayed as inherently flawed in
assessing new types of risk; there was an "in built bias against discovering
health impacts" because it was "difficult to detect significant differences
with a small number of cases" (ibid.: 491). The explicitly anti-scientific
orientation of the anti-toxic movement was celebrated in this account.
Irrationality was no longer felt to be a slur by those activists who were
fearful that "citizens will be 'converted' to a rationalist, probabilistic approach to the problems" (ibid.: 489).

Toxic poisoning became synonymous with carcinogenic effects. Science pundits appeared on television shows to announce a "plague" of

cancers brought about by chemical exposure, which would be of "epidemic proportions." Others suggested that cancer was indeed essentially man-made. The innovator of consumer safety politics, Ralph Nader, announced America's entrance into the "carcinogenic century" and complained of "corporate cancer" (Wildavsky 1995: 142). *Time* magazine announced a "Poisoning of America," which *Newsweek* interpreted to be a "grim update of the Faustian legend" whereby man's insatiable desire for consumer goods threatened him with destruction through its byproducts. Case studies of the incident bore emotive titles such as *America the Polluted* and *Corporate Crime and Violence* (cited in ibid.: 146–55). Edelstein's study of these "contaminated communities" drew out the logic of a man-made disaster. He concluded that "we are hardly innocent when our actions return to haunt us"; toxic victims required our attention because they were the most visible victims of modernity: "we are they" (Edelstein 1988: 197).

It is through incidents such as Love Canal and many other scares since that we have seen the popularization of the idea that turning nature into an object of our desires and manipulation is wrong. Writing in *Nature*, Storch and Stehr point out that science is now connected less with emancipation from nature, but rather with "possible disaster – nuclear war, genetic manipulation, climate change" (Storch and Stehr 2000). The intimate relationship between this questioning of modernization and the environmental agenda had been well illustrated by Rachel Carson's *Silent Spring*, the seminal environmental text, which came to be influential among the disaffected intellectuals of the 1960s. "The control of nature is a phrase conceived in arrogance," she insisted, that was "born of the Neanderthal age of biology and society..." (Carson 1962: 257). Carson indicted pesticides as "elixirs of death" resulting from the zealous pursuit of modernization. Although the limited-resources thesis on which this and the later OECD report *The Limits to Growth* (Meadows 1972) were based were subsequently discredited, the sense that human behavior had precipitated disaster grew stronger and was articulated more widely: "Our simple chemicals had been revealed to be as potent as the atom bomb" (Appleyard 1992: 128). Weir and Shapiro's influential *Circle of Poison: Pesticides and People in a Hungry World* (1981) broadened concern about pesticides from an impact on nature to individual health risks.

The idea that man was unleashing forces and processes on nature, the effects of which could be devastating and uncontainable, was compounded by increasing fears about nuclear power. The nuclear accident at Three Mile Island in 1979 and later the Chernobyl "meltdown" in the Ukraine in the 1980s meant that the destructive power of the atom was no longer confined to the bomb in the American imagination. The celebrated "clean energy" of nuclear technology came to symbolize dangers. While none of these incidents (including Chernobyl) was catastrophic in its own terms, the powerful reaction against them marked an important change in attitudes toward the "mixed blessings" of science and technology.

Nuclear energy became connected to influential anti-corporate themes, where power companies appeared interested in profits at the expense of safety and public accountability (Gamson 1992). With the chemical explosions at Seveso and Bhopal over the same period, the claim that society was experiencing a kind of general backlash from nature was appealing. Growing suspicion of political and commercial motives encouraged the idea that there was a conspiracy to ignore the dangers of incessant attempts to master nature. Instead of seeing these incidents in their own specific circumstances, they became symbolic of a broader sense that man's (mis)use of nature had reached its limits, and the future needed to be approached with greater care. For the first time, at Seveso, there had been a dramatic and highly politicized reaction to an accident that had caused no fatalities. The emphasis had been on the possibility of *future* harm. This echoed Ralph Nader's dramatic claim in the Love Canal case that "mutated genes ... will affect all of [the residents'] descendants, one generation after another" (Fumento 1993: 119).

Considered instrumentally, emphasizing possible risks in the future blunted the need to prove that any actual harm had been caused by the environmental threat in question. No one can decisively refute the possibility of future harm. This outlook, which was rapidly being popularized across American and European societies, encouraged a departure from "known" risks into a far more speculative approach, extrapolating into the future whereupon risks lost the restraints of physical reality and grew inordinately. Moreover, the fact that faith in politicians, scientists, and "big business" was declining meant that an ability to deal positively with risks and disasters was not included in the future projections. Caufield's history of our "multiple exposures" to radiation cites the curious calculation (which she calls "conservative") that 4,000 people will die and over 2,500 will be born with genetic defects as a result of the 80 gigawatts of nuclear power generated in 1980. She eventually adds the rider that "the deaths and injuries will be spread over millions of years" (Caufield 1989: 202). The possibility that such conditions may not be a problem in a hundred years, let alone millions of years, escaped her imagination.

It was not only the scale of risks and hidden damage that grew in the popular imagination, but also the breadth. Everyday items that people had taken for granted were increasingly called into question over the 1980s and 1990s. There were "panics" in the United States (many of which diffused internationally) over the safety of pesticides, salt, tampons, artificial sweeteners, and foam insulation, among others.[4] In the American context, the cutting edge of the new "risk society" was the civil legal system. Angell (1997) notes that the era of the mass risk tort was announced with the first successful product liability litigation in 1973 over asbestos. Over 200,000 lawsuits were eventually filed. Many others have followed, such as lawsuits over the miscarriage drug DES, the pregnancy drug Bendectin, the Dalkon Shield contraceptive, dioxins in Agent Orange, and artificial heart valves. The case against cell phone EMF is now also being advanced through litigation.

Not surprisingly, questioning society's everyday consumption, the environment, and the health of future generations, combined with flattering fears and concerns as more legitimate than the proclamations of science and its political advocates, has undermined confidence in scientific knowledge and resulted in an unprecedented public sensitivity to risk. Sensitivity toward "unnatural" hazards has acquired a life of its own; it has become part of a risk consciousness that has been consolidated throughout the Western world in the remarkably short space of the last three decades. Bound up with this consciousness is a distinctively fragile conception of human health and the body. With everyday risk concerns such as vaccines, food, and radiation it is not a straightforward threat that so animates responses but subtle changes assumed to be capable of devastating impacts.

Medicine, Cause, and Effect

Not only have there been important shifts in the way in which government policy and academic discourse perceive and respond to risk, but medicine also has been drawn toward entertaining and projecting minor risk associations rather than confining itself to what can be known with greater certainty. An important development in the public interaction with science is the way that scientific knowledge has become bound up with delivering social policy, resulting in scientific facts being distorted in the service of particular policy directives or desired *social* outcomes. The public has

---

[4] For details and a critique of these early "panics," see Sapolsky (1986), Fumento (1993), Wildavsky (1995), Foster, Bernstein, and Huber (1999), and Park 2000.

been encouraged by this policy-led science to believe that many types of behavior will profoundly influence health, for example. Science itself, particularly medicine, appears to have sacrificed some of its own integrity in an environment where funding and interest are bound up with health and environmental risk protection policies (Le Fanu 1999).

In addition to a more "socially relevant" science, there has been a "social transformation of medicine" (Starr 1982). With a turn toward society and away from biology, potential health risks have acquired a new importance, particularly through the expanded discipline of epidemiology. Skolbekken (1995) describes a "risk epidemic" in medical journals, with increasing references to risk in their pages through the 1970s and 1980s. The medical writer James Le Fanu sees the danger in the elevation of epidemiology: "further investigations revealed many more previously unsuspected hazards.... Even the most innocent-seeming inanimate objects, such as electricity pylons, mobile telephones and sewing machines, were all found to be full of menace" (Le Fanu 1999: 373). An article in the journal *Science* observed that "the search for subtle links between diet, lifestyle or the environment and disease is an unending source of fear – but yields little certainty." The result was a "mind-numbing array of potential disease-causing agents from hairdryers to coffee... the pendulum swings back and forth resulting in an "epidemic of anxiety" (cited in ibid.: 380).

Today's anxieties about health bear little resemblance to those at the turn of the century, not least because the populations of countries where health risks are given most attention are no longer confronted with the specter of disease in young life. Most people now live out their natural life span to die from diseases strongly connected with aging. Health instead has become an "imperative" (Lupton 1995), promoted through government education initiatives, dedicated television channels, and product marketing. In the process, there seems to have been a growing belief, endorsed by the pursuit of epidemiological studies, that more nebulous lifestyle issues are the source of health differentials.

Dubos argues that the discovery of the major causes of death meant that specific etiology (the principle that every disease has a specific cause), a cornerstone of scientific medicine, "was reaching the limits of its usefulness" (Fitzpatrick 2001: 132). This development is central to health risk issues such as the effects of cell phone EMF because the impossibility of finding a specific cause sustains the belief that there are reasonable grounds for uncertainty about the technology's safety. Claims about health effects, as we saw in the previous chapter, focus on questioning safety rather than positing a more credible, verifiable mechanism through which EMF harms health. The departure from specific etiology creates a constantly shifting ground for argument and suggests that any number of otherwise improbable "causes" might have an effect.

In the late 1970s, a new critique contested medicine's focus on biomedicine and technological interventions aimed at curing disease. In a highly influential text, McKeown argued that this focus had "led to indifference to the external influences and personal behavior which are the predominant determinants of health" (cited in Le Fanu 1999: 315). The emphasis on social factors proved to be very popular, most likely because it supported the opening up of a new range of policy initiatives in disease control, focused on getting people "to change their diets, control pollution and eradicate poverty" (ibid.: 318). The link between smoking and lung cancer, which was already established, was used as the compelling example of social factors and provided the model for future epidemiological research as well as the inspiration for a new turn toward social engineering. In 1980, in *The Causes of Cancer*, Sir Richard Doll, who had assisted Austin Bradford Hill in establishing the link between smoking and cancer, claimed that nearly three-quarters of cancers were attributable to food consumption. Samuel Epstein of the University of Illinois wrote in Nature in 1980 that another 20 percent of cancers were caused by minute quantities of chemical pollutants.

Health education, which emerged in the later 1970s, heralded the policy concern with environmental factors in health. Its wider appeal lay in contesting the reliance on a medical "establishment" and a new emphasis on personal responsibility. The logic was that changing everyone's behavior regardless of the extent to which all were at risk would be more effective, nondiscriminatory, and cheaper. AIDS was already being dealt with in this way. But the centerpiece of the new approach was the identification of heart disease with poor diet. Major government campaigns were launched to reduce cholesterol, despite the lack of evidence of a causal connection with heart disease. Historical development has shown that man is extremely adaptable for living in many conditions and so it is logically suspect to contend that subtle changes in food consumption alone cause lethal diseases. The body's physiological functions are generally insensitive to small changes; in the case of cholesterol, "many 'feedback' mechanisms ensure the ... levels remain at a steady rate, so if the amount of fat in the diet is reduced, the liver compensates by increasing the amount of cholesterol it makes" (Le Fanu 1999: 324). Extensive trials showed by the early 1980s that radical changes in diet did not reduce the risk of a heart attack.

By the mid-1990s evidence against the dietary theory was overwhelming (ibid.: 348). Yet initiatives to encourage "healthy" behavior across the populations of advanced countries proceeded apace, inspiring their own industry of health products.

The consequence of the emphasis on health, and its foundation on a sense of vulnerability to poorly defined risk factors, is that people have become inclined to believe that unknown agents in the products and environment around them are affecting their health, and they are more mistrustful of established knowledge. The rise in second opinion–seeking is testament to this, as is the expansion of "alternative" medical theories across Western societies. The proliferation of Internet websites through which people can exchange anecdotes about health problems and evolve their own theories of causes, as in the case of cell phone EMF campaigners, is further evidence of the lack of willingness to rely on traditional medicine, science, or established explanations. More recently, there is now less of an emphasis on the social factors and differentials that undoubtedly play a role in some conditions and more on environmental factors per se. An important focus for this new emphasis is the energy now devoted to insisting on an "environmental" connection to breast cancer (Davis et al. 1997; WHO 1999).

Accommodating Science to Society

It is widely acknowledged that there is new uncertainty and ambivalence in public attitudes toward science. Reassurance about the relative safety often appears to strengthen rather than allay suspicion, as it did during the BSE crisis. A House of Lords Select Committee report on science and society in March 2000 suggests that "[t]hese negative responses are expressed as lack of trust" (House of Lords 2000a: 5), elsewhere wondering "whatever precisely this may mean" (ibid.: 20). The erosion of trust is located within the terms of the relationship between science and society, now described as a "difficult interface" (Prost 1998: 31). This emphasis has meant that the problem is examined only within the confines of that relationship, where the range of solutions is limited to how much one should accommodate the other. In the context of disillusionment with scientific progress and distrust of scientific authorities, few feel comfortable asserting that society should accommodate science, and so the only path appears to be the accommodation of science to society. It is symptomatic of the times that Philippe Busquin, member of the European Commission responsible for research, can approvingly proclaim that "the myth of progress has been exploded as a myth."[5] His solution is a new, explicit contract between science and responsible institutions. On both sides of the Atlantic it is insisted that science come to terms with the new public mood and adopt a more open, responsive, transparent approach that incorporates public concerns from the very beginning, arguably at the expense of scientific judgment itself.

The now popular idea that science must be reined in through external, public pressure assumes a deeply flawed enterprise. The first influential attacks on claims to scientific objectivity developed in the late 1960s. In his influential thesis, *The Structure of Scientific Revolutions*, Kuhn suggested that science was structured by its own paradigms and was not simply neutral (Kuhn 1970). Paul Feyerabend, who absolutely opposed the idea of scientific objectivity, provided a more direct attack. Scientific truth, according to Feyerabend, was determined by the decisions of the scientific establishment and by politicians, based on money, interest, and pride. The belief that facts, logic, and methodology reveal truth "is what the fairy-tale tells us" (cited in Cole 1981: 162).

It is too simplistic to present a linear development of challenges to the universal claims of science and technology. Gillott and Kumar (1995) argue that there were approaches from left and right, which converged on questioning progress and promoting a more modest, relativized science. The political right became disillusioned with progress through the experience of war, while those on the left expressed increasing doubt about the social benefits of science. This was clearly expressed in the late 1980s in the French intellectual elite's celebration of the end of "grand narratives," foremost among them the "naive" belief in social progress. The consequence is that "bold expectations of the future give way to concern for the present; optimism transforms into caution" (Bauer 1995a: 11).

Key assumptions of contemporary risk theory exercise increasing influence in debates about science and society. Discussion of a crisis of relations between the general public, science, and government is theoretically derived from Ulrich Beck's critique, which is distinct from the established challenges to positivist science, such as the studies on the social construction of science and technology by Latour and others (Callon et al. 1986; Bijker et al. 1987; Latour 1987). Beck's attack on science is far more thoroughgoing, contesting not simply its claim to absolute truth or inability

---

[5] Speech on "Science, Technology and Society in the 2000s" at "Science, Technology and Society in the 21st Century" conference, Santander, European Commission News Release, 18 September 2000.

to assess risk accurately, but that humanity has little chance of even recognizing, let alone saving itself from, "reflexive risk" so long as it remains
beholden to an outlook underpinned by scientific assumption (Mol and
Spaargaren 1993: 441).

At the core of the science and society debate, particularly in its sociological form, is an attack on science as it was conventionally understood.
In the first instance science and those responsible for decisions affecting
its impact have simply failed to recognize how times have changed. Previous attempts to improve the relationship between science and society,
from the mid-1980s onward, stressed the importance of improving the
public's understanding of science in the belief that people's fears stemmed
from insufficient knowledge. Today such approaches are accused of misunderstanding the true nature of the public's concerns and castigated as
further evidence of the arrogance of scientists who fail to see that concerns
about science are an instinctive, valid understanding of its limitations. The
British government's stance on BSE was to issue public reassurance based
on the best scientific information. It is described as "living in a time-
warp" (Macnaghten and Urry 1998: 257). Commenting on the House of
Lords' report on science and society, the British sociologist Brian Wynne
explains that its "essential message is that the widespread public mistrust
of institutionalized science cannot be remedied by elaborating existing
approaches." He accuses science and its representatives of perpetuating
a "culture of denial," still imagining that facts will speak for themselves
(Wynne 2000: 4–6).

Fierce reactions against science have become commonplace. Our relationship to science is described as "cowering in the shadow of technocratic decrees from experts marshaled behind closed doors and whose
pronouncements always seem to begin with the words 'there is no scientific evidence'" (*Financial Times*, 2 June 2001). The British consumer
affairs journalist Felicity Lawrence goes much further in her attack on
biotechnology, unashamedly describing herself as a "luddite" (*Guardian*,
28 May 2001). Associations with Nazism are also common, illustrated
by television series such as *Science and the Swastika*.[6] When it was first
used by post-war radicals of the Frankfurt School to indict modernity
and technology, the association was far more controversial (Gillott and
Kumar 1995: 180–4). Today the pairing of Nazism with science resonates
more profoundly with sensibilities, particularly around genetic research,
which is bound up with a sinister and unnecessary quest for perfection in

---

[6] Shown on Channel 4 in the United Kingdom during February 2001.

the contemporary imagination rather than potential treatment of diseases such as Parkinson's.

The response of authority to this mood has been largely defensive, reflecting and even running ahead of what is perceived to be public anxiety. In some instances we are witnessing vigorous self-restraint from scientists themselves, in what appears to be an attempt to prove that they share society's concerns and thereby to blunt attacks on science per se. A notable example is that important sections of the scientific community made public their boycotting of the First International Symposium on Cloning in October 2001 because it was presided over by embryologist Severino Antinori. There has been universal condemnation of Antinori, who claimed in August 2001 that he would clone a human being. Suspicion relates to his work on fertility in middle-aged women, which for him "is not an issue of being ethical or unethical, but rather assisting people to have children and that is the business we are in" (cited in the *Herald*, 6 October 2001). The fact that his team is alone in even considering this project underlines the extent to which science is overwhelmed by "ethical" doubts.

The proposition that institutions have been condescending in their estimation of public knowledge is now universally accepted. With the problem defined as elitism, it is not surprising that the routine feature of sociological works on science is a demand for a greater public role in decision making. The House of Lords echoes this demand: its report advocates no fewer than ten avenues through which public engagement must be sought: deliberative polling, national and local consultations, consultative panels, focus groups, citizens' juries, consensus conferences, stakeholder dialogues, Internet dialogues, and a government "foresight" program (House of Lords 2000a: 7). The new view of science even supports concessions to "lay knowledge" rather than simply better presentation and reassurance. Although unclear as to what it might actually be, the report aspires to a "democratic science" (ibid.: 42). The emphasis is away from the one-way communication of science to the public toward an interactive process of mutual learning.

Scientific knowledge is increasingly regarded as a matter of opinion, bias, or disposition. Nelkin (1992) argues that ostensibly scientific technical decision making is actually shaped by politics. The House of Lords report suggests that "[t]here is no such thing as pure science unadulterated by money or greed or personality. It is colored by something" (House of Lords 2000a: 36). That this "something" might be benign is not emphasized, neither is the possibility that being driven by "personality" might be creative and constructive. Suspicion of what scientists do behind closed doors is strong, particularly with regard to commercial funding. Consequently, "openness," "transparency," and "dialogue" are advocated. The House of Lords report even suggests that this more open approach might have averted the BSE crisis, despite the widespread recognition that the issue was driven by far wider sensibilities than public concerns about the closed nature of the scientific establishment (ibid.: 34). Unrealistically counterposed to a scientific establishment entirely blind to the nature of risk, in this discourse "the public" is sometimes endowed with an almost natural insight. Reflecting the input of the sociologist Brian Wynne, the House of Lords report suggests that "the public in fact understands uncertainty and risk well, on the basis of everyday experience" (ibid.: 22). Beyond participatory rhetoric, how a risk such as from radiation or BSE is to be understood on the basis of everyday experience remains unclear.

Prost (1998) remains one of the few scientific commentators to discuss an apparent, unrealistic public expectation that life must be risk-free. He further notes a "victimization culture" that determines that decision makers are held responsible for virtually anything perceived to have gone wrong in society. It could be argued that this victimization culture coupled with a suspicion of innovation render it naive to imagine that simply engaging with public anxiety can restore trust. Faced with a risk culture, it is unclear exactly how authority should go about informing the public of anything (Macnaghten and Urry 1998: 254). There has been a call for "citizens' committees" to debate perceived risks such as from cell phones and towers, but there have been few serious attempts to actually implement such schemes, and it remains unclear how to proceed.

In practice, it is difficult to see how "public accountability" could be implemented, and the absence of models is widely recognized. One example that has been cited is the recent case in the United States of the EPA tendering for public comment on establishing a "safe" level of arsenic in drinking water. It received over 12,000 comments, mostly e-mails, on all aspects of the issue, and plans to finalize a new standard in February 2002 in the light of this public involvement. According to one commentator, there was scientific evidence that the level of arsenic should be lower, following a suggestion from the National Academy of Sciences in 1999 that as many as one in 100 people might contract some form of cancer following regular water consumption. "Even stronger, though, it would seem, is the sense among Americans that picking the right level for the future is a political issue, in the deliberation of which they want to be included" (Barlow 2001). Whatever the desire for inclusion, however, the notion of a referendum on how much arsenic should be in drinking water raises more questions than it answers. While we can assume most people would opt for there being absolutely none (regardless of the reasons for its presence or the cost of removal, in the first place), where would policy makers be left if, for some reason or another, a majority opted for an unsafe level?

In the United Kingdom there are currently attempts to institutionalize concern about the environment through the establishment of an environmental court, such as exists in Australia and New Zealand. Professor Malcolm Grant, in a 2000 report for the House of Commons, recommended the creation of such a court to elevate citizens' rights. His argument is that it would present science "for all to see" and give a voice to all interest groups. The report identifies a need to go further than the inquiries chaired by judges into controversies such as BSE, and to open up governance to wider scrutiny. The proposal involves an expanded role for scientists, who would be given their "due recognition" and interwoven with a new regulatory system. Describing "where the court would rule," it points to mobile phones, foot and mouth disease, BSE, and genetically modified foods (*Independent*, 29 May 2001). Where critics see the legal system as an arena that encourages "junk science" (Huber 1991), those proposing such initiatives suggest that the law can be a democratizing agent in disputes over new technologies, part of a public dialogue and thereby playing a role in putting forward a progressive critique of science and technology (Leone and Jasanoff 1995).

The character of the public "lay knowledge" that needs to exert influence over science is not immediately apparent. In one sense it would seem to be eminently practical and experience-based; but of course most people have very limited experience of scientific matters, and experience rather than intellectual insight is likely to be of limited use in casting judgment on science, in any case. In reality, turning toward public "lay knowledge" can mean only resort to everyday morality. It is in this realm that virtually anyone might make some contribution to science-related debate; it is substantially an "ethical turn" where scientific considerations are made accountable to implicit moral concerns attributed to the people (Wynne 2000: 5). This is evident from Macnaghten and Urry's claim that BSE revealed Britain to be a "laboratory in which cattle were turned into carnivores." Despite contesting the construction of moral dichotomies in other parts of their work, they suggest that the feeding of animal to animal is both unique and uniquely abhorrent. It is perhaps only their enthusiasm for a new ethics to regulate scientific inquiry that explains such blindness to their own moral constructions. Indeed, they celebrate the "liberation" of perception from fact and into ethics (Macnaghten and Urry 1998: 263). What remains curious, however, is that the essentially moral character of the risk approach is itself rarely made explicit. Instead, theorists suggest that a disguised (im)morality is specific to scientific matters; the precautionary principle, for example, being presented as simply "common sense." If the problem were simply the moral blindness of science, it should be noted, then science would simply be engaged once again in its age-old confrontation with values.

A Precautionary Future

On both sides of the Atlantic, science and medicine, as with many more routine aspects of life, are increasingly subject to a precautionary ethos, regardless of the latter's relevance in specific issues. There may have been no formal precautionary warnings to limit children's cell phone use in the United States, for example, but it is evident that the perceived sensitivity of children to environmental contaminants is informing American public health policies. The Food Quality Protection Act of 1996 and recent changes to the Safe Water Drinking Act incorporated additional safeguards for the protection of children from chemical agents. At the American Chemical Society meeting in August 1999, one authority questioned whether these are scientifically derived or "simply reflect normative decisions made by political and regulatory bodies based on perception and the precautionary principle" (Shurdut 1999: 118). Whether or not this trend is to be regretted, there are no grounds for believing that it satisfactorily resolves the problems it purports to address.

The House of Lords' report acknowledges that problems of trust and confidence in science and other forms of authority may not be resolved simply by accommodating to perceived public mistrust. The report demands that scientists endeavor to respond to the negative public mood by declaring their affiliations openly, but at the same time, it notes that "political realities cannot be ignored. Peer review and declarations of interest have not averted the present crisis of trust" (House of Lords 2000a: 7). Greater openness certainly does not militate against the development of negative attitudes and panics. With a tone more of hope than expectation, the report continues that perhaps: "[b]y declaring openly the values which underpin their work, and by engaging with values and attitudes of the public, [scientists] are far more likely to command public support" (ibid.: 24). Arguably, communicating uncertainty to an already uncertain public is as likely to compound unwarranted anxieties as assuage them. One thing we can be sure of is that, regardless of whether a strategy of accommodation is successful, either for authority or society more widely, it will continue nonetheless.

A symbiotic relationship has emerged where society has become more dependent on science, and, equally, science more dependent for its own authority on politics, in what one German academic dubs the "scientification of politics and the politicization of science" (Weingart 1999). Particularly as they are now largely deprived of the traditional political languages of the past, technocratic Western polities are increasingly reliant on the authority of expertise, particularly in its "scientific" form. Special advisers, expert committees, review boards, and inquiries are establishing themselves as mainstays of politics. At the same time, political authorities feel bound to endorse risk-driven perceptions of danger from scientific and medical advance; in effect, *politics has become increasingly dependent on the science it increasingly undermines.*

As the BSE crisis illustrated, the policy orientation of science means that the political class is now implicated in the consequences of societies' "meddling with nature." Incidents that in their own terms might have a negative impact on only particular technologies or scientists have the potential to effect politicians and wider trust in the expertise that underpins society. The resulting attempts to regain trust by accommodating concerns and putting regulation in place only further enmeshes the worlds of science and politics so that, with the next outbreak of risk concern, the demand for accountability is cast ever more widely. Much more, then, gets called into question by even the narrowest of risk-related issues, a point that is not lost on the media, which now routinely seek a path from small errors or reported risks to the actions of government departments, the regulatory systems themselves, and the whole issue of who funds what research. Responses to issues such as BSE have led to the further institutionalization of risk concerns into everyday life, with the creation of the Food Standards Agency in the United Kingdom, for example, a body whose singular purpose is to encourage scrutiny of what we consume. In short, the reaction to the consequences of politicizing scientific issues has become to extend this politicization even further into public domains, rather than to question the wisdom of elevating highly specialized issues into public concerns in the first place.

As the embracing of science by politics continues to prove problematic for the latter, so this relationship has fatally undermined any pretense of science and medicine to neutrality. The problem for science in public

TABLE I. *Polls on degrees of trust in the United States and the United Kingdom (%)*

Q: Now I will read out a list of different types of people. For each, would you tell me whether you generally trust them to tell the truth or not?					
	United States, 1998			United Kingdom, 1999		
	Trust	Not	Net (± %)	Trust	Not	Net (± %)
Doctor	83	13	+70	91	7	+84
Teacher	86	13	+73	89	7	+82
Clergymen/priests	85	13	+72	80	14	+66
Professors	77	19	+58	80	14	+66
Judges	79	18	+61	77	16	+61
Television newsreaders	44	52	−8	74	17	+57
Scientists	79	18	+61	63	27	+36
The police	75	23	+42	61	31	+30
The ordinary man/ woman on the street	71	25	+46	60	28	+32
Pollsters	55	38	+17	49	35	+14
Civil servants	70	27	+48	47	41	+6
Trade union officials	37	58	−21	39	47	−8
Business leaders	49	47	+2	28	60	−32
Congressmen/MPs	46	51	−5	23	70	−47
The President	54	44	+10			
Journalists	43	52	−9	15	79	−64

Courtesy of Bob Worcester, MORI. Base: United States: 1,013; United Kingdom, c. 3000. (1997–1999).

perception is very clearly its relationship to business and government. Opinion polls demonstrate that even in the United Kingdom, let alone the United States, trust in scientists remains relatively high, but that it is its lack of independence from politics and corporate interests that invites public suspicion (see Table 1). Contrariwise, the purported "independence" of the science-related views of lobby groups and environmentalists inspires greater confidence, irrespective of the environmentalists' credentials on the matter in question. Ultimately it is science's intimate relationship with politics and business that is more problematic than directly antiscientific prejudice. This is also why explanations that attempt to situate the problem either in public hostility toward science or in the character of the scientific establishment (as aloof and elitist) miss the point. Yet this is not to suggest that the scope for expanding scientific intervention is likely to decrease. On the contrary, it will increase, albeit in a changed, "ethical" form.

The current powerful imperative for a publicly engaged and accountable science has ended "big" science in one sense, but strengthened it in another. While science has been chastened, even demoralized, its increased integration into policy and regulation means that its remit continues to expand. More "responsive" politics necessarily means setting up more expert committees: an expression of the contradiction between a reliance on experts versus responding to the public. Ironically, more experts and expert committees can lead to even greater uncertainty:

The seeming paradox is that the intensified use of scientific expertise has not increased the degree of certainty on the part of judges, administrators and policy-makers; on the contrary, it has left them witnessing the ongoing debates among scientific experts and forces them to decide between conflicting advice. (Weingart 1999: 158)

As Weingart continues:

The paradox arises because, in principle, the competition for the latest, and therefore supposedly most compelling, scientific knowledge drives the recruitment of expertise far beyond the realm of consensual knowledge right up to the research frontier where knowledge claims are uncertain, contested, and open to challenge. (ibid.)

Ever-increasing demands for certainty and reassurances push us into areas where those expectations are increasingly unlikely to be met. Despite the inability of either science or politics to address hypothetical risks in their own terms, there are likely to be many more science-based dilemmas such as that over cell phone EMF, perhaps based on an even smaller number of claims makers and an even more negligible perception of risk, because the culture of precaution has become politically irresistible.

7

Problems of Precaution and Responsibility

The Panic That Never Was?

The reactions to cell phone risk have been driven and shaped by an increasingly precautionary culture. Nonetheless, it was not inevitable that all societies should have reacted in a precautionary manner to the "phantom" risk of EMF, nor did they. While the precautionary culture does condition a greater sensitivity to risk in general, it does not predetermine which particular concerns are acted on, in what form, and to what degree. In a sense, there is an inexhaustible number of potential health concerns that could be raised and, in an environment in which resources and attentions are competed for, no shortage of claims makers seeking recognition for particular agendas. A recent article in the *British Medical Journal*, noting the "health hazards of mobile phones," asked, "Do laptops also pose a risk?" in a contribution that both stakes a claim on an unrecognized, yet evidently potentially fashionable issue and invites the further reaction that might begin the process of social construction (Vlasov 2000). Others who have been central to the promotion of cell phone risk have moved on to other foci as their campaigning efforts diversify and extend. A major U.K. conference in May 2002 included many of the protagonists in the cell phone scare such as Gerard Hyland, Alan Meyer, and Alasdair Philips. The conference aims to establish an agenda on "Electromagnetic Environments and Health in Buildings."[1]

---

[1] Organized by Abacus Communications at the Royal College of Physicians, London, on 16–17 May 2002.

A variety of factors combine to elevate one particular possible risk over others. Practical imperatives, such as the need to install a modern telecommunications infrastructure, circumscribe adaptation to particular anxieties such as over cell phones. However, policy making and initiatives that respond to concerns about intangible threats to our well being are determined, above all, by political disposition. By historical standards, contemporary Western societies are distinctively depoliticized and disengaged, and there are therefore few irresistible social pressures limiting the options to be pursued by those in power (Boggs 2000). Typically, what society now defines as potential social problems are brought to our attention by groups, even simply individuals, making claims that then interact with an increasingly influential media. Whether those in authority respond, and thereby establish a momentum for these claims, remains, at least partly, their decision.

Science correspondent James Meek painted a hypothetical scenario of "what might have been" had the British response to cell phone risk issued not simply precautionary advice for parents but firm recommendations that effectively ended mobile telecommunications:

Lord Pitkerro drew the curtains to block out the press pack camped outside his house. He had said enough yesterday, and the era of the mobile phone was over. For the hundredth time, he thought over what he and his fellow scientists had told the government. Had they taken caution too far? Had it been right, on virtually no evidence, to recommend banning mobile phone use for the under 18s and setting a five minute a day limit for adults? Had it been right to call for the dismantling of all phone antennae within a kilometer of inhabited buildings, rendering mobiles all but useless? True, nobody knew if they were safe, but nobody knew if they weren't – yet.

The Today program said something about a financial crash brought about by the collapse in telecoms shares. In Finland, home of Nokia, the government had resigned. The papers were calling the Pitkerro report "the safety culture gone mad." The U.S. and E.U. were denouncing him, even as skipfuls of British mobiles headed for the scrap heap. Well one day they would thank him. Perhaps. (*Guardian*, 28 October 2000)

The outcome of the health alarm over cell phones was, in fact, nowhere near as dramatic as in Meek's fictionalized account. Insofar as it is possible to speak of a cell phone "panic," it had limited direct impact, particularly in those societies such as the United States where politicians and state institutions didn't directly respond to media pressures. Although cell phone fears originated in and were a product of American society, the issue was subsequently contained, effectively banished to the interminable world of

U.S. litigation. Attempts have continued over the last decade to establish a legal case for a cancer connection to mobile technology, but seem unlikely to succeed. In Europe and Australia, the concern acquired more momentum as it was in some cases directly politicized and in others flattered with precautionary state action.

Yet certainly in the "consumerist" terms through which public anxieties are now often given expression, the impact has been negligible in comparison with the defining examples of contemporary health anxieties. While European consumers continue to boycott anything tainted with the "genetically modified" label in favor of the "organic," there has been no comparable rejection of cell phones. Intensified risk aversion may have made significant inroads into European consciousness over the last decade, but it is evidently still not all-consuming. Practical considerations continue to determine what is perceived as an important risk and what is not. Particularly because of how the case has been argued, there appears no "need" for genetically modified food, or at least the consumer is in a position to comfortably reject it in favor of an alternative. Assuming the desire to communicate on the move, or make it possible for one's children to do so, there was no such clear choice involved with cell phones. There was no organic cell phone, of course, although there are models that promise less radiation. It is interesting to note, however, that the demand for handsets emitting less radiation was never very great. The fashion for handsfree devices passed by the late 1990s, and more recent models that promise virtual elimination of radiation exposure to the brain were met with little media, let alone consumer, interest.[2] This suggests that in circumstances where risks are accepted, the concern is then effectively closed. Even painless, if time-consuming, risk avoidance such as opting for a phone emitting less radiation appears to have little purchase once a risk is, to all intents and purposes, socially accepted.

Compared with other public health risk issues, cell phone risk is a "panic that never was." The BSE "panic" led to a collapse in demand for beef throughout Europe in the late 1990s and a subsequent devastation of cattle farming. Precautionary responses continue to have alarming consequences. Hospitals across Britain were ordered to use throwaway instruments for routine tonsil surgery as part of hastily introduced measures

---

[2] A new mobile headset that cuts radiation reaching the head by 98.5 percent, "Safe Talk for Life" was unveiled at a press conference at the Institute of Directors, London, on 10 September 2001. Despite extensive press releasing, there was little media interest in the new product.

to combat vCJD. Following two unnecessary deaths and many other operating theater accidents, the clumsy equipment (costing £25 million) was abandoned by the Health Department, to the relief of surgeons in May 2002. Curiously, the Government's Chief Adviser on vCJD subsequently told the media that the risk was negligible and that he would be happy to have his tonsils removed with traditional equipment, as if he had no role whatsoever in continuing the policy of using throwaway instruments (*The Times*, 4 May 2002). It appears that it was a generally precautionary climate, particularly with regard to the human form of "mad cow disease," that determined policy on the issue rather than scientific knowledge.

The European alarm over genetically modified (GM) "Frankenfood" has led to a situation where, in a speech to the national press club in Washington, D.C., European Union Health and Consumer Protection Commissioner David Byrne warned: "Unless we can give EU consumers confidence in this new technology then GM is dead in Europe."[3] As they launched an ambitious policy paper to put Europe at the forefront of biotechnology and lifted its moratorium on more than a dozen genetically modified organisms in operation since the mid-1990s, the European Union now finds itself complaining about the anti–genetic modification attitudes that their precautionary response did so much to encourage. Earlier examples from the United States where consumer anxiety, coupled with the threat of litigation, led to the collapse of an industry or product include light aircraft, some contraceptives, and breast implants. Other consequences of precautionary risk avoidance are more indirect. In a survey of U.K. plant scientists, almost half said that the anti–genetic modification campaign had made a career in plant sciences less attractive, and gaining funding for genetically modified plant research more difficult.[4] Projects have been abandoned, such as virus-resistant potatoes. The cellular communications industry, by comparison, may be facing a serious slowdown, but its crisis is rooted primarily in the onset of global economic recession, particularly in the information technology sector, not a health anxiety–driven boycotting of its product.

---

[3] *Life Sciences and Biotechnology – A Strategy for Europe* (Brussels: European Commission, 2001). Both citations from the European Commission publication *Cordis Focus* 183 (22 October 2001).

[4] Survey published in the *Times Higher Education Supplement*, 20 October 2000. The survey contacted all high-ranking plant science departments in the country. Just under a third (124) recorded their opinions.

As microwave fears had earlier shifted their focus from power lines and computers to cell phones, insofar as the cell phone health issue actively continues, it now concerns base stations rather than handsets. On the basis of original claims about the dangers of cell phones themselves, anxiety has diffused to the supporting network of towers. The fact that objections have decisively shifted to contesting the precise location of cell towers rather than any threat from the billions of cell phones themselves suggests that attempts to stigmatize the cell phone were no more successful than earlier efforts against VDTs or other technologies. In retrospect, the extraordinary barrage of stories linking cell phones to possible health threats appears to have left no enduring mark.

The Lingering Specter of Cell Phone EMF

Despite the relative lack of impact made by health fears on public enthusiasm for cell phones, the phantom risk of EMF is a specter that cannot be definitively banished in its own terms. Few suggest that cell phone EMF is a major threat to human health. Ominous assertions that it might be "the next smoking" were largely rhetorical, drawing on a wider discourse of impending threats. The real dimensions of the issue are more modest, and the case for further investigation remains a relatively straightforward one. Because of the sheer numbers of people using these devices, often for prolonged periods of time, and directly against the head, more research is continuing. Curious effects connected to cell phone EMF have appeared in a few studies, although none suggest actual human harm, but these effects have not been reproduced, indicating that results may be the result of flaws in the design or conduct of research.

Critics argue that there is a fundamental problem with all such research, even into more established, yet still minor risk factors (Le Fanu 1999). Investigation into small effects, difficult to isolate from other influences and posited as a threat through progressive long-term accumulation, necessarily has to significantly amplify their impact. Laboratory animals will thus be exposed to massive and targeted exposure. If there is evidence of harm at this level, a proportionally lower level of harm is usually extrapolated. But we are exposed to all manner of chemicals and phenomena that are dangerous at intense levels, and what is harmful at high exposure can be beneficial in moderation, never mind being simply harmless. There are threshold levels beyond which problems may occur, and it is illegitimate to imply that some degree of harm will be caused before that point is reached. A particular problem facing further inquiry in this field is the absence of even a persuasive theory as to how such radio waves, too weak to cause any direct heating effect, could possibly have a negative impact on human biology.

Theories about how such an effect might occur remain only conjecture (Hyland 2000). What is more, any negative health effect would most probably be evident only over a very prolonged period of time, this being the principal contention of those supporting extensive precautionary measures. In itself, this is not a helpful argument. There remains no evidence of even the smallest negative health impact, and multiplying "no negative effect" into a potential, cumulative "electrosmog" does not compensate for this fact. Emphasizing possible long-term effects is attractive to campaigners because it is a possibility that is so difficult to disprove: it can always be argued that we have not measured possible effects over a long enough time frame. The absence of proof of human harm is not due to a lack of investigation. A vast amount of research has been undertaken into possible biological effects of radio-frequency energy over the last fifty years, much of it close to the frequencies used by mobile phones. In the early 1990s there were evident gaps in research on digital mobile radio-frequency signals, but these are being filled with major studies on cancer connections, in particular.

Further research is unlikely to yield definitive answers, certainly ones that can decisively reassure safety concerns. As with all kinds of scientific inquiry, beginning from abstract possibilities rather than a more concrete problem is not conducive to focused research, let alone clear conclusions. There is an absence even of incidental clusters of association between cell phone EMF and cancer, never mind a statistically significant relationship. The principal consequence of further research may be only further uncertainty, and it is worth considering the remarks of physicist Robert Park in this regard. He is the iconoclastic critic of "junk science," what he defines as "tortured theories of what *could* be so ..." (Park 2000: 9). Park asks with regard to EMF research: "And when that research is done, it can always be asked if a larger study, or more sensitive measurements might reveal a problem at some lower level." To an extent, the scientific process in such areas necessarily proceeds slowly, with each fragment contributing to the sum total of knowledge and thereby shifting the balance of probabilities. Yet it cannot simply be assumed that this will always be the case when considering what are evidently small risk factors whose effects are difficult to isolate. A conclusion of the EMF issue is particularly difficult in charged circumstances where external pressures demand, and some researchers themselves allow, highly tentative research to be thrown immediately into the public sphere. Park suggests that a limit should be imposed on the process of investigation into such phenomena: "At what point should researchers decide that the connection, if there is one, is too weak to identify, or the hazard, if a hazard exists, is too insignificant to be concerned about?" (ibid.: 142).

Ultimately, there are essentially nonscientific decisions to be made about social priorities in considering the scope of investigation into a phenomenon such as cell phone EMF. In a world of infinite resources, criticisms such as Park's might have little force, but clearly this is not the case. Italian health minister and cancer expert Umberto Veronesi is one authoritative individual who contests the scale of response precisely on these grounds. He argues that the estimated 20 to 30 billion lire it will cost to comply with new Italian EMF laws would be better spent elsewhere. For him, possible links between EMF and the two cases of leukemia in Italy at the center of controversy do not justify such expenditure.[5] This argument is not unique to cell phone EMF; precisely the same cost/benefit objections could be made regarding relatively minor, as opposed to phantom, risks. By Lomborg's calculations, allocation of resources away from regulating environmental risks such as toxins could save 60,000 more Americans each year (Lomborg 2001: 338–42). At the global level, problems more fundamental than cell phone EMF continue to blight humanity. There are six diseases that cause 90 percent of the total infectious disease deaths worldwide: measles, malaria, tuberculosis, diarrheal diseases, acute respiratory infections, and AIDS. All but AIDS are curable, at least to some degree. Worms such as hookworm and schistosomiasis infect 1.3 billion people a year, mostly through working or playing in fields that double as latrines or swimming in infected lakes and streams. Some 300,000 of these infections lead to death, and for those that survive, repeated infection and reinfection can stunt growth and produce years of discomfort. Each case of these worms can be treated with one or two pills costing $1.

The resources involved in proposed restrictions on EMF are far smaller than the sort of expenditures involved in slowing global warming. Italian and Swiss restrictions are unusual in the considerable expenditures they would necessitate if they were to be implemented. At the same time, the $100 million estimated to be involved in this research area is hardly trivial. It would appear legitimate to ask at least whether these sums should be deployed in this sphere rather than other research fields, particularly ones that suggest the possibility of more consequential results. While it would

---

5 Cited in Italy Daily, *Wall Street Journal Europe*, 24 April 2001.

be an oversimplification to suggest that phenomena such as cell phone EMF are being investigated at the expense of dealing with more basic health problems in the developing world, it is perhaps useful to remain mindful of the wider global picture and the fact that decisions about priorities should remain open to question.

Devoting increasing resources to researching cell phone EMF also suggests, for some, a limiting of ambition on the part of medical science and society. The *New Scientist* (10 April 1999) pointed out that it is unlikely that even major research programs will succeed in answering doubts about cell phone EMF. It reflected that "[w]hile the bill for the research is peanuts for an industry worth billions, it does make one wonder about the WHO's priorities. Medical passions once devoted to changing the world are apparently being invested in comparatively minor safety concerns."

Results are also unlikely to have any major consequence for the development of cell phone use, even if it can be said they would contribute to more informed choice. Research into mobile radio-frequency effects has something of a curious character in that there is little question that billions of people will continue to use these devices, largely irrespective of research outcomes. It is unlikely that cell phone EMF will be shown to be a serious hazard. In practical terms, even if it were discovered that mobile radio-frequency was a small risk factor over prolonged exposure, what are we to do? What could be done? Would we care to know? Given the demonstrable benefits of this technology in terms of social and physical emergencies, would we be left only with an imponderable dilemma? While decisions to commence or continue scientific investigation should not be determined simply by whether they are potentially (socially) consequential, nor should the broader outcomes of research be ignored. In an age where science is told to escape its "ivory tower" and be mindful of its relationship and responsibilities to society, this might include some consideration of the potential consequences of investigation.

Scientific inquiry in the case of the British Stewart Inquiry has extended its attentions beyond the already difficult area of cell phone health effects to address the health concerns about cell towers. People are sometimes more aware of cell towers with regard to a potential hazard than cell phones themselves, partly because of the sense that exposure to the former is involuntary. Yet while emissions from towers may be more powerful than from a cell phone, actual exposure is comparatively more limited, to the extent that it is difficult to distinguish from the manifold other sources of nonionizing radiation that surround us. It is perhaps the most overwhelming peculiarity of the whole cell phone EMF story that concern has come to center on cell phone towers, rather than handsets. There is no clearer confirmation that this is an essentially social, rather than strictly scientific, story. It could also be argued that it is the clearest failing of scientific authorities' risk communication efforts.

Clearly establishing a distinction between cell phone and tower emissions appears a more difficult task in circumstances where both social fears and scientific realities are addressed at the same time. Aside from the scientific substance of the Stewart Inquiry's review of the research, precautionary health fears concerning towers were described as legitimate, and accommodation of anxieties was urged within the same report. The intention appears to have been to demonstrate that good science was compatible with an understanding attitude toward public concerns, no matter how unfounded these concerns are. This very conscious accommodation reflects a wider trend in risk inquiries to be seen to engage the perspective of the "victim." The Philips Inquiry into BSE extensively consulted the families of sufferers, as if they held special insight into this terrible but fortunately very rare condition. An increasingly "victim-centered" perspective for science-based inquiries appears to have done little to further understanding of the issues involved, however.

The Stewart Report attempted to manage and accommodate both scientific fact and "public" fear. Surprisingly, the report endorsed the "validity" of health concerns about masts in one section, while acknowledging in its scientific capacity that neither handsets, nor especially towers, posed a threat to the "general health of the population." Unsurprisingly, there remains some confusion about the scope of the mobile microwave problem, as a precautionary approach was taken to a hypothetical, rather than proven, risk. If the legitimization of tower concerns did little to assist public understanding, it does appear to have played a role in "socially constructing" determinedly health-based opposition to cell towers. Concerns of local residents in fact often centered on issues of esthetics, impact on property prices, and, above all, lack of consultation. In something of a self-fulfilling prophecy, the health dimension became predominant at least partially only because it was this aspect that was taken most seriously by the official inquiry. This is not to suggest that grievances about tower siting should not have been addressed; on the contrary. Local concerns about cell towers appearing suddenly next to individuals' houses and schools should have been anticipated, let alone acknowledged retrospectively. Better, more anticipatory risk communication would have helped deal with grievances in their own, more manageable terms rather than in relation to the essentially irresolvable health agenda. "Acknowledging" often nonexistent health concerns meant that real issues of establishing an effective consultative framework for tower siting were obscured. *Instead, the extent to which the health dimension was acknowledged became coterminous with how seriously the issue was being taken.*

At the same time as being critical of risk communication efforts, however, one can argue that clearly distinguishing between different exposures to EMF was never going to be an easy task. Given that even handset emissions remain an essentially hypothetical risk in the first place, making a clear distinction between this and the more limited exposure to towers is perhaps not as straightforward as it might appear. EMF from neither cell phones nor towers can be declared "safe." Once risk is elevated in society's consciousness, clarity and proportionality becomes an elusive quantities. To declare that towers were a far smaller risk than handsets appears to acknowledge the existence of an actual risk.

Far from being a straightforward regulatory issue, the story of cell phone risk is very much one of late twentieth-century anxieties. Outside of an environment now instinctively suspicious of the "unnatural" and how it might disrupt a curiously fragile human biology, it is difficult to imagine why the cell phone story should have made an impact, even if it was ultimately of limited consequence. The precautionary principle and, to an extent, the wider contemporary imagination insists on an assumption of "harm unless proven otherwise." What underpins such thinking in many instances is an inflation of the scale of hazards confronting humanity.

Certainty, Precaution, and Public Fears

The British Stewart Inquiry is regarded as an exemplary response that neutralized anti-scientific sensibilities and in the process demonstrated sensitivity to public feeling in a way that has gone beyond tentative early American experiments in "citizen science." The precautionary experiment over cell phone risk may be relatively unimportant in itself, but as a model for future handling of health risk it is more significant.

What is distinctive about the response to cell phone fears is not that relatively extensive funds have been committed to further research, but that the response was shaped by the new politics of precaution. The general background to a contemporary health anxiety such as EMF is the post-1960s questioning of human industrialization and progress, their impact on the environment, and, in turn, the negative consequences back on human health. The expectation that apparent health problems represent only the tip of the proverbial iceberg has been strong, particularly since the 1980s. More specifically, the context in which cell phone fears were negotiated was a culture of precaution on principle that developed in Europe in the 1990s, following more informal applications of precautionary approaches to health concerns earlier in the United States. Official endorsement for routinely acting on the basis of the worst possible outcomes created resonance for alarmist stories of "frying" brains.

The adoption of a precautionary approach was an indirect response to other, unrelated issues, most notably the experience of BSE/vCjD in Europe. The overwhelming, if highly selective lesson of the BSE/vCjD experience was that public authority should amplify even theoretical risks. European societies are subsequently being reshaped around the new politics of risk, which dictate that not being seen to be taking risk sufficiently seriously is now a guiding political principle. Where a failure to deliver on programmatic promises, for example, compromised political careers in the past, the allegation of complacency in the face of potential threats to public health is now at the fore in contemporary Europe. Germany's Health Minister, Andrea Fischer, resigned and accepted responsibility for "mistakes made in managing the BSE crisis" in January 2001, for example (*The Lancet*, 20 January 2001). Having suggested that sausage meat was not a serious risk on 19 December, she was then advised to recall all such meat the following day. The Minister of Agriculture, Karl-Heinz Funke, was also forced to step down for his department's failures. As in the more celebrated incident involving the British Conservative Party's response to BSE, there remains no question that either German sausages or British beef burgers were a serious health hazard. Their mistakes were a failure to appreciate the new, often symbolic politics of precaution. The somewhat ironic consequence of this dynamic is that politicians are more than ever cast as the guardians of public health, even if it is a role that some individuals fail to live up to. Institutions are also recast; following the BSE alarm the former Ministry for Agriculture in Germany was renamed the Ministry for Consumer Protection, Food and Agriculture.

The response to cell phone health concerns furthers the trend toward precautionary responses to small-scale "multifactoral" risk and in the process consolidates very decisive reactions to highly uncertain health issues. By a recent European Commission definition, precautionary action is recommended in circumstances where there is a demonstrable hazard and consequences are likely to be "serious, irreversible and large-scale" (European Union 2000). Such criteria have proven highly elastic and were quickly extended in the cell phone case to a risk that cannot seriously be said to constitute a proven hazard that is "serious, irreversible and large scale." This was to be expected because the essence of precaution is to pre-establish limits for research that has not yet been carried out. One might consider it impossible to define qualities justifying the use of precaution on principle in phenomena that have yet to be investigated. It is particularly unclear how it can be known, a priori, whether consequences will be "irreversible" because it is dependent on the society confronted by the phenomenon. There is now a range of interventions for previously "irreversible" damage to fertility. Until very recently, genetic damage was considered irreversible, but many areas of science research now challenge this notion.

The projection into the future of problems but not solutions is an inherent flaw of the precautionary approach. Seen in terms of social progress, one might readily object to constraining the future on the basis of current perceptions of what society can manage. It is highly unlikely that in thirty years the current generation of children will be working, eating, communicating, or traveling in the same way or with the same technology as we do now. Even the evidence of irreversible, large-scale threat informing the most dominant precautionary imperative of our times is highly uncertain. A recent contribution on global warming reminds us that science is very "fragile" when it comes to offering easy prescription, and on this basis we should exercise "prudent inertia" with regard to precautionary action:

> the truth is that we are no nearer the truth about global warming than we were in 1988. Maybe the earth is warming up to an extent that matters, but maybe not. Maybe humans are driving climate change, but maybe not. Maybe we can change the course of climate's evolution over the next century, but maybe not. . . . There are two very good reasons for science's impotence . . . the situation is impossibly complex, and secondly, it defies proper scientific study. There cannot be experiments or controls. All analyses and interpretations depend on correlation – or correlation of correlations . . . and so on. (Baker 2001: 152–3)

Global warming projections take little account of the greater wealth, technology, and knowledge we could have at our disposal in the future, reflecting environmentalism's highly diminished view of human impacts (Lomborg 2001). The history of humanity is of a progressive limiting of nature's more destructive consequences, and this process continues no matter how ambiguously this dynamic is now regarded. Yet uncertainty about global warming, among other precautionary imperatives, is now largely ignored or even vilified. Instead, it is routinely asserted that we face man-made catastrophe unless drastic action is taken immediately. Such assertions are often substantiated with partial, dramatized statistics, as recent critics point out (Best 2001a; Lomborg 2001; Brignell 2002).

The very uncertain character of purported relationships between risk factors and many contemporary maladies is not translated into more tentative recommendations for how to respond. An example of this is the speculative nature of the "environmental" connection to breast cancer failing to inhibit calls for a vigorous response in the name of precaution (Davis 1997). An authoritative recent report notes that "the links with occupational and environmental factors may be small and the evidence for this is disputed. Disentangling the relative contributions of several factors in an inter-dependent causal chain is always going to be difficult. . . ." The report then leaps to an all-embracing conclusion at odds with the highly uncertain nature of the problem, asserting: ". . . and prevention calls for an integrated, holistic approach, based on the precautionary principle," citing an ecological text that "rethought" the issue two years previously (WHO 1999: 271). Before the advent of this precautionary rethinking, "disputed" evidence and "small" links might have been grounds for continuing to hold back from a large-scale, "integrated" response. The act of seeking such a relationship is likely to be a self-affirming one, and the very fact of initiating major investigation confirms to society the real possibility of such a relationship. It is no wonder that environmental cancer is described as a "political disease" in the title of a recent volume contesting media and activist interpretations of the connection (Lichter and Rothman 1999).

The argument for precautionary action on uncertain, multifactoral environmental risk factors is an attempt to compensate for the lack of any specific knowledge about identifiable relationships with a "holistic" approach that in effect evades the problem of establishing causality. In fact, we are not, and may never be, in a position to say that there are significant environmental risk factors causing breast cancer, for example, against which practicable steps can be taken. A "holistic" approach is also in danger of lapsing into the banal conclusion that society, our environment – perhaps life itself – is dangerous (which, of course, it is). The notion of "electrosmog" similarly makes no serious attempt to quantify any hazard, essentially resting only a sense of "contamination" and linguistic similarity with conventional pollutants. As in many other examples, the powerful sense of potential catastrophe is difficult to reconcile with the reality of a demonstrably safer environment. Hypothetical "electrosmog" hardly bears comparison with the conventional "smog" that blighted major cities such as London until recent times, for example. The last great fog in London, in December 1952, led directly to 4,000 deaths and subsequently led to the passing of the Clean Air Act.

Meanwhile, the extent of public concern on which these precautionary health initiatives are based is questionable and certainly demands further inquiry. Gauging the extent of public concern about health risks is not simply an academic issue. In an age where fears about public disengagement pervade every sphere of life, being guided by public wishes has acquired the status of a moral precept, even in such specialized fields as health. The U.K. government's highly risk-averse Chief Medical Officer, Liam Donaldson, for example, states: "My moral principle is that if ever there is a conflict it is the public who wins" (*Sunday Times*, 28 January 2001). It is not scientific evidence or government priorities but "the public" that will prevail, according to Donaldson, and his actions while in office indicate that his avowed intent is not simply good public relations. He has very publicly supported precautionary recommendations with regard to children's cell phone usage, for example. Sociologists and environmental lobby groups go further and argue that public "lay knowledge" often shows itself to be more useful than unreflective scientific investigation.[6] Yet the areas in which "lay knowledge" can be demonstrated to be especially insightful are limited, and in overgeneralizing from specific examples the approach arguably inflates the significance of social experience in scientific matters.

It has long been considered unwise to base health policy on perceived public feeling. Immunization against infectious disease, for example, is a social necessity regardless of any misgivings held by a minority. Discussing the wider history of product risks as they emerged in contemporary America, one authority was highly critical of the emerging response of authority:

Convinced that they must appear responsive to every public fear, officials make no effort to pursue a consistent, carefully designed policy toward health risks. Whatever the scare of the day, officials stand ready with hastily conceived congressional testimony, briefing papers, news releases, and research programs that demonstrate their commitment to protect the public. The scale of the response matches the fear, not the threat. (Sapolsky 1986: 191)

What is more fundamentally problematic than expedient politics is that they might be based on imagined, rather than real, public fears. The extent and character of public feeling about risk is rarely interrogated and is

---

[6] See, e.g., Greenpeace's contribution to the House of Lords inquiry (House of Lords 2000b).

indeed a difficult task in an age of depoliticization and social disengagement when opinions do not equal consequences. Some European sociological research assumes a fixed hostility toward new technologies without investigating its nuances or how sensibilities have been actively shaped (Grove-White et al. 2000). Widely commented on in the media, this report suggested that only 40 percent of people trusted information from the mobile phone industry about product safety. Regardless of the very small sample from which this conclusion was drawn, confronted with a prompted question, such a response is unsurprising. To affirm one's trust in a corporation is seen to betray naivete, even gullibility in a highly cynical age.

The cell phone example in the United Kingdom illustrates how media agenda setting often now stands as the only available measure of "public opinion," perhaps as even public opinion itself insofar as it has any social power. Invoking supposedly "public" wishes can be a means through which the media and lobby groups lend authority to particularistic claims. By definition, consumer organizations, for example, imply they are representative of all the public (as "consumers"), yet such a claim has little real foundation. More generally, health fears raised by lobby groups and claims makers in the name of "the public" are often, in fact, their own. A common contemporary lobby group tactic is to commission opinion polls that invite confirmation of suspicions about genetically modified foods, for example, apparently proving wider public concern. Yet such initiatives do not fundamentally alter the fact that these are often lobby-group, rather than meaningfully "public," agendas. On this basis it can be suggested that urging greater "public" participation can simply be a cipher to push for the inclusion and extended influence of lobby groups. Questioned about the "democratization of science," the chair of the U.K.'s Committee on the Public Understanding of Science professed that she was not sure what this fashionable concept actually meant. She added that "you have to be very careful not to confuse the very, very successful activities of campaigning groups with the expression of democracy . . ." (House of Lords 2000b: 40). Drawing nongovernmental organizations into consultation and decision making might be a desirable objective, but it is not the same as "public" participation.

Even in the most systematic of responses to cell phone risk, the Stewart Inquiry, there was no attempt to ascertain how much the concern was shared within society, despite the fact that the rationale for its investigation was given precisely as the need to assuage public anxiety. It seems to have become so routine in public life to respond to the media, in the absence of other influences, that its very direct influence on policy is treated as barely worthy of investigation, reflecting a pessimistic assumption that unbalanced media presentation both is inevitable and has a determining impact. It is very striking that the Stewart Inquiry also showed little interest (beyond a cursory review of press cuttings) in how, or why, the media pursued the agenda that they did. It is difficult to see how any review of current scientific controversies that embraces the new emphasis on a wider social dimension could proceed without unraveling the role of the media and the claims makers, who so successfully exploit the opportunities these controversies provide.

While "the public" are often bystanders to problems promoted by claims makers and lobby groups in the wider battle for influence, this is not to argue that "the public" is immune from, or positively rational in the face of, the "risk society." Greater individualization creates in turn a greater receptivity to such anxieties than in the past. But risk consciousness is essentially "free floating"; it is an amorphous anxiety that has difficulty fixing on any one target for any length of time (Furedi 1997). The most dramatically presented contemporary risks actually have little directly negative impact on people's lives by comparison with the "real risks" of the past. The infectious diseases that blighted even the developed world until the early twentieth century had an inescapable impact on life, and "public concern" hardly needed demonstrating. With today's "phantom risks," as the cell phone controversy illustrates, the imperatives of conducting one's life necessarily reintroduce themselves and enforce a more balanced perspective. It is only an issue such as genetically modified food, where rejection appears to carry no consequence for individuals, that a demand for "zero risk" can be given full expression.

At the same time, the absence of overwhelming public concern about cell phone EMF is not in itself a reason for ignoring an issue. Society cannot await majority support before making every health policy decision. Decisions are made on a balance of factors, including the scale of the potential danger, the scale of minority concern, and potential consequences. It is sometimes only a minority, even a lone individual, who brings important issues to the attention of society. Many campaigners on EMF regard themselves in these terms, as voices in the wilderness responsibly alerting society to a danger that it refuses to recognize. The majority of those campaigning against cell towers were by no means exclusively motivated by health concerns, however. Yet it was never made clear by official state responses such as the IEGMP that it was principally because of the actions of a handful of claims makers and media pressure that the concern met with a serious response. No consideration was given to the possible consequences for society and "the public" of pursuing a precautionary approach on health and cell phone EMF or reacting so unhesitantly to such a minority concern, perhaps because it appeared so inconsequential. The British scientific establishment, in particular, appears to have calculated that its precautionary credentials could be safely demonstrated in the relatively unimportant sphere of cell phones. Yet even when exercised in relation to an esoteric area, the application of precaution on principle is not without consequence.

Consequences of the "Panic That Never Was"

In some circumstances there is not only negligible public concern about health risks but positive hostility toward their elevation. Explaining that risk identification remains a "value-laden" activity, a recent contribution highlights the case of a mining town in Colorado where the community was identified as "at risk" from toxic contamination, following the identification of lead poisoning by the EPA. The town was already suffering from long-term economic decline and, in the view of residents, was further threatened by the prospect of mine owners being forced to clear up more than a century of waste.

Not only the mine owners but many of the town's residents

regarded the EPA as the devil incarnate. Grimly they recounted how government bureaucrats had invaded their town uninvited, threatening residents with the prospect of condemned property, involuntary relocation, and unwelcome new legal requirements.... And all, they claimed, over a hazard "that doesn't exist." (Needleman and Leviton 1998: 11)

The point is neither to condemn nor condone the attitudes of the townspeople, but to recognize that the identification of risks often has dramatic, unintended, and unforeseen consequences, which do not necessarily impinge on those making the risk assessment.

The international diffusion of anxiety about cell phone radiation exposure did not lead to panic-induced behavior or the ruin of an industry, in the manner of the MMR, BSE, or breast implant precautionary panics. But it was not without consequence, particularly in some societies. Most obviously, the problematization of cell phone EMF has translated into widespread difficulties with the siting of cell towers.

Reaction to the insensitive and inappropriate siting of towers is relatively spontaneous in many societies. To an extent this is an irresolvable problem, as the towers have to be located somewhere near to population centers and in increasing numbers if an adequate service is to be maintained. Restrictions on tower siting now present a threat to the third-generation mobile network, as it requires a more extensive infrastructure. With near universal acceptance of the need for the cell phone network, this problem has to be negotiated, most suitably at the community level. Yet in many countries, local and regional authorities have attempted to use the health issue to press for greater control over siting policy. The elevation of health anxieties has allowed the creation of a telecommunications infrastructure to become a power struggle between the local and national state. Furthermore, in Europe and Australia the cell phone scare has galvanized local reactions against towers and shaped them around the prism of health. This process has removed the conflict from the relatively straightforward local challenge of ensuring adequate consultation about appropriate siting that considers esthetic and economic impacts, and thus rendered it irresolvable in many instances.

Operators in countries such as Belgium and Switzerland are concerned about their countries becoming mobile-free "oases" in Europe as the blocking actions of local and national authorities and/or prohibitive EMF limits may make it financially unviable to run an effective service. Of broader long-term significance, however, are the implications for national safety and exposure standards. Through the cell phone issue, Italy and Switzerland demonstrated that establishing precautionary limits is a politically driven, essentially arbitrary process. If Italy and Switzerland wish to take extra precautions and establish limits ten times "safer" than anyone else's, why not make it twenty times "safer"? Such decisions clearly have implications for setting international scientific standards for toxicity and exposure, more generally. Once in place the very existence of distinctively precautionary standards compels a response from other nations, unless they are to stand accused of irresponsibility. Cell phone campaigners' principal argument was to point to more restrictive standards implemented in other countries. This is a compelling position, all the more so because few are prepared to explain why extreme precautionary standards have been set by others, let alone criticize the policies of other nations. This dynamic points toward internationally agreed standards being determined by the explicitly nonscientific politics of precaution, in not only this field but others associated with human or environmental risk.

Precaution as specific policy can be arbitrary and confusing, precisely because policy is then driven by the perceived need to accommodate anxieties, rather than to produce necessary and practicable solutions for an evident problem. As discussed, the demand to publish SAR (specific absorption rate) levels of cell phones made by consumer groups and echoed by the Stewart Inquiry was accommodated in 2001. SAR levels are now appearing on cell phone packaging worldwide. Yet it would be wrong to suggest that this move represents the introduction of "informed choice." Becoming "informed" about the significance of SAR levels is no easy task and is the subject of widespread disagreement even among experts. Insofar as there is a hypothetical possibility of harmful interaction of cell phone EMF with human biology, it would not reflect the intensity and direct impact of radiation, the only thing measured by SAR levels. In effect, for the everyday consumer mysterious new figures are appearing on their cell phones that they are not in a position to meaningfully interpret. Other precautionary policy recommendations have not been implemented but would have been problematic in any case. While Australian campaigners have called for a $5 research levy on cell phones, William Stewart has publicly called for increasing the cost of phones and calls as a means of discouraging teenage usage (*Daily Mail*, 5 September 2001). Whether it would be right or effective to compel parents to consider a phantom risk through economic punishment is questionable; insofar as it might, the less well-off might suffer disproportionately.

Precautionary *recommendations* rather than actual restrictions have characterized the cell phone episode. Such initiatives are more in keeping with the character of precaution and are therefore likely to become an attractive option in other fields as well as EMF. Precautionary recommendations, rather than straightforward prescription, emphasize allowing individuals to choose for themselves whether they accept a given risk. For the advocates of precautionary recommendations, they are left free of any responsibility for outcomes; their liabilities being discharged in a legal and moral sense. For the individual, however, "doing the right thing" can become even more confusing as it is left to them to decide the best course of action. The IEGMP proclaimed that children "may be at risk" but could be no more specific, given the speculative character of the risk. Suggesting that parents "limit" their children's' usage was an apparent compromise with the fact that the risk was only theoretical. The result was highly confusing. Even some of the British press that had been so central to generating concern in the first place expressed bafflement at the inquiry's conclusions. "So are mobiles a risk or what? Parents confused at shambolic phone report," declared the headline of the popular newspaper the *Mirror* (12 May 2001). On its front page, the *Evening Standard*, meanwhile, described: "Mobile phone safety chaos. Experts warn of risks to children but issue no clear guidance" (11 May 2001). There is a fundamental difficulty in the communication of scientific risk analyses, which do not lend themselves to totalizing declarations, and the demands of the media for conclusions of definite safety or demonstrable hazard. Yet the precautionary "compromise" does not appear to have improved risk communication. The prior problem is that, having elevated the concern in the first place by staging a major scientific inquiry, the expectation of greater clarity was heightened and subsequently all the more dramatically deflated.

Conflicting messages can create anxiety, particularly when choices are extremely difficult. Banning one's children from using mobile phones in the twenty-first century would be a dramatic step in many societies, comparable with insisting that children never watch television or play video games. It is difficult to imagine how an injunction to a teenager instead to "limit" their use might be interpreted. Precaution suggests limiting usage to "essential" purposes, but no doubt many young people would consider maintaining a social life, now intertwined with the cell phone, to be "essential." Complicating the picture is that many parents allow their children to have cell phones precisely because they suggest risk aversion of a more tangible character, allowing easy contact in case of emergency, for example. This appears to be an increasingly powerful imperative in post-Columbine, post–September 11 America. British parents, meanwhile, were presented with a very difficult choice between the recommendation of one of the country's leading scientific authorities and their own more immediate concerns. Evidently, they chose the latter. But the rise in calls to cell phone companies, national radiation regulators, and radio shows from worried parents indicates that this was not without some anxiety. It has long been recognized that there is a psychological price to pay for posing such dilemmas. Fumento details the stream of worried phone calls from frightened individuals following the original raising of microwave concerns. One pregnant woman asked whether she should now have an abortion after use of an electric blanket, for example (Fumento 1993: 243).

Precaution ultimately concerns political and moral choices, yet these can be confused with the apparently predominantly scientific basis for recommendations such as to limit children's cell phone usage. Like other invocations of precautionary politics, the unstated intention is actually a broader one. The application of precaution on principle draws its strength from a late twentieth-century mood of mistrust and caution, as the precautionary principle's original elaborator points out (O'Riordan and Cameron 1994). Based on the recognition that we can no longer proceed with bland reassurance of public concerns, it is perceived that institutionalizing precaution is a means of restoring trust in scientific decision making and authority. Implementation of precaution is about assuaging the mood of mistrust and countering public skepticism, proceeding on the assumption that if authorities can demonstrate similar levels of concern as they imagine exist among the public, they will be seen in a more favorable light. Yet there is no evidence to suggest this is the result nor even a strong logical case for believing so. It is evidently more likely that institutionalizing precaution on principle only consolidates mistrust as a matter of course, as society is implored to anticipate the worse possible outcomes from technologies and those promoting them. Certainly, confidence in the cell phone industry has not been restored as precautionary advocates such as Stewart continue to attack the industry's alleged "irresponsibility." Suggesting that science and government are on the consumers' "side" against malevolent corporations not only is, at best, a partial truth, but more importantly compounds the sense that we must be constantly vigilant and never merely assume that something is not harmful. Moreover, the act of dismissing risks and at the same time advising precaution can appear duplicitous and implies trying to please too many masters, which itself gives cause for mistrust.

The experience of risk communication from the fluoridation controversy onward is that no strategy is a panacea. Precaution on principle is no more effective as a blanket prescription than is a policy of denying that risks are worthy of our attentions. Often momentary pleas for the recognition of negligible dangers have their roots in real social discontents and insecurities, and are therefore not readily susceptible to even the most sensitive solutions in their own terms. If we do not feel our children are "safe" and secure more generally, it is unlikely we will be made to feel so by government inquiries about cell phone radiation.

At a social level, precautionary responses are becoming routinized to a point that it is now very difficult to reorientate policy making in a different, less "consumer friendly" direction even when it is manifestly imperative to do so. In the controversy over the MMR vaccine that raged from February 2002, the U.K. government insisted on unequivocal rejection of the apparent precautionary alternative of allowing parents the choice of single injections. With all parties accustomed to the new norm of accommodating minority concerns, suddenly attempting to confront precautionary fears becomes especially difficult and suggests a panic-like reaction on the part of authority that confirms public suspicions.

Media and claims maker publicity about an unproven connection between the triple vaccine, MMR, and autism continued to have a severe impact on the British vaccination program in 2002. By February 2002 the Department of Health announced that national use of the vaccine had dropped below the critical level of 85 percent, the threshold below which epidemics become a serious risk. In response to the growing precautionary panic over MMR, the British Prime Minister Tony Blair attempted to decisively reinforce confidence in February 2002, asserting that it was "safe" and that the consequences of "media scare mongering" would be an increasing threat from measles. In Parliament, he said that often such "scare mongering" did not matter, but in this case it certainly did (*The Times*, 7 February 2002). Discarding his stated preference for "what the public wants, must be right," Chief Medical Officer Liam Donaldson declared: "To capitulate to media pressure in light of strong scientific evidence ultimately damages children." Dramatically, he asserted that a switch to offering single jabs in addition to the multiple MMR would be like "playing Russian roulette with children's lives" and threatened his resignation if such a policy were introduced (*The Times*, 8 February 2002).

The government's response to the MMR issue has been belated, assertive, and heavy handed, reflecting an institutional machine that is not accustomed to attempting to confront, rather than only mirror, "public" fears. Following further suggestions that parents not using the vaccine might be summoned to their local doctor, the leader of "Jabs," the campaign for a choice of single vaccinations, denounced the move as intimidation characteristic of a "Big Brother" society (*Daily Mail*, 20 February 2002). It is now difficult to insist on "holding the line" on MMR when the government so recently adopted a precautionary approach to cell phones and towers, among other things. Implementing a precautionary approach even to a relatively unimportant issue such as cell phones establishes a distinctive culture among those charged with responsibility for health issues. In the MMR case, the swing from one extreme to another might only further alienate suspicious parents.

Restoring Balance and Responsibility

Bringing society's attention to possible risks in a way that previously may have been considered irresponsible can now be the "responsible thing to do." Taking responsibility is a key demand of our times, particularly in relation to scientific innovation. Science and technology must take responsibility for both its actions and the consequences of its breakthroughs, according to the new sensibility insisting on greater accountability and ethical strictures. Science and scientists have become more defensive as a result, calling into question the picture of a brash and thoughtless science on which the demand for scientific "accountability" draws its strength. However, the alleged problem of an overconfident, "Frankenstein-like" science is less evident or problematic than the extent to which policy on science, technology, and health issues are determined by unelected claims makers and lobby groups, who now wield significant influence on decision making, often through the media, but lack the professional accountability of established authorities.

The media has become more than simply a messenger, as it has taken on an explicitly campaigning role, in the United Kingdom in particular. This is noticeable in the self-congratulations that newspapers advertise when their "issues" receive a government response. In a relatively typical incident, *The Times* (28 January 2002) claimed with some justification that safety advice on a drug given to pregnant women is now under review by the government, "after *The Times* highlighted dangers associated with it." An article centering simply on one mother's story, dramatically headlining her opinion that the drug in question was "like the new thalidomide," had substantiated the authority of their claims. Yet alongside this development, the media's reputation for accuracy and trustworthiness has declined dramatically in the last decades. Journalists consistently figure lowest in opinion polls, below ratings for doctors, scientists, and even politicians (see Table 1). This raises the irony that government has become increasingly responsive to media influence precisely when the media's moral status in society has diminished.

Media campaigning seems to be at its most advanced in Britain. The House of Lords science and technology committee's fact finding tour of the United States noted, with regard to newspapers: "The writing tends to have less of an editorial slant, and so 'snowballing' stories or series of campaigning articles are far less common. The *Globe* journalists felt that in the U.S. there was greater requirement to 'show your working' in an article – any sensational assertions needed to be backed up . . . " (House of Lords 2000b: 10). Yet as the important role of television programs such as *Larry King Live* and *Eye to Eye* in the cell phone story illustrates, other forms of media are important in the American case. The FDA appears to have been influenced by the media in deciding to impose a precautionary ban on breast implants, for example.

Perversely, amid demands for institutions to assume greater responsibility for risks, sense of responsibility and consideration for longer term impacts appear to have diminished, as individual doctors, officials, and others almost casually pronounce the *possibility* of danger. In the

United Kingdom, Dr. Andrew Wakefield publicized the unsubstantiated risk of autism from the triple vaccine, MMR, with apparently little regard for its impact on the majority of parents and society. Dr. Peter Mansfield has subsequently advertised himself as a brave individual willing to administer single injections in response to the panic. Risk concerns socially constructed through an interaction between claims makers and the media have the potential to spin out of control to the extent of threatening public health, supposedly the concern that motivates the raising of alarm in the first place. In a welcome development, recent U.K. guidelines on communicating science and health issues argue that potentially problematic consequences of decision making and how this information is communicated should now be carefully considered (SIRC 2000).

In a rare interrogation, the House of Lords scrutinized the role of the media in health risk alarms recently. The Lords' committee on science and technology interviewed Rosie Boycott, former editor of the *Express* newspaper, and her science editor, Michael Hanlon. She is the editor of the newspaper that, more than any other, adopted an explicitly campaigning stance against cell phones and towers, innovating targets and themes along the way. The paper also played a pioneering role in creating hostility toward genetically modified foods, breaking the later discredited story that they caused harm to laboratory rats, promoted by Dr. Arpad Pusztai.

Boycott made plain the media's interest in "sexy risks" (such as cell phones) as opposed to less interesting, if more objectively important, dangers such as smoking and driving. She initially asserted before the committee: "We always endeavor on a science story . . . to make sure that it will always have a scientific basis." When presented with one of the newspaper's genetically modified foods headlines, however, she backtracked. Questioned about the headline "Mutant Crops could kill you," she conceded that perhaps it was exaggerated. "I think sometimes we possibly make it a bit too scary. It is a hard call," she replied, while remaining proud of breaking the "story" and still regarding such an act as a public warning service of "putting our hands up" (House of Lords 2000b: 213). She continued with the curious proposition that "[p]eople can say it is scaremongering but actually I think it is *correct scaremongering*" (emphasis added). The expertise available among the Lords themselves meant they were aware that the scientists backing the original claim of harm from genetically modified foods used by the media were in fact a group organized and backed by Greenpeace, rather than simply a random or representative group of scientists. It is to be regretted that there has been no opportunity to question newspaper editors and television program

producers on the cell phone issue, let alone claims makers such as Gerard
Hyland and George Carlo.

Contemporary risk assessment has become unbalanced and one-sided.
Cell phones have saved lives. The more mundane fact that they have
improved quality of life, at least in the majority's estimation, is also highly
pertinent to any consideration of society's reaction to the possible health
risks they might pose. Risk always needs to be put into context. After
questioning the "damaging" presentation of risks by the media, Lord
Quirk asked: "Why not encourage the beleaguered expert to turn around
and say 'Crossing the road is not safe. Driving a car is not safe.' . . . put the
risk into some kind of perspective." Another concurred, adding that the
death toll from "mad cow disease" amounted to just four days' casualties
on Britain's roads (ibid.: 192). There may be far more to risk perception
than comparative statistics, but it is at least a useful starting point from
which to proceed.

Angell's response to the FDA in the light of its precautionary ban on
breast implants points out that the agency is never supposed to insist that
a "drug or device be risk free, only that the risks be commensurate with
the potential benefits. . . . The job of the FDA . . . is to gather information
on both benefits and risks, and balance them" (Angell 1997: 62). Importantly in the case of breast implants, there were thirty years of experience,
with between 1 and 2 million women having used them, without major
problems occurring. Angell suggests that because the (male) head of the
FDA considered breast implants trivial (forgetting they are used after mas-
tectomies, for example, not just for cosmetic enlargement), he "seemed
to be introducing an impossibly high standard for the devices: since there
were no benefits, there should be no risks" (Angell 1997: 63).

In the case of the cell phone radiation concerns, public pragmatism
significantly tempered the potential for heightened risk consciousness to
develop into a more significant social reaction. Armed with judgment and
intelligence we accept that some assertions about potential harm are not
strictly true, and others do not need to be spelled out. The suspicious
assumption that something must be harmful unless proven otherwise is
as likely to result in a distorted view as its naive opposite. Angell makes a
useful distinction between the cynicism that characterizes precautionary
thinking, and a more engaged skepticism:

Cynicism is much easier than skepticism, because it requires no distinctions. We
needn't distinguish between reliable evidence and unreliable evidence, between
big dangers and small ones, between likely effects and unlikely ones, between the

reasonable and the bizarre. Yielding to cynicism over skepticism is therefore an easy way out. (Angell 1997: 158)

Equally, she points out that "the opposite side of the coin of cynicism is gullibility." This is the gullibility that is predisposed to accept at face value the claims about "organic" foods or about crystals that promise to enhance our well being or allow a radiation-free existence. Perhaps inconsequential for the individual, self-doubt at the institutional level leads to a more worrying accommodation to these, and more important, "ethical" anxieties. The attempts by scientific and political authorities to ingratiate themselves through such anxieties isolates others who are prepared to make clearer distinctions between the scale and character of problems we are said to confront.

Human beings, both biologically and socially, have shown themselves to be extraordinarily robust and capable of adaptation throughout history. Those charged with the responsibility of leading society now often appear to assume that we are, instead, unnaturally fragile. Authorities increasingly take it upon themselves to safeguard public health even against phantom risk, oblivious to the danger that they might be only chasing phantoms of their own making. In the elusive quest to establish a risk-free existence, our autonomy, intelligence, and capacity for change and enlightenment stand in danger of being compromised and diminished.

Works Cited

Adam, B. 1998. *Timescapes of Modernity*. London: Routledge.

Adey, W. R., et al. 2000. Spontaneous and Nitrosourea-Induced Primary Tumors of the Central Nervous System in Fischer 344 Modulated Rats Chronically Exposed to Frequency Modulated Microwave Fields. *Cancer Research* 60: 1857–1863.

Ames, B., and Gold, L. S. 1999. Environmental Pollution and Cancer: Some Misconceptions. In Foster, Bernstein, and Huber, eds., *Phantom Risk*: 153–182.

Angeli, F. 1999. *Social Picture and Trends: Italy Today*. Milan: Censis Foundation.

———. 2000. *Social Picture and Trends: Italy Today*. Milan: Censis Foundation.

Angell, M. 1997. *Science on Trial: The Clash of Medical Evidence and the Law in the Breast Implant Case*. New York: W. W. Norton.

Appleyard, B. 1992. *Understanding the Present: Science and the Soul of Modern Man*. London: Quality Paperbacks Direct.

ARPA. 2001. *Campi Electromagnetici: Prevenzione, Communicazione, Controllo e Ricerca* (Conference Proceedings). Bologna: Agenzia Regionale Prevenzione e Ambiente dell'Emillia-Romagna.

Ashwood, R. 1999. The Mobile Revolution: Is the Future Really Bright? *Engineering Technology* (June): 38–41.

Baker, R. 2001. *Fragile Science*. London: Macmillan.

Barlow, T. 2001. The Appliance of Science: There's the Evidence but What Does It Say? *Financial Times*, 2/3 June 2001.

Bate, R. 2000. *Life's Adventure: Virtual Risk in a Real World*. London: Butterworth Heinemann.

Bauer, M. 1995a. Resistance to New Technology and Its Effects on Nuclear Power, Information Technology and Biotechnology. In M. Bauer, *Resistance to New Technology*. Cambridge: Cambridge University Press: 1–44.

Bauer, M. 1995b. "Technophobia": A Misleading Conception. In M. Bauer, *Resistance to New Technology*: 97–124.

Beck, U. 1992. *Risk Society: Towards a New Modernity*. London: Sage.

———. 1995. *Ecological Politics in an Age of Risk*. Cambridge: Polity.

Becker, R. O. 1991a. *The Body Electric: Electromagnetism and the Foundation of Life*. New York: Selden, Becker and Guarnascheli.

———. 1991b. *Cross Currents: The Promise of Electromedicine, the Perils of Electropollution*. New York: J. P. Tarcher.

Begich, N., and Roderick, J. 2000. Cell Phone Convenience or 21st Century Plague? www.earthpulse.com.

Bennett, P., and Calman, K. 1999. *Risk Communication and Public Health*. Oxford: Oxford University Press.

Berry, J. M. 1999. *The New Liberalism: The Rising Power of Citizen Groups*. Washington , D.C.: Brookings Institution.

Best, J., ed. 1995. *Images of Issues: Typifying Contemporary Social Problems*. New York: Aldine de Gruyter.

———. 2001a. *Damned Lies and Statistics: Untangling Numbers from the Media, Politicians and Activists*. Berkeley: University of California Press.

———, ed. 2001b. *How Claims Spread: Cross National Diffusion of Social Problems*. New York: Aldine de Gruyter.

Bewers, J. M. 1995. The Declining Influence of Science on Marine Environmental Policy. *Chemistry and Ecology* 10: 9–23.

Bijker, W., et al. 1987. *The Social Construction of Technological Systems: New Directions in the Sociology and History of Technology*. Cambridge, Mass.: MIT Press.

Bleich, A. R. 1961. *The Story of X Rays from Roentgen to Isotopes*. New York: Dover.

Blumberg, P. 1991. Paul Brodeur's War on Electromagnetic Fields. *Washington Journalism Review* 13 (1).

Blumer, H. 1971. Social Problems as Collective Behavior. *Social Problems* 18: 298–306.

Bodansky, D., 1991. Scientific Uncertainty and the Precautionary Principle. *Environment* 33 (7): 4–5 and 43–44.

Boggs, C. 2000. *The End of Politics: Corporate Power and the Decline of the Public Sphere*. New York: Guilford Press.

Braune, S., et al. 1998. Resting Blood Pressure During Exposure to Radiofrequency Electromagnetic Field. *Lancet* 351: 1857–8.

Brauner, C. 1996. *Electrosmog: A Phantom Risk*. Zurich: Swiss Reinsurance Co.

Brignell, J. 2001. *Power Cables: What Risk?* London: Spiked.com (13 March).

———. 2002. *Sorry, Wrong Number: The Abuse of Measurement*. Hampshire: Brignell Associates.

Brobeck, S. 1993. *Encyclopedia of the Consumer Movement*. Santa Barbara, Calif.: ABC-CLIO.

Brodeur, P. 1977. *The Zapping of America: Microwaves, Their Deadly Risk and Cover Up*. New York: W. W. Norton.

———. 1989. *Currents of Death: Power Lines, Computer Terminals, and the Attempt to Cover Up the Threat to Your Health*. New York: Simon and Schuster.

———. 1993. *The Great Power Line Cover Up: How the Utilities and the Government Are Trying to Hide the Cancer Hazard Posed by Electromagnetic Fields*. New York: Simon and Schuster.

Brown, B. 2002. Studying the Use of Mobile Technology. In Brown, Green, and Harper, eds., *Wireless World*: 1–25.

Brown, B., Green, N., and Harper, R., eds. 2002. *Wireless World: Social and Interactional Aspects of the Mobile Age*. London: Springer-Verlag (pre-publication version).

Brown, P., and Mikkelsen, E. 1990. *No Safe Place: Toxic Waste, Leukemia and Community Action*. Berkeley: University of California Press.

Brown, T. 2002. The Social Costs of a Compensation Culture. In *Compensation Crazy: Do We Blame and Claim Too Much?* London: Institute of Ideas/Hodder and Stoughton. Pre-publication version.

BSE Enquiry. 2000. *The Report*. London: HMSO.

Buderi, R. 1996. *The Invention That Changed the World*. New York: Touchstone.

Burgess, A. 2001. Flattering Consumption: Creating a Europe of the Consumer. *Journal of Consumer Culture* 1 (1): 93–117.

Burguière, A., et al. 1996. The Family: What Next? In A. Burguiere et al., eds., *A History of the Family*, vol. 2: *The Impact of Modernity*. Cambridge, Mass.: Belknap Press of Harvard University Press: 531–537.

Burkart, G. 2000. Mobile Communication: The Cultural Significance of the "Handy." *Soziale Welt-Zeitschrift fur Sozialwissenschaftliche Forschung und Praxis* 51 (2): 209–230.

Bush, V. 1946. *Endless Horizons*. Washington, D.C.: Public Affairs Press.

Callon, M., et al., eds. 1986. *Mapping the Dynamic of Science and Technology*. London: Macmillan.

Capek, S. 1993. The Environmental Justice Frame: Conceptual Discussion and an Application. *Social Problems* 40 (1): 5–24.

Carlo, G., and Schram, M. 2001. *Cell Phones: Invisible Hazards in a Wireless Age*. New York: Carroll and Graf.

Carra, L. 1994. *Onde Sospette: Elettricità e Salute* (Suspect Waves: Electricity and Health). Roma: Editori Riuniti.

Carson, R. 1962. *The Silent Spring*. Boston: Houghton Mifflin.

Carstensen, E. 1987. *Biological Effects of Transmission Line Fields*. New York: Elsevier.

Castells, M. 2000. *The Network Society*, 2nd ed. Malden, Mass.: Blackwell Publishers.

Caufield, C. 1989. *Multiple Exposures: Chronicles of the Radiation Age*. London: Penguin.

Chapman, S. 1995. Rationality Cut Off in Mobile Phone Row. *British Medical Journal* 311: 1046.

Chapman, S., and Schofield, W. N. 1998. Lifesavers and Samaritans: Emergency Use of Cellular Phones in Australia. *Accident Analysis and Prevention* 30 (6): 815–819.

Chapman, S., and Wutzke, S. 1998. Community Panics About Mobile Phone Towers. *Australian and New Zealand Journal of Public Health* 21 (6): 614–620.

Chou, C. K., et al. 1992. Long term, low level microwave irradiation of rats. *Bioelectromagnetics* 13: 469–96.

Clarke, L. 1989. *Acceptable Risk? Making Decisions in a Toxic Environment*. Berkeley: University of California Press.

Cohen, S. 1972. *Folk Devils and Moral Panics*. Harmondsworth: Penguin.

Cole, L. 1981. *Politics and the Restraint of Science.* Totowa, N.J.: Rowman and Allanheld.

―――. 1993. *Element of Risk: The Politics of Radon.* New York: Oxford University Press

Commission of the European Communities. 2000. *Communication on the Precautionary Principle.* Brussels. (2 February). See http://europa.eu.int/comm/off/com/health_consumer/precaution.htm.

Cooper, G. 2002. The Mutable Mobile: Social Theory in a Wireless World. In Brown, Green, and Harper, eds., *Wireless World:* 26–54.

Crain, R. L., et al. 1967. *The Politics of Community Conflict: The Fluoridation Decision.* Indianapolis: Bobbs-Merrill.

Dalrymple, T. 1998. *Mass Listeria: The Meaning of Health Scares.* London: André Deutsch.

Davies, A. 1994. *Telecommunications and Politics.* London: Pinter.

Davis, D. L., et al. 1997. *Rethinking Breast Cancer Risk and the Environment: The Case for the Precautionary Principle.* Washington, D.C.: World Resources Institute.

Dendy, P. 2000. Mobile Phones and the Illusory Pursuit of Safety. *The Lancet* 356: 1782.

Department of Health. 2000. *Mobile Phones and Health.* London: Department of Health.

Direct Line Insurance. 2002. *The Mobile Phone Report: A Report on the Effects of Using a "Hand Held" and "Hands Free" Mobile Phone on Road Safety.* Croydon: Direct Line Insurance.

Directeur General de la Sante. 2001. *Rapport Zmirou: Les Telephones mobiles, leurs stations de base et la sante.* Paris.

Douglas, M., and Wildavsky, A. 1982. *Risk and Culture.* Berkeley: University of California Press.

Dreyer, N. A., Loughlin, J. E., and Rothman, K. J. 1999. Cause Specific Mortality in Cellular Phone Users. *Journal of the American Medical Association* 282: 1814–1816.

Dunbar, R., and Lycett, J. 2000. Mobile Phones as Lekking Devices Among Human Males. *Human Nature: An Interdisciplinary Biosocial Perspective* 11 (1): 93–104.

Durodie, B. 1996. *Poisonous Dummies.* Cambridge: European Science and Environment Forum.

Edelstein, M. 1988. *Contaminated Communities.* Boulder, Colo.: Westview Press.

EEA (European Environment Agency). 1999. *Environment in the European Union at the Turn of the Century.* Brussels: EEA.

Elliott, E. D., and Charnley, G. 2000. The Rise, Fall and Rebirth of the Precautionary Principle. Paper presented at the 2000 annual meeting of the Society for Risk Analysis.

Ellman, M. 1994. The Increase in Death and Disease under "Katastroika." *Cambridge Journal of Economics* 18: 331–376.

Elzinga, A., and Jamison, A. 1995. Changing Policy Agendas in Science and Technology. In S. Jasanoff et al., *Handbook of Science and Technology Studies.* Thousand Oaks, Calif.: Sage: 572–598.

Englehardt, H. T., and Caplan, A. L., eds. 1987. *Scientific Controversies*. Cambridge: Cambridge University Press.

European Commission. 1998. Health Scientific Committees Scientific Steering Committee (Former MDSC) Outcome of Discussions on Possible Health Effects from Exposure to Electromagnetic Fields (oHz-300GHz) – Report and Opinion Adopted at the Meeting of the Scientific Steering Committee of 25–26 June 1998. Available at europa.eu.int/comm/food/fs/sc/ssc/out19_en.html.

European Union. 2000. *EU Communication on the Precautionary Principle* (IP/OO.96) (February).

Ewald, F. 1993. Two Infinities of Risk. In B. Massumi, ed., *The Politics of Everyday Fear*. Minneapolis: University of Minnesota Press: 215–234.

Farley, T. 2000. Mobile Phone History. Private Lines: A Website of Enquiry into the Telephone System. Available at: www.privateline.com.

Feshbach, M., Friendly, A., and Brown, L. 1993. *Ecocide in the USSR: Health and Nature Under Siege*. New York: Basic Books.

Feychting, M., and Ahlbom, A. 1993. Magnetic Fields and Cancer in Children Residing Near Swedish High-Voltage Power Lines. *American Journal of Epidemiology* 138: 467–81.

Fischer, C. S. 1992. *America Calling: A Social History of the Telephone*. Berkeley: University of California Press.

Fitzpatrick, M. 2001. *The Tyranny of Health*. London: Routledge.

Fitzpatrick, M., and Milligan, D. 1987. *The Truth About the Aids Panic*. London: Junius.

Flickinger, R. 1983. The Comparative Politics of Agenda Setting: The Emergence of Consumer Protection as a Public Policy Issue in Britain and the United States. *Policy Studies Review* 2: 429–444.

Flynn, C. B. 1984. The Local Impacts of Three Mile Island. In W. R. Freudenberg and E. A. Rosa, eds., *Public Reactions to Nuclear Power: Are There Critical Masses?* Boulder, Colo.: American Association for the Advancement of Science/Westview.

Flynn, J., Slovic, P., and Kunreuther, H. 2001. *Risk, Media and Stigma: Understanding Public Challenges to Modern Science and Technology*. London: Earthscan.

Foster, K. R. 1986. The VDT Debate. *American Scientist* (74): 163–168.

———. 1999a. Weak Magnetic Fields: A Cancer Connection? In Foster et al., eds., *Phantom Risk*: 47–86.

———. 1999b. Miscarriage and VDTs: An Update. In Foster et al., eds., *Phantom Risk*: 123–135.

Foster, K. R., and Moulder, J. E. 2000. Are Mobile Phones Safe? *IEEE Spectrum* 37 (8): 17–32.

Foster, K. R., and Pickard, W. F. 1987. Microwaves: The Risks of Risk Research. *Nature* 330: 531–2.

Foster, K. R., Bernstein, D. E., and Huber, P., eds. 1999. *Phantom Risk: Scientific Inference and the Law*. New York: MIT Press.

Foster, K. R., Vecchia, P., and Repacholi, M. H. 2000. Science and the Precautionary Principle. *Science* 288: 979–981.

Fowlkes, M., and Miller, P. 1987. Chemicals and Community at Love Canal. In Johnson and Covello, *Social and Cultural Construction of Risk*: 55–80.

Fox, K., et al. 2001. *Evolution, Alienation and Gossip: The Role of Mobile Telecommunications in the 21st Century*. Oxford: Social Issues Research Centre.

Freude, G., Ullsperger, P., Eggert, S., Ruppe, I. 1998. Effects of Microwaves Emitted by Cellular Phones on Human Slow Brain Potentials. *Bioelectromagnetics* 19: 384–7.

Fröhlich, H. 1980. The Biological Effects of Microwaves and Related Questions. *Advanced Electronics Electron Physics* 53: 85–152.

Fuller, J. G. 1977. *The Poison That Fell from the Sky*. New York: Random House.

Fumento, M. 1993. *Science Under Siege: Balancing Technology and the Environment*. New York: William Morrow.

Furedi, F. 1997. *The Culture of Fear*. London: Cassell.

———. 2001. *Paranoid Parenting*. London: Penguin Press.

Furedi, F., and Brown, T. 1999. Complaining Britain. *Society* 36 (4): 72–79.

Future Foundation. 1999. *Mapping the New Web of Life*. London: Future Foundation.

Gamson, W. 1992. *Talking Politics*. New York: Cambridge University Press.

Gant, D., and Kiesler, S. 2002. Blurring the Boundaries: Cell Phones, Mobility and the Line Between Work and Personal Life. In Brown, Green, and Harper, eds., *Wireless World*: 231–247.

Garrison, N. 2001. Towering Menace. *Now Toronto* (15–21 February).

Giddens, A. 1990. *The Consequences of Modernity*. Cambridge: Polity.

———. 1991. *Modernity and Self Identity*. Cambridge: Polity.

Gillott, J., and Kumar, M. 1995. *Science and the Retreat from Reason*. London: Merlin.

Glassner, B. 1999. *Culture of Fear*. New York: Basic Books.

Gottlieb, S. 2001. Evidence Grows for the Safety of Mobile Phones. *British Medical Journal* 322 (7279): 129.

Gotzsche, A. 1975. *The Fluoride Question*. London: David Poynter.

Gray, J. S. 1990. Statistics and the Precautionary Principle. *Marine Pollution Bulletin* 21 (4): 174–6.

Green, N. 2002. Who's Watching Whom? Monitoring and Accountability in Mobile Relations. In Brown, Green, and Harper, eds., *Wireless World*: 55–81.

Greenbaum, S. D., et al. 2000. Doing Good: Work as Mission in Silicon Valley and Beyond. Paper presented to the 99th meeting of the American Anthropological Association, San Francisco, November 17.

Grove-White, R., Macnaghten, P., and Wynne, B. 2000. *Wising Up: The Public and New Technologies*. Lancaster University: Centre for the Study of Environmental Change.

Hadfield, P. 2000. Emerging Technologies: Synonara WAP. *New Scientist* (21 October).

Hall, P. A. 1999. Social Capital in Britain. *British Journal of Political Science* 29 (3): 417–461.

Hammitt, J. K. 1990. Risk Perceptions and Food Choice: An Exploratory Analysis of Organic versus Conventional Produce Buyers. *Risk Analysis* 10 (3): 367–374.

Hannigan, J. A. 1995. *Environmental Sociology: A Social Constructionist Perspective*. London and New York: Routledge.

Hansard Society. 2001. The Challenge for Parliament: Making Government Accountable. Executive Summary. London. http://www.hansardsociety.org.uk/ChallengeforParliament.htm.

Hardell, L., et al. 1999. Use of Cellular Telephones and the Risk for Brain Tumors: A Case Control Study. *Journal of Oncology* 15: 113–116.

Harremoës, P., et al. 2002. *The Precautionary Principle in the 20th Century: Late Lessons from Early Warnings*. London: Earthscan/European Environmental Agency.

Harvard Center for Risk Analysis. 1995. Cellular Telephones and Brain Cancer. *Risk in Perspective* 3 (4): 1–2.

Hays, S. P. 2000. *A History of Environmental Politics Since 1945*. Pittsburgh: University of Pittsburgh Press.

Healey, P. 1999. Popularising Science for the Sake of the Economy: The UK Experience. In R. Miettinen, ed., *Biotechnology and Public Understanding of Science*: 68–81.

Health Council of the Netherlands. 2002. *Mobile Telephones: An Evaluation of Health Effects*. The Hague: Health Council of the Netherlands.

Helyar, V. 2002. Usability of Portability: The Case of WAP. In Brown, Green, and Harper, eds., *Wireless World*: 355–74.

Hermann, D. M., and Hossmann, K. A., 1997. Neurological Effects of Microwave Exposure Related to Communication. *Journal of Neurological Science* 152: 1–14.

Hobsbawm, E., and Ranger, T., eds. 1992. *The Invention of Tradition*. Cambridge: Cambridge University Press.

Holsworth, R. D. 1980. *Public Interest Liberalism and the Crisis of Affluence*. Boston: G. K. Hall and Co.

Home Office. 2002. *Mobile Phone Thefts*. London: Home Office.

House of Commons. 1999. *Science and Technology Committee – Minutes of Evidence* (9 June). London: Stationery Office.

House of Lords. 2000a. Select Committee on Science and Technology 3rd Report: *Science and Society*. London: Stationery Office.

House of Lords. 2000b. Select Committee on Science and Technology 3rd Report: *Science and Society – Minutes of Evidence*. London: Stationery Office.

Huber, P. 1989. Electrophobia. *Forbes* (September 4): 313.

———. 1991. *Galileo's Revenge: Junk Science in the Courtroom*. New York: Basic Books.

Hyland, G. 1999a. Fundamental Inadequacy of Current Safety Safety Limits Covering Public Exposure to Radiation from Mobile Phones and VDU Terminals Mandates. London: Tecno AO.

———. 1999b. How Low Intensity Microwave Radiation from Mobile Phone Base Stations Can Affect Humans. Unpublished paper (March).

———. 1999c. On the Fundamental Inadequacy of Existing Safety Guidelines. Submission to House of Commons Seminar (June 15).

———. 2000. Physics and Biology of Mobile Telephony. *The Lancet* 356 (November 25): 1833–36.

ICNIRP. 1998. Guidelines for Limiting Exposure to Time-Varying Electric, Magnetic and Electromagnetic (up to 300GHz). *Health Physics* 75 (4): 442–522.

IEE (Institute of Electrical Engineers). 2001. FactFile on Mobile Phones and Power Lines. London: IEE. http://www.iee.org.uk/Policy/Areas/BioEffects/emchealth.pdf.

IEEE Standards Coordinating Committee 28 on Non-Ionizing Radiation Hazards. 1992. Standard for Safety Levels with Respect to Human Exposure to Radiofrequency Electromagnetic Fields, 3 kHz to 300 GHz (ANSI/IEEE C95.1-1991). The Institute of Electrical and Electronic Engineers, New York.

IEGMP. 2000. *Mobile Phones and Health*. Didcot, U.K.: NRPB.

Inskip, P. D. 2001. Cellular Telephone Use and Brain Tumors. *New England Journal of Medicine* study 344 (2): 459–519.

Irwin, A. 2001. *Sociology and the Environment*. Cambridge: Polity.

Irwin, A., and Wynne, B. 1996. *Misunderstanding Science? The Public Reconstruction of Science and Technology*. New York: Cambridge University Press.

Jacoby, R. 1999. *The End of Utopia: Politics and Culture in an Age of Apathy*. New York: Basic Books.

Jasanoff, S. 1994. *The Fifth Branch: Science Advisers as Policymakers*. Cambridge, Mass.: Harvard University Press.

———. 1995. Product, Process, or Programme: Three Cultures and the Regulation of Biotechnology. In M. Bauer, ed., *Resistance to Technology*: 311–334.

Jauchem, J. R. 1995. Alleged Health Effects of Electromagnetic Fields: The Misconceptions Continue. *Journal of Microwave Power and Electromagnetic Energy* 30 (3): 165–177.

———. 1998. Health Effects of Microwave Exposures: A Review of the Recent (1995–1998) Literature. *Journal of Microwave Power and Electromagnetic Energy* 33 (4): 263–274.

Johnson, B. B., and Covello, V. T., eds. 1987. *The Social and Cultural Construction of Risk*. Dordrecht: D. Reidel.

Jordan, A., and O'Riordan, T. 1999. The Precautionary Principle in Contemporary Environmental Policy and Politics. In O'Riordan and Cameron, eds., *Interpreting the Precautionary Principle*: 12–30.

Jowell, R., et al., eds. 1996. *British Social Attitudes: The 13th Report*. Aldershot: Dartmouth Publishing.

Katz, J., and Aakhus, M. 2002. *Perpetual Contact: Mobile Communication, Private Talk, Public Performance*. Cambridge: Cambridge University Press.

Kepplinger, H. M. 1995. Individual and Institutional Impacts upon Press Coverage of Sciences: The Case of Nuclear Power and Genetic Engineering in Germany. In M. Bauer, ed., *Resistance to Technology*: 357–378.

Knight, N. 1986. "The New Light": X Rays and Medical Futurism. In J. J. Corn, ed., *Imagining Tomorrow*: 10–34.

Koivisto, M., et al. 2000. Effects of a 902 MHz Electromagnetic Field Emitted by Cellular Telephones on Response Times in Humans. *Neuroreport* 11: 413–5.

Kopomaa, T. 2002. Finns Keep Friends at Arm's Length. *Times Higher Education Supplement*, 22 February.

Kuhn, T. S. 1970. *The Structure of Scientific Revolutions*. Chicago: University of Chicago Press.

Lai, H. 1997. Neurological Effects of Radiofrequency Electromagnetic Radiation Relating to Wireless Communication Technology. Paper presented at the IBC-UK Conference: Mobile Phones – Is There a Health Risk? Brussels, Belgium, 16–17 September.

Lai, J., and Singh, N. P. 1996. Single and Double Stranded DNA Breaks in Rat Brain Cells After Acute Exposure to Radiofrequency Electromagnetic Radiation. *International Journal of Radiation Biology* 69: 513–21.

Latour, B. 1987. *Science in Action: How to Follow Scientists and Engineers Through Society*. Milton Keynes, U.K.: Open University Press.

Laurier, E. 2002. The Region as Socio-Technical Accomplishment of Mobile Workers. In Brown, Green, and Harper, eds., *Wireless World*: 82–114.

Le Fanu, J. 1999. *The Rise and Fall of Modern Medicine*. London: Abacus.

Leone, R. C., and Jasanoff, S. 1995. *Science at the Bar*. Cambridge, Mass.: Harvard University Press.

Leung, L., and Wei, R. 2000. More Than Just Talk on the Move: Uses and Gratifications of the Cellular Phone. *Journalism and Mass Communication Quarterly* 77 (2): 308–320.

Leviton, L. C., Needleman, C. E., and Shapiro, M. A. 1998. *Confronting Public Health Risks: A Decision Maker's Guide*. Thousand Oaks, Calif.: Sage.

Lichter, S. R., and Rothman, S. 1999. *Environmental Cancer: A Political Disease?* New Haven, Conn.: Yale University Press.

Lipset, S. M., and Schneider, W. 1983. *The Confidence Gap*. New York: Free Press.

Lomborg, B. 2001. *The Skeptical Environmentalist*. Cambridge: Cambridge University Press.

London, S., et al. 1991. Exposure to Residential Electric and Magnetic Fields and Risk of Childhood Leukemia. *American Journal of Epidemiology* 134: 923–37.

Lotti, M., and Nicoterra, P. 2002. Toxicology: A Risky Business. *Nature* 416: 481.

Lupton, D. 1995. *The Imperative of Health: Public Health and the Regulated Body*. London: Sage.

MacGregor, D. G., Slovic, P., and Morgan, M. G., 1994. Perception of Risks from Electromagnetic Fields: A Psychometric Evaluation of a Risk Communication Approach. *Risk Analysis* 14 (5): 815–28.

MacHamer, P., Pera, M., and Baltas, A. 2000. *Scientific Controversies: Philosophical and Historical Perspectives*. New York: Oxford University Press.

MacKenzie, D., and Wacjman, J. 1999. *The Social Shaping of Technology*, 2nd ed. Buckingham, U.K.: Open University Press.

MacLeod, R. 1997. Science and Democracy: Historical Reflections on Present Discontents. *Minerva* 35: 369–384.

Macnaghten, P., and Urry, J. 1998. *Contested Natures*. London: Sage.

Maier, M., Blakemore, C., and Koivisto, M. 2000. The Health Hazards of Mobile Phones – The Only Established Risk Is of Using One While Driving. *British Medical Journal* 320: 1288–89.

Malyapa, R. S., et al. 1997. Measurement of DNA Damage by the Alkaline Comet Assay in Rat Brain Cells Aafter in vivo Exposure to 2450 MHz Electromagnetic Radiation. In: *Proceedings of Second World Congress for Electricity and Magnetism in Biology and Medicine*, Bologna, Italy.

Massachusetts Municipal Association. 2000. *Working with Wireless: The Massachusetts Municipal-Industry Wireless Collaborative.* Boston: Massachusetts Municipal Association.

Masterson-Allen, S., and Brown, P. 1990. Public Reaction to Toxic Waste Contamination. *International Journal of Health Services* 20 (3): 487–97.

Mayer, R. N. 1988. Consumer Safety and the Issue Emergence Process. In E. S. Maynes, ed., *The Frontier of Research in the Consumer Interest.* University of Missouri: American Council on Consumer Interests: 83–96.

———. 1989. *The Consumer Movement: Guardians of the Marketplace.* Boston: G. K. Hall.

Mazur, A., 1989. Communicating Risk in the Mass Media. In D. L. Peck, ed., *Psychological Effects of Hazardous Toxic Waste Disposal on Communities.* Springfield, Ill.: Thomas Publishers.

McAdam, D., and Rucht, D. 1993. The Cross-National Diffusion of Movement Ideas. *Annals of the American Academy of Political and Social Science* 528: 56–74.

McGrath, A. 2001. Wireless Data: The World in Your Hand? *Communication Technology Decisions* (Spring): 66–69.

McKeown, T. 1979. *The Role of Medicine.* Oxford: Basil Blackwell.

Meadows, D. H., et al. 1972. *The Limits to Growth.* New York: Universe.

Miettinen, R., ed. 1999. *Biotechnology and Public Understanding of Science: Proceedings of the UK–Nordic Co-operative seminar, Helsinki, October 25–27, 1998.* Helsinki: Academy of Finland/Edita.

Miettinen, R., and Väliverronen, E. 1999. In Science and Technology We Trust: On the Public Understanding of Science in Finland. In R. Miettinen, ed., *Biotechnology and Public Understanding of Science*: 11–21.

Mol, A. P. J., and Spaargaren, G. 1993. Environment, Modernity and the Risk Society: The Apocalyptic Horizon of Environmental Reform. *International Sociology* 8 (4): 431–459.

Morgan, M. G., et al. 1985. Powerline Frequency Electric and Magnetic Fields: A Pilot Study of Risk Perception. *Risk Analysis* 5: 139–149.

Morgan, R. W., et al. 2000. Radiofrequency Exposure and Mortality from Cancer of the Brain and Lympthatic/Hermatopoietic Systems. *Epidemiology* 11: 118–127.

Morris, J., ed. 2000. *Risk and the Precautionary Principle.* London: Butterworth Heinemann.

Moulder, J. E., et al. 1999. Cell Phones and Cancer: What Is the Evidence for a Connection? *Radiation Research* 151 (5): 513–31.

———. 2000. Cellular Phone Antennas and Human Health: http://www.mcw.edu/gcrc/cop/cell-phone-health-FAQ/toc.html.

Mudu, P. P., and Pessina, D. 2000. Rome: Administrative Spatial Divisions and Citizens Mobilization Boundaries. Conference paper presented at "Roma-New York City: Comparative Urban Projects." Rome, 19–23 June.

Muller, J., and Nyevriekel, E. 1991. Closing the Technology Gap in East European Telecommunication Services. ITU European Regional Telecommunication Development Conference (EU-RDC), Prague.

Muller, J., and Toker, S. 1994. Mobile Communications in Europe. In C. Steinfield et al., *Telecommunications in Transition.*

Murtagh, G. 2002. Seeing the Rules: Preliminary Observations of Action, Interaction and Mobile Phone Usage. In Brown, Green, and Harper, eds., *Wireless World*: 148–72.

Muscat, J. E., et al. 2000. Handheld Cellular Phone Use and the Risk of Brain Cancer. *Journal of the American Medical Association study* 284 (23): 3001–3007.

Myerson, G. 2001. *Heidegger, Habermas and the Mobile Phone*. London: Icon Books.

Nadel, M. V. 1971. *The Politics of Consumer Protection*. Indianapolis: Bobbs-Merrill.

Nader, R. 1965. *Unsafe at Any Speed: The Designed in Dangers of the American Automobile*. New York: Grossman.

Needleman, C. E., and Leviton, L. C. 1998. Confronting Risk: A Value-Laden Activity. In Leviton, Needleman, and Shapiro, *Confronting Public Health Risks*: 1–20.

Nelkin, D. 1995. Forms of Intrusion: Comparing Resistance to Information Technology and Biotechnology in the USA. In M. Bauer, ed., *Resistance to Technology*: 379–390.

Nelkin, D., ed. 1992. *Controversy Politics of Technical Decisions*. Thousand Oaks, Calif.: Sage.

Nocenzi, M. 2000. Il rischio ambientale nella politica communitaria. Come vivere con l'incertezza? (Environmental risk in community politics. How to live with uncertainty?) Doctoral thesis. University of Rome Faculty of Political Science.

Nolan, J. L. 1998. *The Therapeutic State*. New York: New York University Press.

OECD. 2000. *Mobile Phones: Pricing Structures and Trends*. Paris: OECD.

O' Riordan, T., and Cameron, J., eds. 1994. *Interpreting the Precautionary Principle*. London: Earthscan.

Paarlberg, R. 2000. The Global Food Fight. *Foreign Affairs* 79 (3): 24–38.

Park, R. 2000. *Voodoo Science*. New York: Oxford University Press.

Pearce, D. 1994. The Precautionary Principle in Economic Analysis. In Cameron and O'Riordan, eds., *Interpreting the Precautionary Principle*: 56–73.

Pertschuk, M. 1982. *Revolt Against Regulation: The Rise and Pause of the Consumer Movement*. Berkeley: University of California Press.

Petrie, K. J., et al. 2001. Thoroughly Modern Worries: The Relationship of Worries about Modernity to Reported Symptoms, Health and Medical Care Utilization. *Journal of Psychosomatic Research* 51 (1): 395–401.

Pielke, R. A. 2002. Science Policy: Policy, Politics and Perspective. *Nature* 416: 367–368.

Plant, S. 2002. *On the Mobile*. Libertyville, Ill.: Motorola. http://www.motorola.com/mediacenter/industry/background/0,1083,,00.html.

Pool, I. D. S., ed. 1977. *The Social Impact of the Telephone*. Cambridge, Mass.: MIT Press.

Porritt, J. 2000. *Playing Safe: Science and the Environment*. London: Thames and Hudson.

Preece, A. W., et al. 1999. Effect of a 915 MHz simulated mobile phone signal on cognitive function in man. *International Journal of Radiation Biology* 75: 447–56.

Prost, A. 1998. Science and Society: The Dilemma Facing the Policy Makers. *Eurohealth* 4 (4): 31–33.

Puttnam, R. D. 2000. *Bowling Alone: The Collapse and Revival of American Community.* New York: Simon and Schuster.

Raffensberger, C., and Tickner, J., 1999. *Protecting Public Health and the Environment: Implementing the Precautionary Principle.* Washington, D.C.: Island Press.

Repacholi, M. H. 2001. Health Risks from the Use of Mobile Phones. *Toxicology Letters* 120 (1–3): 323–331.

Repacholi, M. H., et al. 1997. Lymphomas in Em-Pim 1 Transgenic Mice Exposed to Pulsed 900-MHz Electromagnetic Fields. *Radiation Responses* 147: 631–40.

Rifat, T. 1999. *Remote Viewing.* London: Century.

Roberts, J. T., and Toffolon-Weiss, M. M. 2001. *Chronicles from the Environmental Justice Frontline.* Cambridge: Cambridge University Press.

Robison, R., and Goodman, D. S. G. 1996. *The New Rich in Asia: Mobile Phones, McDonalds and the Middle Class Revolution.* London: Routledge.

Rootes, C. 2001. Discourse, Opportunity or Structure? Determining Outcomes of Local Mobilizations Against Waste Incinerators in England. Paper presented to workshop on Local Environmental Politics at the 29th Joint Sessions of the European Consortium for Political Research, Grenoble, 6–11 April.

Rose, H., and Rose, S. 1969. *Science and Society.* Harmondsworth: Pelican.

Rothman, K. J., et al. 1996. Overall Mortality of Cellular Telephone Customers. *Epidemiology* 7: 303–5.

Royal Society. 1985. *The Public Understanding of Science.* London: Royal Society.

Sagan, L. 1996. *Electric and Magnetic Fields: Invisible Risks?* Amsterdam: Gordon and Breach.

Sapolsky, H. 1969. Social Science Views of a Controversy in Science and Politics. *American Journal of Clinical Nutrition* 22 (10): 1397–1406.

———. 1986. Introduction. In H. Sapolsky, ed., *Consuming Fears: The Politics of Product Risks.* New York: Basic Books: 3–18.

Sapolsky, H., et al., eds. 1996. *The Telecommunications Revolution.* London: Routledge.

Savitz, D. 1988. Case Control Study of Childhood Cancer and Residential Exposure to Electric and Magnetic Fields. *American Journal of Epidemiology* 128: 21–38.

Selden, G., Becker, R. O., and Guarnascheli, M. D., eds. 1997. *The Body Electric: Electromagnetism and the Foundation of Life.* New York: William Morrow.

Shephard, B. 2000. *A War of Nerves: Soldiers and Psychiatrists 1914–1994.* London: Jonathan Cape.

Shepherd, I., ed. 2000. *Science and Governance in the European Union: A Contribution to the Debate.* Draft papers to the European Union. 9 March. London: Institute for Systems, Informatics and Safety.

Sherry, J., and Salvador, T. 2002. Running and Grimacing: The Struggle for Balance in Mobile Work. In Brown, Green, and Harper, eds., *Wireless World*: 205–30.

Shurdut, B. 1999. Legislating Children"s Health: Can and Should Science Meet the Challenge? *Preprints of Extended Abstracts* 39 (2) Symposia Papers Presented Before the Division of the American Chemical Society, New Orleans, La., 22–26 August: 112–128.

Silver, B. L. 1998. *The Ascent of Science*. New York: Oxford University Press.

SIRC (Social Issues Research Council). 2000. *Guidelines on Science and Health Communication*. Oxford: SIRC.

Sjostrom, H., and Nilsson, R. 1972. *Thalidomide and the Power of the Drug Companies*. Harmondsworth: Penguin Books.

Skolbekken, J. 1995. The Risk Epidemic in Medical Journals. *Social Science and Medicine* 40 (3): 291–305.

Slesin, L. 1990. Uncovering Radiation. *Columbia Journalism Review* 29 (2): 13–29.

Slesin, L., and Zybko, M. 1983. *Video Display Terminals: Health and Safety*. New York: Microwave News.

Slovic, P. 1987. Perception of Risk. *Science*. 230: 280–285.

Slovic, P., et al. 1997. Evaluating Chemical Risks: Results of a Survey of the British Toxicology Society. *Human and Experimental Toxicology* 16: 289–304.

Smyth, P. 2000. A History of Mobile Communications. *BT Technology Journal* 18 (1): 60–61.

Snow, D. A., and Benford, R. D. 1999. Alternative Types of Cross-National Diffusion in the Social Movement Arena. In D. Della Porta, H. Kriesi, and D. Rucht, eds., *Social Movements in a Globalizing World*: 23–39. London: Palgrave.

Spector, M., and Kitsuse, J. I. 1987. *Constructing Social Problems*. New York: Aldine de Gruyter.

Standage, T. 1998. *The Victorian Internet*. London: Phoenix.

Stang, A., and Jockel, K. H. 2001. Mobiles Phones, Epidemiology and the Media. *Epidemiology* 12 (4): Supplement 536.

Starr, C. 1969. Social Benefit versus Technological Risk. *Science* 165 (19 September): 1232.

Starr, P. 1982. *The Social Transformation of American Medicine*. New York: Basic Books.

Stein, J. A., and Renn, O. 1998. *Transparency and Openness in Scientific Advisory Committees: The American Experience*. Luxembourg: European Parliament Scientific Technological Options Assessment.

Steinfield, C. 1994. An Introduction to European Telecommunications. In Steinfield et al., eds., *Telecommunications in Transition*. London: Sage.

Steneck, N. H.1984. *The Microwave Debate*. Cambridge, Mass.: MIT Press.

Stetz, P. 1999. *The Cell Phone Handbook : Everything You Wanted to Know About Wireless Telephony (But Didn't Know Who or What to Ask)*. New York: Aegis.

Stirling, A. 1999. *On Science and Precaution in the Management of Technological Risk: A Synthesis Report of Case Studies*. Brussels: ECSC/EEC/EAEC.

Storch, H. V., and Stehr, N. 2000. Climate Change in Perspective. *Nature* 405: 615.

Tarr, J. A., and Jacobson, C. 1987. Environmental Risk in Historical Perspective. In Johnson and Covello, eds., *Social and Cultural Construction of Risk*: 317–344.

Tenner, E. 1996. *Why Things Bite Back*. London: Fourth Estate.

Therborn, G. 1995. *European Modernity and Beyond*. London: Sage.

Toffler, A. 1981. *The Third Wave*. London: Pan Books.

Touraine, A. 1995. The Crisis of "Progress." In M. Bauer, ed., *Resistance to Technology*: 45–56.

Townsend, A. M. 2002. Life in the Real-Time City: Mobile Telephones and Urban Metabolism. In Brown, Green, and Harper, eds., *Wireless World*: 115–147.

Troyer, W. 1977. *No Safe Place*. Toronto: Clarke and Irwin.

Tubiana, M. 2000. The Precautionary Principle: Its Benefits and Risks. *Bulletin de l'Academie Nationale de Medecine* 184 (5): 969–993.

Tuesley, M. J. 1999. Not in My Backyard: The Siting of Wireless Communication Facilities. *Federal Communications Law Journal* 51 (3): 887–911.

Vanderzwaag, D. 1999. The Precautionary Principle. *Journal of Environmental Law Practice* 8: 355.

Vecchia, P. 2000a. Controversies About Power Lines in Italy. Unpublished paper.

———. 2000b. Electromagnetic Fields and Precautionary Policies. *IEEE Journal*: 261–262.

———. 2000c. Radiofrequency and Electromagnetic Fields: Health Policies and Public Controversies in Italy. Unpublished paper.

———. 2000d. The Swiss Ordinance on Protection Against Electromagnetic Fields in the Perspective of Other National and International Standards. Unpublished paper.

Verschaeve, L. 1995. Can Non Ionizing Radiation Induce Cancer? *Cancer Journal* 8: 237–249.

Vlasov, V. 2000. Health Hazards of Mobile Phones. Do Laptops Also Pose a Risk? *British Medical Journal* 321 (7289): 1156.

Vodafone. 1998 (September). *Environmental Handbook for Radio Site Selection*. London: Vodafone.

———. 1999 (September). *Health and Safety Issues*. London: Vodafone.

Vyner, H. 1987. *Invisible Trauma: The Psychosocial Effects of Invisible Environmental Contaminants*. Lexington, Ky.: Lexington Books.

Ward, N., and Lowe, P. 1999. Insecurities in Contemporary Country Life. In J. Vail, ed., *Insecure Times*. London: Routledge: 155–170.

Webb, W. T. 1998. *Understanding Cellular Radio: Mobile Communications Series*. Boston: Arlech House.

Weingart, P. 1999. Scientific Expertise and Political Accountability: Paradoxes of Science in Politics. *Science and Public Policy* 26 (3): 151–161.

Weintraub, J., and Kumar, K., eds. 1997. *Public and Private in Thought and Practice*. Chicago: Chicago University Press.

Weir, D., and Shapiro, M. 1981. *Circle of Poison: Pesticides and People in a Hungry World*. New York: Food First Books.

Wertheimer, N., and Leeper, E. 1979. Electrical Wiring Configurations and Childhood Cancer. *American Journal of Epidemiology* 109: 273–284.

Wildavsky, A. 1995. *But Is It True? A Citizen's Guide to Environmental Health and Safety Issues*. Cambridge, Mass.: Harvard University Press.

Wilmott, P., and Young, M. 1960. *Family and Class in a London Suburb*. London: Routledge and Kegan Paul.

Winston, B. 1998. *Media, Technology and Society: A History: From the Telegraph to the Internet*. London: Routledge.

WHO (World Health Organization). 1999. *Overview of Environment and Health in Europe in the 1990s*. Prepared for the 3rd European Conference on Environment and Health, London.

———. 2000. Fact Sheet No. 193, *Electromagnetic Fields and Public Health*. Revised ed., June.

———. n.d. International EMF Project Home Page: http://www.who.int/peh-emf.

———. 2002. *The World Health Report: Reducing Risks, Promoting Healthy Life*.

Wynne, B. 2000. Retrieving a Human Agenda for Science. *RSA Journal* 2 (4).

Index